The Best
AMERICAN
ESSAYS
2003

GUEST EDITORS OF
THE BEST AMERICAN ESSAYS

1986 ELIZABETH HARDWICK
1987 GAY TALESE
1988 ANNIE DILLARD
1989 GEOFFREY WOLFF
1990 JUSTIN KAPLAN
1991 JOYCE CAROL OATES
1992 SUSAN SONTAG
1993 JOSEPH EPSTEIN
1994 TRACY KIDDER
1995 JAMAICA KINCAID
1996 GEOFFREY C. WARD
1997 IAN FRAZIER
1998 CYNTHIA OZICK
1999 EDWARD HOAGLAND
2000 ALAN LIGHTMAN
2001 KATHLEEN NORRIS
2002 STEPHEN JAY GOULD
2003 ANNE FADIMAN

The Best AMERICAN ESSAYS® 2003

Edited and with an Introduction
by ANNE FADIMAN

Robert Atwan, Series Editor

HOUGHTON MIFFLIN COMPANY
BOSTON • NEW YORK   2003

ISSN 0888-3742
ISBN 0-618-34160-9
ISBN 0-618-34161-7 (pbk.)

Printed in the United States of America

MP 10 9 8 7 6 5 4 3 2 1

"Lavender" by André Aciman. First published in *Harvard Review*, Spring 2002. Copyright © 2002 by André Aciman. Reprinted by permission of the author.

"I Bought a Bed" by Donald Antrim. First published in *The New Yorker*, June 17 and 24, 2002. Copyright © 2002 by Donald Antrim. Reprinted by permission of the author.

"Lost Cities" by Rachel Cohen. First published in *The Threepenny Review*, Winter 2002. Copyright © 2002 by Rachel Cohen. Reprinted by permission of the author. Poetry and prose excerpts from *C. P. Cavafy: Collected Poems* by C. P. Cavafy, translated by Edmund Keeley and Philip Sherrard. Translation copyright © 1972 by Edmund Keeley and Philip Sherrard. Reprinted by permission of Princeton University Press. Excerpt from *The Book of Disquiet* by Bernardo Soares/Fernando Pessoa, translated by Alfred MacAdam. Translation copyright © 1991. Reprinted by permission of Pantheon Books, a division of Random House, Inc. Excerpts from *The Book of Disquietude* by Fernando Pessoa, translated by Richard Zenith. Translation copyright © 1996 by Richard Zenith. Reprinted by permission of Carcanet Press, Ltd. Lines from "Lisbon Revisited" from *Poems of Fernando Pessoa*. Copyright © 1988 by Edwin Honig and Susan M. Brown. Used by permission of Ecco.

"Yes" by Brian Doyle. First published in *The Georgia Review*, Summer 2002. Copyright © 2002 by Brian Doyle. Reprinted by permission of the author.

"In a Snob-Free Zone" by Joseph Epstein. First published in *The Washington Monthly*, June 2002. Copyright © 2002 by Joseph Epstein. Reprinted from *Snobbery: The American Version* by permission of Houghton Mifflin Company.

"Memoria ex Machina" by Marshall Jon Fisher. First published in *DoubleTake*, Summer 2002. Copyright © 2002 by Marshall Jon Fisher. Reprinted by permission of the author.

"Home Alone" by Caitlin Flanagan. First published in *The Atlantic Monthly*, September 2002. Copyright © 2002 by Caitlin Flanagan. Reprinted by permission of the William Morris Agency, Inc., on behalf of the author.

"Researchers Say" by Ian Frazier. First published in *The New Yorker*, December 9, 2002. Copyright © 2002 by Ian Frazier. Reprinted by permission of the author.

Contents

Foreword

THIS YEAR marks the bicentennial of Ralph Waldo Emerson, who was born on May 25, 1803, in Boston, not far from the present editorial offices of Houghton Mifflin, the publisher of this series. When I first suggested the idea of an annual collection of the best essays, back in 1985, I called it *The Emerson Awards*, in honor of America's greatest essayist. Though my title didn't stick (wiser heads prevailed), I continue to find it satisfying that the essay series has been published by two of Emerson's own publishers — first by Ticknor & Fields and then, starting with the 1994 book, by Houghton Mifflin, which celebrated Emerson's centennial by publishing a magnificent twelve-volume edition of his *Complete Works* in 1903–04.

At first, I was disappointed to abandon the idea of the Emerson Awards. He is, after all, the presiding genius of American literature. He means to us what Montaigne means to France, Cervantes to Spain, or Goethe to Germany. Emerson defines and epitomizes the American spirit and imagination. But the sad truth is that he is not read much any longer outside college literature departments, and even there his presence has diminished. Emerson's former publisher was correct to find its renowned author's name in the title a risky proposition: it would sound academic and obsolete, perhaps even pedantic. Besides, at that time publishers were so worried about using the dreaded word "essay" in any way, shape, or form that it was easy to imagine the combination of essays and Emerson amounting to a double whammy.

There's another reason that an Emerson Award was inappropriate, one I didn't fully consider then but would soon begin to notice. The essays that would be under consideration for an Emerson would for the most part bear little resemblance to the essays Emerson wrote. Hardly anyone today writes in the Emersonian style. Occasionally we find various strands of Emerson in the contemporary essay, especially when it embraces nature and spirituality, but his highly aphoristic style with its lack of smooth transitions, his utter disregard for episodic narrative, and his amazing autobiographical reticence are hardly models for today's creative nonfiction writers. It's extremely rare to find a single Emerson essay (even a classic like "Experience" or "Self-Reliance") in any of the numerous college textbooks used in today's introductory or advanced writing classrooms.

This is not to say that Emerson's literary legacy has come to an end. On the contrary, he is as powerful an influence today as ever. It's simply that the influence is now largely invisible. We may not find Emerson on the page, but he's in the air. Beneath the expressive surface of our current literary forms, we still find enduring Emersonian values: the importance of process, renewal, and originality, a respect for the individual angle of perception and the common flow of experience. These values can be found aplenty in today's best essayists, though the essays they write look and behave unlike anything Emerson ever wrote. We admire a familiar, conversational, even intimate voice, but Emerson sounds chilly and philosophically remote; we love to hear anecdotes and personal stories, but Emerson stubbornly refuses to tell them; we're partial to concrete details, but Emerson prefers what he calls "severe abstraction"; we relish memoirs, but Emerson never comes close to writing one, though it would be an interesting exercise for someone to reconstruct one from his voluminous notebooks and journals. It's possible to hate reading Emerson (I know some essayists who do) but still reflect and promote his values, which — given his tremendous influence on the national consciousness — are perhaps inescapable.

In "The American Scholar," a talk delivered in Cambridge in 1837 to the Phi Beta Kappa Society, Emerson wrote what Oliver Wendell Holmes (a member of the audience) called "our intellectual Declaration of Independence." In this landmark essay, one of the best American essays ever, written shortly after one of the worst financial panics in our history, Emerson introduced a topic that would remain central to his thinking and one that would be brilliantly repurposed nearly a century and a half later by Harold Bloom into a formidable literary theory Bloom called "the anxiety of influence." "The American Scholar" explores the hidden powers and awesome dangers of influence, whether in its well-known call for a new American literature that would reject the authority of Europe or in its urgent message to college students to trust themselves more than their academic institutions — a message intentionally designed to disturb some of the hard-line Harvard faculty who attended the address. Read closely and honestly, the essay remains a stiff challenge to American culture and our institutions of higher learning. And therein lies much of Emerson's relevance today.

Emerson's address that late-summer day contains a paradox that has come to characterize his best writing: he invariably uses his enormous powers of persuasion to persuade us *not* to be persuaded. Here is a mode of persuasion that flies in the face of conventional rhetoric and which may be one of his greatest achievements as an essayist. As he says in "The American Scholar," "Genius is always sufficiently the enemy of genius by over influence." Emerson wanted us to remain always wary of persuasive claims, to worry about the slippery slope between intellectual influence and intellectual tyranny. This vigilant skepticism is an inseparable part of our experience in reading the essays, as we encounter a mind in constant struggle with (as Wittgenstein wonderfully put it) "the fascination that forms of language exert upon us." If you miss this internal compositional conflict, you're missing the intellectual and artistic excitement of reading Emerson.

In his bicentennial year we should celebrate the Emerson who so combatively struggles against conventional forms of persuasion that he wants his audience to resist even his own exhortations. Emerson doesn't seek an audience's identification or conversion. "Do not," he writes, "set the least value on what I do, or the least discredit on what I do not, as if I pretended to settle anything as true or false. I unsettle all things." The essays pioneered an entirely new model of communication (one that apparently defies traditional rhetoric) that we have not yet culturally assimilated and that makes Emerson so intellectually refreshing and so worth reading still. As unique and inimitable as they are, however, Emerson's essays continually instruct us on how to read an essay: as the enactment of an individual mind in process. Or as William H. Gass (one of our true Emersonians) aptly puts it: "Emerson made the essay into the narrative disclosure of a thought." Although this series was never called *The Emerson Awards,* it nevertheless pays tribute in volume after volume to one of the world's greatest essayists.

It turns out to be a delightful coincidence that Anne Fadiman, the guest editor of this year's volume, should also be the editor of *The American Scholar.* One of our finest quarterlies, the magazine was founded in 1932 as a publication of the Phi Beta Kappa Society and appropriately named after the famous address. The editors chose the title to reflect Emerson's anti-pedantic and anti-academic attitudes, hoping the journal would fulfill his desire for a literature that confronted life broadly, vigorously, and intelligently outside the narrow confines of specialized disciplines and institutions. This goal is also reflected in the magazine's current motto, taken from Emerson's address: "Life is our dictionary." Anne Fadiman, who herself gave the Phi Beta Kappa address in Cambridge in 1997, had been named editor of *The American Scholar* earlier that year. At first, Anne thought the magazine would have to recuse itself this year, but her concerns over a conflict of interest between editing the magazine and making the selections for this series were solved when the *Scholar*'s editorial board decided (with "Solomonic" wisdom, as Anne says) that — to be fair to its writers — she should stay out of the selection process in this case and the final selections, if any, be left to me. Therefore, I personally made the decision to include Francine du Plessix Gray's magnificent slice of private and public history, "The Debacle."

The Best American Essays features a selection of the year's outstanding essays, essays of literary achievement that show an awareness of craft and forcefulness of thought. Hundreds of essays are gathered annually from a wide variety of national and regional publications. These essays are then screened, and approximately one hundred are turned over to a distinguished guest editor, who may add a few personal discoveries and who makes the final selections.

To qualify for selection, the essay must be a work of respectable literary quality, intended as a fully developed, independent essay on a subject of general interest (not specialized scholarship), originally written in English (or translated by the author) for publication in an American periodical during the calendar year. Today's essay is a highly flexible form, however, so these criteria are not carved in stone. Magazine editors who want to be sure their contributors will be considered each year should submit issues or subscriptions to: Robert Atwan, Series Editor, The Best American Essays, P.O. Box 220, Readville, MA 02137. Writers, editors, and readers can also contact me by writing to: Robert Atwan, Director, The Blue Hills Writing Institute, Curry College, 1071 Blue Hill Avenue, Milton, MA 02186-2395. You can also visit www.curry.edu and look for the writing institute under "Continuing Education." If you use the Curry College address, please be sure to put "Attention: Best American Essays" on the envelope. Writers and editors are welcome to submit published essays from any American periodical for consideration; unpublished work does not qualify for the series and cannot be reviewed or evaluated.

I would like to dedicate this eighteenth volume in the series to two previous contributors who died in the past two years: Lucy Grealy (1963–2002) and Vicki Hearne (1946–2001). "Mirrorings," Lucy Grealy's essay that would be turned into her award-winning memoir, *Autobiography of a Face*, appeared in the 1994 volume, edited by Tracy Kidder. Her essay, in fact, appears right next to Vicki Hearne's "Can an Ape Tell a Joke?" Another of Vicki Hearne's essays had been selected by Susan Sontag for the 1992 collection. These two young writers — both poets and essayists — will be deeply missed. As always, I appreciate the support I receive from the Houghton Mifflin staff, especially Erin Edmison, Eric Chinski, Larry Cooper, Liz Duvall, and Janet Silver. It was a great pleasure to work on the essays this year with Anne Fadiman, who knows this elusive genre inside out. Her keen sense of craft and style, and her editorial acumen, are reflected throughout this collection. Like Emerson, she believes that "Life is our dictionary," and this volume — like all the issues of *The American Scholar* she's edited — abundantly demonstrates that she takes Emerson's motto to heart.

R. A.

Introduction

YOU CAN TELL a lot about people from the books they sleep with. Alexander the Great is said to have slept with a copy of the *Iliad* under his pillow. Charlemagne slept with Saint Augustine's *The City of God*. When Edwin Herbert Land, the founder of Polaroid, was a boy, he snuggled up to Robert Wood's *Physical Optics*.

I used to sleep with a copy of the essays of Montaigne. It was a thick volume — 1,035 pages long, a 1933 Modern Library edition with a threadbare gray cover and a missing spine — that would have made a sizable lump under my pillow. (Those other guys must have had cast-iron cheeks. Or maybe they owned abridged versions.) Montaigne reposed on my bedside table. What our relationship lacked in propinquity it made up in constancy, since I was confined to bed twenty-four hours a day for the first eight months of a fragile pregnancy. I'd spent the previous two decades as a wandering journalist, but now I required a literary trade that could be plied from a horizontal position: hence, my hasty metamorphosis from reporter to essayist. Who better to guide me than the ur-essayist, the inventor of the genre, the man who had retreated from public life at age thirty-eight to a round, bay-windowed, book-lined library on the third floor of a tower at his ancestral château: a solitary room, intentionally difficult of access, its silence broken only by the tolling of the *Ave Maria* on a great bronze bell?

Montaigne's famously meandering essays — "Of Idlenesse," "Of Lyers," "Of Vanitie," "Of Smels and Odors," "Of Vaine Subtilties, or Subtill Devices" (my edition was the creatively spelled 1603 translation by John Florio) — were just the ticket for a supine pregnant

woman who was drifting in and out of sleep and incapable of remembering what she'd been thinking five minutes earlier. They
were, after all, *essaies* — a word their author chose in order to em-
phasize that he was attempting something, not perfecting it —
and therefore didn't aspire to military regimentation. Montaigne
would start talking about the fallibility of human experience, quot-
ing Aristotle and Manilius and Epicurus and sounding splendidly
high-minded, and then he'd drift off into an aside on how he
hated to be interrupted when he sat on his chamberpot. Or he'd
be in the middle of a sober discussion of inherited traits, and all of
a sudden he'd scoot into a three-page detour on his kidney stones
("Oh why have not I the gift of that dreamer, mentioned by *Cicero*,
who dreaming that hee was closely embracing a yong wench;
found himself ridde of the stone in his sheetes!"). This was exactly
the way my own mind was working at the time — it could travel
from motherhood to hemorrhoids at the speed of light — and, far
from being intimidated by Montaigne, I began to think: Hey,
maybe this *is* something I could do. And so, at the age of forty, lying on my left side, wrapped in a sweaty tangle of sheets, propping
a laptop computer on the pillow under which Montaigne might
have rested had I been less princess-and-the-pea-like, I wrote the
first essay I ever submitted to a magazine.

Phillip Lopate has called the personal essay the voice of middle
age. After compiling this volume, during the course of which I
read essays of every conceivable stripe, I'd extend that statement
by saying that *any* essay — personal, critical, expository — is more
likely to be written by someone with a few gray hairs than by a
twenty-five-year-old. (He's too busy finishing his first novel.) Activity and reflection tend to be sequential rather than simultaneous.
And it takes at least a dozen years before the taint of the school-
room — the "essay question," the college application "essay," the
"essay on the principal exports of Bulgaria, due Thursday at
10:00," all of which have as much in common with an essay by
Montaigne as a vitamin pill does with a chocolate truffle — wears
off completely.

By the time Robert Atwan asked if I'd collaborate with him on
this anthology, I had left the world of the dreaded blue-book essay
far behind. The associations of the word were entirely hedonic. For

several years I had worked as the editor of a small literary quarterly, a job I took because I could not imagine a more pleasurable way to make a living than reading essays all day long. The downside, of course, is that most of those essays are unsolicited manuscripts about the application of postcolonialist theory to the works of Beatrix Potter. You can therefore imagine how pleased I was to be invited to spend a few months reading essays that had not only been published but *vetted*. Bob Atwan would swim through the oceans of the year's periodicals like a great baleen whale, letting most of their contents flow through unencumbered, and filtering out only the most delicious bits of plankton for my delectation.

I owned a whole shelf of *Best American Essays* — my favorite color was indigo blue with red and green lettering (1994), my favorite introductions were by Elizabeth Hardwick (1986) and Geoffrey Wolff (1989) — and I'd always wondered how the volumes had been compiled. What criteria were used? What exactly was that list of "Notable Essays" in the back (in which I myself had been sequestered for years before finally making it into the sacred precincts of the collection itself)? How many essays did the "series editor" read, and how many did the "guest editor" read? Perhaps other readers have been similarly curious about the process, so I'll tell you how it went this year.

Though I've met Bob Atwan only once, a year before we embarked on this project together, we've spent the last six months in a frenzy of communication by phone, letter, and e-mail. (He recently confided that I was the first guest editor of this series who used e-mail. By that point, we'd exchanged at least a hundred e-mails, both about this volume and about essays in general. Our correspondence resembled that of two rabid collectors of Hummel figurines, brief and businesslike at the outset but incrementally loosened up by their shared passion.) Bob had started the series in 1986, successfully resisting the advice of one publisher who, leery of the word *essay*, told him, "It's a lovely idea, but shouldn't we call it something else?" Every year he screens about two hundred small and large periodicals and reads about five hundred essays, of which he forwards a hundred or so to the guest editor. (He sent me a hundred and forty-two. Either it was a particularly fertile year or my e-mails gave him the impression that I was insatiable.) Bob's Notable Essays list consists of those hundred or so essays, minus the ones selected as *the* best American essays, plus a few dozen that he considers unsuitable for the collection (too long, too short, too far to one end or the other of the journalistic-academic spectrum) but that nonetheless deserve recognition. The guest editor is also free to select essays from outside the Atwan pool; I picked three.

Twelve batches arrived by FedEx on my doorstop between the end of October and the middle of March. (The process oozed into the spring because so many understaffed quarterlies publish their winter issues long after the snow melts.) The first few were from what Bob called "especially rich sources" — mostly *The New Yorker* and *Harper's Magazine* — and, indeed, I ended up choosing six from the original batch of fifteen. But I didn't start reading right away. I waited until about forty essays had accumulated on my bedside table. The first essay I picked up started like this:

> Life begins somewhere with the scent of lavender. My father is standing in front of a mirror. He has just showered and shaved and is about to put on a suit. I watch him tighten the knot of his necktie, flip down his shirt collar, and button it up. Suddenly, there it is, as always: lavender.

Whoa! I thought. There was a little neck-prickle. The prose was simple, almost hushed, but I got the feeling that the author was just revving up, that complexity and voluptuousness and clangor would follow in due time, and that I was going to be taken somewhere unexpected. I was already certain that I wanted this essay — "Lavender," by André Aciman — and although of course it *could* have taken a turn for the worse, I knew it wasn't going to, and it didn't. When I got to the end — an intricate, heartbreaking sentence three times as long as that taciturn first paragraph — I said to my husband, "I've got the first one."

They weren't all that good. At first I wondered if I could find two dozen that I didn't just like, I loved. What captivated me? A memorable voice, like Brian Doyle's wild Irish tenor in "Yes." (In an article, content trumps style; in an essay, style trumps content.) Shapeliness, like the graceful arc of Atul Gawande's "The Learning Curve," which starts and ends with the insertion of a central line into a surgical patient's vena cava. (The best writers had wonderful beginnings and endings; the less skilled ones were comfortable in the midzone, but they got self-conscious in the places they thought were Important and started sounding orotund or abstract or corny.) Restraint, as in Myra Jehlen's "F. P.," an essay about death that had innumerable opportunities for melodrama and turned its back on every one. (Why is it assumed that personal essays must be self-indulgent?) Attention to detail, as in Frederic Morton's "A Delivery for Fred Astaire," which describes the narrator's hunger to sound American as precisely as it describes the apricot tarts he attempts to deliver to Mr. Astaire. (Vagueness is the essayist's mortal enemy.) The determination to explore one thing deeply, as in "Wooden Dollar," Ben Metcalf's revisionist portrait of Sacajawea, rather than cover the waterfront. (Given the essay's space constraints, monumentality can be catastrophic.) Vitality, as in Edward Hoagland's "Circus Music," which contains enough life to fill ten tents. (Some essays were craftsmanlike but desiccated; I wanted to hear the pulsing of blood through their veins.) Density, as in Marshall Jon Fisher's "Memoria ex Machina," whose paragraphs are assembled as tightly as the machines they describe. (By density, I don't mean obscurity; I liked essays that were as clear as newly Windexed windowpanes, and if I couldn't understand something, out it went. I mean the sort of density my daughter had in mind when, in the course of her seventh-grade science fair project, she discovered that a pint of cheap ice cream is pumped full of air and is therefore as light as a feather, whereas a pint of Häagen-Dazs weighs a ton. It's *crammed*. The essays in this book, even the long ones, have no extra air. They're all Häagen-Dazs.)

Some of my favorite essays demanded a loose-constructionist interpretation of the anthology's rules. Conventional reviews are barred from this volume's precincts. Caitlin Flanagan's "Home Alone" was a review of two books about Martha Stewart, but it was also *about* Martha Stewart; Judith Thurman's "Swann Song" was a review of Yves Saint Laurent's final haute couture show, but it was also about Saint Laurent, and fashion, and Judith Thurman. I had admired both essays from the get-go, partly because they were so beautifully written and partly because they were about subjects that rarely make it into this collection. Like doormen at an after-hours club who size up potential patrons to see if they're wearing the right clothes, Bob and I decreed that these were both bona fide essays and let them in. Book excerpts are supposed to be admitted only if they're freestanding sections or chapters; Francis Spufford's "The Habit" was drawn from several parts of a memoir. But the assembly, done jointly by the author and his editor at *Granta,* was so elegant that the result was no mere patchwork: the only word that could possibly describe it was *essay.* We were delighted to open the door.

As Bob explains in his Foreword, I did not participate in selecting essays from *The American Scholar,* the journal I edit. He did it solo, with no *sub rosa* whispers from my direction, though when he told me he had chosen Francine du Plessix Gray's "The Debacle," I was overjoyed. Gray's account of fleeing Paris in 1940, set against the larger backdrop of France's role in the Second World War, had knocked me out the first time it tumbled out of my fax machine and continued to knock me out every time I read it.

As the batches poured in, I started seeing common themes. Dozens of essayists wrote — some very well — about illness, their own or others': depression, dementia, breast cancer, intestinal blockage, autoimmune dysautonomia, posterior cortical atrophy, cystinosis, cerebral palsy, diabetic peripheral circulatory disease. (Bob Atwan wrote me that he had also read essays about acid indigestion and ingrown toenails, but had spared me.) Happy essayists were rare; those who weren't sick had lost a friend or a partner or a dog or their hair, or they'd fallen in love with the wrong person, or they'd gotten into car accidents. (I read four essays on driving — Katha Pollitt's "Learning to Drive" had the keenest edge and the best sense of humor — not one of which was about the joys of tooling down a country road in a convertible. Their authors were all *bad* drivers.) Amid this misery, good cheer stood out like a beacon. When I read "The Reporter's Kitchen," the story of Jane Kramer's intertwined lives as writer and cook, I felt like sending her a thank-you note for so thoroughly enjoying her Bumble Bee tuna curry and her Botswanese mealie-mealie. As for Adam Gopnik's "Bumping Into Mr. Ravioli" (along with the Aciman essay, one of a handful for which I felt instant anthology-lust), you know that the author isn't really worried about his daughter's imaginary friend. He loves his daughter, he loves New York, he even loves Mr. Ravioli.

Although three quarters of the candidates Bob sent me were personal essays, some of my favorites, though hardly *im*personal, had little or nothing to do with their authors' lives. Rachel Cohen's

"Lost Cities" did just what a critical essay ought to do: made me itch to read the writers she wrote about (one of whom, Fernando Pessoa, was completely unfamiliar to me). Susan Sontag's "Looking at War" and Michael Pollan's "An Animal's Place" both used the essay form to frame magnificent arguments, strengthening their positions by presenting the other side of every question as carefully as they presented their own. Ian Frazier's "Researchers Say" took aim at the pallid language of the sociological survey and nailed it. Of course, there are times when only the first person will do. Joseph Epstein recused himself from the first two thirds of "In a Snob-Free Zone," but he could not have completed his tour of that utopian kingdom without admitting — candidly, ruefully, wittily — that he didn't live there himself.

There were many essays about September 11, 2001. I chose Elaine Scarry's "Citizenship in Emergency" and John Edgar Wideman's "Whose War," two polemics that couldn't be more different from each other, because each made me look in a new way at something about which I had thought originality was no longer possible. I concluded that the best work on 9/11 was probably written not in 2001 but in 2002. Time allowed these writers to shake off the conventional responses that would have come more easily and find something hard and brilliant and uncomfortable underneath.

Though I read most of the essays for the first time in bed (a good place to forge intuitive bonds) and reread them the next morning in my office, the only occasion on which I read more than five or six at a stretch was on board a plane. I was returning home from California, where I had attended the funeral of a Hmong friend, the father of a large family. The mourners had beaten a death drum, sacrificed a cow, and wept so copiously over the open casket that my friend's blue silk jacket was damp from fallen tears. But the funeral had gone on for three days and three nights, and no one can keep up that sort of thing continuously, so the mourners had taken periodic breathers in the lobby, sitting on folding chairs and playing cards. I didn't think this was disrespectful. I had recently lost my mother, and I knew that's what grief is like: one minute you cry so hard you think you'll burst, and the next minute you play cards. Among the twenty or thirty essays I read on the way home were Cheryl Strayed's "The Love of My Life" and Donald Antrim's "I Bought a Bed." Both writers had lost their mothers. Afterward, Strayed slept with men she hardly knew and Antrim went bed-shopping. I thought both of them got it exactly, and excruciatingly, right: tears and cards.

"Let us here by the way insert a tale," wrote Montaigne, announcing that he was about to steer an essay on habit into a digression on nose-blowing. (A gentleman of his acquaintance, criticized for sneezing into his hand, pointed out that it was far less civilized to reserve a piece of delicate linen for this purpose, fold it tidily, and carry it around all day long.) My tale is about editing, and its purpose is to explain why this collection contains eight essays from *The New Yorker* and four from *Harper's Magazine* even though, as the editor of a "little magazine," I vowed at the ouset that this would be the volume in which the *The Suburban Cincinnati Aviation and Dentistry Review* would finally be granted its place in the sun.

A few years ago, the author of an autobiographical essay I was planning to publish in *The American Scholar* — a very fine writer — died suddenly. The writer had no immediate relatives, so I asked his longtime editor at *The New Yorker* if he would read the edited piece, hoping he might be able to guess which of my minor changes the writer would have been likely to accept and which he would have disliked. Certainly, said the editor. Two days later, he sent the piece back to me with comments on my edits and some additional editing of his own. "My suggestions are all small sentence tweaks," he wrote. "I could hear ———— 's voice in my head as I did them and I'm pretty sure they would have met with his approval — most of them, anyway." Some examples: "A man who looked unmusical" became "a man so seemingly unmusical." "They made a swift escape to their different homes" became "They scattered swiftly to their various homes." "I felt that that solidity had been fostered by his profession" became "That solidity, I felt, had been fostered by his profession." These were, indeed, only small tweaks, but their precision filled me with awe. Of *course* you couldn't look unmusical. Of *course* it was awkward to use "escape" (singular) with "homes" (plural). Of *course* I should have caught "that that." I faxed the piece to my entire staff because editors rarely get a chance to see the work of other editors; we see only its results. This was like having a front-row seat at the Editing Olympics.

Five days later, the editor sent the piece back to us, covered with a second round of marginalia. "No doubt this is more than you bar-

gained for," he wrote. "It's just that when the more noticeable imperfections have been taken care of, smaller ones come into view
. . . I've even edited some of my own edits — e.g., on page 25,
where I've changed 'dour,' which I inserted in the last go-round, to
'glowering.' This is because 'dour' is too much like 'pinched,'
which I'm also suggesting."

If you're not a writer, this sort of compulsiveness may seem well
nigh pathological. You may even be thinking, "What's the difference?" But if you *are* a writer, you'll realize what a gift the editor
gave his old friend. Had not a word been changed, the essay would
still have been excellent. Each of these "tweaks" — there were perhaps a hundred, none more earthshaking than the ones I've
quoted — made it a little better, and their aggregate effect was to
transform an excellent essay into a superb one.

Now, back to *The Best American Essays*. (The writer Emily Fox
Gordon once told me that narratives are like expressways — once
you're on, you have to keep going — but essays let you get on and
off your main subject whenever you want.) One of the rules of the
series is that although typos, factual errors, and grammatical mistakes may be corrected, nothing may be rewritten. It upset me that
so many intelligent and deeply felt essays ended up not (quite) being admitted into these pages because they were occasionally
clumsy or wordy or repetitive — because, in other words, they
needed the kind of editing I've just described. Most of those essays
had appeared in small quarterlies that could never lavish the sort
of care a large, solvent, glossy magazine can afford. "It's not fair!" I
said to my husband, who had read many of these essays alongside
me. "This series should be renamed *The Best-Edited American Essays!*"

Was it unfair? Was it like running a beauty contest in which most
of the winners had had collagen injections?

No. Most of the candidates from *The New Yorker* and *Harper's*
were — I hate to admit it — just plain better. I have no idea how
extensively they had been edited before I saw them. Some of their
authors had doubtless polished their own sentences to a high
gloss, and others, no less talented, had left that final step to editors
graced with more anally retentive personalities.

Wouldn't Montaigne, the champion of the itinerant, risk-taking,
tentative *essaie*, have voted for the scruffy underdogs?

Probably. But these were supposed to be the *best* American essays. I had to judge them on merit. And, as an editor, I had to think of my profession not as a guilty secret but as part of a proud collaboration: 95 percent writing, 5 percent editing. If you don't get that 5 percent, you're not as good as you could be. Or as good as you deserve to be.

At first there were three piles: YES, NO, and MAYBE. After a while, I divided MAYBE into HIGH MAYBE, LOW MAYBE, and PROBABLY. Then I subdivided PROBABLY into PROBABLY PLUS and PROBABLY MINUS. My husband shook his head. I knew that nothing below PROBABLY PLUS had a chance, but there were some essays to which I had grown so attached that I needed to honor them in some way even if their authors would never know.

I had worried I might not fall in love with enough essays, but of course, the day before the deadline, there were thirty-six essays in my YES and PROBABLY PLUS piles. Why couldn't the book be five hundred pages long? The final cut was painful. I did it late at night, reducing my six piles to two: NO (teetering) and YES (short and sturdy). There were twenty-four essays in the YES pile. I arranged them alphabetically, the way they would appear in the book, and saw for the first time who would sit next to whom. Some of the writers probably knew each other already — wouldn't André Aciman and Donald Antrim be invited to the same parties? — but I was pretty sure that others would be meeting for the first time. Edward Hoagland, this is Myra Jehlen. Susan Sontag, this is Francis Spufford. I hope you enjoy each other's company.

Then I read through all twenty-four essays, marking my favorite parts. This is the moment at which editors always say, "I've chosen these passages at random." Don't believe them. From the many passages I underlined that night, I've chosen the following five because I enjoy rereading them and because they show that when it comes to essays, there are many ways to skin a cat.

> It seems that the appetite for pictures showing bodies in pain is almost as keen as the desire for ones that show bodies naked. For a long time, in Christian art, depictions of Hell offered both of these elemental satisfactions . . . No moral charge attaches to the representation of these cruelties. Just the provocation: Can you look at this? There is the satisfaction of being able to look at the image without flinching. There is the pleasure of flinching.
> — Susan Sontag

Hear what I'm saying. We ain't going nowhere, as the boys in the hood be saying. Nowhere. If you promote all the surviving Afghans to the status of honorary Americans, Mr. President, where exactly on the bus does that leave me. When do I get paid. When can I expect my invitation to the ranch. I hear Mr. Putin's wearing jingle-jangle silver spurs around his dacha. Heard you fixed him up with an eight-figure advance on his memoirs. Is it true he's iced up to be the Marlboro man after he retires from Russia. Anything left under the table for me. And mine.

— John Edgar Wideman

Not much was left on the sale rack, but the marvelously refined skirt with its cavalry swagger and feline nap had been marked down to fifteen pounds — one of its zippers was "as seen." I had a week's pay in my pocket: fifteen pounds. Many of my romances would begin, like this one, as a chance encounter sparked by an obscure hunger, a neat coincidence, and a fatal attraction for the defective.

— Judith Thurman

By the time I reached *The Hobbit*'s last page, though, writing had softened, and lost the outlines of the printed alphabet, and become a transparent liquid, first viscous and sluggish, like a jelly of meaning, then ever thinner and more mobile, flowing faster and faster, until it reached me at the speed of thinking and I could not entirely distinguish the suggestions it was making from my own thoughts.

— Francis Spufford

I say yes to them, yes yes yes, and to exhaustion I say yes, and to the puzzling wonder of my wife's love I say O yes, and to horror and fear and jangled joys I say yes, to rich cheerful chaos that leads me sooner to the grave and happier along that muddy grave road I say yes, to my absolute surprise and with unbidden tears I say yes yes O yes.

— Brian Doyle

To the glories of essays I say yes.

For six months, where Montaigne once rested, a pile of essays overflowed my bedside table. That table is now empty. I miss the mess.

ANNE FADIMAN

The Best
AMERICAN
ESSAYS
2003

ANDRÉ ACIMAN

Lavender

FROM HARVARD REVIEW

I

LIFE BEGINS somewhere with the scent of lavender. My father is standing in front of a mirror. He has just showered and shaved and is about to put on a suit. I watch him tighten the knot of his necktie, flip down his shirt collar, and button it up. Suddenly, there it is, as always: lavender.

I know where it comes from. An elaborately shaped bottle sits on the dresser. One day, when I'm having a very bad migraine and am lying on the living room sofa, my mother, scrambling for something to take my mind off the pain, picks up the bottle, unscrews the cap, and dabs some of its contents onto a handkerchief, which she then brings to my nose. Instantly, I feel better. She lets me keep the handkerchief. I like to hold it in my fist, with my head tilted slightly back, as if I'd been punched in a fistfight and were still bleeding — or the way I'd seen others do when they were feeling sick or crushed and walked about the house taking occasional sniffs through crumpled handkerchiefs in what looked like last-ditch efforts to avoid a fainting spell. I liked the handkerchief, liked the secret scent emanating from within its folds, liked smuggling it to school and taking furtive whiffs in class, because the scent brought me back to my parents, to their living room, and into a world that was so serene that just inhaling its scent cast a protective cloud around me. Smell lavender and I was sheltered, happy, beloved. Smell lavender and in came good thoughts — about life, about those I loved, about me. Smell lavender and, no matter how far from each other, we were all gathered in one warm, snug room stuffed with pillows, close to a crackling fire, with the patter of rain outside to remind us our lives were secure. Smell lavender and you couldn't pull us apart.

My father's old cologne can be found the world over. I have only to walk into a large department store and there it is. Half a century later it looks exactly the same. I could, if I were prescient enough and did not want to risk walking into a store one day and not finding it, purchase a tiny bottle and keep it somewhere, as a stand-in for my father, for my love of lavender, or for that fall evening when, as an adolescent, I'd gone with my mother to buy my first aftershave lotion, but couldn't make up my mind and returned alone the next evening after school, happy to discover, among so many other things, that a man could use shaving as an excuse for wearing perfume.

I was baffled to find there were so many scents in the world, and even more baffled to find my father's scent among them. I asked the salesman to let me sample my father's brand, mispronouncing its name on purpose, overdoing my surprise as I examined its slanted shape as though it were a stranger whom I had hailed in error, knowing that the bottle and I were on intimate terms at home, that if it knew every twist my worst migraines took — as I knew every curve on its body — it knew of my imaginary flights from school in Mother's handkerchief, knew more about my fantasies than I dared know myself. And yet, in the shop that was about to close that day and whose owner was growing ever more impatient with my inability to choose, I felt mesmerized by something new, something at once dangerous and enticing, as though these numberless bottles, neatly arranged in stacks around the store, held the promise of nights out in large cities where everything from the buildings, lights, faces, foods, places, and the bridges I'd end up crossing made the world ever more desirable, if only because I too, by virtue of this or that potion, had become desirable — to others, to myself.

I spent an hour testing bottles. In the end I bought a lavender cologne, but not my father's. After paying and having the package gift-wrapped, I felt like I'd been handed a birth certificate or a new passport. This would be me — or me as long as the bottle lasted. Then we'd have to look into the matter again.

*

Over time, I discovered all kinds of lavenders. There were light, ethereal lavenders; some were mild and timid, others lush and overbearing, some tart, as if picked from the field and left to parch in large vats of vinegar; others were overwhelmingly sweet. Some lavenders ended up smelling like an herb garden; others, with hints of so many spices, were blended beyond recognition.

I experimented with each one, purchased many bottles, not just because I wanted to collect them all or was searching for the ideal lavender — the hidden lavender, the ur-lavender that superseded all other lavenders — but because I was eager to either prove or disprove something I suspected all along: that the lavender I wanted was none other than the one I'd grown up with and would ultimately turn back to once I'd established that all the others were wrong for me. Perhaps the lavender I wanted was basic lavender. Ordinary lavender. Papa's lavender. You go out into the world to acquire all manner of habits and learn all sorts of languages, but the one tongue you neglect most is the one you've spoken at home, just as the customs you feel most comfortable with are those you never knew were customs until you saw others practice completely different ones and realized you didn't quite mind your own, though you'd strayed so far now that you probably no longer knew how to practice them. I collected every fragrance in the world. But my scent — what was *my* scent? Had I ever had a *scent*? Was there going to be one scent only, or would I want all of them?

What I found after purchasing several aftershave lotions was that they would all lose their luster, like certain elements in the actinide series that have a brief radioactive life before turning into lead. Some smelled too strong, or too weak, or too much of such and such and not enough of this or that. Some failed to bring out something essential about me; others suggested things that weren't in me at all. Perhaps finding fault with each fragrance was also my way of finding fault with myself, not just for choosing the wrong fragrance each time, or for even thinking I needed a fragrance in the first place, but for believing that the blessings conferred by cologne could ever bring about the new life I yearned for.

And yet, even as I criticized each fragrance, I found myself growing attached to it, as though something that had less to do with the fragrances themselves than with that part of me that had sought them out and been seduced by them and finally blossomed because of them should never be allowed to perish. Sometimes the history of provisional attachments means more to us than the attachments themselves, the way the history of a love affair stirs more love than the affair itself. Sometimes it is in blind ritual and not faith that we encounter the sacred, the way it is habit, not character, that makes us who we are. Sometimes the clothes and scents we wear have more of us in them than we do ourselves.

The search for ideal lavender was like the search for that part of me that needed nothing more than a fragrance to emerge from the sleep of thousands. I searched for it the way I searched for my personal color, or for a brand of cigarettes, or for my favorite composer. Finding the right lavender would finally allow me to say, "Yes, this is me. Where was I all this time?" Yet, no sooner is the scent purchased, than the me who was supposed to emerge — like the us who is about to emerge when we buy new clothes, or sign up for a magazine that seems so thoroughly right for us, or purchase a membership to a health club, or move to a new city, or discover a new faith and practice new rituals with new congregants among whom we make new friends — this me turns out to be, of course, the one we'd always wished to mask or drive away. What did I expect? Different scent, same person.

Over the past thirty-five years I have tried almost all the colognes and aftershave lotions that perfume manufacturers have concocted. Not just lavenders, but pine, chamomile, tea, citrus, honeysuckle, fern, rosemary, and smoky variations of the most rarefied leathers and spices. I liked nothing more than to clutter my medicine cabinet and the entire rim of my bathtub with bottles two and three deep, each vial like a tiny, unhatched effigy of someone I was, or wished to be, and, for a while, thought I'd finally become. Scent A: purchased in such and such a year, hoping to encounter happiness. Scent B: purchased while scent A was almost finished; it helped me abandon A. C, marking sudden fatigue with B. D was a gift. Never liked it; wore it to make the giver happy, stopped using it as soon as she was gone. Comes E, which I loved so much that I eventually purchased F, along with nine of its sibling scents made by the same house. Yet F managed to make me tire of E and its isotopes. Sought out G. Disliked it as soon as I realized that someone I hated loved it. Then H. How I loved H! Stayed with H for years. They don't make it any longer, should have stocked up on it. But then, much as I loved it, I had stopped using it long before its man-ufacturer discontinued it. Back to E, which I had always liked. Yes, definitely E. Until I realized there had always been something slightly off, something missing about E. I stopped using it again. Of the woman who breezed through my life and, in the ten days I knew her, altered me forever, all I remember is her gift. I contin-ued to wear the fragrance she'd given me as a way of thinking she'd be back soon enough. Now, twenty years later, all that's left of her is a bottle that reminds me less of her than of the lover I once was.

I have thrown many things away in life. But aftershave bottles, never. I take these bottles wherever I move, the way the ancients traveled with their ancestral masks. Each bottle contains a part of me, the formaldehyded me, the genie of myself. One could, as in an Arabian tale, rub each bottle and summon up an older me. Some, despite the years, are still alive, though not a thing they own or wear is any longer in my possession; others have even died or grown so dull I want nothing more to do with them; I've forgotten their phone number, their favorite song, their furtive wishes. I take up an old scent and, suddenly, I remember why this scent always re-minds me of the most ardent days of my life — ardent not because they were happy times, but because I had spent so much time thirsting for happiness that, in retrospect, some of that imagined happiness must have rubbed off and scented an entire winter, cast-ing a happy film over days I've always known I'd never wish to re-live. And as I hold this bottle, which seems more precious than so many things, I begin to think that one day someone I love — par-ticularly someone I love — will happen along and open it and won-der what this scent could possibly have meant to me. What was it I'd wished to keep alive all these years? This is the scent of early spring when they called to say things had gone my way. This of an evening with my mother, when she came to meet me downtown and I thought how old she looks — now I realize she was younger by ten years than I am today. This the night of the A-minor. "And this?" they'll want to ask. "How about this one?"

Fragrances linger for decades, and our loved ones may remem-ber us by them, but the legend in each vial clams up the moment we're gone. Our genie speaks to no one. He simply watches as those he's loved open and investigate. He's dying to scream with the agony of ten Rosetta stones begging to be heard across the centuries. "This was the day I discovered pleasure. And this — how couldn't any of you know? — this was the night we met, standing outside Carnegie Hall after a concert, and how simply one thing led to another, and afterward, when it rained, we had waited a while under the cantilever, both reluctant to leave, having found a pretext in rain, strangers starting to talk, making a quick dash into a nearby coffee shop — deplorable coffee, damp shoes, wet hair, surly foreign waiter mumbling Unspeakanese when we tipped him kindly — and sat and spoke of Mahler and *The Four Quartets,* and no one would have guessed, not even us, we'd end up together in a studio on the Upper West Side." But the voice cannot be heard. To die is to forget you ever lived. To die is to forget you loved, or suffered, or got and lost things you wanted. Tomorrow, you say to yourself, I won't remember anything, won't remember this face, this knee, this old scar, or the hand that wrote all this.

The bottles are stand-ins for me. I keep them the way the ancient Egyptians kept all of their household belongings: for that day when they'd need them in their afterlife. To part with them now is to die before my time. And yet, there are times when I think there should have been many, many other bottles there — not just bottles I lost or forgot about, but bottles I never owned, bottles I don't even know exist and, but for a tiny accident, might have given an entirely different scent to my life. There is a street I pass by every day, never once suspecting that in years to come it will lead to an apartment I still don't know will be mine one day. How can I not know this — isn't there a science?

Conversely, there are places I bid farewell to long before knowing I must leave, places and people whose disappearance I rehearse not just to learn how to live without them when the time comes but to put off their loss by foreseeing it a bit at a time beforehand. I live in the dark so as not to be blinded when darkness comes. I do the same with life, making it more conditional and provisional than it already is, so as to forget that one day . . . one day my birthday will come around and I won't be there to celebrate it.

It is still unthinkable that those who caused us the greatest pain and turned us inside out could at some point in time have been totally unknown, unborn to us. We might have crossed them in numberless places, given them street directions, opened a door for them, stood up to let them take their seat in a crowded concert hall, and never once recognized the person who would ruin us for everyone else. I'd be willing to shave years from the end of my life to go back and intercept that evening under a cantilever when we both put our coats over our heads and rushed through the rain after coffee and I said, almost without thinking, I didn't want to say goodnight yet, although it was already dawn. I would give years, not to unwrite this evening or to rewrite it, but to put it on hold and, as happens when we bracket off time, be able to wonder indefinitely who I'd be had things taken another turn. Time, as always, is given in the wrong tense.

The walls of the Farmaceutica of Santa Maria Novella in Florence are lined with rows of tiny drawers, each of which contains a different perfume. Here I could create my own scent museum, my own laboratory, my imaginary Grasse, the perfume capital of France, with all of its quaint *ateliers* and narrow lanes and winding passageways linking one establishment to the next. My scent museum would even boast its own periodic table, listing all the perfumes in my life, beginning, of course, with the first, the simplest, the lightest — lavender, the hydrogen of all fragrances — followed by the second, the third, the fourth, each standing next to the other like milestones in my life, as though there were indeed a method to the passage of time. In the place of helium (He, atomic number 2) I'd have Hermès, and in the place of lithium (Li, 3) Liberty; Bernini would replace beryllium (Be, 4), Borsari boron (B, 5), Carven carbon (C, 6), Night nitrogen (N, 7), Oynx oxygen (O, 8), and Floris fluorine (F, 9). And before I know it my entire life could be charted by these elements alone: Arden instead of argon (Ar, 18), Knize instead of potassium (K, 19), Canoë for calcium (Ca, 20), Guerlain for germanium (Ge, 32), Yves Saint Laurent for yttrium (Y, 39), Patou for platinum (Pt, 78), and, of course, Old Spice for osmium (Os, 76).

As in Mendeleyev's periodic table, one could sort these scents in rows and categories: by herbs; flowers; fruits; spices; woods. Or by places. By people. By loves. By the hotels where this or that soap managed to cast an unforgettable scent over this or that great city. By the films or foods or clothes or concerts we've loved. By perfumes women wore. Or even by years, so that I could mark the bottles as my grandmother would when she labeled each jar of marmalade with her neat octogenarian's cursive, noting on each the fruit and the year of its make — as though each scent had its own *werkeverzeichnis* number. Aria di Parma (1970), Acqua Amara (1975), Ponte Vecchio (1980).

The aftershaves I used at eighteen and at twenty-four, different fragrances, yet located on the same column: a voyage to Italy is what they shared in common. Me at sixteen and me at thirty-two: twice the age, yet still nervous when calling a woman for the first time; at forty I couldn't solve the calculus problems I didn't understand at twenty; I had reread and taught *Wuthering Heights* so many times, but the scenes I remembered best at forty-eight were those retained from my very first reading at twelve, four "generations" earlier. Me at 14, 18, 22, 26 — life retold in units of four. Me at 21, 26, 31, 36, of fives. The folio method, the quarto method, the octavo — in halves, in fourths, by eighths. Life arranged in Fibonacci's sequence: 8, 13, 21, 34, 55, 89. Or in Pascal's: 4, 10, 20, 35, 56. Or by primes: 7, 11, 13, 17, 19, 23, 29, 31. Or in combinations of all three: I was handsome at twenty-one, why did I think I wasn't; I had so much going for me at thirty-four, why then was I longing to be who I'd been at seventeen? At seventeen, I couldn't wait to be twenty-three. At twenty-three, I longed to meet the girls I'd known at seventeen. At fifty-one, I'd have given anything to be thirty-five, and at forty-one was ready to dare things I was unprepared for at twenty-three. At twenty, thirty seemed the ideal age. At eighty, will I manage to think I'm half my age? Will there be summer in the snow?

Time's covenants are all warped. We live Fibonacci lives: three steps forward, two steps back, or the other way around: three steps forward, five back. Or in both directions simultaneously, in the manner of spiders or of Bach's crab canons, spinning combinations of scents and elective affinities in what turns out to be an endless succession of esters and fragrances that start from the simplest and fan out to the most complex: one carbon, two carbons, three carbons: six hydrogens, eight hydrogens, ten . . . $C_3H_6O_2$, ethyl formate; $C_4H_8O_2$, ethyl acetate; $C_5H_{10}O_2$, ethyl propionate; $C_5H_{10}O_2$, methyl butanoate (which has an apple aroma); $C_5H_{10}O_2$, propyl ethanoate (pear aroma); $C_6H_{12}O_2$, ethyl butyrate; $C_7H_{14}O_2$, ethyl valerate (banana); $C_8H_{10}NO_2$, methyl anthranilate (grape);

$C_9H_{10}O_2$, benzylyl ethanoate (peach); $C_{10}H_{12}O_2$, ethyl phenyl-ethanoate (honey); $C_{10}H_{20}O_2$, octyl ethanoate (orange-apricot); $C_{11}H_{22}O_2$, ethyl decanoate (cognac); $C_9H_6O_2$, coumarin (lavender). Say lavender and you have a scent, a chain, a lifetime.

And here lay Mendeleyev's genius. He understood that, though he could plot every element, many elements hadn't been discovered yet. So he left blank spaces on his table — for missing elements, for elements to come — as though life's events were cast in so orderly and idealized a numerical design that, even if we ignored when they'd occur or what effect they might have, we could still await them, still make room for them before their time. Thus, I too look at my life and stare at its blind spots: scents I never discovered; bottles I haven't stumbled on and don't know exist; selves I haven't been but can't claim to miss; pockets in time I should have lived through but never did; people I could have met but missed out on; places I might have visited, gotten to love and ultimately lived in, but never traveled to. They are the blank tiles, the "rare-earth" moments, the roads never taken.

II

There is another fragrance, a woman's perfume. No one I know has ever worn it. So there is no one to associate it with.

I discovered it one fall evening on my way home after a graduate seminar. In Cambridge, Massachusetts, there is a high-end drugstore on Brattle Street, and sometimes, perhaps to dawdle and not head home sooner than I had to, I'd take the long way and stop inside. I liked Brattle Street around Harvard Square, especially in the early evening when the shops were all aglow and people were coming back from work, running last-minute errands, some with children in tow, the bustling traffic of people giving the sidewalks a heady feel I grew to love, if only because it seemed rife with prospects for the evening I already knew were false. The sidewalk was the only place I felt at home in this otherwise cold, anonymous part of town where I wasted so much time and so many years alone, and where everyone I knew always seemed so very busy doing such small things. I missed home, missed people, hated being alone, missed having tea, had tea alone to invoke the presence of someone over tea.

On such evenings the Algiers café was always crowded. It was good to drink tea with strangers, even if one didn't talk to them. A ziggurat of Twinings tins stood on a cluttered counter behind the cash register. I would eventually try each tea, from Darjeeling to Formosa Oolong to Lapsang Souchong and Gunpowder Green. I liked the idea of tea more than the flavors themselves, the way I liked the idea of tobacco more than of smoking, of people more than of friendship, of home more than my apartment on Craigie Street.

The pharmacy stood at the end of a stretch of stores near the corner of Church Street. It was the last spot before I'd turn and head home. I stepped in one evening. Inside, I discovered an entirely different world from the one I'd imagined. The tiny pharmacy was filled with luxury beauty products, luxury perfumes, shampoos of all nations, Old World soaps, balms, lotions, striped toothbrushes, badgers, old-empire shaving creams. I liked it in there. The antique cabinets, the ancient wares, the whole obsolescence of the shop, down to its outdated razors and aging, Central European owners, all seemed welcoming, solicitous. So I asked — because you couldn't loiter without buying something — for an aftershave I thought they wouldn't have, only to find that they not only carried it but also sold its many companion products. So I was obliged to buy something I had stopped using a decade earlier.

A few days later I was back, not just because the pharmacy helped put off my unavoidable walk home, or because I wished to repeat the experience of opening a door and lighting upon a universe of bygone toiletries, but because the store had itself become a last stop in an imaginary Old World, before that world turned into what it really was: Cambridge.

I came again early one evening after seeing a French film at the Brattle Theater. During the showing, it had started to snow outside, and the snow, fast piling on Cambridge, gave every sign of turning into a blizzard that night. A luminous halo hung over Brattle Street just outside the theater, as it had in the small town of Clermont-Ferrand in the movie. In the near-total absence of traffic, some neighborhood children had gathered outside the Casablanca with their sleds and were about to head down toward the Charles River. I envied them.

I did not want to go home. Instead, I decided to trundle over to my pharmacy. It seemed as good a destination as any. I pushed in the glass door as fast as I could, stamping my feet outside before taking shelter within. A young blond woman with a boy of about four was standing inside, holding a handkerchief to her son's nose. The boy made an effort to blow but wasn't successful. The mother smiled at him, at the salesgirl, at me, almost by way of apology, then folded the handkerchief and applied it to his nose again. *"Noch einmal,"* she added. The boy, sticking his head out of a red hood, blew. *"Noch einmal,"* she repeated with a tone of gentle entreaty, which reminded me of my own mother when she implored me to do things that were good for me, her voice filled with so vast a store of patience that it suddenly reminded me how distant I'd grown from the love of others. Within moments, a cold whiff of air blew into the store. The mother had opened the door and, with her child bundled up, walked out into the snow.

Only the salesgirl and I were left. Perhaps because she was no longer in the mood for business on such a spellbound evening, or because it was almost closing time, the salesgirl, who knew me by then, said she would let me smell something really special, and named a perfume. Had I heard of it? I thought I had — on second thought, I wasn't sure. She ignored my attempted fib, and proceeded to open a tiny vial. Having moistened the glass stopper with the perfume, she dabbed it on her skin and in a gesture that made me think she was about to caress me on the cheek — which wouldn't have surprised me, because I'd always felt she had a weakness for me, which was also why I'd come back — she brought an exposed smooth wrist gently to my lips, which I would have kissed on impulse if I hadn't seen the gesture performed at perfume counters before.

No fragrance I'd ever known before smelled anything remotely similar to this. I was at once in Thailand and in France and on a vessel bound for the Bosporus with women who wore furs in the summer and spoke of Webern's *Langsamer Satz* as they turned to me and whispered *Noch einmal?* It eclipsed every fragrance I'd known. It had lavender, but lavender derealized, deferred, dissembled, which is why I asked her to let me smell her wrist again, but she'd seen through my request, and wasn't sure, as I wasn't sure, that it was limited to perfume alone. Instead, she dabbed the bottle stopper on a scent strip, which she snapped out of a tiny wad filled with other strips, waved the paper ever so lightly in the air to let it dry, and then handed it to me, with a look of complicity that suggested she wasn't about to be fooled by my curiosity and had already guessed that there were at least two women in my life who'd want nothing more than to see the scent strip I'd bring home that evening turn into a gift vial within days. That look flattered me no end.

I came back two evenings later, and then again, not for the store now, not for the snow, or for the elusive luster that hovered over Brattle Street in the evening, but for the revelation in that perfume bottle, for the women in furs who smoked Balkans aboard a yacht while watching the Hellespont drift in the distance. I did not even know whether the perfume was my reason for being in there or whether it had become an excuse, the mask behind the mask, because if it was the salesgirl I was after, or the women that the flicker in her eyes had invoked, I also felt that behind her was the image of another woman, my mother, in another perfume store, though I sensed that she too, perhaps, was nothing more than a mask, behind which was my father, years and years ago now, as he stood by the mirror, pleased to be the man he was when he dabbed lavender water on his cheeks after shaving. He too, perhaps, like all the others now, reduced to a threadbare mask for the love and the happiness I was trying to find and despaired I'd never know. The scent summoned me like a numinous mirage from across a divide so difficult to cross that I thought it might not have anything to do with love either, for love couldn't be the source of so much hardship, and therefore perhaps that love itself was a mask, and that if it wasn't love I was after, then the very tip of this vortex around which I'd been circling had to do with me — just me — but a me that was squandered on so many spaces, and on so many layers, that it shifted like mercury the moment I touched it, or hid away like lanthanide, or flared up only to turn into the dullest substance a moment later.

The perfume was so expensive that all I could take with me, after coming up with more excuses, which seemed to prove to the salesgirl that there *were* other women in my life, was a sprinkle on a paper swab. I kept the swab with me, as if it belonged to someone who had gone away for a while and wouldn't forgive me if I didn't sniff it each day.

About a week later, after seeing the same film, I rushed out of the theater and headed toward the pharmacy, only to find that it had already closed. I stayed around for a few minutes, thinking back to the evening when I'd seen the mother and son there, remembering her blond hair bundled under her hat and her eyes that had roamed around the store and lingered on mine while she urged her son on, sensing I both wanted and envied her. Had she overplayed her maternal gaze to forestall any attempt at conversation? Had the salesgirl intercepted my glance?

Now I pictured mother and son coming out of the store, the mother struggling to open her umbrella on Church Street as they headed toward the Cambridge Common, plodding across the empty field with their colored boots sinking deep into the snow, their backs forever turned to me. It felt so real, and they seemed to disappear with such haste as the wind gusted at their backs that I caught an impulse to cry out with the only words I knew: "Mrs. Noch Einmal . . . Mrs. Noch Einmal . . ."

At the time I thought they were an imaginary wife and an imaginary son, the ones I so desperately wished might be mine one day. Me coming back from work and getting off at Harvard Square, she on a last-minute errand before dinner, buying him a toy at the drugstore because she'd promised him one that morning — *so what if we spoiled him a bit! Just fancy, running into each other in the snow, on this day of all days.* But now, through the distance of years, I think she may have been my mother, and the little boy, me. Or perhaps all this is, as ever, a mask. I was both me and my father, me as a student who'd gone to the movies instead of the library, me as the boy's better father, who'd probably have let him savor childhood a bit longer, me in the future giving the boy vague tips about things to come, all of it reminding me that the crib notes we sneak through time are written in invisible ink.

The boy from the pharmacy is thirty years old today — five years older than I was on the day I felt old enough to be his father. Yet, if I am younger still today than he is at thirty, I was on that day in the snow far older than either of us is today.

From time to time I revisit that perfume, especially when I wade through the cosmetics counters on the first floor of large department stores. Invariably I play dumb — "What's this?" I ask, playing the hapless husband trying to buy a last-minute gift. And they tell me, and they try it on for me, sometimes on their own wrists, and they give me sample strips, which I stick in my coat pocket, and take them out, and put them back in, dreaming back to those days when I dreamed of a life I'm no longer sure I lived.

Perhaps fragrance is the ultimate mask, the mask between me and the world, between me and me, the other me, the shadow me I trail and get hints of but cannot know, sensing all along that talk of another me is itself the most insidious mask of all. But then perhaps fragrance is nothing more than a metaphor for the "no" I brought to everything I saw when I could so easily have said "yes" — to myself, to my father, to life — perhaps because I never loved any of the things of the world well enough and hoped to hide it from myself by thinking I could do better by looking elsewhere, or because I loved and wanted each and couldn't determine which to settle for, and therefore stored the very best till a second life rolled in. As irony would have it, the one perfume I want is the one I never purchased. It is also the one every woman I've known has cunningly refused to wear. So there is no one to remember it by. The perfume conjures an imagined life, it conjures no one.

Last winter I returned to the same pharmacy with my nine-year-old son. We did the rounds, as I always do nowadays whenever I go back to places I've spun too many coats around to even bother wondering whether I've ever loved them or not. As usual, I pretend to be looking for a perfume for my wife. "Do you think Mom would like this one?" I ask my son, hoping he'll say no, which he does. I apologize. We look at toothbrushes, soaps, ancient toothpastes, even my father's aftershave sits before me, staring almost with reproof. I let him smell it. He likes it. I ask whether he recognizes it. He does. We sample another. He likes that one too. He is, I catch myself hoping, making his own memories.

Finding nothing to buy, we open the glass door and leave. Taking a quick right, we walk toward the Common. I try to tell him that I'd once had a glimpse of him there almost three decades ago. He looks at me as if I'm crazy. Or was it just me I'd seen decades ago, I ask. This is crazy too, he says. I want to tell him about Frau Noch Einmal, but I can't find the right words. Instead I tell him I am glad he is with me. He cracks a joke. I crack one back.

But I stop all the same and stand a moment on the very same spot and remember the night I'd nearly shouted *noch einmal* to the winds on the snowed-on, empty Cambridge streets, thinking of the German woman and of her lucky husband coming back from work every evening. Here, at twenty-five, I had conjured the life I wished to live one day. Now, at fifty, I was revisiting the life I'd dreamed of living.

Had I lived it? Had I lived my life? And which mattered more and which did I recall best: the one I'd dreamed up or the one I led indeed? Or am I already forgetting both before my time, with life taking back, one by one, the things I thought were mine to keep, turning the cards face down, one by one, to deal someone else another hand?

La Bouilladisse, June 2001

The house where we're staying near Aix-en-Provence is surrounded by lavender bushes that seem to billow and wave whenever a wind courses through the fields. Tomorrow is our last day in Provence, and we've already washed all of our clothes to let them dry in the sun. I know that the next time I'll put on this shirt will be in Manhattan. I know too how the scent of sunlight and lavender trapped within its folds will bring me back to this most luminous day in Provence.

It is ten o'clock in the morning and I am standing in this garden next to a wicker hamper that is filled with today's wash. My wife doesn't know it yet, but I've decided to hang the laundry myself. It's meant as a surprise. I've already brewed coffee.

So here I am, hanging one towel after the other, the boys' underwear, their many T-shirts, their socks flecked with the reddish clay from Roussillon which, I hope, will never wash off. I like the smell. I like separating the shirts on the line, leaving no more than half an inch between them. I must manage my pins and use them sparingly, making sure I'll have enough for the whole load. I know my wife will still find something to criticize in my method. The thought amuses me. I like the work, its mind-numbing pace which makes everything seem so simple, so complacent. I want it never to end. I can see why people take forever to hang clothes out to dry. I like the smell of parched wood on the hanging pins, which are stored in a clay pot. I like the smell of clay too. I like the sound of drops trickling from our large towels onto the pebbles, on my feet. I like standing barefoot, like the sheets, which take forever to hang evenly and need three pins, one at each end and one for good measure in the middle. I turn around and, before picking up another shirt, I run my fingers through a stalk of lavender nearby. How easy it is to touch lavender. To think I fussed so much and for so long — and yet here it is, given to me, the way gold was given to the Incas, who didn't think twice before handing it over to strangers. There is nothing to want here. *Quod cupio mecum est.* What I want, I already have.

Yesterday we went to see the abbey of Senanques. I took pictures of my sons standing in front of a field of lavender. From a distance, the lavender is so dark it looks like a bruise upon a sea of green. Closer by, each plant looks like an ordinary overgrown bush. I taught them how to rub their hands along lavender blossoms without disturbing the bees. We spoke of Cistercian monks and the production of dyes, of spirits, balms and scented extracts, and of Saint Bernard de Clervaux, and of medieval commerce routes that still exist today and that spread from these tiny abbeys to the rest of the world. For all I know my love of lavender may have started right here, in an essence gathered from bushes that grow on these very same fields. For all I know this is where it ends, in the beginning. And yet, for all I know, everything could start all over again — my father, my mother, the girl with the perfumed wrist, Frau Noch Einmal, her little boy, my little boy, myself as a little boy, the walk in the evening snow, the genie in the bottle, the Rosetta stone within each one of us which no one, not even love or friendship, can unburden, the life we think of each day, and the life not lived, and the life half lived, and the life we wish we'd learn to live while we still have time, and the life we want to rewrite if only we could, and the life we know remains unwritten and may never be written at all, and the life we hope others may live far better than we have, all of it, for all I know, braided on one thread into which is spun something as simple as the desire to be one with the world, to find something instead of nothing, and having found something, never to let go, be it even a stalk of lavender.

DONALD ANTRIM

I Bought a Bed

FROM THE NEW YORKER

MY MOTHER, Louanne Antrim, died on a fine Saturday morning
in the month of August, in the year 2000. She was lying in new purple sheets on a hospital-style bed rolled up next to the green oxygen tanks set against a wall in what was more or less the living room
of her oddly decorated, dark and claustrophobic house, down near
the bottom of a drive that wound like a rut past a muddy construction site and back yards bordered with chain-link fence, coming to
an end in the parking lot that served the cheerless duck pond at
the center of the town in which she had lived the last five years of
her life, Black Mountain, North Carolina. The occasion for my
mother's move to North Carolina from Florida had been the death
of her father, Don Self, from a heart attack, in 1995. Don Self's
widow, my mother's mother, Roxanne, was at that time beginning
her fall into senility, and was, in any case, unequipped to manage
the small estate that my grandfather had left in her name. What I
mean to say is that my grandmother, who came of age in the Great
Depression and who brought away from that era almost no concept of money beyond the idea that it is not good to give too much
of it to one's children, was unlikely to continue in her husband's
tradition of making large monthly transfers into my mother's bank
account. Don Self had kept his daughter afloat for a long while —
ever since she'd got sober, thirteen years before, and decided that
she was an artist and a visionary, ahead of her time — and now,
suddenly, it was incumbent on my mother to seize power of attor-
ney over her mother and take control of the portfolio, a coup she
might've accomplished from Miami but was better able to arrange
through what in the espionage community is known as closework.

Four years later, Roxanne Self passed away. The funeral was held at the Black Mountain Presbyterian Church in September of 1999. A week after that, my mother — barely days after having got, as I heard her proclaim more than once, "*free* of that woman, now I'm going to go somewhere *I* want to go and live *my* life" — went into the hospital with a lung infection and learned that she, too, would shortly be dead.

She was sixty-five and had coughed and coughed for years and years. There had never been any talking to her about her smoking. The news that she had cancer came as no surprise. It had grown in her bronchi and was inoperable. Radiation was held out as a palliative — it might (and briefly did) shrink the tumor enough to allow air into the congested lung — but my mother was not considered a candidate for chemotherapy. She had, during the course of forty years of, as they say, hard living, progressively and inexorably deteriorated. The story of my mother's lifelong deterioration is, in some respects, the story of her life. The story of my life is bound up in this story, the story of her deterioration. It is the story that is always central to the ways in which I perceive myself and others in the world. It is the story, or at any rate it is my use of the story, that allows me never to lose my mother.

With this in mind — the story of my mother and me, my mother *in* me — I will try to tell another story, the story of my attempt, during the weeks and months following her death, to buy a bed.

I should say to keep a bed. I bought several. The first was a big fat Stearns & Foster queen from Bloomingdale's at Fifty-ninth Street and Lexington Avenue. My then girlfriend, R., came along to the store, and together we lay down and compared. Shifman? Sealy? Stearns & Foster? Soft? Firm? Pillow top? I watched R. crawl across a mattress; she bounced up and down with her ass in the air, and I found myself thinking, delusionally, about myself in relation to my mother, who had died the week before, At last, I'm *free* of that woman! Now I'm going to buy a great bed and do some fucking and live *my* life.

Two thousand dollars.

Three thousand dollars would've got me a bigger, fatter Stearns & Foster (and, by extension, a bigger, fatter amount of comfort, leading to more contented sleeping, a finer state of love, and an all-round happier, more productive life) or a nearly top-of-the-line

Shifman. The Shifmans were appealing, thanks to the company's advertisements describing traditional (anachronistic?) manufacturing details such as the eight-way, hand-tied box spring; and to its preference for natural fibers (compressed cotton and wool) over synthetic foams.

"What do you think, hon? Do you like the pillow top?"

"The big one over there?"

"Yes."

"That one's great."

"How long will one of these things last? Did the guy say?"

"Donald, get the bed that feels best. You'll be able to buy other beds later."

"Later? What do you mean, later? Later in life?"

"If you get a bed and you don't like it you can send it back. Look. You have thirty days. People send beds back all the time. That's what department stores are for."

"Right."

"Donald, this is something to be excited about! You're buying a great bed for yourself. You deserve it! We should celebrate."

"Yeah."

"Are you OK?"

"Huh?"

"Do you want to try them one more time?"

Which is what we — and, increasingly, *I,* alone — did. I bought bed number 1 using my debit card in early September 2000, went home, called the store, and refused to have it delivered, then went back and upgraded, in late September, to another and more expensive bed (the pillow top), and refused to have that one delivered, after which I set out on what amounted, in retrospect, to a kind of quest or even, one might say, pilgrimage, to many stores, where I tossed and turned and held repetitive, obsessive conversations with professionals and, whenever possible, patient, accompanying friends, my lay public, about beds. Three months passed, during which time I came to learn more than I ever thought I would about mattresses and about the mattress industry in general — not only about how and where the beds are made but about how they are marketed and sold, and to whom — and, as it happened, I learned about other things besides actual beds. I'm referring to comforters, pillows, and sheets.

It might be helpful at this point to say that, during this time that was described and possibly defined by compulsive consumerism, I had a keen sense of myself as a matricide. I felt, in some substantive yet elusive way, that I had had a hand in killing my mother. And so the search for a bed became a search for sanctuary, which is to say that the search for a bed became the search for a place; and of course by *place* I mean *space*, the sort of approximate, indeterminate space one might refer to when one says to another person, "I need some space"; and the fact that space in this context generally consists of feelings did not prevent me from imagining that the *space* — considered, against all reason, as a viable location; namely, my bedroom — could be filled, pretty much perfectly, by a luxury queen-size bed draped in gray-and-white-striped, masculine-looking sheets, with maybe a slightly and appropriately feminine ruffled bed skirt stretched about the box spring (all from Bellora in SoHo). And I imagined, quite logically considering my grief over my mother's passing and over my participation not only in the event of her death that August morning but, as a child and as a man, in the larger narrative of her lifelong self-obliteration through alcoholism and alcoholism's chief symptom and legacy, rage — I imagined, or fantasized, that, once cozy and secure in the space filled by the bed, lying alone or with R. atop pillows stacked high like the pillows on beds photographed for home-decorating magazines, I might discover who I would be and how I would carry on without my mother, a woman who died insane and alone, in a dreary little house, in a crappy, rented bed.

There was not much that anybody could do. My mother in the final years of her life had become drastically, clinically paranoid. She cultivated or was the victim of borderline episodes in which she conversed with figures from mythology and religion. Trained as a tailor and costumer, she crafted bizarre, well-made garments that resembled and were meant to be worn as vestments in spiritual ceremonies the purpose of which remained unclear. Everything about these garments — the winglike adornments festooning the back panels, the little baubles and totem objects depending from the sleeves or the lapels, the discordant color palettes displayed in fabric pieces stitched one atop the other like elements in a strange collage — spoke to a symbolism that was deeply private and brilliantly militant. Worn in public, these robes and gowns were guaranteed to cause unease among people accustomed to functioning in society at large. If my mother wore, to an Asheville concert or museum opening, a dark purple jacket fastened with clown-size buttons and adorned on the front and sides with crisscrossing strips of Thai silk in tropical pastels, a coat emblazoned on the back with an enormous white medallion topped with gold cloth gathered and bunched to resemble a floral cake decoration, a coat finished with more strips of colored silk tied off and hung with drapery tassels descending to varying lengths beneath the hemline, she was not merely acting as a free spirit and doing her thing; she was repudiating the patriarchy and proving her burden as an artist.

Her power to drive people away was staggering. She behaved spitefully and was divisive in her short-lived relationships with the similarly disenfranchised people who became her friends. Her laughter was abrasive, sometimes even frightening. She chewed with her mouth open, often spilling food down her front. Her hair looked at times as if she had cut it herself, in the dark. You were either with her or against her. She believed that her father was not her real father; that her mother had tried to drown her in a pond when she was a child; that her pulmonary specialist wanted to have sex with her; that in death she would be met by Carl Jung, the Virgin Mary, and Merlin the Magician; that she had done her work on earth and that her work was good; that she was one of those who had been chosen to herald the coming new order of beautiful humanity; that she had been an alcoholic for only about a year or so; that in a former life she had died a watery death as a Roman galley slave, shackled to the oars; that men were shits and her children were hostile; that her smoking was her business, and so mind your own fucking business; that her son was an artist just like she was; that she and I should go to therapy together.

She was, for anyone close to her, and especially for those depending on her competency, a threatening person. She had, in fact, lived much of her adult life in a blackout, dreamlessly "sleeping" three hours or less most nights. The loss of REM sleep must have had devastating consequences on her body and mind. She went on screaming campaigns that lasted into the wee hours, and in the morning before dawn could sometimes be found lying on the rug in the living room.

Perhaps her mother *had* tried to drown her in a pond. The truth may have been as bad as that or worse. My mother may have been a victim of Munchausen syndrome by proxy, a perversion of caretaking in which a child is subjected to unwarranted medical interventions, even surgeries. It was suspected by her physicians in North Carolina, as well as by members of our family, that my mother's mother had had a curious habit of taking her only child to the doctor. This is not something I can comment on extensively; I wasn't there — and I object for a variety of reasons to the second-hand psychoanalysis of my mother, working backward from the time of her intense paranoia and delusions of grandeur, through her addictions, marriage, and so on, in search of unifying causes — and yet I can imagine my grandmother Roxanne, in the late 1940s or thereabouts, leading my mother by the hand down some country hospital's white aisles, or sitting with her in the waiting room in a Florida doctor's office. I remember that my mother told stories, when I was young, of operations. What exactly these operations were meant to achieve is a bit of a mystery. One, it seems to me, had to do with the removal of a rib. Can that be right? And there was a famous story that had my mother "waking up" as her doctors pronounced her dead on the table. By the time I was born, Roxanne had become a radical nutritionist, intent on controlling her family's diets and moods; she handed out vitamins and advice to cancer patients who learned about her on the Florida cancer grapevine; she prescribed foods whose use, in some cases (broccoli, kale), was later ratified by the national health industry. I believe she saw herself as a folk hero. It is possible to imagine my mother's death trip as an internalized, masochistically directed act of hatred against her own mother, who used health to suppress everyone around her; and against her father, who, in any number of conceivable scenarios, had been unable to acknowledge how things were for his daughter, or to act as her advocate, in her childhood.

When young, my mother had been popular and a beauty. She was a girl in Tennessee and a teenager in Sarasota, Florida, where she met my father. Together, my parents were, as far as I can tell from their yearbooks, one of those successful, envied high school couples. A friend of theirs, a man who was in love with my mother in college, and had never fallen out of love, described her to me in terms that reveal the force of her sexuality and personality in those days. Because she had no siblings, I have no maternal aunts or uncles who can accurately remember her as a girl. And testimony from my parents' old crowd about later years — after she'd left home, married my father, had her children, and settled down as a wife and mother in graduate school housing — is hard to come by, as are my own memories, memories of the sort that could add up to form a coherent . . . what? Picture? Impression? Narrative? I was four, five, six years old. My sister, Terry, was three, four, five. It was the early sixties, the tail end — as I think of that era now, almost forty years after our father fell in love with another woman, and our family began coming apart — of the heyday of Southern intellectualism in the style of the Agrarians, when the newly married Episcopalian children of Presbyterians were reading *Finnegans Wake*, escaping into Ph.D. programs, drinking bourbon, martinis, and bargain beer, and staying up all night quarreling and having affairs and finding out about the affairs, then tossing *their* children into the back seats of VW bugs and driving by night up or down the coast. To this day, I remain unable to reliably document the progress of my parents' migrations and relocations, the betrayals and reconciliations, the reunions, separations, re-relocations, hospitalizations. Suffice it to say that there is no end to the crazy stories, many of which I have already used too many times as opening gambits on dates.

But what about the bed? In December, I allowed delivery of the pillow top. The Bloomingdale's guys carried it up the stairs, and I dressed it with the sheets and whatnot that I had collected for this occasion. The bed in comparison with the futon I had been sleeping on seemed gigantic. It *was* gigantic; not only broad but tall, it overpowered the bedroom. Its phallic implications were evident in my invitations to R. to "come over and see it." Things should've ended there, with some promising rambunctiousness with R. and a gradual acceptance of a new order in my house. But that would've required me to be a different person and much farther removed in time from my mother's death. It would've required, as well, that I had never heard anything about Dux.

Dux is one of those companies that produce esoteric, expensive products scientifically engineered to transform your life. When you buy a Dux bed, you gain membership in a community of people who have bought and believe in Dux beds. A Dux bed at first seems peculiarly soft; if you stay on one for a while, you may experience yourself as "relaxed" in a way that can actually be alarming. The initial impression is of settling onto a well-calibrated water bed — on a Dux, you really climb *into* bed. The company promises a variety of health benefits, some postural, some having to do with increased deep sleep, all having to do with natural latex and with the myriad coils described in the Dux literature as a "system" that allows the bed to shape itself gently to the body, reducing pressure points and therefore the number of times a sleeping person will shift or move about to get comfortable during the night. "Do you have a Dux?" I have heard the cognoscenti say. Dux beds come with a twenty-year warranty — I seem to remember "The Last Bed You'll Ever Buy" as one of the promotional slogans. The beds are manufactured in Sweden, advertised on classical-music radio stations, sold in company-owned stores that look like spas, and they never, ever go on sale.

I don't know how many times, during the early winter of the year my mother died, I marched — typically by myself, though whenever possible with R. or one of those other aforementioned friends — into Duxiana on East Fifty-eighth Street (conveniently adjacent to Bloomingdale's), where I pulled off my shoes and hopped from bed to bed and read and reread the brochures and harassed Pamela, the manager, with every kind of question about this model versus that. I arranged the Hutterite goose-down pillows. I settled in. I turned onto my side. I turned onto my other side. Wonderful. You could choose mahogany or metallic legs that would elevate the bed to a great height, or you could leave the bed low to the floor, in the manner of sleek beds in European hotels. You could tuck the sheets in this way, drape them that way. Cotton top pad? Or latex? I began to sense, during afternoons reclining at the Dux store, that all the decisions I might make from here on out could flow naturally from the purchase of the right bed. Though I already had my new bed (returnable) in my bedroom, I didn't especially like it. I lacked sufficient *desire* to like the bed. It is true that the bed was large, but in every other respect I found it pedestrian and a letdown, because it was not saving my relationship with R. It was not making my apartment feel like home. It was not writing my book. Worst of all — and this was the failing that hurt the most — it was not allowing me to carry on indefinitely in my search for a bed.

How badly did I want a Dux? I wanted one in exactly the manner and proportion that was appropriate with regard to the product.

I wanted one enough to want to buy one.

It was in this way that a novelist with literary-level sales and a talent for remorse came to lay out close to seven thousand dollars for a mattress.

— Almost.

In the year preceding my mother's death, a year that was characterized by the kind of mood oscillations that accompany the routine progress toward failure of medical therapeutic interventions in advanced cancer cases — the tidal-seeming, almost manic rising and falling, with every piece of news, every stressed-out conversation with Mom or her doctors, of hope and depression, hope and depression, hope and renewed hope and more hope, followed by distracted euphoria and a deeper despair and the weird, impulsive anger that can be directed at practically anybody at any time, the continuum of fear and volatility that is familiar in some form or another to just about anyone who has watched a parent or a child, or a husband or a wife or a lover or a friend, get a little better, then a little worse, then a little better, dying according to the program, as it were — during this year, I more or less stopped working, and I stopped exercising. I read less, went out for dinner with friends less, made love less. I am a cyclist, and for years have had a routine of riding training laps around the park near where I live. My body has been accustomed to this regimen, in which a great amount of physical information is available to me, information in the form of sensations, sensations that come with deep inhalations and exhalations as I walk down the street or, while riding, stand in the pedals to climb a hill; or in the awareness I might have of a gain or a loss in my weight; or in the excitement I can feel when touching another person, or when being touched; information in the form of, I suppose, *myself,* proprioceptively living in space. Little by little, that information disappeared. In the dull absence of myself, I did what my mother had done throughout her life. I sat up nights in my kitchen smoking.

People are fond of saying that the truth will set you free. But what happens when the truth is not one simple, brutal thing? I could not imagine life without my mother. And it was true, as well, that only without her would I feel able to live. I had had enough of Louanne Antrim and was ready for her to be gone. I wanted her dead, and I knew that, in the year of her dying, I would neglect her.

I would and I did. In this, at least, I can claim that I was true to

her — to *us*. I was, after all, her man. It had been my impossible
and defining task to be both like and unlike all other men — more
specifically, like and unlike her father and her errant, excommuni-
cated ex-husband, my father. What does this mean? I'm not sure I
can clearly say. I was never to leave her for another woman — even
as this required my having, over the years, a succession of women. I
was never to lie to or deceive her; and I lied to and deceived her
about everything. When I first began to write and publish novels, it
was understood by my mother, and hence unwittingly by me, that I
was exhibiting, in whatever could be called my artistic accomplish-
ments, *her* creative agency, her gifts. I was to have a powerful cock
and, at the same time, no cock at all.

"I'll come down soon and stay a few days."

"You don't have to come."

"I want to come."

"I'm not expecting you."

"I'll come."

"Don't if you don't want to."

"Mom."

"Don't wait too long. I'm going to die soon."

"How do you know?"

"Dr. McCarrick is trying to kill me."

"Excuse me?"

"He won't take my calls."

"He's a doctor."

"What's that supposed to mean?"

"Nothing. It's a joke. Sort of. Never mind."

"Everyone is against me. You're against me."

"Mom, he's not trying to kill you. No one is trying to kill you. No
one wants to kill you."

I put off the visit. I put it off. A dog in the apartment next to
mine started barking, and for a while I lost my mind. Then the dog
stopped barking and a year had passed and my sister and I were
boarding flights from opposite ends of the country to stand beside
my mother's bed in the little house near the bottom of the hill that
pitched down to the parking lot beside the town lake. It was our
practice, my sister's and mine, to fly into Charlotte, rendezvous at
the airport car-rental desk, get the car, stop off at Bridges, in
Shelby, North Carolina, for barbecue, then head west over the

mountains, past Chimney Rock, up around Old Fort, and down into Black Mountain. The drive took three hours. We could've flown to Asheville, thirty minutes from our mother's house. Terry and I traveled this roundabout way, I think, in order to give ourselves time to prepare for the difficult ordeal of being — for one last time, in this case — Louanne's children in Louanne's house. That day, we managed to be in a hurry and to drive slowly at the same time. Terry talked about her children and about a neighbor who, like our mother, had refused nutrition in the final stages of a terminal illness. It was late on a late-summer afternoon. The farms and weathered churches alongside the two-lane highway had never seemed to me so lonely or so lovely, so beckoning, as they did that afternoon. This was our grandfather's country; and it was his father's, and his father's father's; and it was our mother's and, for that brief time — looking out the car windows at the sights along the way, at touristy Lake Lure and the rocky stream descending the grade in low waterfalls beside the road; at the forlorn houses surrounded by irregularly shaped fields planted with corn and beans; at the kudzu that devours more and more of the South, forest and field, every year — it was ours. I remember thinking that, after she died, there would be no one left to bind me to this part of the world, and I wondered what might cause me, in the future, ever to return.

At the house, we found our mother on the hospital bed in the living room. Beside the bed stood the enormous wooden table on which she had measured and scissored fabrics. Bolts of silk leaned in a corner. Bookshelves held paperbacks about Carl Jung and healing. The day nurse left Terry and me alone. Our mother was on her way to dying. She had informed us, earlier in the summer, that sometime before too long, probably before her birthday, in September, she would, as she had put it, "take matters into my own hands," but she had not told us exactly when; there were celestial and astrological considerations that needed factoring, and she was waiting for the right moment. Now the moment had come. Gazing at her emaciated face in the evening light, I discovered something that Terry had known and I hadn't, which was that our mother used dentures. Oh. These had been taken out. Her mouth was collapsed. She made noises and sounds that could not be interpreted as sentences, or even words. Morphine, dropped off earlier by the hospice workers, waited, sealed, in a bottle in the kitchen. No one, not even the nurse, seemed to know precisely when to begin feeding it to her. So, like the morphine in the bottle in the kitchen, we waited, and the next day my mother "woke" — as the dying sometimes will, briefly — and spoke relatively straightforwardly, if disjointedly, about her past. She called up names of people from Charlottesville and Kingsport and Miami, from Knoxville and Gainesville, Johnson City and Sarasota and Tallahassee. We felt her feet; her feet were warm. My sister gave her a sponge bath and changed her clothes, and we arranged the pillows beneath her head, and the nurse put her teeth in, and my mother asked us, in her broken voice, if we would mind, please, bringing her a martini.

Playing the role of guardian, playing at being powerful, I asked if she thought a martini a good idea, and she answered, quite sensibly, "What harm could it do now?"

Had there been gin and vermouth in the house, I would surely have mixed her a cocktail. Or maybe I wouldn't have. Did I offer her a taste of beer? I don't remember. Was she still taking oxygen? I can't remember that, either. Green tanks and plastic hoses were everywhere. The part-time nurse practitioner, a sweet and competent, though hardly medically knowledgeable, hard-line Christian fundamentalist, and my mother's two female friends, pagan Wiccans as far as I could make out, were in a battle over my mother's soul. It was a minor flare-up of social conflicts in the New South of the old Appalachias — the Christers versus the Shamans — staged over the proxy that was Louanne Antrim's wasted body. Back and forth it went, in whispered private conferences that I staged in the form of peace talks out in the yard:

"They're saying occult things. They're going to hand her over to the Devil. I've got three churches praying for your mom to rise into Jesus' arms."

"That Pentecostal girl's trying to convert Louanne to Christ. Your mother left organized religion behind a long time ago. It's not what she wants."

"Every time I pray for your mom, they come in and they stop me. I'm just worried sick over your mom."

In the end, it fell to me to administer the morphine. I should say that I decided, as the man on the scene, to be the one to give the morphine. Every four hours, I pressed a lorazepam tablet to powder in a spoon, introduced into this powder a small measure of the liquid morphine, drew the solution into an oral syringe, and squirted the drug into my mother's partly open mouth. I was careful to squirt toward the side of her mouth. My sister and I swabbed her lips with sponges, and on the third night her death rattle began. I put on Mozart piano sonatas, but after a while, getting into the spirit of things, I switched to Miles Davis, and afterward to one of my mother's god-awful Kitaro CDs, which, in that worldless nontime around three in the morning, I found myself enjoying. At some point before dawn, my mother's face relaxed and her skin cleared, and, though her throat and chest still rattled terribly, she smiled. It was a broad, unambiguous smile. Terry said to me, "Look, she's getting younger." It was true. In the hours before she died, Louanne began to resemble herself as the young woman we had seen in photographs taken before we were born — full of radiance and with her future and whatever crazed or credible hopes she had ahead of her. Amazingly, this effect occurred in spite of the absence of teeth. I sat in a chair beside the bed and read to her from *The Collected Stories of Peter Taylor,* which she did not seem to appreciate at all — her smile vanished and she actually scowled at the opening to "A Wife of Nashville" — and, though I like Peter Taylor well enough, I felt in that instant real camaraderie with my mother. I left off reading and told her that she had been a good mother, a good artist; that Terry and I loved her and were grateful to her for her care; that those years in Tallahassee, in particular, had been pretty good years; that both of us, both her children, however much we might miss her, had a great deal to live for; that we would be all right without her. The sun came up. Terry drove back to the hotel for a shower and a nap. The New Agers and the kind Christian were away somewhere; and I held my mother's hand and told her that the house was empty except for the two of us, it was just her and me in the house, and it was a nice day outside the windows, birds were in trees, a breeze blew the leaves, clouds crossed the sky, and if she wanted she could go ahead and die, which she promptly did. She turned gray.

From 1966 until the summer of 1968, my sister and I lived with our mother in Tallahassee, Florida. Across the street from us was a church whose steeple had been removed and laid on its side to peel and rust in the yard beside the church. At the top of the street was a gas station where Apalachicola oysters could be bought for five dollars a bushel. Our father was teaching in Virginia; though our parents' first divorce was either final or on the way to being so, he visited monthly, pulling up in his black Volkswagen Beetle, parking in the driveway made of seashells and sand — the cue for Terry and me to rush from the house screaming with excitement. Often, the first evening of his visit we would spend as a family, sitting on the concrete-and-brick porch, shucking and eating dozens of oysters and looking out at the church with its decapitated, useless steeple. My sister and I conspire to remember these as good years, primarily because there was sparingly little head-to-head conflict between our parents, given that they were infrequently together; but also because the three of us, Terry, my mother, and I, became a family of our own, a family that existed in the absence of the family we wished we could be. Terry and I did fine in school; we rode our bikes, built forts using lawn furniture, played with friends from across the street. I joined the Cub Scouts; she was a Brownie. Occasionally, our mother allowed us to stay home from school, and our party of three became a tea party in the living room. There was something approaching normalcy in our lives. In retrospect, I would say that it was a forced normalcy. Our happy family was a worrisomely happy performance of family.

This idea calls to mind a particular event. When I was nine, I got to play the part of Young Macduff in the Florida State University production of *Macbeth*. My mother worked as an assistant costumer in the theater department. It was she who would eventually make my costume, a yellow-orange tunic with a sash for a belt. The tunic, despite repeated washing, became bloodier and bloodier with each new performance. Here are some lines from act 4, scene 2, spoken by Lady Macduff and her son before they are murdered by Macbeth's henchmen:

L. MACD: Sirrah, your father's dead,
         And what will you do now? How will you live?
   SON: As birds do, mother.
L. MACD: What, with worms and flies?
   SON: With what I get, I mean, and so do they.
L. MACD: Poor bird, thou'dst never fear the net nor lime,
         The pitfall nor the gin.
   SON: Why should I, mother? Poor birds they are not set for.
         My father is not dead, for all your saying.

> L. MACD: Yes, he is dead. How wilt thou do for a father?
> SON: Nay, how will you do for a husband?

And:

> SON: Was my father a traitor, mother?
> L. MACD: Ay, that he was.
> SON: What is a traitor?
> L. MACD: Why, one that swears and lies.
> SON: And be all traitors that do so?
> L. MACD: Every one that does so is a traitor, and must be hang'd.

It is but a moment before the killers enter. The stage instructions call for Young Macduff to be murdered first, crying out, "He has kill'd me, mother: Run away, I pray you!" and for her to flee into the wings, crying "Murther!" In our production, both deaths occurred onstage. First I went down, stabbed in the back and in the stomach. My pretend mother ran to my side and knelt beside me. Then she was killed. She fell across me and lay dead (though breathing heavily). It was in this way that I came to fall in love with Lady Macduff. I mean that I fell in love with Janice, the college girl playing Lady Macduff. The lights dimmed to end the scene. Each night, I watched from beneath my mother who was not my mother, as the lights' filaments faded; and, when the stage fell dark, I whispered in Janice's ear, which was practically in my mouth, "OK, get up," because the smell of her, and her hair falling across my face, and her ear in my mouth, and the pressure and heat of her body pressing down onto mine, became too intense to bear.

It seems to me that some of the archetypes for my adult life were introduced during the period of the play: the man who appears and withdraws, appears and withdraws; the woman who is both my mother and a girl on whom I have a crush; and the real mother, who dies for want of the love and protection of a man, her husband. These are rudimentary formulations; nevertheless, they point to a fact of large consequence, the fact of my precarious victory over my father and my attainment of my mother. Like Young Macduff in the moments before death, I became my mother's confidant. In doing so, I became her true husband, the man both like and unlike other men. And, in becoming these things, I became sick.

The main ailment was a debilitating asthma that required trips to hospitals and doctors' offices. I swallowed drugs that kept me awake nights, struggling to breathe mist from an atomizer that hummed away on the table next to my bed, while my mother sat at my bedside. She had a way of sitting beside me on the bed — at a certain angle, leaning over, maybe touching my forehead or holding my hand, perched the way mothers everywhere perch on beds beside sick children — that I will never forget. It was our intimacy. In later years, after she and my father had overturned their divorce and disastrously remarried, and her alcoholic deterioration had begun in earnest, the image of her in the Tallahassee days, serving tea in china cups, or sitting up nights with me on the edge of my bed in the little house on Eighth Street, would be supplanted by the more violent image of the increasingly damaged Lady Macbeth she was to become. When we say about something or someone that we are dying for that thing, that person, we may miss the more literal meaning hidden in the metaphor. I was a boy dying *for* his mother, angrily, stubbornly doing her work of dying, the work she had begun before I was born. In this version of the story of my illness — the story of our collusion in illness — I was not merely bringing my mother to my bedside, not simply bringing her close. Rather, I was marrying myself to her, learning to speak the language of her unconscious, which, as time would bear out, was a language of suffocation and death. In sickness, we were joined. She was me and I was her. This is how I come to respect the difficulties of her childhood with her own mother — not from doctors' opinions or from family confidences about ambiguous surgical operations but from my own childhood experience of my mother at my bedside, holding my hand, leaning close, needing me to need her beside me, loving me in the only way she knew how to love, which was in sickness not in health, her sickness and mine, ours.

I bought the Dux. Of course, I bought top of the line. If you're going to buy a brand-new rest of your life, why go halfway? The guys who brought it in and set it up were not only deliverymen; they were true believers, real aficionados. One of the men was large, the other less large. The large man did the talking.

"This is the bed I sleep on."

"Really?"

"Best bed I ever slept on. I've slept on every kind of bed. Take a look at me. I'm a big guy. Most beds, I'd get two, three years and the things wear out. Not this bed."

"Really?"

"I'm telling you. I sleep on this bed. My mother sleeps on this bed. My sister has one of these beds. My mother's sister sleeps on this bed."

"You're kidding."

"Sleep like a baby."

Like a baby? What if I wanted to sleep like a man? It didn't much matter either way, because I wasn't going to get any sleep at all. Not that night. Not the following night. Not the night after that.

"Hey, come over. I got the bed."

"You did?"

"Yeah. It's here."

"I can't believe you got the bed."

"I got the bed. It's here."

"Have you gotten on it?"

"Kind of."

"Have you put the sheets on it?"

"Uh-huh."

"Is my pillow on it?"

"Of course."

"Is it as tall as the other bed?"

"Just about."

"You got the bed!"

"I got the bed!"

Talk about up all night — however, not for reasons one would anticipate or wish. It was a bad night on many counts. In the first place, the bed felt too soft. In the second place, it was too springy. In the third place, it seemed too transmissive of vibrations caused by movement. In the fourth place, it was too final. It represented the end of the quest for itself. The search for the bed had always been a grief-abatement project — it was never meant (though how could I have known this?) to end in a purchase. But, now, here the bed was. It was mine. It would be the place not of love and rest but of deprivation and loneliness. All during that first night, I lay awake and *felt* the bed. I felt myself sinking into it. I felt, sinking into the bed, the absence of familiar pressures against my shoulders and hips; and, without those familiar pressures, I felt adrift. If R. moved even an inch, I felt that. If she turned over, the effect was catastrophic. In the morning I was wrung out, and so was R.

What followed over the next few days was a workshop in hysteria. I called the store. I phoned other stores, in other states. I wanted to know from the Dux community what I could do to join, to make myself on my bed feel the way they said they felt on theirs. Pamela, the manager of the store on East Fifty-eighth Street, lost patience eventually and told me that she would take the bed back — immediately! Against company policy! She'd make an exception in my case! Though not for a full refund! Did I want the bed? Did I want the bed or not? Alone at night, I sank into the bed and tried to want it. And the farther I sank into the bed, the closer I came to knowing what the bed was. It was the last bed I would ever buy. It was the bed that would deliver me into my fate. It was the bed that would marry me again to my mother, the bed Louanne and I would share. When I moved, the bed moved, talking back to me through the echoing of coiled springs, telling me that there would be no rest for me. The bed was alive. It was alive with my mother. I sank into the bed, and it was as if I were sinking down into her arms. She was not beside me on the bed, she was *inside* the bed, and I was *inside* the bed; and she pulled me down into the bed to die with her. It was my deathbed. It was a coffin. It was a sarcophagus. I didn't want to die. Did I? If only I could get the bed to stay still. Why wouldn't the bed leave me alone? Why wouldn't the bed be *my* bed?

In the daytime I worked the phones. A woman in a Southern state referred me to a man in the same Southern state who had sold these beds for twenty years. This man knew everything about the beds.

"What kind of floor is your bed on? Is it a wood floor?"

"Yes, it is a wood floor."

"There's your problem."

"How do you mean?"

"Sometimes on a wood floor these beds can be very reverberant. Do you have carpet under the bed?"

"No."

"You need carpet under the bed. That'll damp the springs."

"I don't have any carpet."

"Go out and get yourself a set of those felt-and-rubber furniture coasters. You'll need six, because on a queen-size bed there are those extra legs supporting the middle of the bed."

Coasters? It was too late for coasters. The bed had to go back to the warehouse! It had to go back the next morning! The large man and the less large man were coming to haul away the bed that I both wanted and did not want, that I both needed and did not need in order to continue being the man who was both better and worse than other men. I ran out, with minutes before the stores closed, bought the coasters, ran back home, and shoved them under the legs of the bed. I bounced on the bed. I hadn't slept in days. Nights. And on and on the night went: My mother. The bed. My mother. The bed. Morphine. The bed. I'd failed her by living. I'd killed her with negligence. Comfort was forbidden. Except in death. In the morning, the men were coming to cart away our bed. I pulled up the covers and sank into the bed and drifted restlessly in that half-awake dream world where I could live and die with and without my dead mother, and I waited for the men.

Then it was morning and the light through the windows was hurting my eyes and I had a cigarette of my own going, and the buzzer rang and they tromped up the stairs and began packing the bed. They took off the legs and broke it down and wrapped it up, and just like that the bedroom was empty, and my mind without sleep was suddenly empty, too.

"Wait!"

They waited.

"This isn't right!"

"What's not right?"

"Everything! All of it!"

I told them the story of the bouncy, springy bed. All that sleeplessness. All those phone calls. The store managers, the furniture coasters. It all poured out. Not about my mother, though. Nothing about Louanne. The men stood in my empty bedroom, listening, paying attention. The large man, who had, I think, a firm grasp of reality, said, "I see that there is a problem. But I have to tell you, I'm just the driver."

I went to the telephone. I called the number for the Swedish president of Dux Interiors in North America. What in the world was I going to say to him? What did I want from him?

"Hello?"

"Hello. Is this Mr. Gustafsson?"

"Speaking."

"Hi. My name is Donald. I'm a customer? I have a bed that's being picked up and returned."

"Returned?"

"Yeah, well."

"You don't like the bed?"

"I like the bed. I like the bed. It's just that there are problems."

"Problems?"

The large man stepped forward. He took control. He said to me, "Let me talk to Bo."

I gave the large man the phone. He stood in my ravaged, empty bedroom and did the talking. He talked for a long time. When he was finished speaking with the president, he passed me my phone. He told me, "Bo wants to talk to you."

"Hello?"

"Hello. Is it Donald? Hello. Let me ask you something. What size bed do you have?"

"Queen."

"Ah. And you say it is too bouncy?"

"That's part of it."

"Hmm."

"It's reverberant."

"Reverberant. How do you mean?"

"I mean you can feel everything. When you're on the bed. When you're in bed. You feel too much. I feel too much."

"Well. I don't know what to tell you. There are many springs in that bed. That is how it works. All the springs work together. There is going to be some movement. Maybe to get a good night's rest you need your own sleeping area. Maybe you need the king."

"I don't have room for a king."

"I don't know what to tell you. You have to decide if you want to keep the bed or not. I cannot decide for you."

"I know."

"The bed is a good bed. I am sure that if you keep it you will get used to it. These beds take some getting used to."

"I know."

"Good luck."

I hung up the phone. I saw the men standing in my house. I saw the crated bed by the door. I saw the sunlight coming through the windows. I saw myself standing there seeing these things. I was a man whose need for love and sympathy had led him to telephone a Swede in the middle of the morning. Perhaps at this point the story of my mother and the bed becomes the story of my father and the bed, the story that remains to be told, the story, you could say, of the king versus the queen.

The bed went away. I let it go. R. was right. I could get another bed later. I stood in my empty room. In place of the bed was — shame? In place of the bed was a question, a question that is at once too simple and too complicated to answer.

RACHEL COHEN

Lost Cities

FROM THE THREEPENNY REVIEW

I. Clerks

THERE IS a certain kind of poet who is a clerk during the day. It seems to be necessary to have mundaneness, which must involve paperwork, the long, slow, soporific afternoons at an office, the sedateness of security, a regular paycheck, a bit too small but reassuring nevertheless, a boss, goodhearted but not sensitive, also reassuring in his way. What does this do for the poet?

The Portuguese poet-clerk Fernando Pessoa wrote business correspondence in English and French in various offices for years; the Greek poet-clerk Constantine Cavafy translated letters for the Third Circle of Irrigation, an office of the British colonial administration in Egypt, in the same office every day for thirty-three years. Both were helped by this in an obvious financial sense. As Cavafy pointed out, the writer who does not rely on his writing for his living "obtains a great freedom in his creative work."

Pessoa and Cavafy both published only a handful of poems in their lifetimes, leaving behind countless drafts of other work. Cavafy revised continually, but he did self-publish in manuscripts he carefully bound together, so there is some sense of what he felt to be the final versions. Pessoa, on the other hand, kept all his manuscript pages in a trunk, where multiple undated versions of the same work appear next to each other, so that there's no knowing which he felt to be complete, or if he wanted them to be complete.

Pessoa wrote in dozens of different voices, each the representative of a person wholly formed, though a resident of his imagination. He was a maritime engineer with a passion for Whitman and a monarchist exile who wrote only Horatian odes; he was a hunch-backed woman who wrote love letters to a steelworker and an accountant who admired Omar Khayyám; he was a baron fallen on hard times; and he was an astrologer. One of these persons (whom he called heteronyms) was Bernando Soares, a dusty gray man and assistant bookkeeper with evening light in his soul. Soares was like Pessoa in many ways (Pessoa called him a semi-heteronym), not least in the way that each maintained a double allegiance to the office and the writer's study. Soares's prose writings are as close as we will get to Pessoa's autobiography. These meditations, called in English *The Book of Disquiet,* have been selected and translated into English by at least four different people. A slightly different Soares emerges from each one.

Many of the fragments begin with the mundane: the account books, Soares's boss Vasques, his occasionally foolish colleague Moreira, the delivery boy, the clock and calendar on the wall. Then there is the feeling of the office when the sky outside darkens in a storm. Anxiety comes with the storm, a sense of menace, and Soares is glad for the company of the office, the joke of the delivery boy, the protection and comfort of this undemanding company. This is the shape of his world in the day and it frees him for the night. In the evening, he walks the streets of Lisbon and returns home to write perfect crystalline meditations on depression, insomnia, nostalgia, memory, the city's geography, anonymity, and mortality. It seems that this work is possible only in his straitened conditions. The city wanderings must have their dusty contrast, must play in relief.

The contrast, the relief, these were also necessary for Cavafy. In the evenings, walking the streets of Alexandria or sitting at his desk working by lamplight, he makes his escape into love, art, history, and memory. He writes and he dreams; he dreams and he writes. He begins to lose a little bit his sense of what is real and what is imagined. In his poem "Morning Sea," he writes to himself,

> Let me stand here. And let me pretend I see all this
> (I really did see it for a minute when I first stopped)
> and not my usual day-dreams here too,
> my memories, those images of sensual pleasure.

(Cavafy, "Morning Sea," 1915,
tr. Edmund Keeley and Philip Sherrard)

He tried to keep them separate, perhaps not to sully the dreams, or not to succumb to their temptation all the time, or perhaps because the dreams were richer if the fussy details of quotidian life were not intermingled.

Cavafy must have daydreamed at the office, too. He did not like going to work, and was always at least an hour late. He had the clerks who worked under him organized to explain his absence to his superiors. He was meticulous, correcting correspondence for several offices, and writing and translating letters into and out of English, but the work cannot have been especially demanding. After Cavafy's death, one of the other clerks who worked in the office, an Egyptian man named Ibrahim el Kayar, was interviewed by Manolis Halvatzakis, and the interview is quoted at length in Robert Liddell's biography of Cavafy. The interview was conducted in French and English and some Arabic; just who wrote the English version is a little unclear. Ibrahim el Kayar describes how, for Cavafy, poetry sometimes interrupted translation:

> On very rare occasions he locked himself into his room. Sometimes my colleague and I looked through the keyhole. We saw him lift up his hands like an actor, and put on a strange expression as if in ecstasy, then he would bend down to write something. It was the moment of inspiration. Naturally we found it funny and we giggled. How were we to imagine that one day Mr. Cavafy would be famous!

The poet-clerk is certainly ridiculous, the relationship between his tedious office work and his moments of inspiration clear only to himself at the time. Cavafy found his poetry in the action of barricading office and home against the encroachments of the Third Circle of Irrigation.

Pessoa and Soares entered into an even more extreme arrangement: their poet-clerk is an impossibly unified being, completely interior, with no delineations at all.

> I write attentively, bent over the book in which with my entries I jot down the useless history of an obscure company; and at the same time, with the same attention, my thoughts follow the progress of a nonexistent ship as it sails for nonexistent, oriental lands. The two things are equally clear, equally visible before me: the lined page on which I carefully write the verses of the commercial epic of Vasques and Co., and the deck where I carefully see, just to the side of the caulked seams of the

boards, the long, lined-up chairs, and the extended legs of those resting on the voyage.

(Bernardo Soares / Fernando Pessoa, *The Book of Disquiet,* tr. Alfred MacAdam)

This is the full doubleness of which poet-clerking is capable. Empires, ships, and kings come and go before the poet-clerk's eyes, as do the columns of figures themselves. He lives in a world where everything is imagined, the office as much an illusion as his dreams.

Cavafy and Pessoa were both quite isolated as children: their fathers died when they were young, and they moved with their mothers to countries where the main language was English. Pessoa later explained that it was shortly after his father died, when he was about five, that he invented a friend for himself — the first of the imaginary boys and men who peopled his interior world — called the Chevalier de Pas. Pessoa's mother remarried, and at the age of seven Pessoa moved from Portugal to Durban, South Africa, where his stepfather was in the diplomatic corps. Pessoa attended an English school. In Durban, the Chevalier de Pas was replaced by a new friend and alter ego who went by the particularly English name of Charles Anon. By the time he was twelve or thirteen, Pessoa had any number of internal friends. They all wrote a newspaper together, each with his own byline. After high school, Pessoa's older stepbrothers settled in England; Pessoa chose Lisbon.

Cavafy's father died when Cavafy was seven, and two years later the family moved to England, where they lived until he turned fourteen. His father, a wealthy merchant, did not leave his affairs in good order, and the family had little money. Cavafy's older brothers went to work in various shipping offices. Cavafy also seems to have gone to school in English, and later, when he was living in Alexandria and Constantinople with his mother, much of his correspondence and reading was in English.

Cavafy and Pessoa wrote their first poems in English and continued to write letters, poems, essays, and notes to themselves in English, as well as translations into and out of English, for the rest of their lives. They read French and Latin, too, and Cavafy claimed some Arabic, although his knowledge seems to have been slight. They wrote in the consciousness of other languages. Both were much affected by Shakespeare; both read Browning with careful attention. Pessoa read and translated the French surrealists; he was the first to publish them in Portugal. Pessoa's heteronyms also translated each other's work, and several of the heteronyms — particularly Charles James Search and the Crosse brothers, Thomas and I. I. — were translators first and foremost.

For Cavafy, translation was a source of income and it was also associated with sensuality. In Cavafy's poems, young men of different backgrounds gather together to read poetry and experience sensual pleasure, and they leave behind their native languages for the Greek more appropriate to the occasion.

Pessoa and Cavafy lived translation as Walter Benjamin (kindred spirit of all poet-clerks) understood it: as ardent entry into another realm of language. Not simply catching the literal meaning of another's words, but actually expanding one's own language under the influence of another's language. Thinking in two languages, like a circus rider standing on two horses, allowing oneself to be carried away by two languages together.

Among Browning's greatest poems are his dramatic monologues of characters revealed in all their complexity, sadness, and depravity. Cavafy and Pessoa scholars often cite the influence of Browning. Cavafy's dramatic monologues work through a similar process of a sympathetic imagination that does not balk at revealing weakness, or in some cases doom. And Pessoa took the idea further by living out the dramatic monologues themselves, inventing not characters but authors, and giving them rein to reveal themselves as they would.

The closest Cavafy comes to Browning is in the poem "Philhellene," which, as Edmund Keeley points out, is very much like Browning's "The Bishop Orders His Tomb at Saint Praxed's Church." Each concerns a man who, facing death, explains how he is to be memorialized. The bishop is to have a tomb of marble, jasper, and lapis, in the niche he has reserved for himself in Saint Praxed's Church. It is to be a tomb to make his rival, long dead and buried in the south corner of the church, unspeakably jealous. The bishop's pettiness does not obscure his tragedy, for aren't we all afraid of how we'll be cared for after death? Cavafy's Hellenic ruler is similarly pathetic as he directs his minister or scribe in the design of the coin that will be his legacy. The coin is to have a beautiful young discus thrower on the back, and is to be inscribed with the word *Philhellene,* to show the ruler's sophistication, his cultural taste. "Philhellene" is one of dozens of Cavafy poems that are written specifically as epitaphs or that consider how best to memorialize someone recently dead or about to die.

Cavafy and Pessoa are like the scribes who appear in these poems, taking down the orders of Vasques and other minor emperors. The clerks' writings reassure petty rulers of the extent of their powers. But the poets are also themselves the leaders who know their own weaknesses, and who dream of a glory that may come after death. Deep is the poet's sympathy with a bishop or a Hellenic ruler, desperate at the end of his life for some sign that his prominence will continue. Even more desperate can be the fear of the poet, almost unpublished in his own lifetime, depending on the support of a few friends to ensure that all is not lost, that the work, like the tomb or the coins, will perpetuate the memory of its first imaginer.

This is precisely the task of the translator, the clerk among poets. Walter Benjamin writes that it is the appearance of great translation that marks the perpetual life of the original work. It is when a work enters into translation that it comes to have an effect on language itself, on the languages of the world. Cavafy and Pessoa, dusty clerks in cities no longer prominent, with few friends, secret reputations, and the dream life of kings, could not wait for readers and translators. They were their own clerks, taking down the words of their inspired dreams, living a memorial to themselves.

Cavafy and Pessoa worked in Greek and Portuguese and English, in the Rua dos Douradores and the time of the conquering kings, in the role of the clerk by day and the role of the king by night, or in both roles at both times. In their dreams and account books, they are both the original and the translator, both king and clerk — clerks to themselves, their own translators, their own tenuous assurance of immortality.

II. Cities

Walking in cities is an accumulation of small fragments of loss. A woman you want to keep looking at turns a corner; two people pass and you hear only, "It cannot be because of the child"; you look through a window at a drawing that looks like a print you have seen somewhere before, and it's obscured when someone pulls a curtain across the window; a woman turns ferociously on the man standing next to her, but by the time you reach home you can no longer remember her face.

You begin to feel weighed down by all these losses, which seem separate from you, from the you that walks and sees and remembers and forgets and returns home. You wonder if the city in which you live is not the right city for you. Some other city might be less oppressive, freer. You dream of moving. And yet, you suspect that

> You won't find a new country, won't find another shore.
> This city will always pursue you. You will walk
> the same streets, grow old in the same neighborhoods,
> will turn gray in these same houses.
> You will always end up in this city. Don't hope for things elsewhere:
> there is no ship for you, there is no road.
> As you've wasted your life here, in this small corner,
> you've destroyed it everywhere in the world.
>
>   (Cavafy, "The City," written 1894, revised 1910, tr. Keeley and Sherrard)

Perhaps you do leave for a little while, as Cavafy left Alexandria for London when he was nine, or as Pessoa left Lisbon for Durban, returning at the age of seventeen.

Like the poets, you return. You, too, resist certain aspects of the city — perhaps its industry, or its violence. Its harshness grates upon you. You cling to the softer spaces: the parks at sunset, the river or the bay, a moment of sensuality, the vulnerability of certain passersby.

> Today walking down New Almada Street, I happened to gaze at the back of a man walking ahead of me. It was the ordinary back of an ordinary man, a modest blazer on the shoulders of an incidental pedestrian. He carried a briefcase under his left arm, while his right hand held a rolled-up umbrella, which he tapped on the ground to the rhythm of his walking.
>
> I suddenly felt a sort of tenderness on account of that man. I felt the tenderness stirred by the common mass of humanity, by the banality of the family breadwinner going to work every day, by his humble and happy home, by the happy and sad pleasures of which his life necessarily

consists, by the innocence of living without analysing, by the animal naturalness of that coat-covered back.

(Bernando Soares / Fernando Pessoa, *The Book of Disquietude*, tr. Richard Zenith)

You find that these glimpses are not only pleasing, they have become necessary to you. You try to remember what it was that you thought you needed. Trees, you think, or was it other people, some more natural way of life. You leave the city:

> I went off to the country with great plans.
> But found only grass and trees there,
> And when there were people, they were just like any others.

> (Alvaro de Campos / Fernando Pessoa,
> "Tobacco Shop," 1928, tr. Edwin Honig and Susan Brown)

You return to the city. If your soul is of this kind, there is no longer any difference between the country and the city: you see everything with the same dreamy eyes, you will always be a stranger, you will always be anonymous. How could you tolerate the country now? To what other city would you go?

> By now I've gotten used to Alexandria, and it's very likely that even if I were rich I'd stay here. But in spite of this, how the place disturbs me. What trouble, what a burden small cities are — what lack of freedom.
> I'd stay here (then again I'm not entirely certain that I'd stay) because it is like a native country for me, because it is related to my life's memories.
> But how much a man like me — so different — needs a large city.
> London, let's say. Since . . . P.M. left, how very much it is on my mind.

> (Cavafy, note, 1907, tr. Keeley)

Somehow the lack of freedom is related to life's memories. Now you have reached a point in your life when you realize that you were not meant for youth, that you were in fact always a little older than everyone else and merely waiting for your age to catch up to you, so that you might live partly through memory, as you were meant to. And now your memories, even the memory of your resistance to the city and its constraints, are all part of the city itself.

You will always return to the city. You know that the feeling of return, and its tension between acceptance and resistance, is your most fundamental feeling. You survive by returning. And now, in this city, you no longer need to leave in order to return.

Then, sad, I went out on to the balcony,
went out to change my thoughts at least by seeing
something of this city I love,
a little movement in the streets and the shops.

(Cavafy, "In the Evening," 1917, tr. Keeley and Sherrard)

You have reached an accommodation with your city, you have
found a way to be seamlessly close and distant. If you are Cavafy, Alexandria comforts you in your regret; if you are Pessoa, Lisbon and
its Tagus River reassure you with their indifference.

Oh, sky of blue — the same sky of my childhood —,
Eternal truth, empty and perfect!
O, gentle Tagus, ancestral and mute,
Tiny truth where the sky reflects itself!
O, suffering revisited, Lisbon of long ago and of today!
You give me nothing, you take nothing from me, you're nothing
    that I feel in
myself.

(Alvaro de Campos / Fernando Pessoa,
"Lisbon Revisited," 1923, tr. Rachel Cohen)

If your city is a Lisbon or an Alexandria, it weighs on you, as Pessoa
wrote, "like a sentence of exile," and this is the only tolerable condition. You must live specifically in this city, the only city on earth
in which you can be certain of denying yourself, in which you will
feel a perpetual stranger in precisely the way that you desire.

Slowly, slowly, you and your city grow into each other. Pessoa addresses his Lisbon:

Once again I see you,
But myself, alas, I fail to see!
Shattered, the magical mirror where I saw myself identical,
And in each fateful fragment I descry only a piece of myself —
A piece of you and of myself . . .

(Alvaro de Campos / Fernando Pessoa,
"Lisbon Revisited," 1926, tr. Honig and Brown)

You have become the tiny pieces of half-forgotten streets and men
with overcoats. If you are Cavafy, you have become the fragments
of your memories and your historical imaginings; if you are Pessoa,
you have become a hundred different personalities writing with

the same pen. If you are a bricklayer, then this feeling will be in the bricks, and the way they have been laid, and it will be sensed, though rarely understood, by the people who walk on them. If you are a photographer, you will only take pictures of your city, and even your photographs of fruit on tables will still be pictures of the city. And if you are a poet, then there is some chance that you will become the poet of your city, that people will come to see the city that you became.

They will stop and wonder at the plaque on the Rue Lepsius in Alexandria where your house no longer stands. They will smile wistfully at the statue of you perched forever on a metal chair in front of your café, the Café Brasileira on the Largo do Rato. And they will feel vaguely disappointed that they cannot quite locate the feeling of your poems in the city itself, for the city in places is ugly, and has been garishly modernized, and the people on the buses seem utterly unaware that they live in the city of the poet — they are contemporary and mundane, not so different really from the people in the city where the admirers of the poet live themselves.

The people who go to visit the city of the poet find it hard to make sense of the sight of garbage in alleyways, of blue and yellow tiles behind doors, of mosques, of beggars. These are not in the poems of the poet they love so well. This is not the city they had imagined, though they believe the city of the poet lies buried beneath its stones or is hidden behind its walls. Once or twice perhaps they catch a glimpse of sky, or light reflecting on the river; they see an encounter between two men that the poet might have described, and they nod to themselves, ah, there, just for a minute, I thought I saw it.

And they return to their own city, which is, after all, theirs, and they are comforted.

In the evening, when they come home from walking the streets of their city, they take the poet's books down from the shelf and read a few lines, quietly, in the more comfortable of the two chairs, by the light of the lamp. Ah, yes, they think to themselves, what a beautiful city, if only it existed, if only we could go there.

BRIAN DOYLE

Yes

FROM THE GEORGIA REVIEW

LATELY I HAVE been delving early Irish literature and language, and so have been raiding cattle in Cuailnge, and pondering the visions of Oenghus, and feasting at Bricriu, and wooing Etain, which last has led to some tension with my wife, who is of Belgian extraction and does not like to hear me tell of the beautiful Etain, the loveliest woman in all Ireland, although Etain was changed to an insect and banished for a thousand years, until she was reborn as the wife of Eochaid Airem, king of the green lands.

I try to explain to my wife that I am only wooing by proxy, as it were, and that Eochaid has the inside track, he being in the story and me only reading it. This line of talk leads me inevitably to Flann O'Brien and Myles na gCopaleen and Brian O'Nolan, all of whom I wheel into the conversation, the three men standing all in the same spot, as if they were the same man, which they were, except when O'Nolan was writing, which is when he became one of the others, depending on what he was writing — novels as O'Brien, journalism as na gCopaleen ("of the little horses") or sometimes Count O'Blather, or James Doe, or Brother Barrabus, or George Knowall.

My wife is unmoved; she will not have Etain in the house.

After a while I realize that the problem is the word *woo*. *It is a word that may be applied to your wife and your wife only, if you have a wife*, she is saying without saying. She is a subtle woman, which is part of the reason I wooed her some years ago, and won her from various rivals, who did not woo so well, and went away, one may say, full of rue.

I spent some time after that saying *woo*, which is a very fine word, rife with meaning, and emitted with a lift from the lips, like *whee* and *who*, or *no*. By chance I happened to be saying *woo* in the presence of my new son Joseph, a curious young man three months of age. Like his father he is intrigued by sounds, and soon enough he too was saying *woo*, and then my other new son, Liam, also three months old, picked it up, and the three of us were wooing to beat the band, although then Liam burst into tears, and had to be carried away to another room for milk.

Joe and I kept it up, though; he is an indefatigable fellow. After a while he switched to *who*, and I went with him, to see where this would go, and it went back and forth between us for a while, and then it went to *whee*, and then back to *woo*, and then my wife came back in the room and found us wooing like crazy men. By then it was Joe's turn for a suckle and off he went, and I went downstairs to raid cattle in Cuailnge, and ponder Oenghus, and feast at Bricriu, and woo Etain, of whom the less said the better.

The wooing of Etain demands a certain familiarity with the Gaelic tongue, which has fascinated me since I was a boy in my grandmother's lap listening to the swell and swing of Irish from her lips, which more often than you might expect had Gaelic oaths on them, as she was a shy woman with a sharp temper, though gentle as the night is long, and much mourned by many to this day. I still hear her voice on windy nights, banshee nights, saying to me, gently, *bi I do bhuachaill mhaith*, be a good boy, or *go mbeannai Dia thu*, God bless you. So partly in memory of my grandmother, a McCluskey before she was a Clancey giving her daughter to a Doyle, I have been marching through the thickets of the Irish tongue, the second oldest in Europe behind Basque, and the cold hard fact is that the Gaelic language is a most confusing creature, and although I don't understand very much of it, I read about it at every opportunity, and have been able to note several interesting observations on small scraps of paper, which are then distributed willy-nilly in various pants pockets, emerging here and there like crumpled fish, and reminding me that I had meant to write an essay on the topic at, or more accurately in, hand.

Thus this essay, which was supposed to be about the fact that there is no way to say the words *yes* and *no* in Gaelic, but which has swerved unaccountably into a disquisition about sounds, of which some are exuberant, like Joe's *woo*, and some affirmative, like *sa*, which is Gaelic for *it is*, and *yes* and *sí* and *ja* and *oui*, which are English and Spanish and German and French for *yes*, which there is no way to say in Gaelic, try as you might.

Is it sayable in the Irish?

Nil — it is not.

Nil is as fascinating as *sa* to me, especially so lately because my daughter, Lily, a rebellious angel, age three, is fixated on *no*, which she says often, in different accents, with various degrees of vehemence. She says it morning, noon, and night, particularly at night, when she wakes up screaming *no no no no no,* and answers *nooooo* when I ask what is the matter. Sometimes she says *neuwh*, which is a sort of *no*, which is said usually after she has been watching *Mary Poppins* and is afflicted with a sort of stiffening of the upper lip which prevents proper pronunciation of simple words like *no*. It is interesting that she is riveted by *no* because her brother Liam is riveted by *ho*, which is the only word he owns at the moment. Like a geyser he emits *ho!* regularly and then subsides. I expect him to pick up *no* pretty soon, his sister being a whiz at it and the boys certain to learn at her knee, and then Joe will get *no* too, and then my children will be saying *no* to beat the band, not to mention the thin stretched rubber of their father's patience, which they hammer upon like a bodhran, the wee drum of my Wicklow ancestors.

But their father is in the basement at the moment musing over the fact that Gaelic is the only language on the Continent that always uses *tu,* or thou, when speaking to one person, or *sibh,* you, for more than one, which habit, he thinks, reflects a certain native friendliness in the tongue and in its speakers; and he further puzzles over the fact that Irish counts in twenties, not tens; and further he muses that Gaelic, at least in Ireland, has no terms for the *Mister* and *Señor* and *Herr* that English and Spanish and German use as terms of bourgeois respect, which makes him wonder about Irish independence as well as rural isolation. Also he spends a good deal of time pondering ogham, the alphabet used in Ireland for writing on wood and stone before the year 500 or so, when Christianity and the Latin alphabet rode into Ireland together on strong winds, and the fact that Gaelic has perhaps sixty phonemes, which are sounds that convey meaning, and of which there are perhaps forty-four in English, which comparative fact makes me wonder about the width of the respective languages, so to speak, which width is also reflected in the simple spelling and pronunciation of terms in each tongue: I might say of Liam that he is *an buachaill,* the boy, for example, and roll the former off my tongue and pop the latter out rather like ho!, which is what Liam is saying as I am calling him *an buachaill.*

Further, I am fascinated by the fact that Gaelic is a language in love with nouns, as can be seen with a phrase that often occurs to me when I think about my daughter's and my sons' futures, *ta eagla orm,* which in English would be I fear, but in Gaelic is fear is upon me, which it is, like a demon between my shoulders. To exorcise it I sometimes whistle; in English I whistle, just so, but in Gaelic *ligim fead,* I let a whistle, or *taim ag feadail,* I am at whistling.

I am at whistling a great deal these days, it turns out, trying to get the fear off me. For I am terrified of the fates that may befall my children — fates over which I have no power at all, not the slightest, other than keeping my little children close to me in the presence of cars and dogs and such. So there are times now, I can honestly say — for I am sometimes an honest man, and admiring always of honesty — that I am exhausted by, and frightened for, my raft of children, and in the wee hours of the night when up with one or another of the little people, I sometimes, to be honest, find myself wondering what it might have been like not to have so many.

It would have been lonely.

I know this.

I know it in my heart, my bones, in the chalky exhausted shiver of my soul. For there were many nights before my children came to me on magic wooden boats from seas unknown that I wished desperately for them, that I cried because they had not yet come; and now that they are here I know I pay for them every minute with fear for their safety and horror at the prospect of losing them to disease and accidents and the harsh fingers of the Lord, who taketh whomever He wishes, at which time He alone appoints, and leaves huddled and broken the father and the mother, who begged for the joy of these round faces groping for milk in the dark. So as I trudge upstairs to hold Lily in my lap, and rub my old chapped hands across the thin sharp blades of her shoulders, and shuffle with sons on shoulders in the blue hours of the night, waiting pa-

tiently for them to belch like river barges, or hear Joe happily blowing bubbles of spit in his crib simply because he can do it and is
pretty proud of himself about the whole thing, or hear Liam suddenly say ho! for no reason other than Liamly joy at the sound of
his own voice like a bell in his head, I say yes to them, yes yes yes,
and to exhaustion I say yes, and to the puzzling wonder of my
wife's love I say O yes, and to horror and fear and jangled joys I say
yes, to rich cheerful chaos that leads me sooner to the grave and
happier along that muddy grave road I say yes, to my absolute surprise and with unbidden tears I say yes yes O yes.

Is this a mystery and a joy beyond my wisdom?

Sa — it is.

JOSEPH EPSTEIN

In a Snob-Free Zone

FROM THE WASHINGTON MONTHLY

BY THE LATE 1960S, the old Wasp social ascendancy in American life, after showing many cracks, was beginning to break up in earnest. The Ivy League colleges, as Nicholas Lemann has shown in *The Big Test,* had begun to turn from places where students were admitted by ancestral right into meritocratic institutions that looked to SAT tests to direct their admissions policy. The old Society page, with its news of old-family weddings, cotillions, and charity balls, began everywhere to be replaced in newspapers by the Style page, a very different thing. The Social Register became the subject of jokes. The Episcopal Church, once a bastion of Wasp life — an Episcopalian, the old joke had it, was a Presbyterian who lived on his investments — turned sentimental leftist. How many heterosexual Episcopal priests does it take to elect a bishop? a new joke asked. All three, the answer is. Soon one began to hear reports that many children of established Wasp families — Rockefellers and others — were feeling guilty about their inherited wealth, and looking for ways to redistribute it in the larger society.

The Wasp old guard put up the white flag without a shot being fired. Suddenly bars began to drop: in formerly restricted neighborhoods, in previously elite country and city clubs, in once white-shoe banking, law, and investment firms. Once-snobbish institutions loosened up, opened up, disappeared. The closest thing to an aristocracy that America had known was now most prominently in evidence in the magazine ads of a small gray-haired Jewish designer named Ralph Lauren (né Lifschitz). Perhaps the best analogy to the Wasp self-divestment of power is that of the British giving up their empire. Both may have felt that the need to do so was inevitable — and quite possibly it was — but each came away diminished, disliked, even a little despised for having done so. To this day in America, the Wasps are the one group about which — in a politically correct atmosphere — jokes can be made with impunity.

One might have thought that the steep decline, if not the complete demise, of the Wasps would have put a powerful crimp in snobbery itself. Quite the reverse. What in fact happened is that snobbery became open to everyone: one could claim an essentially snobbish superiority on the basis of one's ethnicity, one's status as a victim, one's children's achievements, one's good taste, one's with-it-ness, one's culture, one's knowledge of wine, grub, or movies. We were all free to be snobs now, and the temptation to act on newfound freedom is never all that easily resisted. Who among us, after all, doesn't, not so deep down, feel rather superior to the next person? And yet, might there be a place where one could be outside all this madness?

Is there a snob-free zone, a place where one is outside all snobbish concerns, neither wanting to get in anywhere one isn't, nor needing to keep anyone else out for fear that one's own position will somehow seem eroded or otherwise devalued? A very small island of the favored of the gods, clearly, this snob-free zone, but how does one get there?

To be wellborn is a start. To be blessed with ample talent cannot hurt. To have been fortunate in one's professional, marital, or personal life will provide a genuine boost. To have won the lottery on an $80 million payoff week would be a serious help. And the easiest way into this zone may be not to care at all, to feel no aspiration, envy, resentment, anger at social arrangements, to live contentedly within oneself and be shut off from the whole damn social racket. Yet this last, the cultivation of sublime indifference, may be not the easiest but the toughest way of all into the snob-free zone.

Let me attempt to draw the portrait of a man (one could do something similar for a woman) who might have a chance for a life in the snob-free zone. I would begin by placing him on the lower edge of the old upper class. The poet Robert Lowell seems to have been in this condition: a Lowell, but not one of the inner circle of Lowells — those Lowells who spoke only to Cabots, and, of course, we all know the only grand party to whom the Cabots spoke. I imagine him, then, to have upper-class family connections, but not be quite of the upper class, lest he seem to share too completely in that class's dreariness and likely snobbery. He should be slightly of the upper class, in other words, but not enough to be tainted by it.

His schooling ought to be mixed, public and private. All private might make him seem too privileged, too lucky. A taste of public schools — perhaps through grade school — would show him not to have existed exclusively in cushy surroundings; it wouldn't do to make him look as if he's had too easy a ride. Having gone to public school, too, will give him a democratic touch — in a democracy, not a bad thing to have. (Paul McCartney and his wife sent their daughters to public — in the American sense of the word — schools, which could be interpreted as a brilliantly snobbish move.) He will have been a respectably good student, but not a great, off-the-boards astonishing one.

I would have him go to Andover or Groton, thence to Harvard or Princeton, and put in a year at Oxford or Cambridge, the last to Anglicize, cosmopolitanize, and polish him a bit. I don't believe any of these places is so wonderful, please understand, but the world seems to believe they are, so if our man is to enter the snob-free zone, he must do so in terms the world recognizes. Besides, having gone through such institutions, he will come to understand that the world, in its estimates, is often stupid, and never more than in recent years, when everything has begun to break down, especially in education. Having gone to what are thought very good schools, he will have taken their measure and never have to think — yearningly, in part snobbishly — as so many people seem to do, how different his life would've been had he only taken thought to have got "a better education." Unlike, say, poor Jay Gatsby, he will not have to falsify an educational résumé.

He'll require money. "A man may be despised," said Balzac, "but not his money." Our man doesn't have to be a billionaire, but he ought to have enough to take him out of the financial wars, so he need never do anything despicable for reasons of money alone. Being in possession of serious money — "holding," as they used to say at the racetrack — will give him freedom in other ways, not least by cutting down on his longing, which in turn reduces his susceptibility to material snobberies of various kinds, from cars to summer houses.

He will have earned his own money. At . . . what? Something for which he has an inherent skill, or a craft he learned by sedulous application of his talents: he could be an artist of some sort, possibly an architect, or maybe he has begun a business, manufacturing or selling something useful and well made. His work gives him pleasure and no cause to believe his days misspent.

His wife, unlike him, is Jewish, a pediatrician perhaps, also happy in her work, physically attractive, a respectable money earner, kindly, large-hearted. They have two children, a son and a daughter, good enough at school, with no known hang-ups or other problems or disabilities.

The family is never put to any of the tests of snobbery. They are never excluded, everywhere thought to be winning and always wanted; and, because so confident are they of their own quality, they have no thought of excluding anyone else. Such clubs as they join — a tennis and swimming club, for their daughter is an ardent tennis player, their son a swimmer of promise — are joined for their utility and pleasantness alone. Status is never a first, nor even a last, consideration. Such judgments as they make about persons, places, and pleasures are made on the basis of intrinsic and therefore genuine merit, never on that of being the right social, professional, or political move. Happy family, I would say, lucky family. Let us hope there are a few such in America, while remaining free to doubt it.

Yet perhaps this is all wrong, and the person who is in the snob-free zone is more likely to be a half-black, half-Hispanic man in dreadlocks who is young, bisexual, and a painter of terrifying pictures of childhood abuse, from which he is known to have suffered, but for which he is everywhere acclaimed.

I can think of a man who lived in a snob-free zone in whom snobbishness, though never justifiable, might have been understandable. He happens to have been a cousin of mine whose name was Sherwin Rosen and who was an economist at the University of Chicago. He was supposed to have been in line for the Nobel Prize in economics before he died, of lung cancer, in 2001, in his sixty-third year.

At his memorial service and at a dinner afterward, I was impressed not only by the range of people who spoke on my cousin's behalf but by their varying personal styles. None seemed particularly elegant, handsome, suave. Neither, for that matter, was my cousin. He was instead immensely winning without any of these qualities, and in part because he didn't seem to care about status at all. He enjoyed owning sporty cars — a white Audi sports coupé was his last — and drinking good wine and listening to classical pianists and playing jazz piano himself, but he made no fuss about these things. He made no fuss about anything, in fact, except economics. He judged his colleagues by their skill at their discipline, and, apart from their characters, nothing else. My guess is that he judged himself by the same criterion.

He once told me that he was offered something called an Albert Schweitzer Professorship in New York, which would have almost doubled his salary, but he said that, even though he could have used the money, he couldn't accept it. He couldn't because he needed the bruising intellectual combat that his colleagues at the University of Chicago Department of Economics gave one another. It wasn't pleasant, but, he felt, he needed it. When one of his best students did not land a job in one of the better-regarded universities, he told the student that it was a good thing, for it would take him outside all the worry about prestige and throw him back on his talent as an economist, which, if his devotion was such as to bring out his potential, would in the end result in his being made offers by better schools. Which, the student said, is exactly what happened.

My cousin Sherwin's way into the snob-free zone was simple enough: care only about one's work, judge people only by their skill at their own work, and permit nothing else outside one's work to signify in any serious way. View the rest of the world as a more or less amusing carnival at which one happens to have earned — through, of course, one's work — a good seat. Judge all things by their intrinsic quality, and consider status a waste of time. One of the reasons I liked him so much is that he brought all this off without any contortion of his essentially kind character.

Now in my seventh decade, am I, at last, anywhere near the snob-free zone? I think it fair to say that I haven't much interest in the social climb. When I think of people for whose company I yearn, I find the majority of them no longer alive. I have a weakness — a snobbish weakness? — for people who exhibit style, but style with the strong suggestion of substance behind it. From the previous generation, I should have liked to have known Noël Coward, Audrey Hepburn, George Balanchine, Marcello Mastroianni, Vladimir Nabokov, George Marshall, Edmund Wilson (when sober), and Billy Wilder. Of people still in full career, I find that, among public figures, I admire Pierre Boulez, whom I met once and found both *haimish* and winning, and Mikhail Baryshnikov, who surmounted the obstacles of being born to wretched parents in a miserable country to go on to become a prominent artist with a selfless devotion to his art; Daniel Patrick Moynihan, who recently died, seemed to me not only the most talented person in political life but the only one with whom I'd care to sit down to lunch.

On the other side — people with whom I wouldn't care to sit down to lunch — I include almost all current university presidents, present members of the U.S. Congress, most contemporary writers and painters, actors, athletes, and anyone vaguely known as a socialite. I came upon twenty-one men and women whom Absolut Vodka featured in an ad in a recent issue of *Vanity Fair,* all photographed by Annie Leibovitz, ranging in age from the architect Philip Johnson to the choreographer Mark Morris, and including Salman Rushdie, Gore Vidal, Spike Lee, Helmut Newton, Sarah Jessica Parker, and other of the usual suspects. They were in this ad because they were supposed to be avant-garde, hip, fascinating; add accomplished, revered, successful. And yet I find I do not long to meet any of them. (My guess is that they can do nicely, thank you, without meeting me, but that is another matter.) I feel about them as the Jews of Russia once felt about the tsars: they should live and be well, but not too close to me.

Does my list of people I wish I had known suggest its own snobbery? Possibly. I prefer to think that I have a bias toward people whose stylishness is informed by an unpredictable but subtle point of view, fine tact, and generosity of spirit. In this line, I have always admired a man named Walter Berry, who was the head of the U.S. Chamber of Commerce in Paris and who shows up in the biographies of such people as Edith Wharton, Marcel Proust, and Bernard Berenson. Edith Wharton conceded that she ought to have married Walter Berry: "He had been to me in turn all that one human being can be to another, in love, in friendship, in understanding." She arranged to be buried near him in the same cemetery in Versailles. Proust immediately recognized him as a man of quality, and Berry once wrote to Proust telling him that, when asked if he had read Proust's novels, he always replied: "Yes, but they have a grave defect: they are so short."

Not yearning to go socially any higher than I am now — content, that is, with the friends I have — I am, in this regard at least, in the snob-free zone. Not so, alas, in other regards. Much as I like to think myself the democrat, I find myself doing a certain amount of snobbish looking down on, in Lyndon Johnson's all too mortal phrase, "mah felluh Amurikuns." On the Outer Drive in Chicago, I am behind a car on whose back window is a decal reading "Illinois State University." My view is that one oughtn't even to have a sticker that reads "All Souls, Oxford," but Illinois State? Of course, the thought is a perfectly snobbish one. The guy driving the car is pleased to have gone to Illinois State; maybe he, or his son or daughter, is the first person in the family to have gone to college; possibly he completed his studies at great financial sacrifice. Still, I almost reflexively look down on that decal.

I do not look down on any of the current American pariahs: cigarette smokers, the overweight, the aged, the unhealthful-food eaters. I rather cherish some among them and feel sorry for others. But I do look down on certain selected people — preferably, it's true, from a distance and until now unbeknownst to them. Yet look down I do, usually with an uncomplicated feeling of satisfaction.

I am at a concert at the Ravinia Summer Music Festival, in Highland Park, on the North Shore outside Chicago. It is a Pops concert, with Erich Kunzel leading the Chicago Symphony Orchestra and a group, made up of six Englishmen, calling itself the King's Singers, since all were once at King's College, Cambridge. Normally, I shouldn't have gone to this kind of concert, but I had to miss another concert date, and in the exchange of tickets this was all that was open to me. I didn't think much of it. Listening to the great Chicago Symphony play the movie and television music of Henry Mancini felt to me like getting into a Rolls-Royce to drive around the block to take out the garbage. The King's Singers weren't much, either. Why, I wondered, am I here?

Bored, I look at the audience of which I am a part in the Ravinia pavilion. It is an older crowd, lots of comb-over hairdos among the men, a fair share of blue rinse among the women. Very suburban, I think: thick-calved younger women, men wearing pastel-colored clothes. They seem happy hearing this stuff, the musical equivalent of chewing gum, which left my mind wandering. The bloody snobbish truth is, I prefer not to think myself part of this crowd. I think myself, if you want to know, much better — intellectually superior, musically more sophisticated, even though I haven't any musical training whatsoever and cannot follow a score.

In part these feelings were justified: the music was terribly thin, leaving no residue, better listened to, if at all, while driving across town on an errand. But why did I have to establish my superiority to my (mildly) detested fellow listeners, even if only in my own mind? Why not simply note them and think about other things? Because, alas, the snob cannot bear to think himself a nobody, even in his own mind, and he certainly doesn't want to think himself included in an audience of what he sees as dull people, who have, as W. H. Auden once said to Nicholas Nabokov about a bureaucratic group in the U.S. Army, the "wrong ideas about everything and belong to that group of people neither you nor I can possibly like or condone." And rather than sit back and enjoy this concert, unmemorable as it was, I had to make plain, if only to myself, that I am a much more serious person than these people sitting around me, and serious in a way that deserves recognition, even if (again) only to myself.

Why do those thoughts play in my head at all? Why did I need to assert my superiority, even to myself, when no one was contesting it? Why cannot I, even so late in the day, grow into one of those admirable fellows — reasonable, tolerant, generous-spirited, honorable — that Jefferson called "natural aristocrats" and that a liberal-arts education is supposed to form but almost never does?

Strange. And ridiculous. Snob-free zone? Haven't myself yet arrived anywhere close. Perhaps in the next life. Or possibly the one after that.

MARSHALL JON FISHER

Memoria ex Machina

FROM DOUBLETAKE

IT WAS A SILVER Seiko watch with a clasp that folded like a map
and snapped shut. The stainless-steel casing was a three-dimen-
sional octagon with distinct edges, too thick and ponderous, it
seems now, for a thirteen-year-old. Four hands — hour, minute,
second, and alarm — swept around a numberless metallic-blue
face. I received it for my bar mitzvah; a quarter century later I can,
in my mind, fingernail the button just one click to set the alarm
hand — not too far, or I'll change the time — and pull out the
other, obliquely positioned button to turn on the alarm. When the
hour hand finally overcame the angle between itself and the alarm
hand, a soft, deep mechanical buzzing would ensue — a pleasant
hum long since obliterated by hordes of digital beeps. I haven't
seen my watch for twenty years, but I can still hear that buzz, feel its
vibrations in my wrist.

What I cannot remember is the timbre or inflection of my sister's voice from that time. She flitted in and out of view, appearing
in the gaps between high school, club meetings, and dates. I can't
even recall her at the dinner table with my parents, my brother,
and me, though she must have been there most of the time.

After she and my brother left for college, when I was in high
school, I spent countless hours lying in bed listening to my clock
radio. I can still see the burnt-amber numerals and the way their
discrete line segments would metamorphose each minute. The
tuning knob on the right-hand side, and the way it resisted torque
as you approached either end of the dial, remain as clear to me as
the remote controls of my new DVD player. I was listening in the

dark to a Monday-night Miami Dolphins game (home, against the New England Patriots) when the radio broadcast broke to the announcement that John Lennon had been shot. I heard Bruce Springsteen singing "Racing in the Street" for the first time on that radio, along with other songs I'd rather forget, like Queen's "We Are the Champions," dedicated one night by a local disc jockey to some high school basketball team. I remember the golden light from within illuminating the frequency band, and I remember tuning by sound for years after that light burned out.

Yet I can't remember what time I went to bed as an adolescent, or anything else about my nocturnal ritual. Did I say goodnight and then go off to my room, or did my parents come in to say goodnight after I was in bed? I don't know. But I do know, decades after it found oblivion, exactly how to set that radio to play for half an hour and then shut off.

The memory of my quotidian habits of those years has been washed away by a thousand new habits, just as my sister's teenage presence has given way to her succeeding selves. In his novel *Vertigo,* W. G. Sebald paraphrases Stendahl's advice "not to purchase engravings of fine views and prospects seen on one's travels, since before very long they will displace our memories completely, indeed one might say they destroy them." "For instance," Sebald continues, "[Stendahl] could no longer recall the wonderful *Sistine Madonna* he had seen in Dresden, try as he might, because Müller's engraving after it had become superimposed in his mind." In the same way, as the people in our lives grow older, their new faces, voices, and demeanors replace those of their former selves in our memory. Yet the new technology that continually replaces old machines fails to have the same effect, because the individuals — the radios, wristwatches, and automobiles that inhabited our lives — never change. That chrome "sleep knob" on my clock radio still looks exactly the same, wherever it may now rest in the center of some unknowable mountainous landfill.

"The past," wrote Proust, "is hidden somewhere outside the realm, beyond the reach, of intellect, in some material object (in the sensation which that material object will give us) which we do not suspect." And just as the taste of the famous *petite madeleine* awakens in Proust's narrator an entire vanished world — the memories of his childhood vacations in Combray — the thought of my old Walkman resurrects my postcollegiate existence. It was a red and black 1985 model, and I've never seen another just like it. The tendency of Sony to constantly bring out new designs lent an air of individuality to one's Walkman, but it also caused successful designs to get lost in the shuffle. Mine was a particularly pleasing construction — sleek, rounded, with an analog radio dial and push buttons that made you feel that you were *doing* something. Unlike many other models, it also worked properly for years, providing the soundtrack to a decade of my life. I can summon the physical memory of squeezing the Play button, the middle of three oblong pieces of silver metal, and suddenly I am back in Munich in 1986, listening to the new Bob Dylan album on a brown threadbare corduroy sofa in my Goethestrasse apartment. Or I'm driving eight hours down I-95 to visit a girlfriend, listening to tapes on the Walkman because my Rabbit's stereo has been stolen. Or I'm riding the Amtrak between New York and Boston, listening to Indigo Girls while the autumn leaves blow by the window. I can even tell you the album and track that unwound on the tape, visible through the tape player's window, in that specific recollection. I have no idea why that moment should survive in my mind, but the red and black Walkman is as much a part of that moment as the music itself, and the leaves, and the dark, sheltering train.

Another machine still lingering in the afterlife: the 1973 Datsun 1200 my dad handed down to me to run into the ground, which I eventually did. A bottom-of-the-line economy model, "the Green Machine," as my friends called it, looked like a vehicle out of Dr. Seuss, but it always started and got forty miles to the gallon — a cause for nostalgia, indeed, in these simmering, gas-guzzling days. I can still see the schematic four-gear diagram on the head of the stick shift and feel the knob — and the worn transmission of the gears — in my right hand. The radio had five black cuboid push buttons for preset stations: the two on the left each sported AM in white indentations, and the other three said FM. It took almost the entire ten-minute ride to school for the anemic defogger to rid the windshield of its early-morning dew. One day that teary outward view was replaced, at forty miles an hour, by green. A rusted latch had finally given out, and the wind had opened the hood and slapped it all the way back against the glass. Luckily, the glass didn't break, and I could see enough through the rust holes to avoid a collision as I braked. Whenever the friend I drove to school was not ready to go, her father would come out and wait with me, looking the Green Machine up and down and shaking his head.

What does it mean that some of my fondest memories are of technology? Have we begun our slide toward the ineluctable merging of man and machine? Are Walkman headphones in the ears the first step toward a computer chip implanted in the brain? Or is it merely that inanimate objects, whether Citizen Kane's wooden "Rosebud" or my handheld electronic circuitry, by virtue of their obliviousness to the passage of time, seize our longing? As photographs do, these objects capture particular periods of our lives. The sense memory of turning that clock-radio knob, or shifting that gear stick, fixes the moment in time as well as any photograph. Just as we painstakingly fit photos into albums or, in the new age, organize them into computer folders and make digital copies for safekeeping, so I hang on to the impression of a stainless-steel wristwatch that once applied a familiar force of weight to my left wrist.

(Where have they gone, these mechanisms of my youth? The Datsun was hauled off for parts. The clock radio and the Walkman no doubt were tossed without a second thought when they no longer functioned properly. But the Seiko? Who would throw out a fine watch that, to my recollection, never broke? My mother swears she wouldn't have. Spring cleaning is not exactly my father's pastime. Could a watch, along with its deep blue case with the silvery embossed square border, vanish into time itself?)

Of course, my memory of these objects may be inaccurate. Were I to come upon my old clock radio, wrapped in old T-shirts inside a threadbare leather overnight bag in the attic, the sensation might be like that felt on entering a high school reunion and being jolted by the discrepancy between the memory of old friends and their current reality. In this case the object has not aged, but the memory has. In his wonderful book-length essay *U and I*, Nicholson Baker practices what he calls "memory criticism": he records his impressions of John Updike's works without allowing himself to re-read them. When he does go back to the texts to check, Baker finds that his memories of many passages, so emblazoned upon his mind, are imperfect. He fashions an argument around a remembered line from a poem, discovers that the actual poem does not support the argument, and finishes off the argument anyway. A story remembered fondly for its metaphor likening a character's sick stomach to "an unprepossessing tuber" turns out not to contain the treasured trope. Baker remembers Updike making a brilliant comparison between "a strange interruption in his act of signature, between the *p* and the *d*," and his verbal stuttering — a comparison that had never in fact been made.

Even Nabokov, that grand master of recollection, with a self-ascribed "almost pathological keenness of the retrospective faculty," is fallible. In the first version of his autobiography, *Speak, Memory*, he describes his family coat of arms as depicting two bears holding up a chessboard. Later, the chess-loving author is chagrined to discover that the bears are lions, and that they support a knight's shield comprising "only one sixteenth of a checkerboard."

So perhaps the clock radio is better off in oblivion. Unearthed, it might strike me as simply a cheap J. C. Penney's item from the 1970s — hardly a golden age for design. Now, for better or worse, holding the object in my hands might remind me of the bored loneliness of the years I spent steering its tuning knob, just as Baker feared being "disappointed by the immediate context of a phrase [of Updike's he] loved, when the context was now hazy and irrelevant."

Once, these humanly flawed recollections were the only means we had of reconstructing the past. And even though our selective memory may have been salubrious, we yearned to possess the past more completely. Now we have created the technology to satisfy our longing. Only machines — tape recorders, cameras, video cameras — can accurately preserve the details of our former selves, of our loved ones' younger faces, of our long-gone possessions. Nostalgia, even for machines, is bolstered by machines of nostalgia.

I am typing this on a Macintosh G4 Powerbook. Will the thought of this laptop someday conjure up such piquant memories? As much as the recollection of my first computer, a 1985 Kaypro I received for college graduation? It was the first "portable" computer — a thirty-pound metal box the size of a small suitcase, with a keyboard that detached from one end. I can still feel the power switch on the right side of the back, where I reached to flick it on thousands of times. The green glow of the characters on screen, the five-and-a-half-inch floppy disks that had to be inserted in order to boot up or run Wordstar, even the control-K commands that brought up various menus — they all seem like the markings of a bygone era, even as they retain an intimate immediacy.

Yet computers, while they have probably replaced the automobile and the television as the most dominating technological feature of our daily lives, seem to have reached a uniformity — as well as a dismayingly short lifespan — that may weaken their nostalgic potential. This laptop isn't very different from past laptops, and I've gone through a succession of desktop computers with almost identical exteriors. I feel little nostalgia for my PCs of the early 1990s. It's hard to get choked up about the fact that a particular box packed only twenty megabytes.

Perhaps, though, this very act of typing is what will linger one day in my mind's reliquary. Voice-recognition software is pounding at the gates; videomail seems every day more feasible. How much longer will our computers even have keyboards? Typing may someday survive only as another sense memory. A writer, while composing with his voice, will still tap his fingers on the desk like an amputee scratching a wooden leg. Rather than the ghost of a particular machine, it will be this metacarpal tapdance, an apparition of the way we used to express language, that will haunt him.

CAITLIN FLANAGAN

Home Alone

FROM THE ATLANTIC MONTHLY

CHRISTOPHER BYRON has had the misfortune of writing a lengthy book on Martha Stewart's business dealings that went to press before news broke of what would surely have been its centerpiece — the Imclone scandal. Nor have the fates been kind to him in the matters of prose style or basic storytelling ability. *Martha Inc.: The Incredible Story of Martha Stewart Living Omnimedia* is a book with rather high literary aspirations, but they go bust from the get-go: in the opening sentences of chapter one, Stewart's father, Eddie Kostyra, is described as a "self-absorbed narcissist." One of Christopher Byron's desires — and not a bad one — is to give readers a sense of Martha Stewart's true nature. Regrettably, his means for achieving this goal border on the comical, as he marshals all of Western art and culture (and, one senses, the entirety of his Yale undergraduate education) to his aid. In the course of the book Stewart is compared to the Romanovs, Richard Nixon, "the ghostly wife of King Popiel the Heartless," elevator music, the Jim Carrey character in *The Truman Show,* the Karl Malden character in *One-Eyed Jacks,* the Jeff Daniels character in *The Purple Rose of Cairo,* a "demonically possessed character out of a horror movie," an unspecified character "out of a Bo Widerberg movie," a central character in *Who's Afraid of Virginia Woolf?,* the Cheshire Cat, Dorothy Gale, Jay Gatsby, Marie Antoinette, Macbeth, Evita Peron, John Fitzgerald Kennedy Jr., Walt Disney, a witch, a saint, a participant in Torquemada's Theater of Tortures, the Ohio State football team, the Chicago Bulls, Chairman Mao, and (perhaps most unlikely of all, and for an entire chapter) Nancy Drew. That this curi-

ous assemblage is incapable of suggesting any one human being —
and least of all Martha Stewart — eludes Byron, although midway
through the book we find a defeated little remark that amounts to
an authorial waving of the white flag: Stewart, he decides, is really
just "like everyone." She has "good qualities and bad qualities, and
still other qualities that seemed to occupy a kind of 'work in progress' niche in between." Well, then maybe we ought to let poor old
Richard Nixon rest in peace.

Byron makes Stewart appear distasteful, but no one could be
more distasteful than Byron himself, as he dredges up news about
Stewart's hysterectomy, does his level best to glean facts from her
sealed divorce file, and reports on the intimate sleeping arrangements of her teenage daughter. In Byron's hands Stewart can't
catch a break. When she and her husband relocated their young
family from Manhattan to Turkey Hill Farm, in Westport, Connecticut, "scarcely had the couple moved to the country than they
found enough money to dump the child in a fancy country day
school a mile from Turkey Hill and left her to fend for herself." It's
a remark that prompts the reader to wonder what the preferable
alternative was — enrolling the little girl in a public school farther
from home and attending classes with her? (He seems also to have
forgotten that in the book's preface he explained proudly that he
and his glamorous subject "had actually been leading parallel
lives"; in fact, Byron and his wife "had sent [their] daughter to the
same country day school where the Stewarts had sent theirs.") We
get the by now familiar litany of offenses (hopped up with a few
spicy new additions) that prove conclusively that Martha Stewart is
the rottenest, nastiest person ever to draw breath: she was mean to
a trick-or-treater, frightened a Boy Scout, jumped to the head of a
line at a tag sale, ran over a kitten, and irritated an employee at
a Chinese restaurant so badly that he blurted out, "I don't give a
fuck." She honked at slowpokes in a bank drive-through. She un-
plugged a guest-room mini-fridge in which a visitor had been stor-
ing yummy "coffee, juice, leftovers and snacks." She once borrowed a large pot and never returned it. A guest at one of her
breakfast meetings was made "instantly nauseous" by the fare. Even
Stewart's breathtaking triumphs (such as seizing and maintaining
control of a Charlie Rose interview) are portrayed in the same
grim light as are her disastrous lapses of judgment (such as actually

dating Charlie Rose). Sometimes Byron's tone is that of a censorious eighth-grade girl, as when he reports that "Martha is not a good mixer at parties." Much has been made in the press of the fact that contrary to expectation, *Martha Inc.* is not the nastiest biography of Stewart yet published. But not for lack of trying. Byron wants us to understand that Stewart is an egomaniac (perhaps even a self-absorbed narcissist), and this should not require much heavy lifting on his part. But oftentimes his evidence lacks punch. When a Cuban tour guide tells her that he learned English by tuning in Tom Brokaw's news broadcasts using a homemade antenna, we get this bit of silliness:

> Whether Martha was genuinely interested or irritated that her "guide" was talking about a rival celebrity isn't known. But whatever her feelings at the new direction in the conversation, she nonetheless quickly managed to steer things back toward something that made her the center of events once again. She said, "I can buy you a satellite dish and send it to you."

Stop this monster before she maims and kills!

Byron performs arabesques of conclusion upon the weakest scaffolding of facts. We learn, for example, that the Kostyra family home "had a single full bath, and two washrooms — one in the basement and the other off the kitchen, where Eddie would shave and relieve himself during mealtimes, whether the family liked it or not." The source for this unlovely revelation seems to be one of Stewart's "Remembering" columns (a regular feature of her *Martha Stewart Living* magazine), in which she remarks of the household facilities, "One of the half-bathrooms was a toilet and a sink off the kitchen — that was really Dad's private domain." How we get from this unremarkable statement to Dad's "reliev[ing] himself during mealtimes" is, I think, what makes so much of this book "The Incredible Story" that it is. Byron is quite rabid on the subject of the "Remembering" columns. In the kind of footnote that makes one think it was really a pity he gave up the law in favor of writing, he tells us, "At the time of this book's writing, ninety-five such columns had been published. Copies of all were obtained and digested for this book." A lesser student of human evil might assume that in ninety-five columns about her childhood, a person might commit a few inconsistencies and repetitions; but Byron is a

stickler for absolute accuracy in such matters. Stewart wrote in
1982 that she first visited Europe with her husband, but then wrote
in a "Remembering" column that she first went to the Continent
with her mother — and Byron cries foul. He is certainly not the
first to sense that collectively these columns leave a telling record
of their author's interests and intentions, but surely it is the biographer's job — if his method is to involve a careful examination of
these things — to make something more of their various obfusca-
tions and revisions than the observation that they all appear to
have been "dashed off on the way to the airport."

But the book just comes apart at the seams when it addresses its
intended main subject — not the personality of Martha Stewart
but, rather, her business acumen and success. Byron, a financial reporter, serves up plenty of blather about "a Harvard B-school concept known as 'synergy'" and the intricacies of television syndica-
tion deals and the dot-com revolution. He tells us that Stewart is
"the human embodiment of an abstract marketing message," but
what, exactly, that message might be is beyond him. I knew that we
might be in the hands of someone distinctly unsuited to write
about a woman whose financial success is based, in large part, on
cooking and fine dining when he described the faces of the girls in
her high school yearbook as appearing to be "frozen in aspic." But
at every turn he fails to understand what, precisely, Stewart is selling, and to whom and how. For her followers he has at best a kind
of pity, finding in them a group of hausfraus completely worn
down by the one-two punch of women's liberation and housework,
and desperate for a messiah. Stewart's fans, we learn, are women
"in fly-over America," women who "toiled in Norman Rockwell's silent rituals of life and death and yearned for something more."
They are women "who came home exhausted from jobs they didn't
really want, to confront equally exhausted husbands and resentful
latchkey children," women severely disillusioned by the fact that
the women's movement has "morphed into an array of more than
500 increasingly shrill special interest groups, with a thousand different issues and arenas for action" — this disillusionment somehow causing them to run willy-nilly toward Stewart's world of gracious living and entertaining. At worst Byron has contempt for
Stewart's fans, especially those who are Kmart shoppers, whom
he characterizes as broke, tasteless, rural, and harried. That the

chain's executives seem also to have underestimated its customers is clear, although Stewart (perpetually blasted as elitist) never has — which is perhaps why the retailer is in Chapter 11 while Martha Stewart Living Omnimedia is thriving.

Over and over, Byron presents scenes in which Stewart doesn't "get" Kmart shoppers; "She didn't really understand what was appropriate merchandise for Kmart . . . and what was not," says a former Kmart consultant, to which Byron adds, "Martha had become like the single out-of-step soldier in the army — yet week after week, month after month, she kept pushing to get the whole army to shift to her cadence." He reports that what Kmart wanted from Stewart was merely a little of her allure, a few of her "daffodil daydreams." What she gave the retailer — and what any more competent outfit ought to have been able to turn into a gold mine — was a line of products called Martha Stewart Everyday, which was founded on a simple principle: not that Betty Friedan has left all of womankind hungering for pastels but, rather, that cheap things don't have to be ugly. For dime-store prices she came up with some attractive merchandise, decorated with a restraint not often seen in discount items, that women (and, in not insignificant numbers, gay men) loved buying. Shortly after Kmart announced its financial woes, the *New York Observer* ran a Simon Doonan column titled "Domestic Slaves of New York Confess Dependency on Kmartha," in which he reported panic buying of Martha Stewart Everyday ware and said that "these middle-class groovers are not slumming for a hit of reverse chic: They are sincerely appreciative of the amazing value and quality that Martha offers." Typical of the line is a very pretty white eyelet shower curtain with a scalloped hem, a product with which I am intimately familiar, because it is hanging in my bathroom. And typical of Byron's inability to understand these products or their appeal is his characterization of Stewart as a control freak "who turned up at every meeting, determined to elbow and nudge her way into every decision made in her name . . . all the way down to demanding to know the thread-count per square inch in sheets and towels sold under her name." It's a foolish remark, because, of course, the only really important thing about sheets is their thread count. He later notes snidely that reporters at a publicity event for Stewart's linens thought the patterns were lovely but "once [they] touched the sheets they were reminded where they came from," because "they weren't as soft as [Ralph] Lauren's or Calvin Klein's." Why? Because the thread count was too low, you idiot.

Martha Inc. is so bloated, repetitive, and overwrought that the reader is much more often frustrated by Byron's meanderings and hypotheses than enlightened by his perceptions. Happily, another recent biography tackles the subject of Stewart's business success with clarity and precision: the Martha Stewart volume in the Women of Achievement series, which you can find in the young-adult section of your local public library. (Stewart is apparently someone whom educational publishers think schoolchildren ought to know about; there are also Martha Stewart volumes in the People to Know and the Library of Famous Women series.) Skip the introductory essay on women's history that is printed in each volume (written by Matina S. Horner, the president emerita of Radcliffe College, it evokes Abigail Adams and Ralph Waldo Emerson, two thinkers who may be fine guardians of the volumes on Eleanor Roosevelt and Elizabeth Cady Stanton, but who may strike too resounding a gong for Women of Achievement such as Cher, Gloria Estefan, and Barbara Walters).

Charles J. Shields, the author of the Stewart volume, trots us through the high points of Stewart's early life and career in short order, making astute observations as to how these various experiences may have shaped her as a businesswoman. Compared with Byron's fervid ramblings, this clear analysis is a welcome relief. In his attempt to provide a brief, vivid sketch of Stewart's domineering father, Byron puts his shoulder to the wheel: Eddie Kostyra was a Captain Queeg, a Stanley Kowalski, a "nobly born" character from an Hilaire Belloc rhyme, both faces of Janus. It's a bravura display of the Byron technique, but it can't compare with Shields's fascinating revelation that Eddie Kostyra's mother "had taught him how to cook, sew, and garden, in the hope of encouraging his creative side," and that Eddie decorated the high school gym for the prom during Martha's junior year. Of her early modeling career Byron says that Stewart lacked the "erotic and sexually charged" quality of the sixties model Veruschka and failed to capture the attention of Richard Avedon as had Twiggy. Why he sees a need to compare Stewart's modeling work (conducted part-time while she was a student in high school and college) with that of two of the most famous fashion models of the era is unclear, although he misses an obvious point that Shields does not: "Working with photographers gave her a sense of how things should look, or be presented." Byron on Stewart's work as a stockbroker: "What was Martha's job? The same job any good-looking young woman got in the 1960s in a world dominated by men: Walk into the room, sit down, and cross her legs." Shields on the same topic: "She was learning the ropes of big business and its key elements — investment, negotiation, and finance." (Whether she was also learning the rudiments of insider trading has turned out to be one of the most gleefully debated questions of the summer. To borrow a page from the Byron style book, not since Marie Antoinette got hauled off to the Conciergerie — or Leona Helmsley to federal prison — has there been the potential of such a thrilling new addition to the female prison population.) Shields gives us Stewart's own take on her Kmart experiences, which brings the conflict between her and the retailer into much sharper focus than any of Byron's hyperbole: "When I first started with Kmart, I was very enthusiastic to build a fine business with them. Little did I know that management was extremely weak and their inventory control and computer programs a complete disaster."

What no biography of Stewart has yet accomplished is an insightful analysis of the core questions that her phenomenal success prompts. Many writers — especially male writers, such as Byron and Jerry Oppenheimer, the author of *Martha Stewart: Just Desserts* (1997) — have been fascinated by her famously mercurial temperament and the unsavory details of her personal life. But other than indulging in juicy speculation (such as Oppenheimer's creepy fascination with Stewart's heavy menstrual periods and Byron's notion that she had a hysterectomy as a form of birth control, a notion that only a man could believe and only a jerk could promulgate), they don't know what to do with these supposed secrets except to humiliate Stewart by making them public. The notion of an attractive late-midlife woman who offers homemaking advice on television but leads an off-camera life marked by nastiness and single-girl liberty is rife with comedic possibility (it is the basis for the Sue Ann Nivens character on *The Mary Tyler Moore Show*), and this type draws the cruelest of the biographers. But these writers' books fail because they assume that Stewart's success is based on the stupidity of women, their inability to see through her many inconsistencies and hypocrisies. If only those dumb clucks would read the "Remembering" columns more critically! They'd cancel their subscriptions in an instant! Byron misses nothing less than the heart of Stewart's appeal to women.

In the first place there is the incontrovertible fact of her tremendous style. The photography in her various publications seems to reduce all of female longing to its essential elements. A basket of flowers, a child's lawn pinafore draped across a painted rocking chair, an exceptionally white towel folded in thirds and perched in glamorous isolation on a clean and barren shelf: most of the pictures feature a lot of sunlight, and many show rooms that are either empty of people or occupied solely by Martha, evoking the profound and enduring female desires for solitude and silence. No heterosexual man can understand this stuff, and no woman with a beating heart and an ounce of femininity can resist it. I can unpack a paragraph of Martha Stewart prose with the best of them, but I also fall mute and wondering at the pages of *Martha Stewart Living*.

Stewart's aesthetic has been steadily evolving over the past two decades, and at this point it has reached a peak of almost unbearable perfection. To compare her two wedding volumes — published in 1987 and 1999 — is to see just how far things have come. The first appeared at the precise moment when Americans by the millions were returning to formal weddings; in fact, its publication was so timely and so influential that it's hard to know to what extent Stewart predicted the craze and to what extent she created it. The book has a documentary quality: it features photographs of actual weddings she catered during the summers of 1984 and 1985 and also some that she heard about and asked if she might photograph and include in the book. The pictures are full of the mess and indignity of real life. There are a few unattractive brides and a couple of chubby ones (as well as several couples of such heartrending youth and hopefulness that I banished a vague notion of doing a longitudinal study of the fate of these marriages as soon as it flitted through my head). There are wedding guests in shorts and shirtsleeves, several preparing to board a Greyhound bus, a couple of Porta Potties nestled into a leafy corner of a reception site. On one table there's a two-liter bottle of Coca-Cola, on another a fifth of cheap Scotch. But to look at the more recent volume is to see all this unpleasantness burnished away. Actual brides are for the most part relegated to small black-and-white photographs; the full-color spreads feature models and careful art direction and receptions unsullied by actual guests. The venues for these stage-set weddings seem to be a collection of New England chapels of the highest caliber. Whitewashed shingles and gleaming wooden pews provide austere backdrops for garlands of flowers, wreaths of flowers, paper cones of flowers; espaliered bushes are covered in clouds of white tulle and tied with silk ribbons; walkways are blanketed in thick drifts of petals; oak trees are hung with white Japanese lanterns. Flower girls wear wreaths of roses and carry more of them; winter weddings feature severe Christmas trees and tall centerpieces of sugared fruit. My attraction to these images has nothing to do with "Norman Rockwell's silent rituals of life and death," nor is it compromised by my knowledge of Stewart's complex personal life. It is rooted in a truth far less mysterious: women like pretty things. Stewart's magazines (she has four titles: *Living, Baby, Kids,* and *Weddings*) all seem to depict some parallel universe in which loveliness and order are untrammeled by the surging chaos of life in session, particularly life as it is lived with small children. In an issue of *Martha Stewart Kids,* I recently saw a photograph of a pair of old-fashioned white baby shoes with their laces replaced by two lengths of grosgrain ribbon. The result was impractical in the extreme, and very, very pretty. Which is a fair summation of many Stewart projects. In one of his few apt observations, Christopher Byron calls Stewart's "the face of the age." I would also say that the look of her magazines has become the look of women's magazines of the age: the photography, art direction, and layouts in many contemporary publications — including the recent magazine *Real Simple,* the redesigned *Child,* and all the craft and decorating features in *Rosie* (the revamped *McCall's*) — are clearly and deeply influenced by Stewart's.

Much of the Stewart enterprise, of course, involves a certain level of fantasy and wish fulfillment, having to do not only with the old dreams of wealth and elegance but also with the new one of time. That many of Stewart's projects are time-consuming is in fact part of their appeal. A risibly complicated recipe for sandwiches that are a "tempting snack for a 1-year-old," which ran in a recent issue of *Baby* (flower-shaped, their bright-yellow centers were created by mashing cooked egg yolk with butter, rolling the resulting paste into a tube, wrapping the tube in parchment paper, refrigerating it, and then slicing it into half-inch-thick rounds), is attractive not in spite of its ludicrous complexity but because of it — *imagine having enough time to do something like that!* The question of whether Stewart is indeed the "teacher" she has always professed to be or whether she is a kind of performance artist is an old one; I think that a significant number of women — including some of Stewart's staunchest defenders — appreciate what she does but never personally attempt it. *Martha Stewart Living* is filled with recipes for complicated restaurant-type food — caramelized fennel, warm goat cheese with wasabi-pea crust, and the like — but the ads are for Wendy's Mandarin Chicken Salad, and Hormel's precooked roast beef, and Jell-O. One gets the sense that women enjoy reading about the best way to select a leg of lamb, but when it's dinnertime, they give an exhausted shrug and settle for the ease and convenience of Campbell's 2-Step Beefy Taco Joes, the recipe for which appears in a Campbell's ad in the magazine's recent hundredth issue.

The true engine of her success has much to do with a remark Stewart makes in chapter one of her first book, the phenomenally successful *Entertaining* (1982).

> Entertaining provides a good excuse to put things in order (polish silver, wash forgotten dishes, wax floors, paint a flaking windowsill) and, sometimes, to be more fanciful or dramatic with details than usual. It is the moment to indulge in a whole bank of flowering plants to line the hall, or to organize a collection of antique clothes on a conspicuous coat-rack, or to try the dining-room table at an odd angle.

The second sentence, of course, is the stuff of a thousand jokes and parodies — not just a vase of flowers but a "bank" of them; the elaborate clothing display that no normal householder has the resources or the willingness to pull off. But the first sentence is the one to keep your eye on, with its unremarkable but attractive suggestion of a house put in order: a windowsill painted, floors gleaming under a new coat of wax. In the hundredth issue of *Martha Stewart Living*, Stewart says that she recently came across a memo she wrote at the magazine's inception, one that she feels expresses her vision as clearly today as it did then. "Our reader," the memo states, "still wants to iron, to polish silver, to set a sensible table, to cook good food." She's right, of course; millions of women still "want" to do these things, although an astonishing number of them (myself included) don't do much ironing or polishing anymore, and are repeatedly frustrated by the nightly return to the kitchen. Our desire to reconnect with these tasks — which we fear are crucial to a well-run home — is commensurate with our uncertainty about what, exactly, they entail. Just as Disneyland presents a vision of Main Street, USA, that is very far afield from the real thing, so Stewart presents a vision of domesticity that involves as much make-believe as practicality, that is filled with allure and prettiness rather than the drudgery and exhaustion of which we are all so wary. She lectures not on the humdrum reality of sweeping the kitchen floor every night but on the correct way to store two dozen specialty brooms. Not on washing the dishes meal after relentless meal but on the advisability of transferring dishwashing liquid from its unattractive plastic bottle to a cut-glass cruet with a silver stopper. The Stewart fantasy encompasses the feminine interest in formal weddings and gracious entertaining, but principally — and more powerfully — it turns on a wistful and almost shameful attraction to ironing boards and newly washed crockery and good meals sensibly prepared. And on this wan longing, Stewart has built an empire.

None of which is to suggest that I have any fondness for Stewart, whom I find the most unpleasant person on television. She is stern and exacting about things for which I have only the fondest and gentlest associations: flower beds and freshly laundered clothes and home-cooked food. That millions of people are happy to be lectured on "family" and "tradition" by a woman whose own marriage imploded and whose relations with her only child have been famously stormy used to drive me wild with frustration; but lately I've softened on the old girl. She is the producer of a myth about American family life that is as old as Hollywood — and if we expected the men who make our best-loved "family movies" to comport themselves honorably as husbands and fathers, we'd be sunk at matinee time. Her faltering confessions about her private domestic bewilderments (she should have "read more psychology books," she has said about her early career as a mother; it was "a big mistake" to have had an only child) provide her most humanizing moments. And I find something touching and almost elegiac in her memories of the family that raised her, for all the ridicule they receive: "We all sat down to dinner at the same time, and we all got up at the same time and we were very close-knit."

Clearly, something powerful is at work here, some weaving together of the dream of a "close knit" family with rigid adherence to complicated baking and gardening protocols. There was a time when the measure of a home was found in the woman who ran it — who was there all day long, who understood that certain aspects of "hominess" had less to do with spit and polish than with continuity and permanence. As these old standards wane, a new one has emerged, and it is Stewart's. No human effort is so fundamentally simple and pleasurable that she cannot render it difficult and off-putting (we are to be grateful that thus far she has not produced a marriage manual). But almost any project she cooks up is less daunting than the one it is meant to replace: keeping a family together, under one roof, home.

IAN FRAZIER

Researchers Say

FROM THE NEW YORKER

ACCORDING TO a study just released by scientists at Duke University, life is too hard. Although their findings mainly concern life as experienced by human beings, the study also applies to other animate forms, the scientists claim. Years of tests, experiments, and complex computer simulations now provide solid statistical evidence in support of old folk sayings that described life as "a vale of sorrows," "a woeful trial," "a kick in the teeth," "not worth living," and so on. Like much common wisdom, these sayings turn out to contain more than a little truth.

Authors of the twelve-hundred-page study were hesitant to single out any particular factors responsible for making life tough. A surprise, they say, is that they found so many. Before the study was undertaken, researchers had assumed, by positive logic, that life could not be *that* bad. As the data accumulated, however, they provided incontrovertible proof that life is actually worse than most living things can stand. Human endurance equals just a tiny fraction of what it should be, given everything it must put up with. In a personal note in the afterword, researchers stated that, statistically speaking, life is "just too much," and as yet they have no plausible theory how anyone gets through it at all.

A major disadvantage to living that the study called attention to is, of course, death. In fact, so obvious are its drawbacks that no one before had thought to examine or measure them empirically. Death's effects on life, the scientists pointed out, are two: First, death intrudes constantly and unpleasantly by putting life at risk at every stage, from infancy through advanced adulthood, degrading its quality and compromising happiness. For individuals of every species, death represents a chronic, worrisome threat that they can never completely ignore.

Secondly, and far worse, death also constitutes an overwhelmingly no-win experience in itself. Many of life's well-known stress producers — divorce, loss of employment, moving, even fighting traffic — still hold out hope of a better outcome in the future. After all, one may end up with a better spouse, exciting new job, beautiful home, or fresh bottle from the drive-through liquor store. Death, by contrast, involves as much trouble as any conventional stress, if not more. Yet, at the end of the medical humiliations, physical suffering, money concerns, fear, and tedium of dying, one has no outcome to look forward to except being dead. This alone, the study found, is enough to give the entire life process a negative tinge.

Besides dying, life is burdened with countless occurrences that are almost equally unacceptable to active and vital individuals. In many cases that the scientists observed, humans no longer functioned properly after the age of seventy or seventy-five. A large majority of subjects in that age range exhibited significant loss of foot speed, upper-body strength, reflexes, hair, and altitude of vertical leap. Accompanying these impairments were other health glitches, sometimes in baffling number and variety. Such acquired traits carried the additional downside of making their possessors either "undesirable" or "very undesirable" to members of the opposite sex in the key eighteen-to-thirty-five demographic. Researchers were able to offer no credible hope for the development of treatments to deal with these creeping inadequacies.

Somewhat simplifying the study's collection of data was the natural law first discovered by Newton that things are rough all over. Thus, what happens to you will always be just as bad (relatively speaking) as what happens to anybody else. Or, to frame it another way, no problem is effectively "minor" if you yourself have it. One example is the mattress cover, or quilted pad, that goes over the mattress before you put on the fitted sheet, and that pops loose from one corner of the mattress in the middle of the night nearly sixty percent of the time, experts say. After it does, it will often work its way diagonally down the bed, taking the fitted sheet with it, until it becomes a bunched-together ridge of cloth poking up at about kidney level. The problem it represents to the individual experiencing it at that moment is absolute, in the sense that it cannot usefully be compared with difficulties in the lives of people in China or anywhere. The poke in the kidneys and the press of bare mattress against the face are simply the accumulating misery of life making itself known.

Nine out of ten of the respondents, identified by just their first initials for the purpose of the survey, stated that they would give up completely if they knew how. The remainder also didn't see the point of going on any longer but still clung to a slight hope for something in the mail. Quitting the struggle and lying face down on the floor was a coping strategy favored by most or all. Situations like having to wait an entire day for a deliveryman to deliver a breakfront and the guy didn't say exactly when he would be there and in the end didn't come and didn't even bother to call were so pointless and awful that the hell with the whole deal, many respondents said.

Interestingly, the numbers bear them out. The point, or points, of going on with existence, when charted and quantified, paint a very grim picture indeed. Merely trying to get a shoe off a child has been shown to release a certain chemical into the system that causes a reaction exactly opposite to what the task requires. Despite vigorous effort and shouting, the thing won't come off, for Christ's sake, as can be seen in the formula written out in full in figure 7. Furthermore, that level of suffering doesn't include the additional fact that a person's spouse may not consider what the person does every day to be "work," because he or she happens occasionally to enjoy it; so what is he or she supposed to do, get a job he or she hates, instead? From a mathematical standpoint, this particular problem is an infinite regression.

Flammia Brothers Pharmaceuticals, which paid somebody to say it paid for the study, frankly admits that it does not as yet have the answers. In the interim, it offers a wide array of experience-blocking drugs, which consist of copyrighted names without pills to go with them, and which certainly might work, depending on one's susceptibility, financial history, and similar factors. Hundreds of thousands of notepads with the Flammia Brothers' logo and colorful drug names at the top of every page are already in circulation in doctors' offices and examining rooms, and a soothing poultice may be made of these pages soaked in water and driveway salt from Ace Hardware. (Most health-insurance plans may or may not cover the cost of the salt, excluding delivery.)

Other large drug manufacturers, while not willing to go quite as far, still substantially follow the Flammia Brothers' program. The fact that life is beyond us has been firmly established by now. All the information is in, and no real dispute remains. But with the temporary absence of lasting remedies, and looking to a future when they won't be necessary, the manufacturers' consortium suggests that consumers send them money in cash or check, no questions asked. Major health organizations have unanimously endorsed this goal. Originally, the consortium explained that the companies might need the money to develop a new generation of drugs narrowly focused on curing many previously uncured problems. More recently, however, they have backed off of that.

Why we were brought into the world in the first place only to suffer and die is an area of research in which much remains to be done. Like other problems thought impossible in the past, this one, too, will someday be solved. Then anybody afflicted with questions like "Why me?," "What did I do to deserve this?," "How did I get in this lousy mess?," and so on could be given a prescription, maybe even through diagnostic services provided online. The possibilities are exciting. At the same time, we must not underestimate our adversary, life itself. Uncomfortable even at good moments, difficult and unfair usually, and a complete nightmare much too often, life will stubbornly resist betterment, always finding new ways of being more than we can stand.

ATUL GAWANDE

The Learning Curve

FROM THE NEW YORKER

THE PATIENT needed a central line. "Here's your chance," S., the chief resident, said. I had never done one before. "Get set up and then page me when you're ready to start."

It was my fourth week in surgical training. The pockets of my short white coat bulged with patient printouts, laminated cards with instructions for doing CPR and reading EKGs and using the dictation system, two surgical handbooks, a stethoscope, wound-dressing supplies, meal tickets, a penlight, scissors, and about a dollar in loose change. As I headed up the stairs to the patient's floor, I rattled.

This will be good, I tried to tell myself: my first real procedure. The patient — fiftyish, stout, taciturn — was recovering from abdominal surgery he'd had about a week earlier. His bowel function hadn't yet returned, and he was unable to eat. I explained to him that he needed intravenous nutrition and that this required a "special line" that would go into his chest. I said that I would put the line in him while he was in his bed, and that it would involve my numbing a spot on his chest with a local anesthetic, and then threading the line in. I did not say that the line was eight inches long and would go into his vena cava, the main blood vessel to his heart. Nor did I say how tricky the procedure could be. There were "slight risks" involved, I said, such as bleeding and lung collapse; in experienced hands, complications of this sort occur in fewer than one case in a hundred.

But, of course, mine were not experienced hands. And the disasters I knew about weighed on my mind: the woman who had died within minutes from massive bleeding when a resident lacerated her vena cava; the man whose chest had to be opened because a resident lost hold of a wire inside the line, which then floated down to the patient's heart; the man who had a cardiac arrest when the procedure put him into ventricular fibrillation. I said nothing of such things, naturally, when I asked the patient's permission to do his line. He said, "OK."

I had seen S. do two central lines; one was the day before, and I'd attended to every step. I watched how she set out her instruments and laid her patient down and put a rolled towel between his shoulder blades to make his chest arch out. I watched how she swabbed his chest with antiseptic, injected lidocaine, which is a local anesthetic, and then, in full sterile garb, punctured his chest near his clavicle with a fat three-inch needle on a syringe. The patient hadn't even flinched. She told me how to avoid hitting the lung ("Go in at a steep angle," she'd said. "Stay *right* under the clavicle"), and how to find the subclavian vein, a branch to the vena cava lying atop the lung near its apex ("Go in at a steep angle. Stay *right* under the clavicle"). She pushed the needle in almost all the way. She drew back on the syringe. And she was in. You knew because the syringe filled with maroon blood. ("If it's bright red, you've hit an artery," she said. "That's not good.") Once you have the tip of this needle poking in the vein, you somehow have to widen the hole in the vein wall, fit the catheter in, and snake it in the right direction — down to the heart, rather than up to the brain — all without tearing through vessels, lung, or anything else.

To do this, S. explained, you start by getting a guide wire in place. She pulled the syringe off, leaving the needle in. Blood flowed out. She picked up a two-foot-long twenty-gauge wire that looked like the steel D string of an electric guitar, and passed nearly its full length through the needle's bore, into the vein, and onward toward the vena cava. "Never force it in," she warned, "and never, ever let go of it." A string of rapid heartbeats fired off on the cardiac monitor, and she quickly pulled the wire back an inch. It had poked into the heart, causing momentary fibrillation. "Guess we're in the right place," she said to me quietly. Then to the patient: "You're doing great. Only a few minutes now." She pulled the needle out over the wire and replaced it with a bullet of thick, stiff plastic, which she pushed in tight to widen the vein opening. She then removed this dilator and threaded the central line — a spa-ghetti-thick, flexible yellow plastic tube — over the wire until it was all the way in. Now she could remove the wire. She flushed the line with a heparin solution and sutured it to the patient's chest. And that was it.

Today, it was my turn to try. First, I had to gather supplies — a central-line kit, gloves, gown, cap, mask, lidocaine — which took me forever. When I finally had the stuff together, I stopped for a minute outside the patient's door, trying to recall the steps. They remained frustratingly hazy. But I couldn't put it off any longer. I had a page-long list of other things to get done: Mrs. A needed to be discharged; Mr. B needed an abdominal ultrasound arranged; Mrs. C needed her skin staples removed. And every fifteen minutes or so I was getting paged with more tasks: Mr. X was nauseated and needed to be seen; Miss Y's family was here and needed "someone" to talk to them; Mr. Z needed a laxative. I took a deep breath, put on my best don't-worry-I-know-what-I'm-doing look, and went in.

I placed the supplies on a bedside table, untied the patient's gown, and laid him down flat on the mattress, with his chest bare and his arms at his sides. I flipped on a fluorescent overhead light and raised his bed to my height. I paged S. I put on my gown and gloves and, on a sterile tray, laid out the central line, the guide wire, and other materials from the kit. I drew up five cc's of lidocaine in a syringe, soaked two sponge sticks in the yellow-brown Betadine, and opened up the suture packaging.

S. arrived. "What's his platelet count?"

My stomach knotted I hadn't checked. That was bad: too low and he could have a serious bleed from the procedure. She went to check a computer. The count was acceptable.

Chastened, I started swabbing his chest with the sponge sticks. "Got the shoulder roll underneath him?" S. asked. Well, no, I had forgotten that, too. The patient gave me a look. S., saying nothing, got a towel, rolled it up, and slipped it under his back for me. I fin-ished applying the antiseptic and then draped him so that only his right upper chest was exposed. He squirmed a bit beneath the drapes. S. now inspected my tray. I girded myself.

"Where's the extra syringe for flushing the line when it's in?" Damn. She went out and got it.

I felt for my landmarks. *Here?* I asked with my eyes, not wanting to undermine the patient's confidence any further. She nodded. I numbed the spot with lidocaine. ("You'll feel a stick and a burn now, sir.") Next, I took the three-inch needle in hand and poked it through the skin. I advanced it slowly and uncertainly, a few millimeters at a time. This is a big goddamn needle, I kept thinking. I couldn't believe I was sticking it into someone's chest. I concentrated on maintaining a steep angle of entry, but kept spearing his clavicle instead of slipping beneath it.

"Ow!" he shouted.

"Sorry," I said. S. signaled with a kind of surfing hand gesture to go underneath the clavicle. This time, it went in. I drew back on the syringe. Nothing. She pointed deeper. I went in deeper. Nothing. I withdrew the needle, flushed out some bits of tissue clogging it, and tried again.

"Ow!"

Too steep again. I found my way underneath the clavicle once more. I drew the syringe back. Still nothing. He's too obese, I thought. S. slipped on gloves and a gown. "How about I have a look?" she said. I handed her the needle and stepped aside. She plunged the needle in, drew back on the syringe, and, just like that, she was in. "We'll be done shortly," she told the patient.

She let me continue with the next steps, which I bumbled through. I didn't realize how long and floppy the guide wire was until I pulled the coil out of its plastic sleeve, and, putting one end of it into the patient, I very nearly contaminated the other. I forgot about the dilating step until she reminded me. Then, when I put in the dilator, I didn't push quite hard enough, and it was really S. who pushed it all the way in. Finally, we got the line in, flushed it, and sutured it in place.

Outside the room, S. said that I could be less tentative the next time, but that I shouldn't worry too much about how things had gone. "You'll get it," she said. "It just takes practice." I wasn't so sure. The procedure remained wholly mysterious to me. And I could not get over the idea of jabbing a needle into someone's chest so deeply and so blindly. I awaited the X-ray afterward with trepidation. But it came back fine: I had not injured the lung and the line was in the right place.

Not everyone appreciates the attractions of surgery. When you are a medical student in the operating room for the first time, and you see the surgeon press the scalpel to someone's body and open it like a piece of fruit, you either shudder in horror or gape in awe. I gaped. It was not just the blood and guts that enthralled me. It was also the idea that a person, a mere mortal, would have the confidence to wield that scalpel in the first place.

There is a saying about surgeons: "Sometimes wrong; never in doubt." This is meant as a reproof, but to me it seemed their strength. Every day, surgeons are faced with uncertainties. Information is inadequate; the science is ambiguous; one's knowledge and abilities are never perfect. Even with the simplest operation, it cannot be taken for granted that a patient will come through better off — or even alive. Standing at the operating table, I wondered how the surgeon knew that all the steps would go as planned, that bleeding would be controlled and infection would not set in and organs would not be injured. He didn't, of course. But he cut anyway.

Later, while still a student, I was allowed to make an incision myself. The surgeon drew a six-inch dotted line with a marking pen across an anesthetized patient's abdomen and then, to my surprise, had the nurse hand me the knife. It was still warm from the autoclave. The surgeon had me stretch the skin taut with the thumb and forefinger of my free hand. He told me to make one smooth slice down to the fat. I put the belly of the blade to the skin and cut. The experience was odd and addictive, mixing exhilaration from the calculated violence of the act, anxiety about getting it right, and a righteous faith that it was somehow for the person's good. There was also the slightly nauseating feeling of finding that it took more force than I'd realized. (Skin is thick and springy, and on my first pass I did not go nearly deep enough; I had to cut twice to get through.) The moment made me want to be a surgeon — not an amateur handed the knife for a brief moment but someone with the confidence and ability to proceed as if it were routine.

A resident begins, however, with none of this air of mastery — only an overpowering instinct against doing anything like pressing a knife against flesh or jabbing a needle into someone's chest. On my first day as a surgical resident, I was assigned to the emergency room. Among my first patients was a skinny, dark-haired woman in her late twenties who hobbled in, teeth gritted, with a two-foot-long wooden chair leg somehow nailed to the bottom of her foot. She explained that a kitchen chair had collapsed under her and, as she leaped up to keep from falling, her bare foot had stomped down on a three-inch screw sticking out of one of the chair legs. I tried very hard to look like someone who had not got his medical diploma just the week before. Instead, I was determined to be nonchalant, the kind of guy who had seen this sort of thing a hundred times before. I inspected her foot, and could see that the screw was embedded in the bone at the base of her big toe. There was no bleeding and, as far as I could feel, no fracture.

"Wow, that must hurt," I blurted out idiotically.

The obvious thing to do was give her a tetanus shot and pull out the screw. I ordered the tetanus shot, but I began to have doubts about pulling out the screw. Suppose she bled? Or suppose I fractured her foot? Or something worse? I excused myself and tracked down Dr. W., the senior surgeon on duty. I found him tending to a car-crash victim. The patient was a mess, and the floor was covered with blood. People were shouting. It was not a good time to ask questions.

I ordered an X-ray. I figured it would buy time and let me check my amateur impression that she didn't have a fracture. Sure enough, getting the X-ray took about an hour, and it showed no fracture — just a common screw embedded, the radiologist said, "in the head of the first metatarsal." I showed the patient the X-ray. "You see, the screw's embedded in the head of the first metatarsal," I said. And the plan? she wanted to know. Ah, yes, the plan.

I went to find Dr. W. He was still busy with the crash victim, but I was able to interrupt to show him the X-ray. He chuckled at the sight of it and asked me what I wanted to do. "Pull the screw out?" I ventured. "Yes," he said, by which he meant "Duh." He made sure I'd given the patient a tetanus shot and then shooed me away.

Back in the examining room, I told her that I would pull the screw out, prepared for her to say something like "You?" Instead she said, "OK, Doctor." At first, I had her sitting on the exam table, dangling her leg off the side. But that didn't look as if it would work. Eventually, I had her lie with her foot jutting off the table end, the board poking out into the air. With every move, her pain increased. I injected a local anesthetic where the screw had gone in and that helped a little. Now I grabbed her foot in one hand, the board in the other, and for a moment I froze. Could I really do this? Who was I to presume?

Finally, I gave her a one-two-three and pulled, gingerly at first and then hard. She groaned. The screw wasn't budging. I twisted, and abruptly it came free. There was no bleeding. I washed the wound out, and she found she could walk. I warned her of the risks of infection and the signs to look for. Her gratitude was immense and flattering, like the lion's for the mouse — and that night I went home elated.

In surgery, as in anything else, skill, judgment, and confidence are learned through experience, haltingly and humiliatingly. Like the tennis player and the oboist and the guy who fixes hard drives, we need practice to get good at what we do. There is one difference in medicine, though: we practice on people.

My second try at placing a central IV line went no better than the first. The patient was in intensive care, mortally ill, on a ventilator, and needed the line so that powerful cardiac drugs could be delivered directly to her heart. She was also heavily sedated, and for this I was grateful. She'd be oblivious of my fumbling.

My preparation was better this time. I got the towel roll in place and the syringes of heparin on the tray. I checked her lab results, which were fine. I also made a point of draping more widely, so that if I flopped the guide wire around by mistake again, it wouldn't hit anything unsterile.

For all that, the procedure was a bust. I stabbed the needle in too shallow and then too deep. Frustration overcame tentativeness and I tried one angle after another. Nothing worked. Then, for one brief moment, I got a flash of blood in the syringe, indicating that I was in the vein. I anchored the needle with one hand and went to pull the syringe off with the other. But the syringe was jammed on too tightly, so that when I pulled it free I dislodged the needle from the vein. The patient began bleeding into her chest wall. I held pressure the best I could for a solid five minutes, but still her chest turned black and blue around the site. The hematoma made it impossible to put a line through there anymore. I wanted to give up. But she needed a line and the resident supervising me — a second-year this time — was determined that I succeed. After an X-ray showed that I had not injured her lung, he had me try on the other side, with a whole new kit. I missed again, and he took over. It took him several minutes and two or three sticks to find the vein himself, and that made me feel better. Maybe she was an unusually tough case.

When I failed with a third patient a few days later, though, the doubts really set in. Again, it was stick, stick, stick, and nothing. I stepped aside. The resident watching me got it on the next try.

Surgeons, as a group, adhere to a curious egalitarianism. They believe in practice, not talent. People often assume that you have to have great hands to become a surgeon, but it's not true. When I interviewed to get into surgery programs, no one made me sew or take a dexterity test or checked to see if my hands were steady. You do not even need all ten fingers to be accepted. To be sure, talent helps. Professors say that every two or three years they'll see someone truly gifted come through a program — someone who picks up complex manual skills unusually quickly, sees tissue planes before others do, anticipates trouble before it happens. Nonetheless, attending surgeons say that what's most important to them is finding people who are conscientious, industrious, and boneheaded enough to keep at practicing this one difficult thing day and night for years on end. As a former residency director put it to me, given a choice between a Ph.D. who had cloned a gene and a sculptor, he'd pick the Ph.D. every time. Sure, he said, he'd bet on the sculptor's being more physically talented; but he'd bet on the Ph.D.'s being less "flaky." And in the end that matters more. Skill, surgeons believe, can be taught; tenacity cannot. It's an odd approach to recruitment, but it continues all the way up the ranks, even in top surgery departments. They start with minions with no experience in surgery, spend years training them, and then take most of their faculty from these same homegrown ranks.

And it works. There have now been many studies of elite performers — concert violinists, chess grand masters, professional ice skaters, mathematicians, and so forth — and the biggest difference researchers find between them and lesser performers is the amount of deliberate practice they've accumulated. Indeed, the most important talent may be the talent for practice itself. K. Anders Ericsson, a cognitive psychologist and an expert on performance, notes that the most important role that innate factors play may be in a person's *willingness* to engage in sustained training. He has found, for example, that top performers dislike practicing just as much as others do. (That's why, for example, athletes and musicians usually quit practicing when they retire.) But, more than others, they have the will to keep at it anyway.

I wasn't sure I did. What good was it, I wondered, to keep doing central lines when I wasn't coming close to hitting them? If I had a clear idea of what I was doing wrong, then maybe I'd have something to focus on. But I didn't. Everyone, of course, had suggestions. Go in with the bevel of the needle up. No, go in with the bevel down. Put a bend in the middle of the needle. No, curve the needle. For a while, I tried to avoid doing another line. Soon enough, however, a new case arose.

The circumstances were miserable. It was late in the day, and I'd had to work through the previous night. The patient weighed more than three hundred pounds. He couldn't tolerate lying flat because the weight of his chest and abdomen made it hard for him to breathe. Yet he had a badly infected wound, needed intravenous antibiotics, and no one could find veins in his arms for a peripheral IV. I had little hope of succeeding. But a resident does what he is told, and I was told to try the line.

I went to his room. He looked scared and said he didn't think he'd last more than a minute on his back. But he said he understood the situation and was willing to make his best effort. He and I decided that he'd be left sitting propped up in bed until the last possible minute. We'd see how far we got after that.

I went through my preparations: checking his blood counts from the lab, putting out the kit, placing the towel roll, and so on. I swabbed and draped his chest while he was still sitting up. S., the chief resident, was watching me this time, and when everything was ready I had her tip him back, an oxygen mask on his face. His flesh rolled up his chest like a wave. I couldn't find his clavicle with my fingertips to line up the right point of entry. And already he was looking short of breath, his face red. I gave S. a "Do you want to take over?" look. Keep going, she signaled. I made a rough guess about where the right spot was, numbed it with lidocaine, and pushed the big needle in. For a second, I thought it wouldn't be long enough to reach through, but then I felt the tip slip underneath his clavicle. I pushed a little deeper and drew back on the syringe. Unbelievably, it filled with blood. I was in. I concentrated on anchoring the needle firmly in place, not moving it a millimeter as I pulled the syringe off and threaded the guide wire in. The wire fed in smoothly. The patient was struggling hard for air now. We sat him up and let him catch his breath. And then, laying him down one more time, I got the entry dilated and slid the central line in. "Nice job" was all S. said, and then she left.

I still have no idea what I did differently that day. But from then on my lines went in. That's the funny thing about practice. For days and days, you make out only the fragments of what to do. And then one day you've got the thing whole. Conscious learning becomes unconscious knowledge, and you cannot say precisely how.

I have now put in more than a hundred central lines. I am by no means infallible. Certainly, I have had my fair share of complications. I punctured a patient's lung, for example — the right lung of a chief of surgery from another hospital, no less — and, given the odds, I'm sure such things will happen again. I still have the occasional case that should go easily but doesn't, no matter what I do. (We have a term for this. "How'd it go?" a colleague asks. "It was a total flog," I reply. I don't have to say anything more.)

But other times everything unfolds effortlessly. You take the needle. You stick the chest. You feel the needle travel — a distinct glide through the fat, a slight catch in the dense muscle, then the subtle pop through the vein wall — and you're in. At such moments, it is more than easy; it is beautiful.

Surgical training is the recapitulation of this process — floundering followed by fragments followed by knowledge and, occasionally, a moment of elegance — over and over again, for ever harder tasks with ever greater risks. At first, you work on the basics: how to glove and gown, how to drape patients, how to hold the knife, how to tie a square knot in a length of silk suture (not to mention how to dictate, work the computers, order drugs). But then the tasks become more daunting: how to cut through skin, handle the electrocautery, open the breast, tie off a bleeder, excise a tumor, close up a wound. At the end of six months, I had done lines, lumpectomies, appendectomies, skin grafts, hernia repairs, and mastectomies. At the end of a year, I was doing limb amputations, hemorrhoidectomies, and laparoscopic gallbladder operations. At the end of two years, I was beginning to do tracheotomies, small-bowel operations, and leg-artery bypasses.

I am in my seventh year of training, of which three years have been spent doing research. Only now has a simple slice through skin begun to seem like the mere start of a case. These days, I'm trying to learn how to fix an abdominal aortic aneurysm, remove a pancreatic cancer, open blocked carotid arteries. I am, I have found, neither gifted nor maladroit. With practice and more practice, I get the hang of it.

Doctors find it hard to talk about this with patients. The moral burden of practicing on people is always with us, but for the most part it is unspoken. Before each operation, I go over to the holding area in my scrubs and introduce myself to the patient. I do it the same way every time. "Hello, I'm Dr. Gawande. I'm one of the surgical residents, and I'll be assisting your surgeon." That is pretty much all I say on the subject. I extend my hand and smile. I ask the patient if everything is going OK so far. We chat. I answer questions. Very occasionally, patients are taken aback. "No resident is doing my surgery," they say. I try to be reassuring. "Not to worry — I just assist," I say. "The attending surgeon is always in charge."

None of this is exactly a lie. The attending *is* in charge, and a resident knows better than to forget that. Consider the operation I did recently to remove a seventy-five-year-old woman's colon cancer. The attending stood across from me from the start. And it was he, not I, who decided where to cut, how to position the opened abdomen, how to isolate the cancer, and how much colon to take.

Yet I'm the one who held the knife. I'm the one who stood on the operator's side of the table, and it was raised to my six-foot-plus height. I was there to help, yes, but I was there to practice, too. This was clear when it came time to reconnect the colon. There are two ways of putting the ends together — handsewing and stapling. Stapling is swifter and easier, but the attending suggested I handsew the ends — not because it was better for the patient but because I had had much less experience doing it. When it's performed correctly, the results are similar, but he needed to watch me like a hawk. My stitching was slow and imprecise. At one point, he caught me putting the stitches too far apart and made me go back and put extras in between so the connection would not leak. At another point, he found I wasn't taking deep enough bites of tissue with the needle to ensure a strong closure. "Turn your wrist more," he told me. "Like this?" I asked. "Uh, sort of," he said.

In medicine, there has long been a conflict between the imperative to give patients the best possible care and the need to provide novices with experience. Residencies attempt to mitigate potential harm through supervision and graduated responsibility. And there is reason to think that patients actually benefit from teaching. Studies commonly find that teaching hospitals have better outcomes than nonteaching hospitals. Residents may be amateurs, but having them around checking on patients, asking questions, and keeping faculty on their toes seems to help. But there is still no avoiding those first few unsteady times a young physician tries to put in a central line, remove a breast cancer, or sew together two segments of colon. No matter how many protections are in place, on average these cases go less well with the novice than with someone experienced.

Doctors have no illusions about this. When an attending physician brings a sick family member in for surgery, people at the hospital think twice about letting trainees participate. Even when the attending insists that they participate as usual, the residents scrubbing in know that it will be far from a teaching case. And if a central line must be put in, a first-timer is certainly not going to do it. Conversely, the ward services and clinics where residents have the most responsibility are populated by the poor, the uninsured, the drunk, and the demented. Residents have few opportunities nowadays to operate independently, without the attending docs scrubbed in, but when we do — as we must before graduating and going out to operate on our own — it is generally with these, the humblest of patients.

And this is the uncomfortable truth about teaching. By traditional ethics and public insistence (not to mention court rulings), a patient's right to the best care possible must trump the objective of training novices. We want perfection without practice. Yet everyone is harmed if no one is trained for the future. So learning is hidden, behind drapes and anesthesia and the elisions of language. And the dilemma doesn't apply just to residents, physicians in training. The process of learning goes on longer than most people know.

I grew up in the small Appalachian town of Athens, Ohio, where my parents are both doctors. My mother is a pediatrician and my father is a urologist. Long ago, my mother chose to practice part-time, which she could afford to do because my father's practice became so busy and successful. He has now been at it for more than twenty-five years, and his office is cluttered with the evidence of this. There is an overflowing wall of medical files, gifts from patients displayed everywhere (books, paintings, ceramics with biblical sayings, hand-painted paperweights, blown glass, carved boxes, a figurine of a boy who, when you pull down his pants, pees on you), and, in an acrylic case behind his oak desk, a few dozen of the thousands of kidney stones he has removed.

Only now, as I get glimpses of the end of my training, have I begun to think hard about my father's success. For most of my residency, I thought of surgery as a more or less fixed body of knowledge and skill which is acquired in training and perfected in practice. There was, I thought, a smooth, upward-sloping arc of proficiency at some rarefied set of tasks (for me, taking out gallbladders, colon cancers, bullets, and appendixes; for him, taking out kidney stones, testicular cancers, and swollen prostates). The arc would peak at, say, ten or fifteen years, plateau for a long time, and perhaps tail off a little in the final five years before retirement. The reality, however, turns out to be far messier. You do get good at certain things, my father tells me, but no sooner do you master something than you find that what you know is outmoded. New technologies and operations emerge to supplant the old, and the learning curve starts all over again. "Three quarters of what I do today I never learned in residency," he says. On his own, fifty miles from his nearest colleague — let alone a doctor who could tell him anything like "You need to turn your wrist more" — he has had to learn to put in penile prostheses, to perform microsurgery, to reverse vasectomies, to do nerve-sparing prostatectomies, to implant artificial urinary sphincters. He's had to learn to use shock-wave lithotripters, electrohydraulic lithotripters, and laser lithotripters (all instruments for breaking up kidney stones); to deploy Double J ureteral stents and Silicone Figure Four Coil stents and Retro-Inject Multi-Length stents (don't even ask); and to maneuver fiberoptic ureteroscopes. All these technologies and techniques were introduced after he finished training. Some of the procedures built on skills he already had. Many did not.

This is the experience that all surgeons have. The pace of medical innovation has been unceasing, and surgeons have no choice but to give the new thing a try. To fail to adopt new techniques would mean denying patients meaningful medical advances. Yet the perils of the learning curve are inescapable — no less in practice than in residency.

For the established surgeon, inevitably, the opportunities for learning are far less structured than for a resident. When an important new device or procedure comes along, as happens every year, surgeons start by taking a course about it — typically a day or two of lectures by some surgical grandees with a few film clips and step-by-step handouts. You take home a video to watch. Perhaps you pay a visit to observe a colleague perform the operation — my father often goes up to the Cleveland Clinic for this. But there's not much by way of hands-on training. Unlike a resident, a visitor cannot scrub in on cases, and opportunities to practice on animals or cadavers are few and far between. (Britain, being Britain, actually bans surgeons from practicing on animals.) When the pulse-dye laser came out, the manufacturer set up a lab in Columbus where urologists from the area could gain experience. But when my father went there the main experience provided was destroying kidney stones in test tubes filled with a urinelike liquid and trying to penetrate the shell of an egg without hitting the membrane underneath. My surgery department recently bought a robotic surgery device — a staggeringly sophisticated $980,000 robot, with three arms, two wrists, and a camera, all millimeters in diameter, which, controlled from a console, allows a surgeon to do almost any operation with no hand tremor and with only tiny incisions. A team of two surgeons and two nurses flew out to the manufacturer's headquarters, in Mountain View, California, for a full day of training on the machine. And they did get to practice on a pig and on a human cadaver. (The company apparently buys the cadavers from the city of San Francisco.) But even this was hardly thorough training. They learned enough to grasp the principles of using the robot, to start getting a feel for using it, and to understand how to plan an operation. That was about it. Sooner or later, you just have to go home and give the thing a try on someone.

Patients do eventually benefit — often enormously — but the first few patients may not, and may even be harmed. Consider the experience reported by the pediatric cardiac-surgery unit of the renowned Great Ormond Street Hospital in London, as detailed in the *British Medical Journal* last April. The doctors described their results from 325 consecutive operations between 1978 and 1998 on babies with a severe heart defect known as transposition of the great arteries. Such children are born with their heart's outflow vessels transposed: the aorta emerges from the right side of the heart instead of the left, and the artery to the lungs emerges from the left instead of the right. As a result, blood coming in is pumped right back out to the body instead of first to the lungs, where it can be oxygenated. The babies died blue, fatigued, never knowing what it was to get enough breath. For years, it wasn't technically feasible to switch the vessels to their proper positions. Instead, surgeons did something known as the Senning procedure: they created a passage inside the heart to let blood from the lungs cross backward to the right heart. The Senning procedure allowed children to live into adulthood. The weaker right heart, however, cannot sustain the body's entire blood flow as long as the left. Eventually, these patients' hearts failed, and although most survived to adulthood, few lived to old age.

By the 1980s, a series of technological advances made it possible to do a switch operation safely, and this became the favored procedure. In 1986, the Great Ormond Street surgeons made the changeover themselves, and their report shows that it was unquestionably an improvement. The annual death rate after a successful switch procedure was less than a quarter that of the Senning, resulting in a life expectancy of sixty-three years instead of forty-seven. But the price of learning to do it was appalling. In their first seventy switch operations, the doctors had a twenty-five percent surgical death rate, compared with just six percent with the Senning procedure. Eighteen babies died, more than twice the number during the entire Senning era. Only with time did they master it: in their next hundred switch operations, five babies died.

As patients, we want both expertise and progress; we don't want to acknowledge that these are contradictory desires. In the words of one British public report, "There should be no learning curve as far as patient safety is concerned." But this is entirely wishful thinking.

Recently, a group of Harvard Business School researchers who have made a specialty of studying learning curves in industry decided to examine learning curves among surgeons instead of in semiconductor manufacture or airplane construction, or any of the usual fields their colleagues examine. They followed eighteen cardiac surgeons and their teams as they took on the new technique of minimally invasive cardiac surgery. This study, I was surprised to discover, is the first of its kind. Learning is ubiquitous in medicine, and yet no one had ever compared how well different teams actually do it.

The new heart operation — in which new technologies allow a surgeon to operate through a small incision between ribs instead of splitting the chest open down the middle — proved substantially more difficult than the conventional one. Because the incision is too small to admit the usual tubes and clamps for rerouting blood to the heart-bypass machine, surgeons had to learn a trickier method, which involved balloons and catheters placed through groin vessels. And the nurses, anesthesiologists, and perfusionists all had new roles to master. As you'd expect, everyone experienced a substantial learning curve. Whereas a fully proficient team takes three to six hours for such an operation, these teams took on average three times as long for their early cases. The researchers could not track complication rates in detail, but it would be foolish to imagine that they were not affected.

What's more, the researchers found striking disparities in the speed with which different teams learned. All teams came from highly respected institutions with experience in adopting innovations and received the same three-day training session. Yet, in the course of fifty cases, some teams managed to halve their operating time while others improved hardly at all. Practice, it turned out, did not necessarily make perfect. The crucial variable was *how* the surgeons and their teams practiced.

Richard Bohmer, the only physician among the Harvard researchers, made several visits to observe one of the quickest-learning teams and one of the slowest, and he was startled by the contrast. The surgeon on the fast-learning team was actually quite inexperienced compared with the one on the slow-learning team. But he made sure to pick team members with whom he had worked well before and to keep them together through the first fifteen cases before allowing any new members. He had the team go through a dry run before the first case, then deliberately scheduled six operations in the first week, so little would be forgotten in between. He convened the team before each case to discuss it in detail and afterward to debrief. He made sure results were tracked carefully. And Bohmer noticed that the surgeon was not the stereo-typical Napoleon with a knife. Unbidden, he told Bohmer, "The surgeon needs to be willing to allow himself to become a partner [with the rest of the team] so he can accept input." At the other hospital, by contrast, the surgeon chose his operating team almost randomly and did not keep it together. In the first seven cases, the team had different members every time, which is to say that it was no team at all. And the surgeon had no prebriefings, no de-briefings, no tracking of ongoing results.

The Harvard Business School study offered some hopeful news. We can do things that have a dramatic effect on our rate of im-provement — like being more deliberate about how we train, and about tracking progress, whether with students and residents or with senior surgeons and nurses. But the study's other implications are less reassuring. No matter how accomplished, surgeons trying something new got worse before they got better, and the learning curve proved longer, and was affected by a far more complicated range of factors, than anyone had realized.

This, I suspect, is the reason for the physician's dodge: the "I just assist" rap; the "We have a new procedure for this that you are per-fect for" speech; the "You need a central line" without the "I am still learning how to do this." Sometimes we do feel obliged to ad-mit when we're doing something for the first time, but even then we tend to quote the published complication rates of experienced surgeons. Do we ever tell patients that, because we are still new at something, their risks will inevitably be higher, and that they'd likely do better with doctors who are more experienced? Do we ever say that we need them to agree to it anyway? I've never seen it. Given the stakes, who in his right mind would agree to be prac-ticed upon?

Many dispute this presumption. "Look, most people understand what it is to be a doctor," a health policy expert insisted when I vis-ited him in his office not long ago. "We have to stop lying to our patients. Can people take on choices for societal benefit?" He paused and then answered his question. "Yes," he said firmly.

It would certainly be a graceful and happy solution. We'd ask pa-tients — honestly, openly — and they'd say yes. Hard to imagine, though. I noticed on the expert's desk a picture of his child, born just a few months before, and a completely unfair question popped into my mind. "So did you let the resident deliver?" I asked.

There was silence for a moment. "No," he admitted. "We didn't even allow residents in the room."

One reason I doubt whether we could sustain a system of medical training that depended on people saying "Yes, you can practice on me" is that I myself have said no. When my eldest child, Walker, was eleven days old, he suddenly went into congestive heart failure from what proved to be a severe cardiac defect. His aorta was not transposed, but a long segment of it had failed to grow at all. My wife and I were beside ourselves with fear — his kidneys and liver began failing, too — but he made it to surgery, the repair was a success, and although his recovery was erratic, after two and a half weeks he was ready to come home.

We were by no means in the clear, however. He was born a healthy six pounds plus, but now, a month old, he weighed only five and would need strict monitoring to ensure that he gained weight. He was on two cardiac medications from which he would have to be weaned. And in the longer term, the doctors warned us, his repair would prove inadequate. As Walker grew, his aorta would require either dilation with a balloon or replacement by surgery. They could not say precisely when and how many such procedures would be necessary over the years. A pediatric cardiologist would have to follow him closely and decide.

Walker was about to be discharged, and we had not indicated who that cardiologist would be. In the hospital, he had been cared for by a full team of cardiologists, ranging from fellows in specialty training to attendings who had practiced for decades. The day before we took Walker home, one of the young fellows approached me, offering his card and suggesting a time to bring Walker to see him. Of those on the team, he had put in the most time caring for Walker. He saw Walker when we brought him in inexplicably short of breath, made the diagnosis, got Walker the drugs that stabilized, him, coordinated with the surgeons, and came to see us twice a day to answer our questions. Moreover, I knew, this was how fellows always got their patients. Most families don't know the subtle gradations among players, and after a team has saved their child's life they take whatever appointment they're handed.

But I knew the differences. "I'm afraid we're thinking of seeing Dr. Newburger," I said. She was the hospital's associate cardiologist in chief and a published expert on conditions like Walker's. The young physician looked crestfallen. It was nothing against him, I said. She just had more experience, that was all.

"You know, there is always an attending backing me up," he said. I shook my head.

I know this was not fair. My son had an unusual problem. The fellow needed the experience. As a resident, I of all people should have understood this. But I was not torn about the decision. This was my child. Given a choice, I will always choose the best care I can for him. How can anybody be expected to do otherwise? Certainly, the future of medicine should not rely on it.

In a sense, then, the physician's dodge is inevitable. Learning must be stolen, taken as a land of bodily eminent domain. And it was, during Walker's stay — on many occasions, now that I think back on it. A resident intubated him. A surgical trainee scrubbed in for his operation. The cardiology fellow put in one of his central lines. If I'd had the option to have someone more experienced, I would have taken it. But this was simply how the system worked — no such choices were offered — and so I went along.

The advantage of this coldhearted machinery is not merely that it gets the learning done. If learning is necessary but causes harm, then above all it ought to apply to everyone alike. Given a choice, people wriggle out, and such choices are not offered equally. They belong to the connected and the knowledgeable, to insiders over outsiders, to the doctor's child but not the truck driver's. If everyone cannot have a choice, maybe it is better if no one can.

It is 2 P.M. I am in the intensive-care unit. A nurse tells me Mr. G.'s central line has clotted off. Mr. G. has been in the hospital for more than a month now. He is in his late sixties, from South Boston, emaciated, exhausted, holding on by a thread — or a line, to be precise. He has several holes in his small bowel, and the bilious contents leak out onto his skin through two small reddened openings in the concavity of his abdomen. His only chance is to be fed by vein and wait for these fistulae to heal. He needs a new central line.

I could do it, I suppose. I am the experienced one now. But experience brings a new role: I am expected to teach the procedure instead. "See one, do one, teach one," the saying goes, and it is only half in jest.

There is a junior resident on the service. She has done only one or two lines before. I tell her about Mr. G. I ask her if she is free to do a new line. She misinterprets this as a question. She says she still has patients to see and a case coming up later. Could I do the line? I tell her no. She is unable to hide a grimace. She is burdened, as I was burdened, and perhaps frightened, as I was frightened.

She begins to focus when I make her talk through the steps — a kind of dry run, I figure. She hits nearly all the steps, but forgets about checking the labs and about Mr. G.'s nasty allergy to heparin, which is in the flush for the line. I make sure she registers this, then tell her to get set up and page me.

I am still adjusting to this role. It is painful enough taking responsibility for one's own failures. Being handmaiden to another's is something else entirely. It occurs to me that I could have broken open a kit and had her do an actual dry run. Then again, maybe I can't. The kits must cost a couple of hundred dollars each. I'll have to find out for next time.

Half an hour later, I get the page. The patient is draped. The resident is in her gown and gloves. She tells me that she has saline to flush the line with and that his labs are fine.

"Have you got the towel roll?" I ask.

She forgot the towel roll. I roll up a towel and slip it beneath Mr. G.'s back. I ask him if he's all right. He nods. After all he's been through, there is only resignation in his eyes.

The junior resident picks out a spot for the stick. The patient is hauntingly thin. I see every rib and fear that the resident will puncture his lung. She injects the numbing medication. Then she puts the big needle in, and the angle looks all wrong. I motion for her to reposition. This only makes her more uncertain. She pushes in deeper and I know she does not have it. She draws back on the syringe: no blood. She takes out the needle and tries again. And again the angle looks wrong. This time, Mr. G. feels the jab and jerks up in pain. I hold his arm. She gives him more numbing medication. It is all I can do not to take over. But she cannot learn without doing, I tell myself. I decide to let her have one more try.

ADAM GOPNIK

Bumping Into Mr. Ravioli

FROM THE NEW YORKER

MY DAUGHTER, Olivia, who just turned three, has an imaginary friend whose name is Charlie Ravioli. Olivia is growing up in Manhattan, and so Charlie Ravioli has a lot of local traits: he lives in an apartment "on Madison and Lexington," he dines on grilled chicken, fruit, and water, and, having reached the age of seven and a half, he feels, or is thought, "old." But the most peculiarly local thing about Olivia's imaginary playmate is this: he is always too busy to play with her. She holds her toy cell phone up to her ear, and we hear her talk into it: "Ravioli? It's Olivia . . . It's Olivia. Come and play? OK. Call me. Bye." Then she snaps it shut and shakes her head. "I always get his machine," she says. Or she will say, "I spoke to Ravioli today." "Did you have fun?" my wife and I ask. "No. He was busy working. On a television" (leaving it up in the air if he repairs electronic devices or has his own talk show).

On a good day, she "bumps into" her invisible friend and they go to a coffee shop. "I bumped into Charlie Ravioli," she announces at dinner (after a day when, of course, she stayed home, played, had a nap, had lunch, paid a visit to the Central Park Zoo, and then had another nap). "We had coffee, but then he had to run." She sighs, sometimes, at her inability to make their schedules mesh, but she accepts it as inevitable, just the way life is. "I bumped into Charlie Ravioli today," she says. "He was working." Then she adds brightly, "But we hopped into a taxi." What happened then? we ask. "We grabbed lunch," she says.

It seemed obvious that Ravioli was a romantic figure of the big exotic life that went on outside her little limited life of parks and

playgrounds — drawn, in particular, from a nearly perfect, mynah
bird–like imitation of the words she hears her mother use when
she talks about *her* day with *her* friends. ("How was your day?"
Sighing: "Oh, you know. I tried to make a date with Meg, but I
couldn't find her, so I left a message on her machine. Then I
bumped into Emily after that meeting I had in SoHo, and we had
coffee and then she had to run, but by then Meg had reached me
on my cell and we arranged . . .") I was concerned, though, that
Charlie Ravioli might also be the sign of some "trauma," some
loneliness in Olivia's life reflected in imaginary form. "It seems
odd to have an imaginary playmate who's always too busy to play
with you," Martha, my wife, said to me. "Shouldn't your imaginary
playmate be someone you tell secrets to and, I don't know, sing
songs with? It shouldn't be someone who's always *hopping* into
taxis."

We thought, at first, that her older brother, Luke, might be the
original of Charlie Ravioli. (For one thing, he is also seven and a
half, though we were fairly sure that this age was merely Olivia's
marker for As Old as Man Can Be.) He *is* too busy to play with her
much anymore. He has become a true New York child, with the
schedule of a cabinet secretary: chess club on Monday, T-ball on
Tuesday, tournament on Saturday, play dates and after-school conferences to fill in the gaps. But Olivia, though she counts days,
does not yet really *have* days. She has *a* day, and into this day she
has introduced the figure of Charlie Ravioli — in order, it dawned
on us, to insist that she does have days, because she is too harried
to share them, that she does have an independent social life, by virtue of being too busy to have one.

Yet Charlie Ravioli was becoming so constant and oddly discour-
aging a companion — "He canceled lunch. Again," Olivia would
say — that we thought we ought to look into it. One of my sisters is
a developmental psychologist who specializes in close scientific
studies of what goes on inside the heads of one- and two- and
three-year-olds. Though she grew up in the nervy East, she lives in
California now, where she grows basil in her garden and jars her
own organic marmalades. I e-mailed this sister for help with the
Ravioli issue — how concerned should we be? — and she sent me
back an e-mail, along with an attachment, and, after several failed
cell-phone connections, we at last spoke on a land line.

It turned out that there is a recent book on this very subject by the psychologist Marjorie Taylor, called *Imaginary Companions and the Children Who Create Them,* and my sister had just written a review of it. She insisted that Charlie Ravioli was nothing to be worried about. Olivia was right on target, in fact. Most under-sevens (sixty-three percent, to be scientific) have an invisible friend, and children create their imaginary playmates not out of trauma but out of a serene sense of the possibilities of fiction — sometimes as figures of pure fantasy, sometimes, as Olivia had done, as observations of grownup manners assembled in tranquillity and given a name. I learned about the invisible companions Taylor studied: Baintor, who is invisible because he lives in the light; Station Pheta, who hunts sea anemones on the beach. Charlie Ravioli seemed pavement-bound by comparison.

"An imaginary playmate isn't any kind of trauma marker," my sister said. "It's just the opposite: it's a sign that the child is now confident enough to begin to understand how to organize her experience into stories." The significant thing about imaginary friends, she went on, is that the kids know they're fictional. In an instant message on AOL, she summed it up: "The children with invisible friends often interrupted the interviewer to remind her, with a certain note of concern for her sanity, that these characters were, after all, just pretend."

I also learned that some children, as they get older, turn out to possess what child psychologists call a "paracosm." A paracosm is a society thought up by a child — an invented universe with a distinctive language, geography, and history. (The Brontës invented a couple of paracosms when they were children.) Not all children who have an imaginary friend invent a paracosm, but the two might, I think, be related. Like a lonely ambassador from Alpha Centauri in a fifties sci-fi movie who, misunderstood by paranoid Earth scientists, cannot bring the life-saving news from his planet, perhaps the invisible friend also gets an indifferent or hostile response, and then we never find out about the beautiful paracosm he comes from.

"Don't worry about it," my sister said in a late-night phone call. "Knowing something's made up while thinking that it matters is what all fiction insists on. She's putting a name on a series of manners."

"But he seems so real to her," I objected.

"Of course he is. I mean, who's more real to you, Becky Sharp or Gandalf or the guy down the hall? Giving a manner a name makes it real."

I paused. "I grasp that it's normal for her to have an imaginary friend," I said, "but have you ever heard of an imaginary friend who's too busy to play with you?"

She thought about it. "No," she said. "I'm sure that doesn't occur anywhere in the research literature. That sounds *completely* New York." And then she hung up.

The real question, I saw, was not "Why this friend?" but "Why this fiction?" Why, as Olivia had seen so clearly, are grownups in New York so busy, and so obsessed with the language of busyness that it dominates their conversation? Why are New Yorkers always bumping into Charlie Ravioli and grabbing lunch, instead of sitting down with him and exchanging intimacies, as friends should, as people do in Paris and Rome? Why is busyness the stuff our children make their invisible friends from, as country children make theirs from light and sand?

This seems like an odd question. New Yorkers are busy for obvious reasons: they have husbands and wives and careers and children, they have the Gauguin show to see and their personal trainers and accountants to visit. But the more I think about this, the more I think it is — well, a lot of Ravioli. We are instructed to believe that we are busier because we have to work harder to be more productive, but everybody knows that busyness and productivity have a dubious, arm's-length relationship. Most of our struggle in New York, in fact, is to be less busy in order to do more work.

Constant, exhausting, no-time-to meet-your-friends Charlie Ravioli–style busyness arrived as an affliction in modern life long after the other parts of bourgeois city manners did. Business long predates busyness. In the seventeenth and eighteenth centuries, when bourgeois people were building the institutions of bourgeois life, they seem never to have complained that they were too busy — or, if they did, they left no record of it. Samuel Pepys, who had a navy to refloat and a burned London to rebuild, often uses the word "busy" but never complains of busyness. For him, the word "busy" is a synonym for "happy," not for "stressed." Not once in his diary does Pepys cancel lunch or struggle to fit someone in for coffee at four-thirty. Pepys works, makes love, and goes to bed, but he does not bump and he does not have to run. Ben Franklin, a half century later, boasts of his industriousness, but he, too, never complains about being busy, and always has time to publish a newspaper or come up with a maxim or swim the ocean or invent the lightning rod.

Until sometime in the middle of the nineteenth century, in fact, the normal affliction of the bourgeois was not busyness at all but its apparent opposite: boredom. It has even been argued that the grid of streets and cafés and small engagements in the nineteenth-century city — the whole of social life — was designed self-consciously as an escape from that numbing boredom. (Working people weren't bored, of course, but they were engaged in labor, not work. They were too busy to be busy.) Baudelaire, basically, was so bored that he had to get drunk and run out onto the boulevard in the hope of bumping into somebody.

Turn to the last third of the nineteenth century and the beginning of the twentieth, though, and suddenly everybody is busy, and everybody is complaining about it. Pepys, master of His Majesty's Navy, may never have complained of busyness, but Virginia Woolf, mistress of motionless lull, is continually complaining about how she spends her days racing across London from square to square, just like — well, like Charlie Ravioli. Ronald Firbank is wrung out by his social obligations; Proust is constantly rescheduling rendezvous and apologizing for being overstretched. Henry James, with nothing particular to do save live, complains of being too busy all the time. He could not shake the world of obligation, he said, and he wrote a strange and beautiful story, "The Great Good Place," which begins with an exhausting flood of correspondence, telegrams, and manuscripts that drive the protagonist nearly mad.

What changed? That James story helps supply the key. It was trains and telegrams. The railroads ended isolation, and packed the metropolis with people whose work was defined by a complicated network of social obligations. Pepys's network in 1669 London was, despite his official position, relatively small compared even with that of a minor aesthete like Firbank, two centuries later. Pepys had more time to make love because he had fewer friends to answer.

If the train crowded our streets, the telegram crowded our minds. It introduced something into the world which remains with us today: a whole new class of communications that are defined as incomplete in advance of their delivery. A letter, though it may enjoin a response, is meant to be complete in itself. Neither the Apostle Paul nor Horace Walpole ever ends an epistle with "Give me a call and let's discuss." By contrast, it is in the nature of the telegram to be a skeletal version of another thing — a communication that opens more than it closes. The nineteenth-century telegram came with those busy threatening words "Letter follows."

Every device that has evolved from the telegram shares the same character. E-mails end with a suggestion for a phone call ("Anyway, let's meet and/or talk soon"), faxes with a request for an e-mail, answering-machine messages with a request for a fax. All are devices of perpetually suspended communication. My wife recalls a moment last fall when she got a telephone message from a friend asking her to check her e-mail apropos a phone call she needed to make vis-à-vis a fax they had both received asking for more information about a bed they were thinking of buying from Ireland online and having sent to America by Federal Express — a grand slam of incomplete communication.

In most of the Western world outside New York, the press of trains and of telegraphic communication was alleviated by those other two great transformers: the car and the television. While the train and the telegram (and their love children, subways and commuter trains and e-mail) pushed people together, the car and the television pulled people apart — taking them out to the suburbs and sitting them down in front of a solo spectacle. New York, though, almost uniquely, got hit by a double dose of the first two technologies, and a very limited dose of the second two. Car life — car obsessions, car-defined habits — is more absent here than almost anywhere else in the country, while television, though obviously present, is less fatally prevalent here. New York is still a subject of television, and we compare *Sex and the City* to sex and the city; they are not yet quite the same. Here two grids of busyness remain dominant: the nineteenth- and early-twentieth-century grid of bump and run, and the late-twentieth- and early-twenty-first-century postmodern grid of virtual call and echo. Busyness is felt so intently here because we are both crowded and overloaded. We exit the apartment into a still dense nineteenth-century grid of street corners and restaurants full of people, and come home to the late-twentieth-century grid of faxes and e-mails and overwhelming incompleteness.

We walk across the Park on a Sunday morning and bump into our friend the baker and our old acquaintance from graduate school (what the hell is she doing now?) and someone we have been avoiding for three weeks. They all invite us for brunch, and we would love to, but we are too . . . busy. We bump into Charlie Ravioli, and grab a coffee with him — and come home to find three e-mails and a message on our cell phone from him, wondering where we are. The crowding of our space has been reinforced by a crowding of our time, and the only way to protect ourselves is to build structures of perpetual deferral: I'll see you next week, let's talk soon. We build rhetorical baffles around our lives to keep the crowding out, only to find that we have let nobody we love in.

Like Charlie Ravioli, we hop into taxis and leave messages on answering machines to avoid our acquaintances, and find that we keep missing our friends. I have one intimate who lives just across the Park from me, whom I e-mail often, and whom I am fortunate to see two or three times a year. We are always . . . busy. He has become my Charlie Ravioli, my invisible friend. I am sure that he misses me — just as Charlie Ravioli, I realized, must tell his other friends that he is sorry he does not see Olivia more often.

Once I sensed the nature of his predicament, I began to feel more sympathetic toward Charlie Ravioli. I got to know him better, too. We learned more about what Ravioli did in the brief breathing spaces in his busy life when he could sit down with Olivia and dish. "Ravioli read your book," Olivia announced, for instance, one night at dinner. "He didn't like it much." We also found out that Ravioli had joined a gym, that he was going to the beach in the summer, but he was too busy, and that he was working on a "show." ("It isn't a very good show," she added candidly.) Charlie Ravioli, in other words, was just another New Yorker: fit, opinionated, and trying to break into show business.

I think we would have learned to live happily with Charlie Ravioli had it not been for the appearance of Laurie. She threw us badly. At dinner, Olivia had been mentioning a new personage almost as often as she mentioned Ravioli. "I talked to Laurie today," she would begin. "She says Ravioli is busy." Or she would be closeted with her play phone. "Who are you talking to, darling?" I would ask. "Laurie," she would say. "We're talking about Ravioli." We surmised that Laurie was, so to speak, the Linda Tripp of the Ravioli operation — the person you spoke to for consolation when the big creep was ignoring you.

But a little while later a more ominous side of Laurie's role began to appear. "Laurie, tell Ravioli I'm calling," I heard Olivia say. I pressed her about who, exactly, Laurie was. Olivia shook her head. "She works for Ravioli," she said.

And then it came to us, with sickening clarity: Laurie was not the patient friend who consoled you for Charlie's absence. Laurie was the bright-toned person who answered Ravioli's phone and told you that unfortunately Mr. Ravioli was in a meeting. "Laurie says Ravioli is too busy to play," Olivia announced sadly one morning. Things seemed to be deteriorating; now Ravioli was too busy even to say he was too busy.

I got back on the phone with my sister. "Have you ever heard of an imaginary friend with an assistant?" I asked.

She paused. "Imaginary friends don't have assistants," she said. "That's not only not in the literature. That's just . . . I mean — in California they don't have assistants."

"You think we should look into it?"

"I think you should move," she said flatly.

Martha was of the same mind. "An imaginary playmate shouldn't have an assistant," she said miserably. "An imaginary playmate shouldn't have an agent. An imaginary playmate shouldn't have a publicist or a personal trainer or a caterer — an imaginary playmate shouldn't have . . . *people*. An imaginary playmate should just *play*. With the child who imagined it." She started leaving on my pillow real-estate brochures picturing quaint houses in New Jersey and Connecticut, unhaunted by busy invisible friends and their entourages.

Not long after the appearance of Laurie, though, something remarkable happened. Olivia would begin to tell us tales of her frustrations with Charlie Ravioli, and, after telling us, again, that he was too busy to play, she would tell us what she had done instead.

Astounding and paracosmic tall tales poured out of her: she had been to a chess tournament and brought home a trophy; she had gone to a circus and told jokes. Searching for Charlie Ravioli, she had "saved all the animals in the zoo"; heading home in a taxi after a quick coffee with Ravioli, she took over the steering wheel and "got all the moneys." From the stalemate of daily life emerged the fantasy of victory. She had dreamed of a normal life with a few close friends, and had to settle for worldwide fame and the front page of the tabloids. The existence of an imaginary friend had liberated her into a paracosm, but it was a curiously New York paracosm — it was the unobtainable world outside her window. Charlie Ravioli, prince of busyness, was not an end but a means: a way out onto the street in her head, a declaration of potential independence.

Busyness is our art form, our civic ritual, our way of being us. Many friends have said to me that they love New York now in a way they never did before, and their love, I've noticed, takes for its object all the things that used to exasperate them — the curious combination of freedom, self-made fences, and paralyzing preoccupation that the city provides. "How did you spend the day?" Martha and I now ask each other, and then, instead of listing her incidents, she says merely, "Oh, you know . . . just . . . bumping into Charlie Ravioli," meaning, just bouncing from obligation to electronic entreaty, just spotting a friend and snatching a sandwich, just being busy, just living in New York. If everything we've learned in the past year could be summed up in a phrase, it's that we want to go on bumping into Charlie Ravioli for as long as we can.

Olivia still hopes to have him to herself someday. As I work late at night in the "study" (an old hallway, an Aalto screen) I keep near the "nursery" (an ancient pantry, a glass-brick wall), I can hear her shift into pre-sleep, still muttering to herself. She is still trying to reach her closest friend. "Ravioli? Ravioli?" she moans as she turns over into her pillow and clutches her blanket, and then she whispers, almost to herself, "Tell him call me. Tell him call me when he comes home."

The Debacle

FROM THE AMERICAN SCHOLAR

As MY MOTHER and I left Paris on the gloriously sunny morning of June 10, 1940, four days before the Germans took the city, we became part of a panic-stricken caravan whose surreal mayhem still haunts me. The road to Tours, the destination of most Parisians (and also of the French government, which decamped for Tours that very day), was clogged with every possible invention that could move on wheels. Amid a cacophonous din of bleating horns, fire trucks, ambulances, ice cream vendors' vehicles, funeral carriages, municipal street-sweeping trucks, tourist buses racily labeled "Paris La Nuit," even wheelbarrows and prams mingled with the chic limousines, sports cars, and family sedans that were all heading south toward the Loire, where, so deluded gossip had it, French troops might still "reconstitute a front." Barely moving at the pace of a human stride — it was taking three days to travel a distance usually covered in three hours — these vehicles, crammed with children, women of all ages, old men, and boys under the age of eighteen, were surmounted by an astounding variety of hastily assembled personal possessions. Tied onto their roofs amid mounds of sheets, blankets, and mattresses, there were birdcages, bicycles, cradles, sewing machines, saucepans and other cooking utensils, collapsible tents, cuckoo clocks. Swarming amid the vehicles, at times totally stopping their advance, large bands of haggard, desperate-eyed soldiers in search of their retreating units stumbled alongside hordes of pedestrian refugees who carried their possessions on their backs: a portion of the millions of citizens who had taken to the roads, in the past four weeks, in the wake of one of the most catastrophic defeats in military history.

Beginning its onslaught on May 10, in a mere two days the German army had pierced the rugged Ardennes region and crossed the Meuse River, terrains that France's tragically incompetent High Command had thought impregnable to the German panzer divisions. In the ensuing fortnight they had swept through Holland and Belgium, forcing the capitulation of both countries, and bolted across France's Département du Nord, necessitating the heroic evacuation, at Dunkirk, of more than 330,000 Allied troops. At the end of May, German forces had obliged the French army to reconstitute its front at the Somme River, a two-hour drive north of Paris. And on June 6, they had broken through that last defense line, causing such panic among French troops that generals, their originally scheduled maneuvers made impossible by the tide of civilians clogging the country's roads, ceased to accept commands from the general staff, and hundreds of thousands of soldiers of all ranks abandoned their regiments to seek refuge in their homes throughout France. Now, on June 10, the day my mother and I left Paris, German forces were speedily approaching the capital, having overwhelmed what had only recently been considered continental Europe's most powerful army.

No wonder that the word used ever since for this tragic sequence of events and Marshal Pétain's ensuing armistice — *débâcle* — does not mean merely "defeat." Its overtones of shame, of communal failure, of widespread social disintegration, were recorded in the faces of the civilians and soldiers who crowded the tragic caravan my mother and I had joined. This torrent of humanity registered no ill will and little rage, simply a shared despair and a benumbed stupor. Few members of that exodus knew where their relatives were. It was as if a monstrous explosion had blown hundreds of thousands of families into fragments, scattering them all over the landscape, causing the ones left behind to phone every possible hostelry in the country and place ads in papers ("Jules Monnet, your loving parents are in Auxerre").

As our tiny Peugeot wheezed and spluttered southward in the bumper-to-bumper traffic, we knew that throughout France hundreds of thousands of our compatriots were searching for loved ones, and wondering about their survival, with an anxiety equal to ours.

I imagine that most of us can cite a particular historical event — Pearl Harbor, D-day, the assassination of John Kennedy, 9/11 — that we look on as a defining moment, the specific encounter of self and world that became the cradle of our historical consciousness. That event, for me, was the fall of France. I was nine years old in June 1940, but this milestone drew a curtain on my innocence; made me unable, from that time on, to have any sense of identity not linked to some precise historical context; stamped me with a dual sense of uprootedness and engagement.

Throughout that summer of 1940, there were numerous personal factors that intensified my sense of deracination. Upon leaving Paris, I had been separated from the two women who had been my principal mentors since my infancy: my governess and my beloved Russian great-aunt, both of whom had chosen to stay behind. I worried despairingly about the idol of my childhood, my father, an officer in the air force who was somewhere in France, looking for his disintegrated squadron and grieving over his American mistress's enforced return to the United States. I sensed that the elegant blond beauty sitting at the wheel of our little Peugeot, my mother, was desperate for news of her own lover, who had left Paris for the South a few days earlier — as a Russian Jew with a Nansen passport, he was particularly vulnerable to persecution. Moreover, my mother had only recently learned to drive and was totally confounded by the clutch. As we sputtered toward Tours at the rate of five kilometers an hour, the engine constantly stalling, I was aware that, notwithstanding the kisses she kept blowing me to boost my spirits, she was very worried about whether we'd make it to Tours ahead of the Nazis. So, to cheer her up, I kept humming a ditty that had been the rage since the war's outbreak, and that has summed up to me, ever since, the delusions the entire nation had been steeped in. It went: "Nous allons pendre notre linge sur la ligne Siegfried . . . Si la ligne Siegfried est encore là" (We're going to hang our linen on the Siegfried line . . . If the Siegfried line is still there).

Most of those whose lives have been transformed by a historical crisis are impelled to return, at some point, to the site where the crisis occurred. The doughty octogenarians who flocked to Normandy Beach on the fiftieth anniversary of D-day, the millions of Americans who have visited Pearl Harbor, the millions who will visit Ground Zero, testify to our perennial need to attune memory to the concrete reality of place. But in the case of the fall of France, which manifested itself in dispersion and dislocation, a return to those sites in which the tragedy was experienced may not be enough. Unlike the Normandy Beach landing or 9/11, the debacle of 1940 was a process rather than an event, a phenomenon whose nature was as psychological as it was physical. Rather than a visit to a material site, it calls for a patient, diligent examination of the historical givens that led to the tragedy. This is what I've recently attempted to engage in as I reflected on the role played by my parents' and grandparents' generations — France's intellectual and military elite — in the most agonizing defeat of their nation's history.

The first step in such a process of reflection, I soon realized, is to recognize how deeply the tragedies of World War I influenced France's attitude toward the events of 1939. Beyond its reckless wasting of a million and a half French lives — a sizable portion of the nation's young male population — World War I was a conflict that France won by a very small margin, through one freakish reversal of fortunes that occurred at the Marne in 1918. Yet it created a massive network of delusions about France's role in the world, as well as a determination to avoid another war at all costs, to preserve "peace at any price." Few writers of the *entre deux guerres* period expressed these convictions better than the novelist and essayist Maurice Sachs in his memoir of the 1920s and 1930s, *Le Sabbath:*

> The War of 1914 was a crisis deeper than any of those that France had lived through since 1789. Neither 18 Brumaire, nor the Empire, nor Waterloo, nor the return of the royalty . . . nor the Second Republic, nor the Second Empire, nor Sedan, nor the Commune, nor the birth of the Third Republic shook France as profoundly, to the depths of its entrails, as the war of 1914 and the peace that followed . . . The peace of 1919 announced an eternal peace . . . The French, charmed by delicious illusions, were the first to think that this peace (which . . . differed from others only by the demented hopes it created) once more marked the Fatherland for a unique destiny: . . . All excesses, all licenses, all fol-

lies became authorized, crowned as they were by the charming attributes of victory.

As crucial to any discussion of the 1940 debacle as these delusions of "eternal peace" is the hardware-versus-software debate: How much blame should be placed on the inferiority of France's material weapons? Or should one principally fault the nation's psychological and cerebral equipment — the attitudes and tactical intellect of its general staff? Of the many historical works that have focused on the fall of France, the most memorable is *Strange Defeat* by Marc Bloch, the leading historian of his generation, who wrote it in a blaze of anger in the summer of 1940, immediately after being demobilized after the fall of France. He later became a legendary Resistance leader and was captured, tortured, and shot by the Nazis in 1944, shortly after the Allies landed in Normandy.

It has become a truism to say that the French were defeated because they continued to wage the same "war of the trenches" they had waged in World War I. Exploring that very issue, Bloch, a decorated veteran of the 1914 conflict who served as a captain in army intelligence in World War II, proves how deeply intertwined the issues of software and hardware can be. He asserts that the archaic tactics of the nation's military leaders — General Maurice Gamelin's response to the German onslaught proved so patently inept that he was replaced within a fortnight by seventy-three-year-old General Maxime Weygand — were caused by the fact that they were still "soaked . . . to the very marrow of their bones" with memories of their 1918 victory.

Like Marshal Philippe Pétain, who would become head of state the following month, Gamelin and Weygand were, in Bloch's view, "ancient fossils . . . trailing clouds of former glory" who suffered from such "moral and intellectual sclerosis" that they could not begin to grasp the new metaphysics of time and distance implicit in the German blitzkrieg. The term means "lightning war," and it denoted a revolutionary blend of three assault forces: 1) a spearhead of panzer divisions, powerful tanks supported by large contingents of motorized infantry and motorcycle troops that buzzed like wasps about the armored columns; 2) the well-protected infantry divisions, which followed a few miles behind; and 3) the Luftwaffe, which softened up the enemy shortly before the panzer charge with several kinds of planes, including the Stuka dive-bomber, whose horrendous whistling sound, according to Bloch, contributed greatly to the demoralization of French forces, and the Me 109 fighter, one of the fastest airborne vehicles in existence.

Bloch was the first of many historians who have pointed out the deficiency of French weaponry — both the intellectual and material kinds — in confronting these highly sophisticated German tactics. In contrast to the streamlined Luftwaffe, France's air power was notably weak. Its intelligence services were rendered pathetically inefficient by bureaucratic bumbling and overcentralization. The members of its High Command were notorious Anglophobes, ill suited to collaborate efficiently with their allies. French tanks were as powerful as German tanks, but they were less mobile and far less strategically positioned. The High Command, heedless of the warnings of a few *frondeur* officers — including an obscure colonel named Charles de Gaulle, who as early as 1933 had published an article predicting that the next war would be based on tank power — had completely discounted their effectiveness as attack weapons. (De Gaulle's work, in contrast, was read by many German military leaders.)

Instead of focusing on tank warfare, the French High Command had put most of its energy and faith into the obsolete concrete of the Maginot Line, a fortification made all the more irrelevant by the fact that it did not extend beyond the Belgian frontier, which is precisely where the Germans launched their flanking attack. Bloch points out that the French generals' most mind-boggling mistake was to overlook the lessons learned in the Polish campaign of September 1939, when the Germans' tank-based onslaught had swept through the country in a mere fortnight. Gamelin argued that the panzer divisions' conquest of the Polish plains would be unthinkable in the hilly, densely forested Ardennes, which, he alleged, tanks could not cross. He was proved disastrously wrong when those hills offered the panzer divisions all the more protection.

As Bloch put it, "It is as if the two opposing forces belonged . . . to entirely different epochs of human history." The French High Command was a group of men who "in a century of chemists had retained the outlook of alchemists." France was waging "a war of old men . . . bogged down by errors engendered by the faulty teaching of history. It was saturated by the smell of decay rising from the Staff College . . . the offices of the General Staff, and the barrack-square." Bloch's comments on the decay of the barrack square, alas, constitute the saddest segment of his remarkable book, for they highlight the roles that various ideological segments of the French citizenry played in the debacle of 1940. The right wing's hysterical dread of Bolshevism had led it to look on Germany as the last bastion of defense against the Soviet Union. The strong pacifist streak that developed in France's left wing directly after World War I — Socialist deputy Pierre Laval would be an outstanding example — led many citizens to believe that wars are waged for the interest of the rich and powerful, and that France would save itself a great deal of suffering by opening its gates to the enemy — an argument that, as Bloch puts it, "worked unconsciously to produce a nation of cowards."

Throughout the 1930s, a pervasive disenchantment with the French political system led others to the dubious consolation that beneath the ruins of France a shameful regime would be crushed to death; that defeat would be, as one observer put it, "a punishment meted out by Destiny to a guilty nation." (Simone Weil believed this for years.) Bloch's bitter conclusions about the moral and intellectual bankruptcy of the French military elite have never, to my knowledge, been challenged. As Tony Judt, a distinguished historian of twentieth-century France, has recently written: "All subsequent commentators on 1940, including Ernest May, the most recent historian of the battle . . . describe their own efforts as a mere footnote or amendment to [Bloch's] penetrating analysis . . . a rotting, divided polity collapsed unprotesting when its incompetent military caste caved in before a magnificent war machine."

The Nazis caught up with us in mid-June, a few days after my mother and I had arrived in the Touraine at the end of a harrowing three-day trip. We had slept in the car, living on the reserves of bread, water, and hard-boiled eggs we had brought from Paris, supplemented by occasional scraps of fruit we scrounged in local cafés. The Touraine was where my father had bidden us to go if Paris fell; he had been an early convert to de Gaulle's theories of tank warfare, and his acerbic disenchantment with the French High Command had led him to predict the debacle since the beginning of the war. My mother, who, notwithstanding their marital difficulties, greatly trusted my father's wisdom, had abided by his wishes. We had sought refuge at Villandry, a Renaissance château graced with one of France's loveliest gardens. It belonged to a friend of my mother's, Isabelle Carvallo de la Bouillerie, a woman of considerable mettle and generosity who had recently turned her residence into a guest house for acquaintances seeking shelter in the region.

Our room at Villandry was at the end of one of the two main wings of the U-shaped château, and looked out, on the left, to its celebrated boxwood gardens. Straight ahead we could see the little country road that linked the village of Villandry to Tours. Soon after our arrival from Paris, on June 18 — it was a very sunny morning; I remember that entire tragic month as being drenched in sunlight — we woke before seven to the sound of powerful young voices singing. My mother leapt out of bed, exclaiming, "Les Boches sont arrivés!" She grabbed my hand as she ran to the window, and we looked down upon a German regiment's first parade on their newly conquered terrain: goose-stepping smartly, four abreast, a few hundred yards from our window, fresh-faced, very young, their heads held high toward us, their helmets and bayonets blazing in the sun. If my memory serves me right, their marching song that day was "Lili Marlene":

> Vor der Kaserne, vor dem grossen Tor
> stand eine Laterne, und steht sie noch davor . . .

As children, I suspect, we are all born collaborationists; we do everything in our power to enchant and charm the enemy, to save our skins, to survive. I thrilled to the radiance of the young Germans' stern faces with an enjoyment I knew to be infamous. I wanted to kill them, yet I felt a child's admiration for anything sleek, streamlined, powerful. My crass little soul delighted in the pomp of uniforms, in all appurtenances of rank and might. I thought back with pity and rage to the haggard, desperate French soldiers we had seen on the road out of Paris. I stared hard at the Nazis, trying to summon up hatred, feeling disloyal to my father (who might at any moment, wherever he was, be killed by one of them) for admiring their beauty, their futurity. I know my mother felt no such ambivalence. She stood defiantly at the window, her hands on her hips, as if confronting someone in a brawl, and quietly whispered, loathing in her voice, "Quelle merde."

Throughout that week we had kept up with events on the château's wireless, some twenty of us gathering nightly in the living room to hear the calamitous news. On June 16, Premier Paul Reynaud had resigned after his cabinet voted down Churchill's extraordinary offer to fuse the British and French nations into a single temporary union. Marshal Pétain was named head of state in his stead. And on June 17 — this time we were bidden to gather in the living room earlier than usual, at noon — we heard the eighty-four-year-old leader announce the end of the war in his quivering, curiously high-pitched voice: "I make to France the gift of my person to allay its misery . . . It is with a heavy heart that I tell you today to cease all combat."

As for reports of de Gaulle's appeal of June 18, which was broadcast by the BBC and heard by only a very small minority of citizens, these reached us in the following days. I remember our hostess, Madame de la Bouillerie, rushing into our room to give us the news. General Charles de Gaulle, she announced, was calling on all French to join him in London and to continue the struggle against Germany! Upon hearing this — I suspect it was around June 19 or 20 — my mother grew very quiet. She waited until we were alone, took my hand, and whispered excitedly, "I suspect that your father will at any moment join him, join de Gaulle!" She was absolutely right.

Shortly thereafter, perhaps a fortnight into the Occupation, my mother and I had our first face-to-face encounter with the Nazi regime. We had driven in our little Peugeot to Tours to renew my mother's driving permit. A few blocks from the Préfecture, where the Germans had established their Kommandantur, our tiny car collided with a huge Mercedes three times the size and weight of our vehicle, filled with German officers. Glass from the windshield shattered on our foreheads, hitting particularly hard on the passenger side, and my memories of the next few minutes are drenched in blood. Although my mother's terrible driving may have been to blame, she bounded out of the car, seething with rage, and in her limited German accused the officers of causing the accident. The officers may have been taken aback by her vehemence — these were the days when docility was counseled upon any encounter with the occupying forces — but she was gorgeous and distinguished-looking enough to keep them temporarily at bay, and they limited themselves to asking for our identity papers. She whipped them out, along with her visiting card. Seeing the title "Vicomtesse" engraved on the card, the officers, apparently sensitive to issues of social hierarchy, offered to take us to the hospital. "Not at all," my mother demanded. "I want to see the Kommandant." Startled but bowing, they acceded. Our Peugeot was still drivable, and we followed the Germans' Mercedes, amid a blaze of Klaxons, to the Kommandantur.

My mother was a shrewd and cunning woman. And I suspect that for the past few weeks, ever since the armistice had divided France into an Occupied Zone and a so-called Free Zone, she had been wondering how to obtain an Ausweis, a permit, to get us to the Free Zone. What luck! she had immediately thought when the accident occurred. She could finally meet the Kommandant of Tours! I was a brave child who had survived some serious illnesses, and as our car reached our destination, she lovingly commended me for my calm as she wiped blood from my face and combed my hair for our important visit.

We were ushered into the main office, where a French Préfet had reigned until a few weeks before. The Kommandant was a tall, courtly, scholarly-looking man in his late thirties, with horn-rimmed glasses and a handsome mustache. The Kommandant perused our identity papers and then asked, in accent-free French, "Is your husband by any chance descended from the Cardinal de Richelieu?"

"Anyone in his right mind," my mother answered snappily, "would rather be descended from La Dame aux Camélias." (Cardinal de Richelieu's full name was Armand-Jean du Plessis, Duc de Richelieu. The courtesan who is the heroine of Dumas's novel, on which Verdi's opera *La Traviata* is based, is called Camille Duplessis.)

The Kommandant gave a broad, enchanted smile, and called his orderlies to come dress my wounds. As I was being tended to, he held a lively discussion with my mother concerning the relative merits of Dumas *père* and Dumas *fils*. We learned that Kommandant Hebert had been a professor of French literature at the University of Heidelberg. A box of chocolates was offered us, a car was called for to take us home to Villandry. "Schön kleine Kontessen," he whispered as he kissed my hand in parting. I'll never forget the graze of his mustache on my wrist, the very great kindness — an almost pleading kindness — of his eyes, my deepening confusion about whether it was permissible to like a highly placed member of the armed forces that were my father's enemy.

Kommandant Hebert's kindness was revealed to us once more in an episode that I did not witness, but that I heard my mother relate many times in later years. In July, barely ten days after our first meeting with the Kommandant, my mother had been called down to the Ministry of War at Vichy, where she was given the news of my father's death. Just as she had predicted, he had set out to join de Gaulle the very day after the general's radio appeal (the loving letter he wrote us telling us of his decision would not reach us for some months). He had flown to Casablanca and organized the first squadron of the Free French air force. He was shot down over the Mediterranean on his very first mission, and became one of the first five Frenchmen to be decorated with de Gaulle's highest honor, the Croix de la Libération. (Over the following years, some 850 men would be so honored, many of them, like my father, posthumously.) I was not told of my father's death until a year later.

A fortnight or so after my mother received the news, she received a message from Kommandant Hebert asking her to visit him in his office, alone. The way she related it years later, he sat her down courteously in an armchair and said words to this effect: "I hear from our intelligence reports that your husband was shot down over the Mediterranean. There may be problems. You and your child might be safer in the Free Zone." And he offered her an Ausweis, the very document she had been gathering the courage to ask him for. They parted on the best of terms.

A week later we were back in our little Peugeot, sputtering and stalling every few minutes — my mother never did learn to work a clutch properly — toward the Free Zone and the South of France. My mother's lover — my stepfather-to-be — had safely reached his villa there at the end of June, and was anxiously awaiting us. Six months later, the three of us sailed together from Lisbon to New York on a tiny storm-tossed vessel that had never gone farther than the Azores and was making a three-week virgin voyage across the Atlantic. Another banal tale of survival, another instance of Destiny being kind.

*

One of the many maxims I was exposed to during my youth in France — the French love a good abstraction, since it enables them to create yet another aphorism — goes this way: "The British are beastly toward the peoples they colonize, and utterly decent to each other, whereas the French can be relatively democratic colonizers, and are beastly toward each other." I tend to trust the wisdom of that adage, at least in regard to the distaste the French have for their compatriots.

Few books on the debacle of 1940 have been as eloquent on that very issue as Emmanuel Berl's *La Fin de la IIIe République*. This account, published in the late 1960s, offers a sweeping indictment of the shameful scapegoating, masterminded by the Vichy regime, that went on after the fall of France, and of the deep-seated internecine hatreds it revealed. Berl, a French Jew, writes as a onetime insider, for he briefly served as one of Pétain's speechwriters before having a radical change of heart and seeking refuge in southern France. He points out that among the military leaders who headed Pétain's government, there was a code of honor that mandated covering up any mistakes made by the French army. So every possible segment of the French community except the military was held accountable for the debacle of 1940. According to Vichy's propaganda machine, the war was lost because the citizens were too hedonistic; because they were not fertile enough; because French workers, deluded by the left-wing unions, had not fabricated enough weapons; because liberty, equality, and fraternity had been exalted at the price of honor and Fatherland; because France's allies (perfidious Albion again!) let her down; and, above all, because of the Popular Front, led by the Jew Léon Blum, who gave the rabble paid vacations and the forty-hour week. Weygand, who at one point wanted to declare war against England (even Pierre Laval rebuked him, saying "Isn't one defeat enough for you?"), enjoyed tracing the debacle to the French army's "inadmissible proportion of colonial and North African military men" and to France's "massive and regrettable number of naturalizations" (no wonder Jean-Marie Le Pen sounds so familiar to those of us who lived through the debacle).

Surveying the bleak panorama of hatreds and recriminations that followed the armistice of 1940, and the return to primeval chthonic deities summed up in the Pétainist slogan "Work, Family, Fatherland," Berl comes to the following bitter conclusion:

The French cannot love their country without hating a good part, if not the majority, of their compatriots. Without having injured, disqualified, incarcerated, deported, or massacred enough to satisfy the exigencies of their zeal, they accuse themselves of moderation and tepidity. A good Frenchman looks on himself as such only if he has caused death during harsh periods, caused sufficient shame and ruin . . . amid a number of his compatriots to calm his dread that he has not given all the love he has to his fatherland. Unless avarice or personal or family egoism has not already made him indifferent to the public cause, his lack of fervor leads to self-loathing if he has not delivered other Frenchmen to the inquisition, to the police, to the executioners, to the grave-diggers.

Dreadful words. But as our own great historian Robert O. Paxton has proved, the "zeal" shown by the French when they informed on compatriots and delivered them to certain death would be amply manifested in the next shameful chapter of the nation's history — their treatment of Jewish compatriots. I've long been thankful that I did not live on in my native country to witness the infamy of those years, and that my mother brought me to safety when she did, thus preserving herself from the fatally heroic actions she would surely have undertaken as a resister. This sense of gratitude surged in me a few months ago, on my most recent trip to France, when I went to Villandry and stood in the room my mother and I had shared during those first months of the German occupation. It is now a dusty, atticlike storeroom, dense with cobwebs and filled with decrepit sofas, decaying storage bins, rusting furniture, heaps of plaster dust, the very foundation of its walls destroyed — a fitting metaphor, I guess, for the process of memory itself, its profusion and profligate messiness and devious multilayeredness.

As adults remembering a grave historical moment a half century past, we stare at such a room and say to ourselves: I may have gotten a lot of it wrong. Those first young Germans I saw parading down our road may have been singing "Deutschland über Alles" rather than "Lili Marlene." Kommandant Hebert may have been short and clean-shaven, not mustached and tall. The officers' car might have been a Hispano-Suiza, not a Mercedes. No matter. In those months during 1940, the fate of an entire generation was radically changed. In this room, this house, my life was transformed. I have not been the same child since.

EDWARD HOAGLAND

Circus Music

FROM HARPER'S MAGAZINE

A CIRCUS IS BOTH acrobatic and elephantine, wholesome but freakish, and that is partly why we like it so — because we are two-headed, too. A showgirl in the center ring displays her pretty legs to daddy while his children are engrossed in watching a palomino stallion dance to the band's tempo. But that, of course, is an illusion. The bandmaster, flourishing his silver cornet, is actually following the horse's mannered, jerky prance, not vice versa, which in turn is being cued by the same short-skirted lady's cracking whip. And in the old days the sideshow used to be called "The Ten-in-One" because it had "Ten Different Freaks Under One Tent for Only One Dollar! Can you beat that, folks?" as the barkers yelled. Only, I suppose, by looking inside oneself. People too fat or too small, too thin or too tall, remind us of a certain unwieldy, weird, but shrinking-violet personage whom we know all too well — as does the Knife Thrower, the Escape Artist or Contortionist, the Tattooed or Albino Lady, hefting a boa constrictor, perhaps, and the knuckle-walking Wild Man, bearded all over, or the Living Skeleton, and the kinky but outwardly clean-cut gentleman who is wed to the swords and fireballs that he swallows a dozen times a day for our entertainment. Why is it entertainment, if we're not gawking at a caricature of ourselves?

In the big top everybody wears a spiffy uniform, but if yours isn't a one-night stand and they stay until tomorrow, you'll see some of the circus people sleeping in the horse straw on the ground. And when the costumes come off, baby, don't imagine they'll remember you, no matter how hard you may think you clapped. Behind the greasepaint is quite a different sort of face and person. You wouldn't necessarily trust one of the clowns or animal handlers who give such intense pleasure to tens of thousands of children with the downright raising of even a couple; they might already have abandoned a family. Like actors only more so, circus performers are expected to be manic and depressive, and we accept the paradox that a real genius at making little kids laugh, like Danny Kaye or Charlie Chaplin, could verge on frightening them as a father. The funniness is vertiginous, and the hippodrome food is too sweet. Too much is going on in the rings to absorb it all, and the physical stunts sometimes edge toward the suicidal. Maybe the grisly part of the bargain is that we, the "lot lice," the Elmers, rubes, towners, hayseeds, hicks, yokels, are paying green money to watch the star troupers risk their lives. If a trapeze artist falls and hits the ground, he'll lie in front of a grandstand of utter strangers, whimpering, jactitating, and dying alone.

A circus is high and low, piccolos and trombones. The edgy tiger roars and charges, but then licks her trainer at the end, as if they had been friends all along. A clown meanly tricks his chum, dunks him treacherously in a barrel of water, and gloats for the crowd, but then the high-wire walker steals all his thunder as soon as the whistle blows. The ringmaster, though he seems the boss, is curiously not the star; the saddest puss gets the biggest laugh; and the innocence is raunchy (those leggy girls who strut their stuff alongside a whiteface Bozo so that dad has his own reasons to snicker). The clowns teach most memorably that if you trust anybody he will betray you.

We want circus people to be different from us — homeless and garish, heedless and tawdry (otherwise why pay to watch?) — yet to connect with us in deeper currents that we share. Our fear of heights and ridicule, our complicated fascination with animals (whips, but kindness), our love of grace and agility, of stylish vanity and splendid boasting, of dressing in spangles yet living in tents and trailers. As an element of rooting our children in a stable home, we nourish them with this annual spectacle of the elaborately raffish and picaresque. Therefore, we want the show people to be outlandish but never outrageous, to hide from us their perverse, larcenous, or alcoholic tendencies that may accompany the tramping life. A guy who just got out of the county jail (we hope not the Big House) for doing whatever (and we don't want to know the whatever) and then hit the road because his wife didn't want him is coiling and flinging the ropes around that keep the aerialists' rigging up; and somehow it has become the kind of responsibility he can handle. And without quite articulating it, we want our offspring to be flexible and adventurous as well as predictable, tolerant as well as ethical, capable of flights of delight as well as down-to-earth. Also, we want circus people to know us better than we know them, in a sense: to be wise beyond what their education and social status should officially warrant in gauging human nature, and cater to and inspire our children, even though we have come to watch some of them risk breaking their necks — which is base of us — and even if they can't always manage their own private behavior. People are juggling themselves, hand-to-mouth, in brassy penury, in the circus, not just tossing torches or chancing an awful clawing. Then they'll live in back-street rented rooms during the winter until they can take to the road again.

It's no coincidence that circus music is often identical to the sort of marches that soldiers used to go off to die to. The stakes are high. Bravery, resourcefulness, pinpoint concentration, and self-containment are what make it work, and one reason why so many losers and handicapped souls have found their footing in the circus may be because they see in the crowds how thin a veneer conventional society paints upon our basic greed, inertia, and callousness. So why worry that you're an oddball and have to move somewhere new every other day to keep your haywire impulses under control and sublimate them into stunts? Like rich people, you have that privilege. New audience, new town, never seen you before, never'll see you again. It's anesthetic. If you screw up one of the acts today, you'll get it right tomorrow — so, no sweat, you get it right today.

"We have the fattest woman in the world, and the tallest man, and a girl who has no arms or legs, and midgets who are married! Have you ever seen a camel spit, or seals play catch, or elephants stand on their heads? A man with reptile's scales, who was once just like you! And the Good Lord made him. Can you finish your ice cream after you have looked at him?"

Good question. In the pre-television era, when much of the novel technology related to transportation, not electronics, live entertainment toured between cities by train or motor vehicle. Repertory-stage and opera companies, evangelist preachers, Chautauqua lecturers, freelance physic salesmen, vaudeville magicians, humorists, and strippers, who formerly had gone by riverboat or wagon, would troop through town — as well as the more celebrated Sells-Floto, or Sparks, or Hagenbeck-Wallace, or Sam B. Dill's, or Walter L. Main, or Robbins Bros., and Christy Bros. circuses, not to mention Ringling Bros. and Barnum & Bailey, The Greatest Show on Earth. There was Downie Bros. Wild Animal Circus, The Largest Motor Circus in the World (families and brothers stuck together in business in those days), and the famous Clyde Beatty–Cole Bros. big show, and Col. Tim McCoy & His Indian Village, or his Congress of Rough Riders of the World, and Marcellus' Golden Models (with the men's pectorals as big as the women's breasts), and Tommy Atkins' Military Riding Maids.

Fortunately, we aren't entirely bereft of a visual record of these arcane marvels. A Manhattan banquet photographer named Edward Kelty, whose usual venue was hotel ballrooms and Christmas parties, went out intermittently in the summer from the early 1920s to the mid-1940s, taking panoramic tripod pictures of circus personnel, in what could only have constituted a labor of love. He was expert, anyway, from his bread-and-butter job, at joshing smiles and camaraderie out of disparate collections of people, coaxing them to drape their arms around each other and trust the box's eye. He had begun close to home, at Coney Island freak shows, when the subway was extended out there, and Times Square flea-circus "museums" and variety halls, and the Harlem Amusement Palace. Later, building upon contacts and friendships from those places, he outfitted a truck for darkroom purposes (presumably to sleep in too) and sallied farther to photograph the tented circuses that played on vacant lots in New Jersey, Connecticut, or on Long Island, and gradually beyond. He would pose an ensemble of horse wranglers, canvasmen, ticket takers, candy butchers, teeterboard tumblers, "web-sitters" (the guys who hold the ropes for the ballet girls who climb up them and twirl), and limelight daredevils, or the bosses and moneymen. He took everybody, roustabouts as conscientiously as impresarios, and although he was not artistically very ambitious — and did hawk his prints both to the public and to the troupers, at "6 for $5" — in his consuming hobby he surely aspired to document this vivid, disreputable demimonde obsessively, thoroughly: which is his gift to us.

More of these guys may have been camera-shy than publicity hounds, but Kelty's rubber-chicken award ceremonies and industrial photo shoots must have taught him how to relax jumpy people for the few minutes required. With his Broadway pinstripes and a newsman's bent fedora, as proprietor of Century Flashlight Photographers, in the West Forties, he must have become a trusted presence in the "Backyard" and "Clown Alley." He knew show business and street touts, bookies and scalpers — but also how to flirt with a marquee star. Because his personal life seems to have been a bit of a train wreck, I think of him more as a hat-check girl's swain, yet he knew how to let the sangfroid sing from some of these faces, or simple good rolling-stone mischief, while doing justice to the ragged stringbeans, ranked in another line. These zany tribes of showboaters must have amused him, after the wintertime's chore of recording for posterity some forty-year drudge receiving a gold watch. Other faces look muddied with inchoate emotions, however, as if the man indeed had just gotten out of the penitentiary, or were mentally retarded, or could already feel the dreadful undertow of an illness like epilepsy, schizophrenia, pedophilia, kleptomania, tuberculosis, or diabetic collapse that had choked off so many fresh starts he had attempted before. You wouldn't see *him* in a hotel ballroom, even as a waiter.

The ushers, the prop men and riggers, the cookhouse crew, the elephant men and cat men, the showgirls arrayed in white bathing suits in a tightly chaperoned, winsome line, the hoboes who had put the tent up and, in the wee hours, would tear it down, and the bosses whose body language, with arms akimbo and swaggering legs, tells us something of who they were: these collective images telegraph the complexity of the circus hierarchy, with stars at the top, winos at the bottom. Except that still below the winos were the "jigs," or Negroes, whom you may notice in uneasily angular positions as they perch semi-perilously on a wagon roof behind everybody else, up in "nigger heaven" (as expressed in movie-house terms), signifying their loose-balloon moorings in this segregated world, based on the mores of winter quarters, which were usually down South. There may even be two bands in the picture, a black one and a white one, that might have sounded better playing together.

While arranging corporate personnel in the phony bonhomie

of an office get-together for a company's annual report, Kelty
must have longed for summer, when he would be snapping "Con-
gresses" of mugging clowns, fugueing freaks, rodeo sharpshooters,
plus the train crews known as "razorbacks" (*Raise your backs!*), who
loaded and unloaded the wagons from railroad flatcars at midnight and dawn. That was the way a chug-a-lug bar fighter might
wind up, in this era when "rootless" was a pejorative word, like "hedonistic" or "atheistic," and a new face in town was cause for suspicion. These ladies toted pythons, strolling around the hippodrome
track, and didn't wear enough clothes; and some of the men
looked as bathless as the guys from a hobo jungle who would steal
your wife's apple pie that she'd left to cool on the kitchen windowsill, yet had skills you hadn't imagined. Circuses flouted convention as part of their pitch — flaunted and cashed in on the
romance of outlawry, like Old World Gypsies. If there hadn't
been a crime wave when the show was in town, everybody had
sure expected one. And the exotic physiognomies, strangely cut
clothes, and oddly focused, disciplined bodies were almost as disturbing — "Near Eastern," whatever Near Eastern meant (it somehow sounded weirder than "Middle Eastern" or "Far Eastern"),
Bedouin Arabs, Turks and Persians, or Pygmies, Zulus, people
cicatrized, "platter-lipped," or nose-split. That was the point. They
came from all over the known world to parade on gaudy ten-hitch
wagons or caparisoned elephants down Main Street, and then, like
the animals in the cages, you wanted them to leave town. Yet if you
were a farmer who thought a bear that had killed a pig was scary to
come to grips with, try managing half a dozen snarling lions! Or
maybe you had screwed up your nerve recently to reroof the barn?
Try walking the high wire, fifty feet up, with just your wife standing
underneath you in case of a slip.

When it rained, the rest of us went indoors, but show folk didn't
have an indoors. They were negotiating with the mud in order to
hit the road. The seat men folded thousands of chairs and "bibles,"
or souvenir programs. The "bull hands," the elephant men, controlled the pachyderms with a club with a hook on the end as the
animals pulled out the quarter poles and the center poles and any
wagons that got stuck. The transience of the circus jibed better
with wild nature than the closely trimmed lawns at home — and
willy-nilly a circus rolled. People with survival skills pitched in to fill

the gaps. The whole grew bigger than the parts, though close to nature meant close to scandal too, as they intersect in such a phrase as "Nature calls." Nature is randy as well as rainy, smelly as well as sunny. Circus Day was uncivilized like the Fourth of July, with candied apples, cotton candy, fireworks, and special dispensation for skimpy costumes, public lust, trials of strength, breakneck stunts, colossal crowds. "It was a circus," we'll still say when some ordinary scene bursts out of control. And if your blouse stuck out farther than the next girl's, that cage boy loafing over there might decide to persuade the hippopotamus to gape her mouth for you and poke his hand inside and scratch her gums the way she liked, to make you ooh and aah at how heroic he was.

I was such a cage boy myself, with Ringling Bros. and Barnum & Bailey in 1951 and 1952, and would also pet the menagerie leopards for the right admirer. I worked for two dollars per sixteen-hour day and slept two to a bunk, three bunks high, on the train, or else could rattle through the night outside on a flatcar. The faces of the drifters I was with sometimes looked as grim and bitter as a Wanted poster, and quite at their wit's end, not having had much wit to begin with, and what they might have had perhaps dispelled in prison. They'd slammed around, with their hats pulled down over their eyes, every mother-in-law's nightmare, and knew how to jump on a moving train without saying goodbye to anybody — knew the Front Range of the Rockies, and the Tex-Mex border. And not even our rumpled banquets guy with the windblown tie — a theater-district barfly and Coney Island dime-museum habitué, who scarcely saw his own sons after they were toddlers — could have coaxed a trustful look out of them.

Up on that giddy wire or the trapeze bar — or in the Iron Jaw act, spinning relentlessly by their teeth — people did things they shouldn't reasonably do, with no ostensible purpose but showing off, while the tuba oompahed, the trombone slalomed, the clarinet climbed a rope, and the cornet hit the canvas's peak line. "Flyers" and slack-wire artists and "risley" foot-jugglers and whiteface or "auguste" clowns hoarded and pruned their skills, like the humble juggler of legend, who during the night tiptoed into the empty cathedral on the Madonna's feast day after the wealthier citizens had long since delivered their heavy gifts, genuflected before her statue, and gone comfortably home. Alone and barefoot, he performed for her with whatever grace and dexterity he could muster.

And for the first time in all of history, tears welled up in her stone eyes.

That's what we try to do, isn't it? Keep rolling, keep juggling and strutting our stuff, honoring our gods; then take a bow and exit smiling? But magic seldom happens unless a structure has been erected — whether a church or a tent — that is hospitable to it. Art is fragile, and a windless silence helps. Then depart just as the applause crests, leaving some emotion for the next act, because the thrust of the circus never stops, whether in mud or sunshine, whether the tickets have sold out or not. High stakes. The aerialist Lillian Leitzel, the most mesmerizing female performer ever, fell to her death in 1931, and afterward Alfredo Codona, her husband and male counterpart, at least on the trapeze, married an aerialist/equestrienne, but injured himself while doing a triple somersault in 1933 and never flew again. Grotesquely, he became his wife's hostler on the Tom Mix Circus — until, estranged, he shot both her and himself in her divorce lawyer's office.

Karl Wallenda, the greatest wire-walker and another compulsive, fell twelve stories off a cable strung 750 feet between two hotels in 1978, at seventy-three. But for some of these plain old Okies, Arkies, Hoosiers, and Wisconsin Cheeseheads and Georgia Crackers who got the show to run on time and then maybe drove a trailer truck all night, the gamble was compelling, too. Their trajectory ran toward alcohol and the jitters of oblivion, even though they had a seaman's way with ropes. And several gaze at Kelty's camera as if reminded of a police-station booking room, whereas the performers pose in a row in profile with their biceps bulged, or ponytail pert. "Is your body as trim as mine?" they seem to ask. "I'll stand on one hand — or one finger! I'll do a back flip from one horse to another and then lie down on the ground and let the elephant put her foot on my nose, but because we're all a family she won't crush it. Instead she'll lift me onto her shoulders and we'll chase that clown until he drops his red bloomers."

The moneymen, gimlet-eyed, with peremptory chests, let their suits, cufflinks and stickpins, their oxblood shoes and railroad men's timepieces, speak for them. They owned the tents and trucks and railroad cars, of course, but also often the lions too, despite the trainer's intimacy with them. He could be fired and have to pack his kit and never see those particular cats again. Similarly, the acrobats were not terribly suited to busking for spare change on the subway. They needed complicated rigging and a spread of canvas overhead — the whole apparatus — to gather an audience sufficient to justify risking their lives, without being clinically crazy. And a run-of-the-mill hobo, who was used to sneaking across the hazardous, lightless bustle of a railroad yard to boost himself into a moving boxcar without being detected, had probably found a raison d'être with Ringling Bros., called by show people "the Big One." In my time, if he was fired with the dreaded words "No Re-hire" scribbled on his pink slip to go into the company's records, it might take the little wind that he had out of his sails. The performance, the crowds and ovations, though not directly for him, had centered and justified his shaky life.

The center poles and brocaded, bejeweled elephant howdahs might be bedecked with the Stars and Stripes, and yet one knew that the entire spectacle, unlike July 4, wasn't quite *American.* The men and women holding hands in the center ring to take a bow after manipulating their bodies on the teeterboard were probably foreigners, and might not even be married to each other — and God knows where they slept. They had somehow jelled their flightiness for professional purposes, but the idea of a new town tomorrow, a new town the next day, and consorting in a business way with freaks whose very livelihood was exhibiting their disfigurements like fakirs in an Asian marketplace (freaks inherently were un-American) was not like the Home of the Brave. What demons in themselves were they trying to anesthetize by harboring values so different from ours? We, the Elmers, the hicks, the towners, the hayshakers, had just put down good money to watch somebody shoot himself out of a cannon on the assurance that it was going to be genuine and he might really die before our eyes. But he landed succinctly on his back in the L-shaped net, swung to the ground, acknowledged our claps — and didn't then thank his lucky stars and settle down to a productive existence like ours. *Eat your heart out, rube* was part of his message. *We'll be gone tomorrow. We'll see Chicago. We'll be in Florida. You stay here and milk your cows!*

To "the Strange People," misshapen on their little stages in the sideshow and peddling 10¢ likenesses of their deformities to the public, the conventional response would be, "There but for the grace of God go I." But why had He withheld His mercy when constructing *them*? Did their burden, as suggested by ancient superstitions, express a spiritual canker? Was external ugliness a punishment laid on the erring soul? My own feeling, while working next to them in Madison Square Garden and other arenas half a century ago, was that the object lesson ran deeper still. People were fascinated not just because of morbid curiosity and schadenfreude but because we saw ourselves incarnate in the Knife Thrower, the Living Skeleton (or "Pincushion," or "Picture Gallery"), the Human Pretzel, the Fat Lady, the lame and wheezing Giant, and were encouraged to stare without being rude. The foxfire flicker of ferocity and awful insecurity that so frequently subverted our genial veneer lay out there exposed — much as the bum, the coward, the fussbudget and spoilsport whom we knew all too well was embodied in some of the skits the clowns performed. (Our Knife Thrower really got to people when, as a pièce de résistance, he "horsewhipped" pretty women who volunteered from the crowd.)

A clown or Santa Claus costume, in my experience of the individuals who wear them, can conceal a multitude of sins. But so does the attire that the rest of us hide in, using blandness to mask our shamefaced failures and maladjustments. We, too, have flat feet and big asses, chalky faces and weepy tendencies when frightened of our shadows or searching through the tanbark for a nickel we have lost, a button that popped off, or a pebble that was in our shoe — we took it out but now we miss it. In the smaller tent shows the Fat Lady in the baby-doll nightie might even *show it all* in a curtained-off area, if you paid an extra four bits (and it was said you could insert them). In a circus you didn't have to — weren't supposed to — avert your eyes, and that may have been its ultimate kick. The guy might die, but without muttering the piety "Oh, I can't watch," we simply did.

Uzbeks rode on saddled camels. Elephants sashayed. A sway-pole acrobat almost seemed to touch the ground on each backswing, then locked his feet and slid down headfirst. A lovely woman with blond hair hanging to her coccyx adjusted her shoulder straps, kicked off her silver slippers, and gripped a knotted rope to ascend for the Cloud Swing. Over at one side, we might not notice a self-effacing clown — not bizarrely loud now to attract attention —

pulling her up with considerable care, then standing underneath in case of a mishap. But if you were observant, you realized there might be some people who had a love life after all.

The black-maned lion roared with bestial fury yet soon lapsed into contented amiability, as if he might be willing to settle in our burg. And the Albino Girl and Snake Charmer and other troupers were said to have bought cough medicine, underpants, and other personal stuff in the local stores. But just when we thought they really liked us and had been converted to our home-sweet-home values, they up and did a disappearing act. Overnight, the magic cavalcade vanished to another state, another climate. We have the gimpy, haywire gene as well, the one that makes you want to hit the road each spring while you last — a hail-fellow who knows that nothing is for keeps. You do your thing, to just whatever tattoo of music and battery of lights are available to you, survive today, sleep it off, and get up on that wire again tomorrow.

MYRA JEHLEN

F. P.

FROM RARITAN

A FRIEND DIED and asked in her will that her ashes be divided between two places. She was French, so one place is in France, under a tree in the field behind a house in a village of the Charente-Maritime. The other is in the United States: a cemetery up a dirt road in Vermont. We who were to do this two-part burial asked the undertaker to give us her ashes in two urns, but he said he was not allowed to divide bodies: "Le corps," he said, "est indivisible." We wondered at this; that a corpse can be divided harmlessly is, after all, one of its defining traits. But the undertaker was adamant, so we said one urn was fine, and to one another said we would do the dividing ourselves.

I looked up the law the undertaker had invoked, which turned out to be a ruling by the court of the city of Lille, which, in 1997, added a provision about ashes to a regulation it already had about bones. The occasion was a suit brought against a widow who had removed her husband's ashes from the cemetery to her house, making it very hard for his sister, who didn't get along with the widow, to visit his tomb. The sister claimed the widow had violated the law against removing bodies from their burial places. The judge, observing that an urn wasn't, like a tomb, a permanent refuge, but a container for ashes whose vocation, as he put it, is to be scattered, ruled the widow could move the urn wherever she wanted. The undertaker had it wrong, or hadn't kept up with recent rulings: it's not ashes but bones that you can't divide. I hadn't thought before about the opposition between burying a body and burning it: by the first, you fix it forever in place, or mean to. But by the second, you transform it into something that flies off with every breeze. The urn is a way to temporize between the two, I suppose. I know several people who have the ashes of their fathers or their mothers in closets, unsure whether to bury or scatter them. Parents being where you leave from, it's hard to imagine them more adrift than you. My friend, who had been born on the left bank of the Seine and never considered living anywhere else, imagined herself dead becoming part of places that alive she would only consider visiting, as if in her life she'd rehearsed leaving and then in death gone and done it.

The cremation was at the Père-Lachaise cemetery, which has the only crematorium in Paris. One crematorium is not enough, and there is a crush. Each burying party gets a half hour in an underground room beyond which, visible through a window, is the place where the coffin will be set on rails to carry it into the furnace. The cemetery personnel call the furnace "the device" (*l'appareil*). But before it goes into the device, there is a ceremonial half hour during which the coffin is in the room with the mourners. It's laid on a wheeled cart in the middle of the room and surrounded by eight chairs. The chief mourners or the oldest sit, and everyone else stands because the room is too small to accommodate the average party sitting down. At the head of the room, the end with the window on the rails, there is a platform on which people who want to speak or have been designated to speak stand up facing the coffin.

There were four people speaking at my friend's funeral, representing stages of her life. She was just coming of age in 1968, and for the next decade she did sixties things. One of these she carried over into the eighties, when she ran her own very small publishing house, which was not an unlikely occupation though fairly heroic. Actually, she was not herself heroic, only ironic, but she kept her house going and proved to be commercially shrewd about writings most people thought commercially impossible. When eventually she moved on to a larger publishing house, she turned out to be remarkably good at navigating the mainstream too. Personally, she held steady where she'd always stood, a yard to the side of everything. The four people spoke well, became interested in their arguments, almost forgot she was dead. We listened carefully.

We had already asked that the speeches be short, but, to move things along just in case, Père-Lachaise provides a master of ceremonies, a young man who keeps his head reverently bent even when speaking directly to you. I'm not sure whether we could have refused his services, but anyway, at the moment we didn't have the presence of mind to send him away. Apparently not remembering the last names of the speakers, he called them Michel, Françoise, Geneviève, and Boris, as in California. At the beginning and again at the end, he urged us to mourn our dead friend and wish her well. Then two young cemetery attendants (all the attendants were in their twenties) wheeled the coffin out of the room through a side door, and the master of ceremonies told us to stand and face the window for the dispatch into the fire, the *mise à la flamme.* Some people did, most didn't; it was confusing because a shade had been dropped over the window while the coffin was lifted onto the rails and the shade stuck, so that the coffin had begun to move forward by the time it became visible again. It disappeared and the attendants were guiding us out. Another party was already coming down the stairs and there was some of the awkwardness of rush hour on the subway. The social services in big cities are always overburdened.

The next day we went to collect the urn, which was to be delivered to a local branch of the funeral parlor. (We hadn't waited because a cremation takes one and a half to two hours.) The urn hadn't arrived due to the heavy traffic. In Paris the traffic is called *la circulation.* The circulation was bad that day and they asked us to return in a half hour. I would be coming back alone, and the man recommended I bring a bag, possibly the one I used for shopping. When I arrived, he insisted I sit down and told me that, amazingly, the urn had gotten there not ten minutes after we'd left. Then he went into a back room and came back with a blue satiny sack tied around the neck with a cord in a darker blue. The outline of a box was visible through the sack. Inside, the man said, was a certificate of cremation. I know, he said, that these ashes will be traveling. I wondered how he knew but then remembered we had told him about our friend's wish. When you travel with the ashes, he urged, be sure to bring the certificate with you. If you are stopped by the police, they will consider that you are transporting a body and you must be able to show them everything is legal.

I was surprised by how heavy the urn was. I had to keep changing hands as I carried it home. By the weight, I could well believe my

friend's body was all in that box. I thought how much I would have
liked to tell her the story of trundling her ashes along the Rue St.
Jacques, and how as we, she and I, passed the church of the Val de
Grâce, the bells were ringing and I looked in the courtyard and saw
a hearse. My friend was neither Christian nor religious, nor am I,
and I didn't go in. When I arrived home, I put the ashes in the corner of the living room, next to a ficus she'd raised from a cutting,
and sat down to think what to do next.

This was self-evident: next was the will. She had left a will written
in ballpoint on two sides of a page of French graph paper. It was eloquent and elegant, and it conducted masterfully for the last time
the ensemble of a complicated life. It was also a sad will, written in
a moment of despair. Legally, however, it was not much. Fortunately, it was handwritten, dated and signed, so it was valid. In the
United States, a will has to be witnessed to be valid. In this matter,
France seems to value vows over contracts, so a will is valid so long
as it clearly denotes personal wishes. My friend's will, being in her
handwriting, met this requirement, but it was lacking in other
ways. She'd written it logically, thinking of her possessions singly
and giving them away singly. There weren't many: she left her
apartment to one, to another some furniture and a few paintings,
and a third was to choose an object or two. But the notary said she
wished my friend had called her so she could have told her a will
should never be a series of gifts but a universal donation; you
should designate a single person to distribute this to that one and
that to this. Otherwise, anything not named in the will goes to a de-
fault heir, a blood relative who also becomes the executor. My
friend had forgotten that she had two small bank accounts, as well
as death benefits from her job, odds and ends, *des poussières* in
French, dust. Her only relatives were a nephew and a niece, children of a brother now dead and long estranged, and she had written in the will that they were not to inherit. They therefore
wouldn't, but their small children could, which came to the same
thing. It wouldn't be much of an inheritance by an accountant's
reckoning, and it would be still less minus the French sixty percent
inheritance tax, but symbolically who inherited mattered very
much.

Henceforth she was all symbols, and those of the will had meanings she had assigned herself. It was essential that her symbols not

be revoked by her relatives. Between us, we referred to them ge-
nerically: *the* nephew, *the* niece. They were *the* children of *the*
brother. She had loved her mother wholly, her father not so much,
and her brother, after a bad time, not at all. Now that she was dead
these distinctions vanished: mother, father, brother . . . her family.
In addition, they were all dead, mother, father, brother; but still
they were an official family more powerful than any relations her
life had bred: the nephew and the niece, banished from her life,
could now become the crux of who she remained. The family, I
thought, gets a lot of its meaning, most of it maybe, from death.

She had written her will as if a child, in drawing a fence around
her picture of a house, had forgotten to extend the line all the way
around. She hadn't said the nephew and the niece mustn't inherit
her bank balance, the miles on her American Express card, the security deposit on her rented apartment. So they would. I imagined
the stuff of the law flowing in over the place in the world where she
no longer was, like water closing, cloth knitting, a hole filling, eras-
ing the perturbations of her ways of living. Strange, no? that a person's absence should restore wholeness. Yet she wasn't a disruptive
person, not difficult to work or live with and no more critical than
comes with a sense of humor. Maybe not quite a member in good
standing, a pillar of society. I thought that it happens like this:
willy-nilly the dead become pillars of society.

We knew what she would have felt about the nephew and the
niece transforming her into their aunt and decided that we
couldn't let them. We said we'd get a lawyer, we swore we wouldn't
let them. Then, in the midst of swearing, I lost the thread of
fierceness. All this about the will was crucial to our keeping faith
with our friend, I thought, but it was also beside the point. A few
months before she died, I saw a child born. The hours it took were
incandescent with consciousness, concentration, fear, hope, work,
curiosity. In the room, everyone was supremely present. Except the
child: at the center of all the sounds of his coming into life, there
was a great silence. He made no sound, and for all that his presence was overwhelmingly impending, I could sense only his absence. When I thought that keeping faith with our friend's will was
perhaps necessary but also irrelevant, I remembered the silence of
the unborn child cutting it off categorically from the world of our
anticipation. While we were swearing we'd not let the nephew and

the niece get away with it, our friend was silent the way the unborn child had been. So, in the middle of it, I fell silent because I saw my swearing on her behalf was nonsense. Literally without sense, which is another word for connection, when there's no connection, no continuity or relevance, between life and death. There's nothing to understand about death, not even that it exists. Epicurus said death was nothing to us, since, as he put it, where we are, death is not, and where death is, we are not. It's well to remember that birth bursts in on a long silence, so as to be prepared for the bursting into silence of death. It's not a diminuendo, it's the absence of all sound.

At first, I wanted burying my friend to be a diminuendo. I was glad she'd asked us to divide her ashes because it was a way for us to continue the story of her life, to add another episode, under her direction. Then I lost my train of thought and, instead of what she had asked us to do, I heard mostly her silence and I found this silence intolerable, and excessive. It was what they call in French English "too much," by which they mean not a relative but an absolute muchness.

I find myself objecting to the excess of her death. At insignificant moments, crossing the boulevard, putting the milk back in the refrigerator, spraying the cactus, I've spoken to her aloud. The last time I spoke so strangely that I heard myself: I was saying, All right, that's enough now, *ça suffit*, it's time you came back, really it's time. I said before that I'm not religious. I don't think there is an afterlife, and certainly not that the dead walk the earth. Yet I meant it when I told her it was time she returned, and I was annoyed that she stayed away. I'd not have been surprised if she'd appeared, and I'm disappointed that she hasn't. I'd have told her that this thing she asked us to do with her ashes was more complicated than she'd realized; she'd have said forget it; I'd have said, no, it was turning out to be very interesting and we wanted to do it, now that she'd mentioned it. I can imagine this conversation very easily. What I can't imagine is that she's dead.

I don't blame my imagination. Death is not a subject for the imagination. Literature, painting, and music only talk around it. Two weeks after my friend's death, I went to hear Haydn's *Orfeo ed Euridice*, about a man penetrating alive into death. Orpheus just will not accept that he can't have Eurydice. She's taken from him once alive, and he gets her back by dint of his music. Then, the fool, he leaves her unguarded and she's taken from him again. This time, fleeing her abductor, she's killed. The question is whether Orpheus's music can bring her back to life. Most people would say no. At the funeral, we played Chopin etudes to acknowledge my friend's death, not to dispute it. Once death has happened, there is nothing to say. All the living can do is show the flag, make a show of force the way a nation might march its army up to the border of an enemy state. The force of the living is in nonetheless giving shape to the world they don't transcend. So when they see death rising up at their borders, they go out and demonstrate this power to give shape. Hence ceremony, and music, the most formal of the arts. A funeral ought to be the most formal of ceremonies, for, there being nothing to see in death but dissolution, a funeral has nothing in view but form.

Orpheus, however, mistook a flexing of muscles, meant to keep up your spirit in the knowledge of ultimate defeat, for having a fighting chance. He was misled by his music's wondrous power over nature and man into thinking it transcendent. Haydn's librettist Badini invented the character Genius, who tries to explain to Orpheus that the best answer to death is philosophy, which, having walked the metes and bounds of life, accepts the limits of the estate in return for getting to furnish it. But Orpheus will have none of such trades, and for a little while he seems to be right, since Genius now tells him that after all he can regain Eurydice, on one not very difficult condition. Which he can't fulfill: the great puzzle of the story of Orpheus is why he turns back to look at Eurydice knowing he'll lose her for it. I thought, watching the opera after my friend's death, that Orpheus had a greater ambition than reviving Eurydice, which was to breach the underworld. He had to see Eurydice while she was still on the ground of death, for, if he saw her again only after her return to life, his invasion of death wouldn't be realized as such. It would have had consequences but no reality of its own. Persuading Pluto to annul Eurydice's death is not enough for Orpheus. What he really wants, what the living want, what I want, is to see with my living eyes the world of death; and, by seeing it, to overcome its discontinuity, to make it another condition of life, so I can go on, or can imagine going on, even though dead. Sight is the most important sense. Emerson insisted that what you see, you possess. Orpheus, for his glimpse of the world of the dead, for thinking he could make the dead Eurydice his, was torn apart by the forces that rule that world, the forces of disorder and the antithesis of the force with which he makes his music. Pluto's prohibition is simple and absolute: you can't with your living mind know death.

Eurydice just faded away from Orpheus's sight, but in real life the way it becomes evident that death is a closed matter feels like mockery. We were in the other room, talking, when my friend died. I went in to check on her and couldn't see her breathing. The doctor came and said she was dead. Then quickly there were other people. The doctor recommended a funeral parlor, and they said they'd come in two hours. This seemed too fast, but, it being Friday, it was then or not until after the weekend. They said to choose clothes in which they would "prepare" her. I thought, having had to die, she shouldn't have to undergo being prepared, and said I would dress her, not knowing how difficult it is to dress a dead person. To begin with, I couldn't pull out the intravenous tube that still connected her to a morphine drip. The tube had been inserted into a catheter through which she had been undergoing chemotherapy. When I tried to pull out the tube, blood seeped from the opening of the catheter. So instead I cut the tube and, so doing, saw that she was dead. I had wanted her to wear a favorite gray cashmere turtleneck, but I couldn't put it on her. She was too heavy, although she weighed less than eighty pounds, and too stiff, so I dressed her in a shirt and pants. She looked terrible, yet fully and definitively herself. You're never so wholly incarnate as in death.

When I was dressing my friend, I expected her to help. The utter stillness of her arms and legs filled me with hopelessness. In French, there are two words that look like "despair," but the second means "hopelessness": *désespoir* and *désesperance*. It's useful to have despair and hopelessness look alike; they correct one another, so that *désespoir* is less sentimental than despair, and *désesperance* less childish than hopelessness. The feeling I had when my friend didn't raise her arm even a little so I could slip on her sweater was *désesperance:* there was nothing anymore to hope for in relation to her.

This feeling had an unwonted finality. I wasn't used to despair.

She had been sick a long time and I knew she would probably, nearly inevitably, die of the disease. But such an eventuality never seemed immediately relevant. Ten days before she died, we went to Nantes, where she had been invited to visit for a course on book editing. She didn't seem strong enough to go alone, so I went with her. We took the TGV and arrived in the rain. I walked with her to the place where she was to talk, stopping on the way to get her some coffee and a raisin bun for strength. Later, the talk having gone very well, we ate at a fish brasserie from the turn of the century, and shared a big platter of shellfish. We were to return to Paris the next morning, but instead we stayed over one more day. It was no longer raining, and we turned the trip into a holiday. We rented a car and, because my friend had passed the summers of her childhood on the Atlantic coast, she knew a place she wanted to go, near Pornic. We drove, in fact she drove, and it all started to come out right. After a while, on the left was a long driveway down to a parking lot on a beach. We parked and walked down to the water. The sky was mostly gray but a bright gray, an ocean gray with white seagulls. It wasn't cold, not cold enough to make the mist uncomfortable. The tide was coming in and, to go all the way to the water, you had to be ready to jump back. She stayed farther up the beach and I went down to the water. A perfect seashell floated in on a small roller and was left behind still cupped upright, the only one on the beach (I checked) that was hollow side up. I told her it was definitely bringing something. Superstitious only to the degree that connotes a proper sense of your own understanding's limits and the infinitude of possibility, still, we took it as a sign. So to drink to the sign, we entered the beach café, which was called Bahia and decorated with plastic parrots two feet tall hanging from the ceiling on round swings. The African owner made us impeccable hot chocolates.

I'm stuck in that day. And I'm simultaneously stuck in the night before she died. She wasn't conscious. I didn't have a view about her unconsciousness. For the moment, I thought only of the night. I lay down beside her. I talked to her and told her she should rest tranquilly; we were there and were taking care of her. I said, *On te soigne.* Sleep. It's all right. I'm stuck in the day on the beach and in that night. Being stuck, I suppose, is a way of dying with the dead by stopping when they do. Yet the mother of the child I saw being born, in whose silence I had sensed a universe outside life, said, when I told her I was stuck in the night of my friend's death, that she was stuck in the night of her child's birth. You get stuck, then, when you meet up with something that makes the limit of your perpetual motion just too obvious.

Stuck, you turn back. My friend didn't appear to me, so I made her appear: one night, I dreamed she had come back to life, or rather, that she hadn't died. At first, in my dream, she was as she was in the moments before she died. But, in the dream, as I bent over to see how she was, she grew better and better, until, in the dream, I called out to the doctor to do something, since something could be done.

JANE KRAMER

The Reporter's Kitchen

FROM THE NEW YORKER

THE KITCHEN where I'm making dinner is a New York kitchen. Nice light, way too small, nowhere to put anything unless the stove goes. My stove is huge, but it will never go. My stove is where my head clears, my impressions settle, my reporter's life gets folded into *my* life, and whatever I've just learned, or think I've learned — whatever it was, out there in the world, that had seemed so different and surprising — bubbles away in the very small pot of what I think I know and, if I'm lucky, produces something like perspective. A few years ago, I had a chance to interview Brenda Milner, the neuropsychologist who helped trace the process by which the brain turns information into memory, and memory into the particular consciousness called a life, or, you could say, into the signature of the person. Professor Milner was nearly eighty when I met her, in Montreal, at the neurological institute at McGill, where she'd worked for close to fifty years, and one of the things we talked about was how some people, even at her great age, persist in "seeing" memory the way children do — as a cupboard or a drawer or a box of treasures underneath the bed, a box that gets full and has to be cleaned out every now and then to make room for new treasures they collect. Professor Milner wasn't one of those people, but I am. The memory I "see" is a kind of kitchen, where the thoughts and characters I bring home go straight into a stockpot on my big stove, reducing old flavors, distilling new ones, making a soup that never tastes the same as it did the day before, and feeds the voice that, for better or worse, is *me* writing, and not some woman from another kitchen.

I knew nothing about stockpots as a child. My mother was an awful cook, or, more accurately, she didn't cook, since in her day it was fashionable not to go anywhere near a kitchen if you didn't have to. Her one creation, apart from a fluffy spinach soufflé that for some reason always appeared with the overcooked turkey when she made Thanksgiving dinner (a task she undertook mainly to avoid sitting in the cold with the rest of us at the Brown Thanksgiving Day home football game), would probably count today as haute-fusion family cooking: matzo-meal-and-Rhode-Island-johnnycake-mix pancakes, topped with thick bacon, sour cream, and maple syrup. Not even our housekeeper and occasional cook could cook — beyond a tepid, sherried stew that was always presented at parties, grandly, as lobster thermidor, and a passable apple filling that you could spoon out, undetected, through the large steam holes of an otherwise tasteless pie. I don't think I ever saw my father cook anything, unless you can call sprinkling sugar on a grapefruit, or boiling syringes in an enamel pan, the way doctors did in those days, cooking. (I use the pan now for roasting chickens.) The only man in my family with a recipe of his own was my brother Bobby, who had mastered a pretty dessert called pumpkin chiffon while courting an Amish girl who liked pumpkins. My own experience in the kitchen was pretty much limited to reheating the Sunday-night Chinese takeout early on Monday mornings, before anyone else was awake to eat it first.

I started cooking when I started writing. My first dish was tuna curry (a can of Bumble Bee, a can of Campbell's cream of mushroom soup, a big spoonful of Durkee's curry powder, and a cup of instant Carolina rice), and the recipe, such as it was, came from my friend Mary Clay, who claimed to have got it directly from the cook at her family's Kentucky farm. It counted for me as triply exotic, being at once the product of a New York supermarket chain, the bluegrass South, and India. And never mind that the stove I cooked on then was tiny, or that "dining" meant a couple of plates and a candle on my old toy chest, transformed into the coffee table of a graduate school rental, near Columbia; the feeling was high sixties, meaning that a nice girl from Providence could look forward to enjoying literature, sex, and cooking in the space of a single day. I don't remember whom I was making the curry for, though I must have liked him, because I raced home from Frederick Dupee's famous lecture on symbolism in *Light in August* to make it. What I do remember is how comforting it was to be standing at that tiny stove, pinched into a merry widow and stirring yellow powder into Campbell's soup, when I might have been pacing the stacks at Butler Library, trying to resolve the very serious question of whether, after Dupee on Faulkner, there was anything left to say about literature, and, more precisely, the question of whether *I'd* find anything to say in a review — one of my first assignments in the real world — of a book of poems written by Norman Mailer on the occasion of having stabbed his second wife. I remember this because, as I stood there, stirring powder and a soupçon of Acapulco Gold into my tuna curry, I began to accept that, while whatever I did say wasn't going to be the last word on the poetics of domestic violence, it would be *my* word, a lot of Rhode Island still in it, a little New York, and, to my real surprise, a couple of certainties: I was angry at Norman Mailer; I was twenty-one and didn't think that you should stab your wife. Mailer, on the other hand, had produced some very good lines of poetry. He must have been happy (or startled) to be taken for a poet at all, because a few weeks after my review ran — in a neighborhood paper you could pick up free in apartment-house lobbies — his friend Dan Wolf, the editor of what was then a twelve-page downtown alternative weekly called the *Village Voice*, phoned to offer me a job.

I bought a madeleine mold, at a kitchen shop near the old *Voice* offices, on Sheridan Square. It was my first purchase as a reporter who cooked — a long, narrow pan of shallow, ridged shells, waiting to produce a Proust — but though I liked madeleines, they didn't collect my world in a mouthful, the way the taste of warm apples, licked from the cool tingle of a silver spoon, still does, or, for that matter, the way the terrible chicken curry at the old brasserie La Coupole, in Paris, always reminded me of Norman Mailer's wife. The mold sat in my various kitchens for ten years before I moved to the kitchen I cook in now, and tried madeleines again, and discovered that, for me, they were just another cookie — which is to say, not the kind of cookie that belonged in the ritual that for years has kept me commuting between my study and my stove, stirring or beating or chopping or sifting my way through false starts and strained transitions and sticky sentences.

The cookies I like to make when I'm writing are called "dream cookies." I made my first batch in my friend John Tillinger's kitchen, in Roxbury, Connecticut, at one in the morning, in a mood perhaps best described by the fact that I'd just been awakened by the weight of a large cat settling on my head. The cookies were a kind of sand tart. They had a dry, gritty, burned-butter taste, and I must have associated them with the taste of deliverance from sweet, smooth, treacherous things like purring cats. I say this because a few years later I found myself making them again, in North Africa, in the middle of reporting a story about a tribal feud that involved a Berber wedding and was encrypted — at least for me — in platters of syrupy honeyed pastries, sugared couscous, and sweet mint tea.

At the time, my kitchen was in the Moroccan city of Meknès, where my husband was doing ethnographic research, but my story took me to a village a couple of hours up into the foothills of the Middle Atlas Mountains. It was a wild, unpleasant place. Even today, some thirty years, a couple of wars and revolutions, and an assortment of arguably more unpleasant places later, I would call it scary. The wedding in question, a three-day, her-house-to-his-house traveling celebration, was about to begin in the bride's village — which had every reason to celebrate, having already provided the groom's village with a large number of pretty virgins and, in the process, profited considerably from the bride-prices those virgins had commanded: goats, chickens, silver necklaces, brass plates, and simple, practical, hard cash, some of it in negotiable European currencies. The problem was that none of the young men in the bride's village were at all interested in the virgins available in the groom's village, whose own supply of goats, chickens, necklaces, plates, and money was consequently quite depleted. All that village had was an abundance of homely daughters — or, you could say, the bad end of the balance of trade in brides. As a result, the men in the groom's village were getting ready to fight the men in the bride's village, a situation that left the women in both villages cooking day and night, in a frantic effort to turn their enemies into guests.

By then, I was close to being an enemy myself, having already broken one serious taboo: I had asked the name of somebody's aunt in a conversation where the naming of paternal aunts in the

company of certain female relatives was tantamount to calling ca-
tastrophe down on the entire family, and the women had had to
abandon their cooking in order to purge the premises, which they
did by circling the village, ululating loudly, while I sat there in the
blazing sun, under strict orders to keep the flies off a platter of
dripping honey cakes. It hadn't helped any that, in a spirit of apology (or perhaps it was malice), I then invited the villagers to
Meknès and served them my special Julia Child's bœuf bourguig-
non, which made them all quite ill. A few days later, I went to the
medina and bought some almonds for dream cookies. I don't
know why I did it. Maybe I was homesick. Certainly, I was being
spoiled, knowing that Malika, the young Arab woman who worked
for me and became my friend, would grind those almonds into a
sandy paste as quickly as she had just peeled peaches for my breakfast — which is to say, in less time than it took me to check for scor-
pions underneath the two cushions and copper tray that were then
my dining room. But I think now that I was mainly trying to find
my voice in a country where some women couldn't mention an
aunt to a relative — where the voices of most women, in fact, were
confined to their ululations. Once, I heard that same shrill, flutey
cry coming from my own kitchen and rushed in to find Malika
shaking with pain and bleeding; she was sixteen, and had taken
something or done something to herself to end a pregnancy that I
had never even suspected. After that, I would sometimes hear the
cry again, and find her huddled in a corner of the room, struck
with a terror she could not describe. No one had ever asked her to
describe it, not even the man she'd married when, by her own
reckoning, she was twelve years old.

I never finished the story about the Berber bride. I was a bride
myself, and this posed something of a problem for my erstwhile village friends, who had wanted to find me a husband from the tribe
and thus assure themselves of the continued use of, if not actually
the title to, my new Volkswagen. In the event, one night, after we'd
been trading recipes, the women sent me home with a complicated (and fairly revolting) "love recipe" to try out on the husband
I already had, and it turned out — at least, according to the neighbors who warned me not to make it — to be a bit of black magic
whose purpose was, to put it discreetly, less amorous than incapaci-
tating. I took this as a sign that it was time to come down from the

mountains. I wrote a book about an Arab wedding instead, and I waited until I was back in my study in New York to finish it. The lesson for me, as a writer, was that I had to burrow back into my own life before I could even start thinking clearly about someone else's, or come to terms with the kinds of violence that are part of any reporter's working life, or with the tangles of outrage that women reporters, almost inevitably, carry home with their notes.

In New York, I cook a lot of Moroccan food. I keep a *couscousière* on the shelf that used to hold the madeleine mold, and then the Swedish pancake skillet and the French crêpe pan and the Swiss fondue set and the electric wok that my husband's secretary sent for Christmas during a year when I was stir-frying everything in sesame oil — something I gave up because stir-frying was always over in a few fraught seconds and did nothing at all for my writing. The cooking that helps my writing is slow cooking, the kind of cooking where you take control of your ingredients so that whatever it is you're making doesn't run away with you, the way words can run away with you in a muddled or unruly sentence. Cooking like that — nudging my disordered thoughts into the stately measure of, say, a good risotto simmering slowly in a homemade broth — gives me confidence and at least the illusion of clarity. And I find that for clarity, the kind that actually lasts until I'm back at my desk, poised over a sentence with my red marker, there is nothing to equal a couscous steaming in its colander pot, with the smell of cumin and coriander rising with the steam. That's when the words I was sure I'd lost come slipping into my head, one by one, and with them even the courage to dip my fingers in and separate the grains.

Some of the food I learned to cook in Morocco didn't translate to New York. I have yet to find a hen in New York with fertilized eggs still inside it — a delicacy that the Meknasi would produce for their guests in moments of truly serious hospitality — not at the halal markets on Atlantic Avenue or even at International Poultry, on Fifty-fourth Street, poulterer to the Orthodox carriage trade. I cannot imagine slaughtering a goat on Central Park West and then skinning it on the sidewalk, if for no reason other than that I'm an ocean away from the old *f'qui* who could take that skin before it stiffened and stretch it into a nearly transparent head for a clay drum with a personal prayer baked into it. I have never again squatted on my heels, knees apart and back straight, for the hours it takes to sift wheat through a wooden sieve and then slap water into it for a flat-bread dough, though in the course of various assignments I have made chapati with Ugandan Asian immigrants in London, stirred mealie-mealie with Bushmen in Botswana, and rolled pâte feuilletée with Slovenian autoworkers in the projects of Södertälje, Sweden. And I am still waiting for permission to dig a charcoal pit in Central Park for the baby lamb that I will then smother in mint and cumin, cover with earth, and bake to such tenderness that you could scoop it out and eat it with your fingers.

But when I'm starting a piece about politics, especially French politics, I will often begin by preserving the lemons for a chicken tagine, perhaps because a forkful of good tagine inevitably takes me back to the home of the French-speaking sheik whose wives taught me how to make it (to the sound of Tom Jones singing "Delilah" on a shortwave radio), and from there to the small restaurant in Paris where I ate my first tagine outside Morocco, and from *there* to the flat of a surly French politician named Jean-Pierre Chevènement, who lived near the restaurant, and who unnerved me entirely during our one interview by balancing cups of espresso on the breasts of a hideous brass coffee table that appeared to be cast as a woman's torso, while barking at me about French nuclear policy. Similarly, I make choucroute whenever I'm starting a piece that has to do with music, because my first proper choucroute — the kind where you put fresh sauerkraut through five changes of cold water, squeeze it dry, strand by strand, and then braise it in gin and homemade stock, with a ham hock and smoked pork and sausages buried inside it — was a labor of love for the eightieth birthday of the composer George Perle; and since then the smell of sausage, gin, and sauerkraut mingling in my oven has always reminded me of the impossible art of composition, and set my standards at the level of his luminous woodwind suites.

On the other hand, when I write about art I like to cook a rabbit. My first rabbit was also, unhappily, my daughter's pet rabbit, and I cooked it with understandable misgiving, one summer in the Vaucluse, after an old peasant sorcerer who used to come over during the full moon to do the ironing took it from its hutch and presented it to her, freshly slaughtered and stuffed with rosemary, on the morning of her first birthday, saying that once she ate it she would have her friend with her "forever." We had named the rabbit Julien Nibble, in honor of our summer neighbor Julien Levy, a man otherwise known as the dealer who had introduced Ernst and Gorky and most of the great Surrealists to New York, and my daughter, who is thirty-one now, has refused to eat rabbit since we told her the story, when she was six or seven. But I have kept on cooking rabbit, changing recipes as the art world changes, and always asking myself what Julien would have made of those changes, and, of course, whether he would have liked the dinner. There was the saddle of rabbit in a cognac-cream sauce that smoothed out my clotted thoughts about a middle-aged Italian painter with what I'd called "an unrequited sense of history." There was the lapin niçoise, with olives, garlic, and tomatoes, that saw me through the first paragraphs of a story about the politics of public sculpture in the South Bronx. There was the rich, bitter rabbit ragout — a recipe from the Croatian grandmother of the Berlin artist Renata Stih — that got me started after a couple of earthquakes hit Assisi, shattering the frescoes on the ceiling of San Francesco into a million pieces. Dishes like these become invocations, little rituals you invent for yourself, in the hope that your life and your work will eventually taste the same.

Good cooking is much easier to master than good writing. But great cooking is something different, and during the years that I've stood at my stove, stirring and sprinkling and tasting, waiting for a sauce to thicken and a drab sentence to settle — if not precisely into echoing, Wordsworthian chords, at least into a turn of phrase that will tell you something you didn't already know about Gerhard Schröder, say, or Silvio Berlusconi — my cooking has leaped ahead by several stars, leaving my writing in the shade. Some dishes have disappeared from my repertoire; tuna curry, for example, has been replaced by the crab-and-spun-coconut-cream curry I first tasted in Hong Kong in 1990 and have been working on ever since, and never mind that the crab in Hong Kong turned out to be doctored tofu, while mine arrives from a Broadway fishmonger with its claws scissoring through the paper bag. Some dishes I've sampled in the course (and cause) of duty are memorable mainly because I've tried so hard to forget them. For one, the crudités I managed to get down at Jean-Marie Le Pen's gaudy and heavily guarded Saint-Cloud villa, with M. Le Pen spinning an outsize plastic globe that held a barely concealed tape recorder, and a couple of Dobermans sniffing at my plate. For another, the rat stew I was served in the Guyana jungle by a visibly unstable interior minister, who had accompanied me there (en route to a "model farm" hacked out of the clearing that had once been Jonestown) in a battered Britten-Norman Islander with no radar or landing lights and a thirteen-year-old air force colonel for a pilot. Some dishes I've repressed, like the cauliflower soup that was ladled into my plate in the dining room of a Belfast hotel just as a terrorist's bomb went off and a wing of the building crumbled, leaving me, the friend whose couch I'd been using for the past week, and a couple of other diners perched in the middle of the sky — "like saints on poles," a man at the next table said, returning to his smoked salmon. Some dishes I've loved but would not risk trying myself, like the pork roast with crackling that Pat Hume, the wife of the politician and soon-to-be Nobel peace laureate John Hume, was in the process of carving, one Sunday lunch in Derry, when a stray bullet shattered the window and lodged in the wall behind her; she didn't stop carving, or even pause in her conversation, which, as I remember, had to do with whether the New York subways were so dangerous as to preclude her visiting with the children while John was in Washington, advising Teddy Kennedy on how to get through a family crisis.

Some dishes I've left in better hands. It's clear to me that I'm no match for the sausage vender at the Frankfurt Bahnhof when it comes to grilling a bratwurst to precisely that stage where the skin is charred and just greasy enough to hold the mustard, and then stuffing the bratwurst into just enough roll to get a grip on, but not *so* much roll that you miss the sport of trying to eat it with anything fewer than four paper napkins and the business section of the *Frankfurter Allgemeine Zeitung*. In the same way, I know that I will never equal my friend Duke, a Herero tribesman known from the Kalahari Desert to the Okavango Delta by his *Dukes of Hazzard* T-shirt, in the art of thickening a sauce for a guinea fowl or a spur-winged goose in the absence of anything resembling flour. Duke was the cook at my fly camp when I was out in the delta researching a piece about "bush housekeeping," and he thickened his sauces there by grating roots he called desert potatoes into boiling fat. But the secret was how many potatoes and, indeed, how to distinguish those potatoes from all the other roots that looked like potatoes but were something you'd rather not ingest. I never found out, because the day we'd planned to fly to the desert to dig some up a tourist camping on a nearby game preserve was eaten by a lion, and my pilot volunteered to collect the bones. Food like that is, as they say in the art world, site-specific.

Take the dish I have called Canard Sauvage Rue du Cherche Midi. I cooked my first wild duck in a kitchen on Cherche Midi in 1982, and during the sixteen years that I lived between Paris and New York I tuned the recipe to what my friends assured me was perfection. But it has never produced the same frisson at my New York dinner table that it did at the picnic table in my Paris garden, if for no reason other than that my neighbors across the court in New York do not punctuate my dinner parties with well-aimed rotten eggs, accompanied by shouts of "Savages!," the way one of my Paris neighbors — a local crank by the name of Jude — always did, and that consequently my New York guests know nothing of the pleasure that comes from pausing between bites of a perfect duck in order to turn a hose full blast on the open window of someone who dislikes them.

Some dishes just don't travel, no matter how obvious or easy they seem. I know this because I tried for a year to duplicate the magical fried chicken known to aficionados as Fernand Point's Poulet Américain — a recipe so simple in itself that no one since that legendary Vienne chef has ever dared to put it on a menu. I have never even attempted to duplicate the spicy chicken stew that the actor Michael Goldman heats up on a Sterno stove in his damp, smelly Paris *cave,* surrounded by the moldy bottles of Lafite and Yquem and Grands Echezeaux that you know he's planning to open as the night wears on. Nor have I attempted the Indonesian rijsttafel — which is basically just a platter of rice with little bowls of condiments and sauces — that my late friend George Hoff, a Dutch kendo master and nightclub bouncer, tossed off one night, in London, after a long and strenuous demonstration that involved raising a long pole and slamming it down to within a centimeter of my husband's head. Or the fish grilled by a group of young Portuguese commandos in the early summer of 1974 — I

was covering their revolution; they were taking a break from it —
over a campfire on a deserted Cabo de São Vicente beach. Or, for
that matter, the s'mores my favorite counselor roasted over a
campfire at Camp Fernwood, in Poland, Maine (and never mind
that I hated Camp Fernwood). Or even popcorn at the movies.

But most things do travel, if you know the secret. A lot of cooks
don't share their secrets, or more often lie, the way my mother-in-
law lied about the proportion of flour to chocolate in her famous
"yum-yum cake," thereby ending whatever relationship we had. *My*
best secret dates from a dinner party at Gracie Mansion when Ed
Koch was the mayor of New York. I had known Koch from his Village Independent Democrat days, when he pretty much starved
unless his mother fed him. But now that he was Hizzoner the
Mayor of New York City he could, as he repeatedly told his guests,
order anything he wanted to eat, no matter what the hour or the
season or inconvenience to a staff best trained in trimming the
crusts off tea sandwiches. The dinner in question got off to an awkward start — "You're Puerto Rican? You don't *look* Puerto Rican"
is how, if I remember correctly, he greeted the beautiful curator
of the Museo del Barrio — and it was frequently interrupted by
phone calls from his relatives, who seemed to be having some sort
of business crisis. But everybody agreed that the food was delicious. It wasn't elaborate food, or even much different from what
you'd cook for yourself on a rainy night at home: pasta in a tomato
sauce, good steaks, and hot-chocolate sundaes for dessert. But the
meal itself was so oddly remarkable that I went back to the kitchen
afterward and asked the cook how he'd made it, and he told me,
"Whatever Ed likes, whatever he says he never got as a kid, I double
the quantity. I doubled the Parmesan on the pasta. I *tripled* the hot-
chocolate sauce on the ice cream." Ed's principle was "More is
more."

It's not a principle I would apply to writing, but it's definitely the
one I cook by now, on my way from excess in the kitchen to a
manuscript where less is more. If my couscous is now the best couscous on the Upper West Side, it's because, with a nod to Ed, I take
my favorite ingredients from every couscous I've ever eaten — the
chickpeas and raisins and turnips and carrots and almonds and
prunes — double the quantity, toss them into the broth, and then
go back to my desk and cut some adverbs. I put too many eggs in
my matzo balls, too much basil in my pesto, too much saffron in

my paella. I have no patience with the kind of recipe that says "1/4 teaspoon thyme" or "2 ounces chopped pancetta." I drown my carrots in chervil, because I like the way chervil sweetens carrots. I even drown my halibut in chervil, because I like what it does to the reduction of wine and cream in a white fish sauce — though, now that I think of it, when I'm on a bandwagon, when I'm really mad at the world I'm writing about and the people in it, I will usually switch to sorrel.

The first time I cooked halibut on a bed of sorrel, I was in New York, laboring over a long piece about liberation theology in South America and, in particular, about a young priest whose parish was in a favela with the unlikely name of Campos Elísios, about an hour north of Rio de Janeiro. I wasn't mad at my Brazilian priest — I loved the priest. I was mad at the bishop of Rio, who was on the priest's back for ignoring orders to keep his parishioners out of politics. At first, I thought I could solve the problem by taking the afternoon off to make moqueca, which was not only my favorite Brazilian dish but, in my experience, an immensely soothing one — a gratin of rice, shrimp, lime, and coconut cream, served with (and this is essential, if you're serious) a sprinkling of toasted manioc flour — which provides the comforts of a brandade without the terrible nursery taste of cod and potatoes mushed together. I made moqueca a lot in Rio, because I was angry a lot in Rio. Angry at the poverty, at the politics, at the easy brutality of people in power and the desperate brutality of people without it. But it's hard to make my moqueca in New York unless you have a source of manioc flour, and the closest I came to that was the seven-foot-long flexible straw funnel leaning against a beam in my living room — an object devised by the Amerindians, centuries ago, to squeeze the poison out of manioc so that they wouldn't die eating it. I had wasted the better part of the afternoon on Amsterdam Avenue, searching for manioc flour, when I happened to pass a greengrocer with a special on sorrel. I bought him out, and a couple of hours later I discovered that the patient preparation of sorrel — the blanching and chopping and puréeing and braising in butter — had taken the diatribe in my head and turned it into a story I could tell.

There are, of course, moments in writing when even the most devoted cook stops cooking. Those are the moments that, in sex, are called "transporting" but in journalism are known as an empty fridge, an irritable family, and the beginnings of a first-name friendship with the woman who answers the phone at Empire Szechuan. When I am lost in one of those moments, I subsist on takeout and jasmine tea, or if takeout is truly beyond me — the doorbell, the change, the tip, the mismatched chopsticks, the arguments when I won't share — on chili-lime tortilla chips and Diet Coke. If the hour is decent, I'll mix a bloody mary or a caipirinha like the ones that the priest and I used to sneak in the kitchen of the parish house of Campos Elísios on evenings when the Seventh-day Adventists would arrive at the favela in force, pitch a tent in a field, and call the poor to salvation through amps rented by the hour from a Copacabana beach band. But moments like those are rare.

My normal state when beginning a piece is panic, and by now my friends and family are able to gauge that panic by the food I feed them. This past spring, in the course of a few weeks of serious fretting over the lead of a story about an Afghan refugee, I cooked a small Thanksgiving turkey, two Christmas rib roasts, and an Easter lamb. I cooked them with all the fixings, from the corn-bread-and-sausage stuffing to the Yorkshire pudding and horseradish cream — though I stopped short of the Greek Easter cheesecake that three cookbooks assured me had to be made in a clean flowerpot. My excuse was that I'd worked through Thanksgiving and been snowbound in Berlin through Christmas, and, of course, it *was* nearly Easter when I began my holiday cooking. Easter, actually, went well. No one mentioned the fact that we were celebrating it on a Saturday night, or, for that matter, that at noon on Sunday we were due, as always, for our annual Easter lunch at the home of some old friends. But Thanksgiving in April brought strained smiles all around, especially since my next-door neighbor had already cooked a lovely Thanksgiving dinner for me in February. And while my first Christmas was a big success — one of the guests brought presents and a box of chocolate mushrooms left over from a bûche de Noël — my second Christmas, a few days later, ended badly when my daughter suggested that I "see someone" to discuss my block, my husband announced to a roomful of people that I was "poisoning" him with saturated fats, and my son-in-law accused me of neglecting the dog. But I did end up with a paragraph. In fact, I thought it was a pretty good paragraph. And I finished the piece the way I usually finish pieces, with notes and cookbooks piled on the floor, working for a few hours, sorting the Postits on my desk into meaningless, neat stacks, and then heading for my big stove to do more cooking — in this case, to add the tomatoes to a Bolognese sauce, because my last paragraph was too tricky to handle without a slow, comfortable Italian sauce, and I'd been using Bolognese for tricky characters since I first tackled the subject of François Mitterrand, in a story on his inauguration, in 1981.

It seems to me that there is something very sensible about keeping your memories in the kitchen, with the pots and the spices, especially in New York. They take up no space; they do not crash with your computer; and they collect the voice that you can't quite hear — in tastes and smells and small gestures that, with any luck, will eventually start to sound like you. I'm not in New York right now. The dinner I was cooking twenty-five pages ago — the clam-and-pork stew with plenty of garlic and piri-piri that I first ate in a Portuguese fishermen's tavern near Salem, the day I tacked wrong and sailed my boyfriend's sixteen-footer into a very big ketch and broke his mast and, with it, whatever interest he had in me — is not the dinner I am cooking today, at a farmhouse in Umbria. My stove is smaller here (though my pots are bigger). I do not write easily about myself. I am not as tasty or exotic as the characters I usually choose. My first attempt at anything like autobiography was a thinly disguised short story, and it was returned with the gentle suggestion that I replace myself with someone "a little less like the kind of person we know everything about already." But twenty years later I did manage to produce a reminiscence of sorts. It was about my mother and my daughter and about being a feminist, and it ended where I am writing now, in Umbria, looking across a pond to a field of wheat and watching a family of pheasants cross my garden. It occurred to me, worrying over *this* ending — not quite a panic but enough of a problem to have already produced a Sardinian saffron-and-sausage pasta, a cold pepper soup with garlic croutons, nightly platters of chicken-liver-and-anchovy bruschetta, pressed through my grandmother's hand mill, and twenty jars of brandied apricot jam — that I might possibly solve the problem by cooking the same dinner that I'd cooked then. It turns out to be one meal I can't remember.

BEN METCALF

Wooden Dollar

FROM HARPER'S MAGAZINE

I have come to debase the coinage.
— Diogenes

1

I AM WRONGED by the United States Mint, as are all those Americans who might have hoped that the "golden" coin stamped with a likeness of the Indian maid Sacajawea was meant not merely to inspire but to represent them, and who dared to believe by the close of the twentieth century that the Mint's worst work lay well in its past. Buffalo nickels, which seemed a denial of the fact that we had killed off most of the buffaloes and stocked our boutique ranches with the remainder, and their Indian Head faces, which likewise seemed to imply that we had never poisoned or starved or hung or gutshot the greater share of the Indians and ranched them out too, were themselves all but extinct and corralled in the dusty coin sets our grandfathers used to keep. Walking Liberty half-dollars were confined there as well, along with Standing Liberty quarters and Seated Liberty dimes and varied treatments of Liberty's detached head. I assumed that the Mint had learned to hold itself to likenesses of party hacks murdered by their own countrymen while still in office, or by time and the bottle once retired, and to stray from this plan only after hard thought, lest we be forced to ignore another Susan B. Anthony at great public outlay. Had it done so the Mint might yet have created the same Sacajawea dollar we disregard today, and are unable in some places even to exchange for candy, but it would not then have had the foolishness to argue that the figure on the coin, a Shoshone girl enslaved by the Minne-tarees and sold if not gambled away to a French-Canadian fur trader later employed by Meriwether Lewis and William Clark, was a beacon of aid and virtue, wholly free of taint and flaw; that is to say, in no real sense an American.

In the three years that the Sacajawea dollar has been among us, our government has spent the equal of 67 million Sacajaweas to persuade us to use just one of them, and the effort has failed so thoroughly that the Mint has for now stopped pressing the coin and at least one congressman, a Senator Byron Dorgan of North Dakota, has announced a personal stake in the native girl's rescue. The senator seems to think that she was a resident of, and not a captive in, the territories his state now comprises, and I do not therefore rate his help very highly, but I agree that the coin is wor-thy of salvage, if only because it is the first with the potential to re-flect something of the ordinary American since those days when the Mercury dime seemed to embody, no doubt by chance, his penchant for haste, and the fickleness of his desires, and the un-holy speed with which the national industry would abandon his blanched and hollow husk. The Mint has heretofore imagined that the American and his deeds must be whitewashed or idealized or avoided altogether if its product is to be welcomed into the na-tion's pockets, but the American, despite a clear taste for being pandered to, can tolerate some shame, and he does not care to be hoodwinked: had the Mercury dime displayed the word HASTE above its principal's head, and had the Buffalo nickel read DEAD BUFFALO on one side and DEAD INDIAN on the other, these coins might still be in demand today. I cannot remove the LIB-ERTY that floats like a rain cloud above Sacajawea's head, and I cannot retrieve the tax dollars squandered on her promotion as a worthless cartoon saint, but I can, and with relative ease, sketch a portrait of her as an American everywoman and possibly even as a human being. Whether my fellow citizens will find this of use, and come to see a suggestion of themselves in the dull relief of a dollar shunned too soon, it is beyond my power to say.

2

Sacajawea was by birth a Snake, or Lemhi-Shoshone, and prior to her capture by the Minnetarees at the age of ten or so, she made her home in what is now the state of Idaho, which for many years had a legal drinking age lower than, and therefore amenable to the youth of, its neighbors. The youth of Sacajawea's day (she was born in or around 1790) also would make for Idaho with an eye toward violence and the theft of local women, though often enough the Shoshones would transport their wives and daughters into western Montana so as to place them more directly in the path of the marauders, an accommodation, I believe, unique to that time. The Minnetarees, situated just upriver from historic Bismarck, lived in a sort of five-towns format with the Wattersoons and the Mandans, the latter of whom had learned from protracted defeat at the hands of the Sioux to employ a rhetoric of peace with all who came near. The Minnetarees claimed likewise to attack only those who had done them grave insult, yet since nearly everyone within a day's ride and even as far away as western Montana evidently had, Lewis and Clark were obliged, upon their arrival in the autumn of 1804, to settle a dispute now and then so as to maintain a climate suitable to the procurement of necessities. When not courting slaughter these villagers practiced a species of free love (or prostitution: the record is unclear), and there seems to have been a steady stream of visitors to the expedition's fort with offers of a wife or two to be "used for the night," as well as invitations to orgiastic rites related in some fashion to the buffalo hunt. (Clark: "We Sent a man to this Medisan Dance last night, they gave him 4 Girls.") So comfortable did the whites become with the arrangement that when an Indian man beat and stabbed his wife for the very behavior he had formerly encouraged in her, Clark simply ordered the company not to fornicate again with this particular woman and advised the couple to "live hapily together in future."

I understand why this sort of thing is kept out of the schoolbooks, but might not some of our more bored and poverty-stricken adults find themselves on familiar ground here? Are such scenes to be tolerated in our trailer communities, and on our television sets, and at times on our own patios, but recast in the national pageant with all-wise chiefs and noble-hippie braves and Land O'Lakes maidens and clean tepees? Sacajawea was several months pregnant when the group first encountered her as the wife, or property, of the trader Touissant Charbonneau, and she may have opted out of, or been excused from, the round robins, but we gain little by the

insistence that she was untutored in her captors' ways, and I suspect that the innocent dignity with which she has been shellacked
in our popular histories serves not some larger truth but rather the
coward's disinclination to offend. I myself owe my presence in this
world to the fact that some fifty years after Sacajawea had left it
my great-great-great-grandfather Joshua thought nothing, or not
enough, of the offense he would give his mother and father by
marrying one Elmira Grush, an Indian of uncertain age and origin, believed possibly to be a Chickasaw or an Illini or a variety
of Sioux, the couple being driven for a spell to flee the judgment
of southern Illinois for land in Minnesota where they were not
known. The family took no umbrage at the introduction into the
line of Indian blood, about which said line has been either overly
proud or entirely ignorant ever since; the protest stemmed, and
rightly so, from the plain and visible truth that Elmira Grush was
pregnant at the time of the wedding, most likely with another
man's child.

So Sacajawea appears before us: with child, and although by
common courtesy the child is agreed to be Charbonneau's, we
must admit that the father, but for the grace of God, might have
been any number of men with the indelicacy required to impreg-
nate what was, after all, a girl of only (and here we must extend another courtesy) fourteen or fifteen. My own people, and I suppose
a great deal of these United States, have in general lacked neither
the young girls nor the indelicacy, and I think it only sensible and
fair that they come to know of their newfound place in the sym-
bology of the republic. In lieu of Sacajawea's LIBERTY, a concept
that figures scarcely more in their lives than it did in hers, they
might imagine the words TEEN and MOTHER.

3

When Lewis wrote of Sacajawea that "if she has enough to eat and a
few trinkets to wear I believe she would be perfectly content anywhere" he meant not to imply that she had achieved the Buddha-
like bliss of which all natives are mistakenly thought to be possessed but that she seemed to pass the journey in an emotionless
daze unbroken even by the thought that she would soon be among
her own people. Although her stupor may have been fed by the

knowledge that her own people lived in a manner no kinder to their women than did the Minnetarees and the Mandans, I tend to think that she preferred simply to save her energy until there arose yet another chance to cover for the spinelessness and patent idiocy of her husband, or owner, Charbonneau. Hardly a figure in history can touch this man for sheer lack of worth. After an initial fit failed to secure him more money for the hire of his meager skills as an interpreter, and very nearly resulted in his and Sacajawea's removal from the roster, he seems to have busied himself with the search for new forms of delay and disaster to visit upon his employers. On those days when a milked injury would not excuse him from honest work or brisk travel, he contrived to get himself chased by a bear; or to misplace a horse; or to imperil a boat and several souls in the wide Missouri; or to risk doom to all by his failure to describe properly the movements of the Indians; or to let a horse throw its load and be stripped of what it still carried by the locals, inspiring in the by then enraged Lewis a threat to "birn their houses"; or to lose yet another horse; or to tip yet another canoe; or to provoke, in countless smaller ways, disgust and fury and chagrin among men already hampered by "Venerials Complaints" connected to their visit with the Mandans and the Minnetarees. That this Charbonneau was a nineteenth-century foreigner I consider a mere accident: he was in action and in purpose an American of the televised lower class, with a wife no less of our time and of that stripe, in that she performed so well the duties of what today we might call an ENABLER.

Almost as soon as the journey began, Sacajawea undertook a great show of her usefulness, possibly at first to compensate for Charbonneau's blunders and afterward, once it became clear to all that this man's moral debt was unpayable, simply to distract from them. She seems to have dug up a good deal of the topsoil along the route in an effort to find edible roots with which to impress Lewis and Clark, and a number of these are detailed in the journals as if they were rare and precious gems, which is no doubt how she presented them in her sign language. Where there were no clods to overturn, and no moccasins to stitch together in a feeble effort to defeat the nettles with Indian know-how, and no landmarks to point out in a display of her acquaintance with the terrain, she kept an uneasy eye on Charbonneau, especially when the party was afloat. Sacajawea's boosters never tire of the fact that one evening in May of 1805 she saved, from a boat full of water and about to sink, several items of value, which earned her a kind word in the journals; less often remarked upon is that Charbonneau, whom Lewis called "perhaps the most timid waterman in the world," was at the boat's helm that night, though he had no call to be, and through his incompetence had let the water in, and by his panic would have caused everyone on board to drown had not a man in the bow "threatened to shoot him instantly if he did not take hold of the rudder and do his duty." Under such conditions, Sacajawea's retrieval of those objects within her reach was no less to be expected, and no more an act of courage, than was Charbonneau's tearful if abrupt retrieval of the helm.

Sacajawea surely profited by the comparison with her keeper, and had he been gunned down in the boat I have little confidence that she would have survived the trip herself, so heavy a BURDEN did she become to the group as it penetrated the great Northwest, and so enormous a DRAIN ON RESOURCES. In the month of June 1805 alone, having acquired a sickness of which Lewis managed to cure himself in a matter of hours, she pestered those around her with such zeal that I am frankly surprised she saw July. "Sahcah-gagweâ our Indian woman verry sick," Clark wrote on the tenth; four days later he recorded that she had been "complaining all night & excessively bad this morning"; by the fifteenth she was still "sick & low spirited." So persistent was this illness, and so unlike the ordinary flu her colleagues had weathered handily, that Lewis assumed it to stem from "an obstruction of the mensis" and chivalrously diverted, as did Clark, a good amount of attention toward her cure. Those Americans on feigned disability will please note that this woman managed to parlay a simple bellyache into a week's vacation during one of the voyage's most difficult legs and could not be convinced to pronounce herself well enough to dig for roots again until treated to the opium I presume was meant for those who had been struck by arrows or by bullets or by bears. Once upright she needed only a few days to locate yet another chance to weigh down and endanger the crew by her tendency, or desire, to fall apart: as a flash flood began to fill a ravine she became "much scared and nearly without motion," and Clark was forced to drop several valuables, including his best compass, in order to push her and her child up the hill to safety. Charbonneau pulled at the other end, perhaps aware that he could no more afford to lose his apologist than she her foil, and together the men got her back to camp, where, sodden and cold, she was quickly availed of what spirits were needed to dissuade her from a relapse of the previous fortnight's "severe indisposition."

Whether Charbonneau beat Sacajawea for this sort of behavior, or for some other sort, I cannot say, but it is widely held that she was a VICTIM OF ABUSE, and at least once on the journey Clark swallowed any anger he himself may have felt toward her and stayed the interpreter's hand with a promise of similar treatment should the practice continue. I do not know that my great-great-great-grandfather ever struck Elmira Grush, but there is cause to suspect that he murdered her; and certainly their descendants, as well as the many other Americans handicapped by poor finances and a poorer choice of mate, have amassed among them an impressive number of hours in family court, where again and again they have read into the record further installments of a saga that has clearly shaped, if not actually defined, this nation but has thus far been denied representation on the currency in which the lawyers are paid. To the abused, as much as to the teen mothers, and the enablers, and the perpetual burdens on our health-care system, the Sacajawea dollar now waits to speak.

4

Sacajawea was a government subcontractor, in that she was not paid directly by Lewis and Clark but toiled instead under Charbonneau, who received "500$ 33-1/3 cents" for the journey and most likely kept even the fraction for himself. In our own time a government subcontractor is often paid a criminally large sum for slipshod work that worsens, if it does not threaten outright, the lives of his peers, and although the last part of this equation might be shown to hold in Sacajawea's case, she was so roughly used on the financial end that the overall parallel collapses and we must be content to deem her a mere FEDERAL EMPLOYEE. My father, himself a descendant of Elmira Grush, has twice been on the federal payroll, the first time being a halfhearted stint in the Syphilis Eradication Program (circa 1965) and the last being when he took a job some years back as a mailman, or rather when he finished the United States Postal Service's paid training course and then promptly quit, his objective clear: to take the government's money but to avoid the humiliation, or even the simple locomotion, implied by actual work. His main words on the subject were, as I recall, "I'm not going to deliver the fucking mail," though he later admitted that if what he had seen on the training course was any hint, he would hardly have been expected to deliver, or to do, much at all.

The goldbricks and incompetents who man the lower decks of our federal workforce might be pleased to learn that their distaste for effort, and their want of skill, and their fear of blame, and their failure to convey crucial information up the chain of command, and their devotion to the spoils system, all are well mirrored in the half-smile of the girl on the coin, as is the deplorable oversight that won them their posts in the first place. Lewis and Clark hired Sacajawea, or allowed her to accompany Charbonneau, because of a belief, fostered in them by the Frenchman, that she would prove handy when they met up with the Shoshones, whom they intended to employ, as we might employ Red Caps on an Amtrak platform, to portage their boats and baggage across the mountains to the Columbia River. By the time I attended school her role had become inflated somewhat, and my classmates and I were led to understand that in addition to her duties as an interpreter for the party, which was taken to mean that she had befriended and debriefed every native from the Black Hills to the Pacific Ocean, she was its primary guide through the wilderness and, by obvious virtue of being the sole woman and Indian along, its guide through the moral and spiritual unknowns as well. Not even the Mint will call her a guide today, so badly does the notion conform to the historical record, and so falsely does the thought strike any sensible adult that a kidnapped and terrified child would possess the capacity to take detailed mental notes on the topography while en route to a distant and uncertain future, and so clearly does the reader of the journals come to see that if Sacajawea had indeed served as a guide to Lewis and Clark they and their party would directly have vanished, and precious time would have been lost in our campaign to diminish and destroy the Indians of the Northwest.

What small guidance Sacajawea did offer proved unsound

enough to suggest that her work for the federal government aided
far less in the fall of her race than might be supposed of the compromised ambassadress in our schoolbooks, and on occasion her
judgment erred so badly as to make one almost believe that she
had resolved to see the members of the expedition pulped in their
canoes. In late July of 1805, Lewis thought the Missouri too gentle
as it wound south past the Big Belt Mountains, and he feared a
"falls or obstruction . . . notwithstanding the information of the Indian woman to the contrary who assures us that the river continues
much as we see it." The next day saw the river not continue as such
but split into three separate streams, and even the choice of the
least treacherous of these did not spare Lewis the horror he had
imagined despite Sacajawea's guess: (August 1) "here the toe line
of our canoe broke in the shoot of the rapids and swung on the
rocks and had very nearly overset"; (August 3) "the men wer compelled to be a great proportion of their time in the water today;
they have had a severe days labour and are much fortiegued"; (August 6) "Whitehouse had been thrown out . . . and the canoe had
rubed him and pressed him to the bottom as she passed over him
and had the water been inches shallower must inevitably have
crushed him to death." Her next gambit, just two days after the
cruelty to Whitehouse, was perhaps better informed, or luckier,
but Lewis was no longer inclined to trust her, if he ever had been:
in response to her assurances that she knew the area, and that he
would soon find her people "on this river or on the river immediately west of it's source," the vagueness of which seemed to exasperate him, he "determined to proceed . . . to the Columbia; and
down that river untill I found the Indians . . . or some others, who
have horses if it should cause me a trip of one month."

Lewis found a Shoshone warrior within three days of that statement, and within five he was engaged with a Shoshone chief,
Cameahwait, in a banter so full of cultural and geographic detail
that the reader of the journals is compelled to flip back through
the pages in an effort to learn where Sacajawea came in; she had
not, nor did her absence seem to impede Lewis as he carried out a
subtle negotiation for Cameahwait's friendship and assistance, and
explained that there would be guns and ammunition in it for the
chief if he complied, and shame and empty-handedness if he did
not, and that "among whitemen it was considered disgracefull to
lye or entrap an enemy by falsehood." By the time Sacajawea ar-

rived there remained only to repeat the offer of firearms, and to lie about the purpose of the journey (which now became "to examine and find out a more direct way to bring merchandize to them"), and to arrange the details of the portage, all of which was put at risk when she recognized Cameahwait as her brother, and indulged herself in an emotional outburst, and was thereafter unable to keep the personal situation from affecting her work. Cameahwait, who was "moved, though not in the same degree," stuck to the question of the guns, which he had hoped to receive up front, and although he seemed to offer what men and horses were needed, Lewis and Clark might have known better than to place their faith in a promise made across four disparate languages and three untried translators, one of whom was in tears. We are inclined to think inefficiency in our government a recent innovation until made aware of how this team actually functioned: Sacajawea, through her sobs, would render in the Hidatsa tongue what Cameahwait had said in the Shoshone; and then Charbonneau would work up some version of the Hidatsa in his frontier French; and then a man named Labiche would convert what little of the original message had made it through to the French, as well as whatever had been added along the way, into English for Lewis and Clark; and then back they would all go the other way. I cannot imagine that what the explorers took away from their end of the conversation bore an especially close relation to what Cameahwait took away from his, and when, a week later, the chief made ready to use the gathered men and horses to help not the expedition but rather his own half-starved people, I am surprised that he did not meet Lewis's chastisement with either confused laughter or violent rage.

Sacajawea had been sent to the Shoshone village "to haisten the return of the Indians with their horses to this place," and if Cameahwait had not heard through the cacophony of the interpreters what he had "promised" to do she may have deprived him of the excuse of ignorance, but she failed to impress strongly enough upon *her own brother* that he was expected to *keep* said promise, and in this dereliction, or lack of ability, we can gauge her true merit as a civil servant. Lewis covered for the error with a forceful return to the matter of the guns and saw both personnel and accoutrements safely removed to the Columbia, by which they would eventually reach the sea. There the party would learn that a whale had climbed up onto a nearby beach and killed itself, and

Sacajawea would demand that she be allowed to see the "monstrous fish." Perhaps she did so in order to establish that a woman had the same right to knowledge and discovery as any man, and if the promotion of such an idea would bring further attention to the coin I cannot in good conscience object, but it is my personal belief that she was far less akin to the feminist of today than to the federal worker who shirks, or is unequal to, assigned responsibility, and whose continued employment admits of no link between performance and reward, and who, in Sacajawea's place, would have understood the chance to view the whale as a relatively straightforward perk.

5

Lewis on Sacajawea's people, the Lemhi-Shoshones:

> They seldom correct their children particularly the boys . . . they give as a reason that it cows and breaks the sperit of the boy to whip him, and that he never recovers his independence of mind after he is grown. They treat their women but with little rispect, and compel them to perform every species of drudgery . . . the man dose little else except attend his horses hunt and fish. the man considers himself degraded if he is compelled to walk any distance . . . the chastity of their women is not held in high estimation, and the husband will for a trifle barter the companion of his bead for a night or longer . . .

Aside from the refusal to whip the boys lest their souls be shattered in the process, this passage might well describe how my own family generally conducts itself today, 140 years after Elmira Grush married Joshua Metcalf and 130 years after she succumbed to the rat poison he may or may not have employed to be rid of her. Whether this was murder by his or by someone else's hand, or was a careless mishap, or was simply another southern Illinois suicide, I cannot say with any certainty, but I do find it odd that Joshua's pious and judgmental father had disappeared just three months prior to the wedding and that the rat poison had been put into milk, which Elmira Grush drank regularly but Joshua knew his sons to despise. Overt concern for the children has not marked the family since, nor has it emerged as a particularly strong trait elsewhere among a people famed for selfishness and inattentive to, if not plainly disdainful of, those who are by nature helpless and needy and small.

In this regard the Sacajawea dollar might be thought of as a medallion issued in remembrance of every UNFIT PARENT in the land, for it will be noticed that the girl on the coin carries with her an infant, the first of its kind to appear on our money and the last, I hope, to suffer such a hardship for the opportunity.

Jean-Baptiste Charbonneau is depicted in Christian repose, his round cheek nestled against the nape of his mother's neck, but there is a clear downward turn to the tiny mouth, and the eyes, although shut, do not strike me as quite restful; if I did not know what the Mint's intentions were in the hire of Ms. Glenna Goodacre to design the coin, I might think the little boy frightened or sick. He was surely acquainted with fear, as any child would be who had fought his way out of the womb only to find himself baked in the hot prairie sun by day, and frozen by the pitiless gusts at night, and forced to run rapids in a poorly built and ineptly manned canoe, and dragged across mountains when no water could be found to risk him in, and dangled before paranoid rattlesnakes and enraged bears, and nearly stomped to death by a confused buffalo, and displayed to the natives as proof of the party's humanity when in fact his very presence on the trek bespoke a certain coldness of heart. For his service as a human shield, he was introduced not merely to fear but to sickness, and only by miracle did he not thenceforth reside in a shallow grave somewhere west of the Bitterroot Mountains, having developed, in May of 1806, a malady so unkind that I wonder if it did not inspire Ms. Goodacre's choice to enlarge his head on the coin to unnatural proportions. An insect had got him, or a rat, or a food allergy, or an airborne germ he was too weak to fend off after so many months spent stiff with terror, and while the fever tried to take him, his neck and jaw became grotesquely swollen and remained so for several days, until the evil beneath his skin burst forth in an "ugly imposthume" just below the ear. That he survived this indignity in no way excuses the mother who brought it upon him, any more than the absence of a Mandan child-care program excuses her for the countless lesser afflictions he endured on the trip. He was probably two, after all, before he learned that a lungful of air was not supposed to have a mosquito in it, and the closed eyes on the coin may have chanced upon another historical truth: the gnats tended to pool there, and an infant would not have known, or been able, to brush them away.

Clark called Jean-Baptiste "Pomp," or "Pompey," after an over-

blown style of dance the little boy had devised, I suspect, in order
to catch the eye of anyone in a position to save his life. Lewis, toward the end of the journey, was distracted from the boy's plight by
an obvious hatred for Indians as well as by the gunshot wound he
had received, perhaps inadvertently, from one Peter Cruzatte, who
had threatened earlier to shoot Charbonneau and who, for all anyone knows, may have followed Lewis along the Natchez Trace
three years later and finished the job. It therefore fell upon Clark
to perform a rite familiar to those many thousands of modern
Americans who have put a child in danger and been caught at it, or
who have themselves been the unfortunate child: with no objec-
tion from either parent, he "offered" to remove Pomp from their
care, or lack thereof, and to raise him properly back in St. Louis.
Clark is usually said to have "adopted" the little boy because he had
grown to love him as he would a child of his own blood, but I think
it more apt to say that he took him on as a FOSTER CHILD and was
motivated to do so less by love than by a simple concern for human
decency; certainly love could not have been a factor when, six years
later, he "adopted" Sacajawea's next product, a little girl named
Lisette, sight unseen. What became of Lisette is not recorded, but
the boy on the coin is known to have received a fine education,
which he then proceeded, in the current American fashion, to
waste. For a time he toured Europe as a *bon sauvage,* with a Prussian
aristocrat for a sponsor, or a pimp, and when he tired of Europe, or
Europe tired of him, he returned to America and found work
among the fur traders, as had his father before him. He is said to
have served as a scout with the United States Army during the Mexican land grab of 1846 and to have taken part in both the California gold rush and a later variant to the north, neither of which
profited him a great deal and the latter of which, in or around
1866, killed him. Before he died he is believed to have worked for
a short time as a PRISON GUARD.

6

I have heard it charged against this coin that the face is host to a
number of flaws: that a Shoshone-Bannock, and not a Lemhi-Shoshone, modeled for the frieze, and so the cheekbones are all
wrong; and that the model was a woman in her twenties and not a
girl of fifteen, which may also have affected the cheekbones; and

that the girl on the dollar carries her child in what appears to be a sack, whereas a Lemhi-Shoshone would have strapped him to a board. What are such petty mistakes next to the enormous lie the Mint has furthered? I have heard it said that the coin depicts a figure of some mystery, for we cannot know if Sacajawea died in 1812 of "putrid fever," or from a long illness quickened by Lisette's birth, or if in fact she did not die in 1812 at all but walked out on Charbonneau, and lived with a goodhearted Comanche man, and bore him strong children, and at last made it home to the Shoshones (home by then being land on a reservation in Wyoming), where she lived as a wise and honored elder among her people until death took her peacefully in 1884. I am of the "putrid fever" camp, but what matter how she died if we cannot allow for the possibility that she ever truly lived, and was no stranger to weakness and futility, and might have put more thought into the welfare of her son, and might have concentrated better at work, and might have covered less for the man who beat and enslaved her and ensured, if the Shoshones and the Minnetarees and the Mandans had not seen to this already, that she would be every bit the casualty of her own time that the modern American is of his?

If my cousin can afford the tank of gas, and if he is not presently incarcerated, and if his work schedule at the nursing home or on the railroad or in the cab of a tractor-trailer permits, and if no one remains at home for him to assault or neglect, and if the drink or the methamphetamine or the ennui has not robbed him entirely of the will to participate in the larger culture, he might make his way to one of the countless NASCAR racetracks that disfigure the landscape, there to learn that the Mint has now deemed these venues proper to a wider distribution of, and perhaps even a popular regard for, the Sacajawea dollar. Traditionally the newer currencies have been hawked through the banks, but I believe the Mint is well aware, despite its daft hagiography of Sacajawea, that the person it must reach with this coin tends to associate "bank" with "missed loan payment" and "foreclosure," and will not go near one except in somebody else's car. Can it honestly be chance that earlier deals to help the coin were struck with Wal-Mart and the International House of Pancakes? Perhaps the Mint might next consider, once it has replaced the word LIBERTY above the head of this poor and put-upon teenage mother, the commissaries of our nation's prisons.

FREDERIC MORTON

A Delivery for Fred Astaire

FROM HARPER'S MAGAZINE

THE FIRST THING to do after climbing down the steep steps into
the bakery cellar is to look at the work sheet Mr. Frosch hangs on
the wall for us. I always wince a little in advance. But I am not prepared for what Mr. Frosch has scrawled on the bottom of a list already heavy with Saturday orders: "15 doz jel donuts (8th ave street
fare tomorro)."

Never mind that his misspelled parenthesis about the street fair
may be a sort of "sorry" for inflicting this on us. Fifteen dozen jelly
doughnuts on top of our normal weekend load! At the end of tonight's shift, the pile that will be facing me in the sink! Not only
the mixing bowls, the cupcake forms, the cake rings, the pie
molds, to soap and scrub and rinse and dry; now I shall also have
to scrape clean that huge vat encrusted with doughnut frying oil.

As for my boss, Bert, the doughnuts threaten his radio-listening
schedule because of the extra heat involved, which in turn requires
the radio-sabotaging fan. So he tries to handle the threat by making the doughnuts first.

In vain. Hours after we have finished them, the sultriness of
their frying persists and combines with the oven's torrid breath.
Steam fogs my glasses. We are soaking in our undershirts. Only the
fan keeps us from suffocation.

That's why he starts to curse Mr. Frosch. Saddling him with child
labor! Bad enough to hire a kid sixteen, worse yet to pick an out-
lander like me, a boy not used to crazy New York summers, let
alone to one hundred goddamn degrees in this crummy cellar!
And no, no goddamn use my protesting I feel fine — something

ever happens to me, on whose goddamn head will it be? His, Bert's! No, tonight, on this goddamn doughnut night, he'll have to wait until the apricot tarts (our final batch) are done before killing the fascist fan.

This fan swings from the ceiling (no other room for it in our cramped cave), cruises through the air like a winged meat slicer, ready to lop off any arm raised too high. And it really is reactionary: its static jams the progressive potential of our radio's shortwave band, yet it never disrupts a single capitalist commercial of any local station on the AM dial. And on this doughnut-ridden night, Bert, stuck with fragile child labor, will have to leave the fan on as long as the oven is on.

Right into a critical broadcasting period. Instead of Bert's beloved Moscow shortwave program, our sooty, wireless set now gives off the bourgeois sounds of WNEW's kitsch. Bert must put up with all that mooning and crooning and Pepsi-Cola jingling until all the apricot tarts are baked through.

Now, the fruit flavor of these tarts is a deliciously nuanced sweet-sour. A dainty scalloping of crust wreathes the filling. They are the most popular pastries in the neighborhood, and Mr. Frosch gets away with charging more for them than he charges for éclairs with more expensive ingredients. These tarts are Bert's pride; therefore he bakes them at the end of the shift so they will be Frosch's freshest offering in the morning. Yet tonight they bedevil him because they take forever in the oven.

Typically enough, that becomes more and more my fault. After a while Bert gets no relief from blasting Mr. Frosch, who is sleeping out of earshot, in plutocratic comfort, three floors up. I make a much more satisfying target, being physically available. It is my presence that's lousing up Moscow. Not that Bert would ever blame a toiling minor for being frail. But he can show impatience with a dawdler and a bungler: Look at me, greasing tart forms slow-motion, like some gentleman of leisure! . . . Am I dreaming by the apricot filler? . . . I must be trying to save Mr. Frosch money, brushing far too little melted butter on the pastry shells — why else are the fuckers browning so slowly, even at four hundred degrees?

Not a word of truth in any of this, of course. If anything, I have used an excess of Mr. Frosch's butter, my one way of getting even with him for the doughnut trouble. It's not because of me that the apricot tarts don't ripen into the right deep gold pastry color until way after ten-thirty P.M. In fact, when Bert peels the last tart tin out of the oven, it is almost eleven. Only then can he kick shut the oven's gas-heat lever while reaching up to kill the fan. Instantly — undawdlingly — I push the shortwave button on the radio.

Too late.

The announcer is signing off at WNEW, Vera Lynn warbling *There'll be blue birds over, the white cliffs of Dover* . . . changes to *Voelker, hoeret die Signale, auf zum letzten Gefecht* . . . a Teutonic chorus of "Die Internationale," introducing Moscow's German-language news. We have missed the English program.

Nothing could frustrate Bert more on a Saturday night. This is the night he listens extra carefully to the Russian truth enunciated in the King's English; when he, having finished his shift but still sweaty, leaning forward rapt from his perch on a flour sack, pad at the ready, pencil in his moist hand, jots down facts to fortify his letter to the editor, his weekly protest against the unheard-of manner in which the *Daily News* disregards the Soviet contribution to the Allied war effort.

But tonight the German gutturals coming out of Russia don't help him at all. Suddenly he tells me I better translate what the hell they are saying.

"What?" I ask.

My sharp italics are my only defense against this imposition. As if I weren't already busy enough, transferring with clumsy asbestos gloves endless tarts out of their sizzling tins onto the display trays.

"You understand them," Bert says, pencil stabbing at his pad. "You're German!"

I am Austrian, but one can't talk to him when he is in this mood. I can't waste my breath with arguments, drudging stooped over the tarts when I am frantic mentally as well, trying to sum up each German bulletin in English in time to absorb the next German one. Under the pressure I deform a number of Bert's exquisitely shaped tart shells — serves him right if he gets bawled out by Mr. Frosch.

My resentment even colors the news the wrong way. Very wrong, because the concentration camp still lives under my father's scalp; his black hair, shaved off by the SS, has grown back gray in New York. Yet tonight — shameful to say — I can't truly enjoy a Nazi setback. Bert doesn't deserve the glad tidings that at Stalingrad the Red Army has captured a Wehrmacht general.

I relate the coup in indifferent tones. Just the same, Bert starts to smile as he scribbles. Indeed, he says "thank you" when the broadcast is over. I give a brief nod. Before changing into his street clothes Bert switches the fan back on and points it helpfully at me. I am too busy to notice, working so hard. This pushes Bert halfway toward an apology, into a sheepish stutter.

Uh, a Nazi general captured, he says, such great stuff, he should put it into really good language, so the goddamn editor will have to publish the letter this time for sure, so the dictionary in my locker where I get all my big words, how about borrowing it? Just for one day?

"At your disposal," I say, not looking up from the tarts.

"You'll have it back Monday guaranteed."

I give another mute, stooped nod.

Whereupon he mutters something about all the stuff I have to lug up to the store tonight, so since he's on his way out up the stairs anyway, so he might as well take along one of the tart trays.

This is an unprecedented gesture.

Now I do look at him (and see that he is already holding my Webster's dictionary). I may even be smiling.

"Don't trouble," I say. "You need both hands for a tray. You already carry the big dictionary."

"You sure? Loads of trays tonight."

"It is OK."

Only after we have waved a friends-again so long, do I realize the foreignness of "It is OK." "It's OK" would have been correct.

But it really is OK, bringing up the finished baked goods, entering from backstairs the locked, empty store, no displays in the window, nothing to block my view of the street. Because at this hour I love to watch Eighth Avenue for those long automobiles with curtained windows, limousines that come from the direction of Fifth Avenue. They may not be faster than ordinary cars; still, the speed with which they glide toward the West Side Highway is supernatural. They are extraterrestrial vehicles issuing from America.

Mr. Frosch's bakery is simply not in America. Proof of that right now (as I am bringing up the first tray) is Jimmy, Mr. Frosch's security guard. He is standing flush against the glass until the slit-skirted woman lounging on the sidewalk turns around; he lip-purses a kiss at her, working the key in the lock with one hand while flashing a ten-dollar bill with the other. And when the woman comes right up and can't rattle open the door Jimmy has left locked after all and sees him bent over with mean laughter, all she can do is spit. Such things don't happen in the true America — neither Jimmy's leering cackle nor the whore's saliva dribbling down the outside of the pane. None of messy Eighth Avenue is anywhere near America. Nor is Washington Heights uptown, where I live with my parents and where on special occasions my mother takes along the white combed-cotton napkins saved from Vienna and spreads them on the cracked plastic table of the Three Star Diner so that the hamburgers will have the same ceremony as a dinner at the Café Restaurant Landtmann on the Ringstrasse.

Nor is downtown New York America, and that includes Thirteenth Street. There I attend Food Trades Vocational High School, whose baking department has found me this summer job. True, Food Trades' baking oven gleams with chrome and is much newer than Mr. Frosch's. But America itself gleams nowhere in the school: its library — two shelves squeezed into a corner of the assistant principal's office — consists of a dog-eared culinary encyclopedia from which two middle volumes are missing, with not a single dictionary to make up for it.

None of the Food Trades kids are in America, though most are born New Yorkers. This they never let me forget during my first semester, saying frequently, "Kraut, get the shit oudda here!" But after I gave Haber a puffy eye and kicked Palusso into a limp (suffering a fat lip my mother, thank God, mistook for a blister) — after that they let me have the outfield at the parking-lot games. Now and then soccer reflexes still louse up my stickball moves, but even so I have proved that I am faster than just about any of them. They still say "Get the shit oudda here!" to me, but no more often than to one another.

They can say that, however, with flawless vowels and perfectly slurred consonants that define them, in contrast to me, as American. Even this does not gain them America, though the superiority of their speech indicates that someday they might well attain it.

Sounding like them has become crucial to me. I have spent

ninety cents of my first Frosch earnings on a dictionary, a used one but sizable, no fewer than eighty thousand entries; expanding my vocabulary might diminish my accent somehow, perhaps by diluting it among a greater number of words. The closer I get to the native tone, the better my chances to arrive in America.

And as a matter of fact, working at Frosch's has helped me track down America's whereabouts. Not the real live movie-America, but at least the site where that America hibernates, the way a rocket hibernates on its launching pad.

Each afternoon around five P.M., when I climb out of the Sixth Avenue subway station on Fiftieth Street and start walking west toward Frosch's, I am briefly on that launching pad: it stretches in this area from Fifth Avenue to Seventh. I walk on a carpet of special smooth asphalt soon to be touched by patent-leather shoes and fantastically high heels, but now still largely empty. I walk under sumptuous silken canopies that lead to paneled restaurant doors still shut, locked tight against me. I pass nightclub entrances, guarded by silver posts with red velvet ropes festooned between them. Guards against what? What fabulous ghosts? There is nobody on the sidewalk — no diners, no dancers, no revelers, no bouncers even. There is just me, shuffling in my brogues toward Mr. Frosch's cellar.

I know that within a couple of hours the transformation will come to pass. About the time I am greasing cupcake forms for Bert, the America on that takeoff ramp will zoom into lustrous orbit. But later, when I walk home at three A.M., nothing will be left of the soaring glamour except debris: thick cigar butts on the curb; perfumed lipsticked crumpled tissues; the dull glint of a dime in the gutter — dregs of some magnificent tip.

No, I can't penetrate America during the hours when it stirs miraculously alive. And yet it is at Frosch's that I get a daily clue about high America still in flight. And I get it, of all people, from Jimmy, who keeps vigil in the nocturnal store.

Jimmy mustn't ever know that, of course. Let him find out he is doing me a favor — and it's goodbye, favor. A toothpick keeps dangling from his mouth, pulling his face into a remarkable variety of sneers; all of them come into play in the course of his diverse functions, all of which involve some cunning dodge. He is Mr. Frosch's night watchman, payroll master, garbage-disposal manager, and tricky-delivery specialist. On the tray I am carrying up from the cellar now sits a basket with twenty of Bert's renowned apricot tarts. Jimmy will bring them to the Pink Banana Club on Fifty-second Street, where the tarts will be devoured for free by any cop checking if the Pink Banana really does serve warm meals till closing as required by its liquor license. This lowdown Jimmy once revealed to me with the bottomless smirk of an insider who has the dirt on the entire universe.

But only very rarely does Jimmy favor me with such privileged information. As a rule I am treated like some juvenile barbarian, there to be jeered at. Handing me my Saturday pay envelope now, he says, his toothpick jerking derisively between smoke-stained teeth, "Sorry, Fritz, it's Hun money. Ain't legal to pay you in dollars till you're a citizen."

"Ha. Ha. Ha," I say slowly, in counter-derision. Which doesn't stop him from the next jeer. He points to the tabloid newspaper on the counter.

"There. Roast a nice rat for me."

That crack refers to my final chore each night. After I have cleaned the whole cellar and washed the pile in the sink, I take the newspaper, twist its sheets into three sausages, stuff them into three mouse holes in our storage room, put a match to them, and have the broom ready for the kill. But before that, the paper serves a very different purpose for me, one of which Jimmy doesn't have the faintest idea.

And so I don't even bother to answer him, just grab the paper and run out of his sight down the stairs. In the cellar I riffle through the pages on the kneading bench. Naturally the sports section is missing, because Jimmy keeps the horse-race listings he has marked up. But the most important part of the paper is intact. The column glows with bulletins from the real America, printed in a magic language fit for a magic planet.

> Ann Sheridan oozing ooooomph all over El Morocco . . . "Oklahoma!" top-boffo again on the Rialto . . . The Franklin Delano Roosevelt Jr.'s infanticipating? . . . Robert Taylor and Barbara Stanwyck one hundred percent guaranteed pffft . . .

And then the jolt. The three dots after "pffft" . . . lead to the bombshell.

Hoofer of hoofers, Fred Astaire raising major moolah for needy terpsi-
choreans at "21" tonight . . .

Is it possible? Truly true?
Sweat drops smudge the page. Flour has clouded my glasses. I
wipe them before rereading the item.
True!
But is it graspable? This key inhabitant of the elusive, authentic
America, this film god of my Vienna childhood, this Manhattan
white-tie deity, live in the undubbed flesh just a few hundred yards
away? Right now, tonight? So close, at the "21" restaurant on West
Fifty-second Street while I am on West Fiftieth? And the Pink Ba-
nana Club even closer, on West Fifty-second itself!

I am less aware of the plan just formed than of the electric energy driving my limbs to effect it. I rush up to the store with a tray
of still hot apricot tarts, snatch a small cake carton, fold it into a
box, select from among Bert's most beautiful tarts two of the very
best, nestle them into the box, close the top, shear off a generous
slice from the gift-paper roll, drape the red-and-white-striped wrapping lavishly around the box — then can't find any tape with
which to hold it together.

That stops me for a moment. But only for a moment: I rush
downstairs for the rubber bands Bert taught me to use as slingshots
against cockroaches. They tie the wrapping very nicely. Then —
stroke of genius — I rip the work-sheet pad off the wall together
with the string-attached pencil with which Mr. Frosch wrote the
abominable doughnut order. Who ever said you have to have a pen
for an autograph?

Upstairs again, I sober up, slow myself down. Now comes the
tough part. Jimmy. At the moment he is not even approachable,
being busy outside the store, which he has temporarily unlocked,
doing the weekly garbage thing. And this is good. It gives me a
chance to collect my wits.

I have a minute while he extends his hand to the municipal sani-
tation foreman meeting him in the street.

"Hey, Big Joe!" I hear him say. "Your nose still in the trash? Lost
the Sweepstakes again? Where's the luck of the Irish?"

"Well you sure ain't got it, wop sonofabitch!" says the foreman,
joining Jimmy's laughter as their palms slap together.

When their handshake is over, the ten-note Jimmy got from Mr.

Frosch (the one he baited the hooker with) is gone from inside his fingers. The foreman's hand sinks closed into his pants pocket. His men are already scraping the metal cans with our bakery trash across the sidewalk toward the truck. That ten-note saves Mr. Frosch the expense of commercial garbage haulers for the entire week. And Jimmy, smirking his way back to the store, comes within reach of the move I must make now.

"Jimmy," I say. "Listen, I will do the delivery to the Pink Banana for you."

The toothpick in his mouth freezes at a suspicious angle.

"Yeah? How come?"

"I just — just want some fresh air before I finish up downstairs."

"Cost you two bucks."

Sheer extortion!

"You jest," I say. He hates hearing words he does not quite understand, especially if they are spoken by a foreigner.

"Highfalutin, huh? Keep it up, I'll make it three bucks."

I realize I am in no position to rile him.

"Come on, Jimmy, I am doing you a favor!"

"I lose the buck tip I get at the Pink Banana."

"All right," I say. "I will give you a dollar."

"Plus another buck I lose, not getting reward money from the FBI."

"What?"

"Not telling 'em a little Nazi spy like you is loose in the streets."

His mouth distends into a grin. The toothpick moves with his evil amusement. But his hand comes at me palm upward, dead serious. I have to peel off two bills from my pay envelope.

A minute later I am out on Eighth Avenue, half running, bound for the Pink Banana. My right hand holds the basket with the cop-bribing tarts; my left shelters, under my apron, the gift-wrapped box for Mr. Astaire. The clatter and screech from the garbage trucks seem to have chased away pedestrians and limousines. It is still quite a bit before midnight, but the light from the streetlamps trickles down humid, groggy, late — not too late, I hope, to see Him at "21."

The Pink Banana Club is still very alive, with a small spotlight glaring at the exclamation on a poster:

JUANA LINU-LINU
THE BALINESE SPICE SENSATION!

"Delivery from the Frosch Bakery," I say to the giant with a black-dyed goatee and a blue turban. He stands inside the sequined curtain serving as door. He takes the basket, a flowered platter with a coffee pot, a cup and saucer, on which he drops one of the tarts from my basket.

"OK, kiddo. That way. Up the stairs."

"Up the stairs?"

I am dumbfounded by the sudden platter in my hands.

"Her door's on the right."

"But — Jimmy never mentioned anything about any coffee up the stairs."

"Oh, Jimmy's gonna eat his heart out when you tell him."

"Jimmy said there will be a dollar tip," I say, out of sheer confusion.

"Sure, she'll give it to you upstairs. Plus a free look at her tits."

"But I have to go somewhere else now, another delivery."

"Kiddo, this you don't want to miss. Just knock on the door and say, 'Compliments of the management.' Only takes a minute."

There is not even a place to put down the platter. That is one reason why I do go to the stairs, though they are a detour from Him, at "21." Another reason is that making Jimmy eat his heart out may be worth a minute's delay. But mostly it is the prospect of that free look. For what if the turban is not lying? What if a freely offered look at a pair of naked breasts — legend of my top-secret dreams — is waiting for me at the top of the stairs? Every other whisper in the Food Trades' locker room rubs in the fact that I am the only fellow in school who has never laid eyes on such a thing.

Abruptly, midway on the steep climb up, the red carpet gives out. The steps become bare wood, dim and creaking. To the right of the even creakier landing is the door with a golden paper star glued over golden paper letters saying JUANA.

The Astaire gift box I hold in my right hand I now must put on the platter I am holding with my left, in order to have my right free for knocking.

"Open," says a husky voice. "Open, open."

In the cubicle a woman sits slumped before a mirror framed

with lightbulbs of which half are burned out. Her bathrobe has come open at the top, but stingily, showing only the middle of a black bra.

"Well, look what's come in!" she says.

At least she is interesting in the sense that one side of her face is Asiatic, the other European. To make her face look exotic, the skin around one eye has been pulled back into an oriental slant with a clamp; but another clamp hangs loosely, leaving the other eye round.

"Compliments of the management," I say.

"No kiddin'!"

Suddenly she has lurched up from her stool, reached out. I pull back, but not fast enough to keep her from grabbing the Astaire gift box on the platter.

"No!" I say.

She presses the box against that stingy little bit of visible black bra. Long green fingernails close around the bright wrapping.

"No! Please!"

"What's the matter, honey?"

I put the platter down on her mirror table between a cosmetic jar brimming with cigarette butts and a tall glass smelling of whiskey.

"*This* tart here and the coffee — *this* is compliments of the management!"

"Aaaah, they just wanna sober me up for the last show."

"Please return the box!"

"It's so pretty! 'S not for me?"

"It is for someone else."

"Your cutie?"

"I just very much need it back!"

"You sound kinda funny. You from the other side?"

"From Vienna, but I really need —"

"Vienna! Wow! Why'd you leave a beautiful place like that?"

"It became too dangerous. But please —"

"Oh yeah, all them canals sinking into the sea."

"You have to give back the box!"

She leans back, box still pressed against her bra, and crosses a fishnet leg high enough to show a garter mid-thigh.

"I'm not as cute as your cutie?"

"That cake box is for Fred Astaire!"

"Haha!" She tosses the box up in the air. "And me, I'm Ginger Rogers!"

"I mean it! He is in the '21' restaurant. Just two blocks down!"

She sits up, uncrosses her legs, thigh and garter vanishing into the robe.

"On the level?"

"It is in the paper!"

"No kiddin'? Fred's expectin' this?"

Fred! Her impudence frees me from any obligation to tell her the truth.

"Yes, he is expecting it! A special order! You have to give it back!"

But she holds on to the box. Worse, I see that she has snapped both rubber bands by tossing it around. The gift paper has come apart, down to the bare cardboard box — which she now actually dares to open.

"Hey, just a couple of apricot tarts," she says.

"You have hurt the wrapping!"

"Same as my tart here. How do you like that? Him and me, same thing."

Her oriental eye remains an impassive slit, but the round European one is utterly delighted, like her smile. At my expense.

"You should not have opened that! You spoiled it!"

"Hey, Vienna, easy." She leans forward, still smiling, her European eye giving me a long-lashed wink. "I'll fix it for you."

"You even tore the rubber bands!"

"So what? Give you somethin' better."

She reaches for a pink band hanging from one of the dead bulbs of her mirror and stretches it around the box on her lap. It is a garter like the one on her thigh, but it doesn't hide the damage.

"The gift-wrapping is all crumpled!"

"Oh, never fear, Juana's here."

She pulls open a drawer on her mirror table, finds a photograph, slides it under the garter, holds up the box for my inspection with a roguish sideward inclination of her head.

"Little better?"

Covering the wrinkled wrapping is a glossy picture of herself in a short skirt made of bananas and a skimpy halter composed of apples, her torso sinuously curved as she bows a violin with slit-eyed passion.

"OK?"

At last she hands back the box.

"Tell Fred that's with *my* compliments!"

Her own joke shakes her with such abrupt, vehement laughter that she nearly topples from her stool. To steady herself she holds on to my arm. A moment later her hand slides up to my shoulder, pats my cheek.

"Go on, Vienna — run along! Catch Fred!"

Outside her door I don't get rid of the photo right away. Perhaps it's the touch of her hand somehow still lingering on my cheek together with a whiff of musk and whiskey. Also it comes to me that when school starts again, a photo like that could make quite a trophy. Passing the turban downstairs, I let him have a glimpse of it and nod a "Yeah, some tits!" grin.

Back on the street I do yank the picture out from under the garter but refrain from throwing it away. I drop it in the pouch of my apron for its locker-room value. Then I start running to make up for the delay.

Not until the traffic on Sixth Avenue brings me to a stop do the brighter lamps of the crossing light up what I myself have done: yanking away the photo made the damage Juana did even worse. I've shredded the gift-wrapping into a completely sleazy mess. No choice but to discard it in the trash basket. Yet this disaster has given her garter a possible value — could its rosy quilted velvet pass as a decorative ribbon? I decide to leave it in place; it might maintain the gift character of the box — a hope dying at the sight of the additional blemish I discover only now: the horrible little grease stain on the box top!

Rush back to the bakery for a new box and a new gift-wrap?

No, I am too time-pressed. I must keep going. Walking fast, I take her photo out of my apron pocket, slide it back under her garter on the box top, but slide it down much farther than before, bending it over the edges of the box so that some of the fishnet scandal of her legs vanishes under the box bottom, yet enough of her picture is left on top to cover the grease stain with her artistic violin.

"Yes?"

A deep voice jars me out of the box-top problem.

I am already there. Before the iron gate of "21."

The doorman here isn't quite as tall as the one at the Pink Banana, but he's much more elegant, with an admiral's cap, a slender blond mustache, and two rows of gold buttons glinting down a dark blue jacket.

"Yes?" he asks again.

The question catches me idiotically unprepared.

"This — it is a delivery."

"At this hour?"

Has America closed down already?

I see just one car by the curb here, but it has a long smart hood and a visored man behind the wheel, leafing slowly through a magazine — no doubt waiting for Him.

I hold up the cake box.

"This is for Mr. Fred Astaire."

But the doorman doesn't even hear. He has turned to attend to a couple flowing out of the restaurant door some inner gatekeeper has opened, the gentleman with a short silver beard matching the silver band of his black fedora, the lady lifting her long silk gown slightly to step up to street level, both flowing in a brief detour around me and my soiled apron, flowing into the taxi the doorman conjures out of nowhere, simply by bowing to them, finger against cap.

After the taxi pulls away, I hold up the cake box again.

"This is for Mr. Fred Astaire," I say again.

"Over there." The doorman points to a smaller gate in the iron railing, some twenty feet down. "Service entrance."

"But this is personal. A gift —"

"You can't keep standing here."

"I have to give it to him in person!"

"All right, let's have it."

He reaches for the box much more slowly than Juana did but with an authority that can't be resisted. I have to give it up.

"Please — I would like a personal answer!"

He nods, points once more.

"Wait at the service entrance."

And then he himself is gone, gone together with the cake box into the restaurant.

There is nothing for it but the service entrance. It leads into an alley flanked by two trash cans the like of which I have never seen before — so new and clean they gleam like platinum pillars. A miniature streetlamp illuminates them, also revealing a bicycle leaning against a wall, a multispeed one I could never afford. But then the light fades. I can barely make out a door — locked, as it turns out. Something like a pearl hovers in the murk. It is a white doorbell button, obviously to be pressed. I press it and take out the work-sheet pad for the autograph.

Nothing happens. Just my heart pounds. I press again. Nothing happens except more pounding. Suddenly a soft purr of a buzz swings the door slowly open into yet another alley, a very short passageway ending in another dim door.

This door, though, opens promptly.

So strong a shaft of light dazzles me that I, blinking in the dark, can at first comprehend no more than a black silhouette in a forked cape. Then, gaining focus, the fork defines itself as tails — white tie and tails — Him! But in the very next moment a belly bulges the white dress shirt. Has He grown fat? . . . No, worse yet, it isn't Him at all. This is a chubby red-haired waiter, a napkin on his arm.

"You the baker boy?" says his munching mouth. "Tasty tart."

This is unbelievable.

"*You* are eating that! That is for Fred Astaire!"

"Oh, he's in dreamland back at the hotel."

"It is a gift! What hotel?"

"Wouldn't do you any good to know. Here."

The arm with a napkin on it holds out a bill. A thousand-dollar bill could not redeem those jowls chomping my gift for Him.

"No!"

"Not enough? Tell you what. The babe in the photo, you write her number on your pad there. Gets you another buck from the guys in the kitchen."

His chewing grin, his fat shirtfront, my foolishness, my futility — enormous anger flares in my chest, boils up in my throat, booms out of my mouth —

"*Fuck you!*"

I turn away. I tear up the work-sheet pad, all the pages left in it. I fling the pieces down together with the pencil, I litter the "21" restaurant, be it only the service entrance, litter it in revenge for I am not quite sure what, and kick the multispeed bicycle on my way back out of the alley.

But then, back on the street again (the street empty now, even that one waiting limousine gone), walking slowly toward an enormous filthy pile in a cellar sink, I feel a flicker of belonging, as if I had connected to a current running underground across the country, even under the flash of Mr. Astaire's feet — and the connection was my shout.

"Fuck you!"

Me, crying out the two most American words. Without any accent whatsoever.

MICHAEL POLLAN

An Animal's Place

FROM THE NEW YORK TIMES MAGAZINE

THE FIRST TIME I opened Peter Singer's *Animal Liberation*, I was dining alone at the Palm, trying to enjoy a rib-eye steak cooked medium-rare. If this sounds like a good recipe for cognitive dissonance (if not indigestion), that was sort of the idea. Preposterous as it might seem, to supporters of animal rights, what I was doing was tantamount to reading *Uncle Tom's Cabin* on a plantation in the Deep South in 1852.

Singer and the swelling ranks of his followers ask us to imagine a future in which people will look back on my meal, and this steakhouse, as relics of an equally backward age. Eating animals, wearing animals, experimenting on animals, killing animals for sport: all these practices, so resolutely normal to us, will be seen as the barbarities they are, and we will come to view "speciesism" — a neologism I had encountered before only in jokes — as a form of discrimination as indefensible as racism or anti-Semitism.

Even in 1975, when *Animal Liberation* was first published, Singer, an Australian philosopher now teaching at Princeton, was confident that he had the wind of history at his back. The recent civil rights past was prologue, as one liberation movement followed on the heels of another. Slowly but surely, the white man's circle of moral consideration was expanded to admit first blacks, then women, then homosexuals. In each case, a group once thought to be so different from the prevailing "we" as to be undeserving of civil rights was, after a struggle, admitted to the club. Now it was animals' turn.

That animal liberation is the logical next step in the forward march of moral progress is no longer the fringe idea it was back in 1975. A growing and increasingly influential group of philosophers, ethicists, law professors and activists are convinced that the great moral struggle of our time will be for the rights of animals.

So far the movement has scored some of its biggest victories in Europe. Earlier this year, Germany became the first nation to grant animals a constitutional right: the words "and animals" were added to a provision obliging the state to respect and protect the dignity of human beings. The farming of animals for fur was recently banned in England. In several European nations, sows may no longer be confined to crates nor laying hens to "battery cages" — stacked wired cages so small the birds cannot stretch their wings. The Swiss are amending their laws to change the status of animals from "things" to "beings."

Though animals are still very much "things" in the eyes of American law, change is in the air. Thirty-seven states have recently passed laws making some forms of animal cruelty a crime, twenty-one of them by ballot initiative. Following protests by activists, McDonald's and Burger King forced significant improvements in the way the U.S. meat industry slaughters animals. Agribusiness and the cosmetics and apparel industries are all struggling to defuse mounting public concerns over animal welfare.

Once thought of as a left-wing concern, the movement now cuts across ideological lines. Perhaps the most eloquent recent plea on behalf of animals, a new book called *Dominion,* was written by a former speechwriter for President Bush. And once outlandish ideas are finding their way into mainstream opinion. A recent Zogby poll found that fifty-one percent of Americans believe that *primates* are entitled to the same rights as human children.

What is going on here? A certain amount of cultural confusion, for one thing. For at the same time many people seem eager to extend the circle of our moral consideration to animals, in our factory farms and laboratories we are inflicting more suffering on more animals than at any time in history. One by one, science is dismantling our claims to uniqueness as a species, discovering that such things as culture, toolmaking, language and even possibly self-consciousness are not the exclusive domain of *Homo sapiens.* Yet most of the animals we kill lead lives organized very much in the spirit of Descartes, who famously claimed that animals were mere machines, incapable of thought or feeling. There's a schizoid quality to our relationship with animals, in which sentiment and brutality exist side by side. Half the dogs in America will receive Christmas presents this year, yet few of us pause to consider the miserable life of the pig — an animal easily as intelligent as a dog — that becomes the Christmas ham.

We tolerate this disconnect because the life of the pig has moved out of view. When's the last time you saw a pig? (Babe doesn't count.) Except for our pets, real animals — animals living and dying — no longer figure in our everyday lives. Meat comes from the grocery store, where it is cut and packaged to look as little like parts of animals as possible. The disappearance of animals from our lives has opened a space in which there's no reality check, either on the sentiment or the brutality. This is pretty much where we live now, with respect to animals, and it is a space in which the Peter Singers and Frank Perdues of the world can evidently thrive equally well.

Several years ago, the English critic John Berger wrote an essay, "Why Look at Animals?," in which he suggested that the loss of everyday contact between ourselves and animals — and specifically the loss of eye contact — has left us deeply confused about the terms of our relationship to other species. That eye contact, always slightly uncanny, had provided a vivid daily reminder that animals were at once crucially like and unlike us; in their eyes we glimpsed something unmistakably familiar (pain, fear, tenderness) and something irretrievably alien. Upon this paradox people built a relationship in which they felt they could both honor and eat animals without looking away. But that accommodation has pretty much broken down; nowadays, it seems, we either look away or become vegetarians. For my own part, neither option seemed especially appetizing. Which might explain how I found myself reading *Animal Liberation* in a steakhouse.

This is not something I'd recommend if you're determined to continue eating meat. Combining rigorous philosophical argument with journalistic description, *Animal Liberation* is one of those rare books that demand that you either defend the way you live or change it. Because Singer is so skilled in argument, for many readers it is easier to change. His book has converted countless thousands to vegetarianism, and it didn't take long for me to see why: within a few pages, he had succeeded in throwing me on the defensive.

Singer's argument is disarmingly simple and, if you accept its premises, difficult to refute. Take the premise of equality, which most people readily accept. Yet what do we really mean by it? People are not, as a matter of fact, equal at all — some are smarter than others, better looking, more gifted. "Equality is a moral idea," Singer points out, "not an assertion of fact." The moral idea is that everyone's interests ought to receive equal consideration, regardless of "what abilities they may possess." Fair enough; many philosophers have gone this far. But fewer have taken the next logical step. "If possessing a higher degree of intelligence does not entitle one human to use another for his or her own ends, how can it entitle humans to exploit nonhumans for the same purpose?"

This is the nub of Singer's argument, and right around here I began scribbling objections in the margin. *But humans differ from animals in morally significant ways.* Yes they do, Singer acknowledges, which is why we shouldn't treat pigs and children alike. Equal consideration of interests is not the same as equal treatment, he points out: children have an interest in being educated; pigs, in rooting around in the dirt. But where their interests are the same, the principle of equality demands they receive the same consideration. And the one all-important interest that we share with pigs, as with all sentient creatures, is an interest in avoiding pain.

Here Singer quotes a famous passage from Jeremy Bentham, the eighteenth-century utilitarian philosopher, that is the wellspring of the animal rights movement. Bentham was writing in 1789, soon after the French colonies freed black slaves, granting them fundamental rights. "The day *may* come," he speculates, "when the rest of the animal creation may acquire those rights." Bentham then asks what characteristic entitles any being to moral consideration. "Is it the faculty of reason or perhaps the faculty of discourse?" Obviously not, since "a full-grown horse or dog is beyond comparison a more rational, as well as a more conversable animal, than an infant." He concludes: "The question is not, Can they *reason?* nor, Can they *talk?* but, Can they *suffer?*"

Bentham here is playing a powerful card philosophers call the "argument from marginal cases," or AMC for short. It goes like this: There are humans — infants, the severely retarded, the demented — whose mental function cannot match that of a chimpanzee. Even though these people cannot reciprocate our moral attentions, we nevertheless include them in the circle of our moral consideration. So on what basis do we exclude the chimpanzee?

Because he's a chimp, I furiously scribbled in the margin, *and they're human!* For Singer that's not good enough. To exclude the chimp from moral consideration simply because he's not human is no different from excluding the slave simply because he's not white. In the same way we'd call that exclusion racist, the animal rightist contends that it is speciesist to discriminate against the chimpanzee solely because he's not human.

But the differences between blacks and whites are trivial compared with the differences between my son and a chimp. Singer counters by asking us to imagine a hypothetical society that discriminates against people on the basis of something nontrivial — say, intelligence. If that scheme offends our sense of equality, then why is the fact that animals lack certain human characteristics any more just as a basis for discrimination? Either we do not owe any justice to the severely retarded, he concludes, or we do owe it to animals with higher capabilities.

This is where I put down my fork. If I believe in equality, and equality is based on interests rather than characteristics, then I have to either take the interests of the steer I'm eating into account or concede that I am a speciesist. For the time being, I decided to plead guilty as charged. I finished my steak.

But Singer had planted a troubling notion, and in the days afterward, it grew and grew, watered by the other animal rights thinkers I began reading: the philosophers Tom Regan and James Rachels; the legal theorist Steven M. Wise; the writers Joy Williams and Matthew Scully. I didn't *think* I minded being a speciesist, but could it be, as several of these writers suggest, that we will someday come to regard speciesism as an evil comparable to racism? Will history someday judge us as harshly as it judges the Germans who went about their ordinary lives in the shadow of Treblinka? Precisely that question was recently posed by J. M. Coetzee, the South African novelist, in a lecture delivered at Princeton; he answered it in the affirmative. If animal rightists are right, "a crime of stupefying proportions" (in Coetzee's words) is going on all around us every day, just beneath our notice.

It's an idea almost impossible to entertain seriously, much less to accept, and in the weeks following my restaurant face-off between Singer and the steak, I found myself marshaling whatever mental power I could muster to try to refute it. Yet Singer and his allies managed to trump almost all my objections.

My first line of defense was obvious. *Animals kill one another all the time. Why treat animals more ethically than they treat one another?* (Ben Franklin tried this one long before me: during a fishing trip, he wondered, "If you eat one another, I don't see why we may not eat you." He admits, however, that the rationale didn't occur to him until the fish were in the frying pan, smelling "admirably well." The advantage of being a "reasonable creature," Franklin remarks, is that you can find a reason for whatever you want to do.) To the "they do it too" defense, the animal rightist has a devastating reply: Do you really want to base your morality on the natural order? Murder and rape are natural too. Besides, humans don't need to kill other creatures in order to survive; animals do. (Though if my cat, Otis, is any guide, animals sometimes kill for sheer pleasure.)

This suggests another defense. *Wouldn't life in the wild be worse for these farm animals?* "Defenders of slavery imposed on black Africans often made a similar point," Singer retorts. "The life of freedom is to be preferred."

But domesticated animals can't survive in the wild; in fact, without us they wouldn't exist at all. Or as one nineteenth-century political philosopher put it, "The pig has a stronger interest than anyone in the demand for bacon. If all the world were Jewish, there would be no pigs at all." But it turns out that this would be fine by the animal rightists: for if pigs don't exist, they can't be wronged.

Animals on factory farms have never known any other life. Singer replies that "animals feel a need to exercise, stretch their limbs or wings, groom themselves and turn around, whether or not they have ever lived in conditions that permit this." The measure of their suffering is not their prior experiences but the unremitting daily frustration of their instincts.

OK, the suffering of animals is a legitimate problem, but the world is full of problems, and surely human problems must come first! Sounds good, and yet all the animal people are asking me to do is to stop eating meat and wearing animal furs and hides. There's no reason I can't devote myself to solving humankind's problems while being a vegetarian who wears synthetics.

But doesn't the fact that we could choose to forgo meat for moral reasons point to a crucial moral difference between animals and humans? As Kant pointed out, the human being is the only moral animal, the only one even capable of entertaining a concept of "rights." What's wrong with reserving moral consideration for those able to reciprocate it? Right here is where you run smack into the AMC: the moral status of the retarded, the insane, the infant and the Alzheimer's patient. Such "marginal cases," in the detestable argot of modern moral philosophy, cannot participate in moral decision-making any more than a monkey can, yet we nevertheless grant them rights.

That's right, I respond, for the simple reason that they're one of us. And all of us have been, and will probably once again be, marginal cases ourselves. What's more, these people have fathers and mothers, daughters and sons, which makes our interest in their welfare deeper than our interest in the welfare of even the most brilliant ape.

Alas, none of these arguments evade the charge of speciesism; the racist, too, claims that it's natural to give special consideration to one's own kind. A utilitarian like Singer would agree, however, that the feelings of relatives do count for something. Yet the principle of equal consideration of interests demands that, given the choice between performing a painful medical experiment on a severely retarded orphan and on a normal ape, we must sacrifice the child. Why? Because the ape has a greater capacity for pain.

Here in a nutshell is the problem with the AMC: it can be used to help the animals, but just as often it winds up hurting the marginal cases. Giving up our speciesism will bring us to a moral cliff from which we may not be prepared to jump, even when logic is pushing us.

And yet this isn't the moral choice I am being asked to make. (Too bad; it would be so much easier!) In everyday life, the choice is not between babies and chimps but between the pork and the tofu. Even if we reject the "hard utilitarianism" of a Peter Singer, there remains the question of whether we owe animals that can feel pain *any* moral consideration, and this seems impossible to deny. And if we do owe them moral consideration, how can we justify eating them?

This is why killing animals for meat (and clothing) poses the

most difficult animal rights challenge. In the case of animal testing, all but the most radical animal rightists are willing to balance
the human benefit against the cost to the animals. That's because
the unique qualities of human consciousness carry weight in the
utilitarian calculus: human pain counts for more than that of a
mouse, since our pain is amplified by emotions like dread; similarly, our deaths are worse than an animal's because we understand
what death is in a way they don't. So the argument over animal testing is really in the details: Is this particular procedure or test *really*
necessary to save human lives? (Very often it's not, in which case
we probably shouldn't do it.) But if humans no longer need to eat
meat or wear skins, then what exactly are we putting on the human
side of the scale to outweigh the interests of the animal?

I suspect that this is finally why the animal people managed to
throw me on the defensive. It's one thing to choose between the
chimp and the retarded child or to accept the sacrifice of all those
pigs surgeons practiced on to develop heart-bypass surgery. But
what happens when the choice is between "a lifetime of suffering
for a nonhuman animal and the gastronomic preference of a human being?" You look away — or you stop eating animals. And if
you don't want to do either? Then you have to try to determine
if the animals you're eating have really endured "a lifetime of suffering."

Whether our interest in eating animals outweighs their interest in
not being eaten (assuming for the moment that is their interest)
turns on the vexed question of animal suffering. Vexed, because it
is impossible to know what really goes on in the mind of a cow or
a pig or even an ape. Strictly speaking, this is true of other humans, too, but since humans are all basically wired the same way,
we have excellent reason to assume that other people's experience
of pain feels much like our own. Can we say that about animals? Yes
and no.

I have yet to find anyone who still subscribes to Descartes's belief that animals cannot feel pain because they lack a soul. The
general consensus among scientists and philosophers is that when
it comes to pain, the higher animals are wired much the way we are
for the same evolutionary reasons, so we should take the writhings
of the kicked dog at face value. Indeed, the very premise of a great

deal of animal testing — the reason it has value — is that animals' experience of physical and even some psychological pain closely resembles our own. Otherwise, why would cosmetics testers drip chemicals into the eyes of rabbits to see if they sting? Why would researchers study head trauma by traumatizing chimpanzee heads? Why would psychologists attempt to induce depression and "learned helplessness" in dogs by exposing them to ceaseless random patterns of electrical shock?

That said, it can be argued that human pain differs from animal pain by an order of magnitude. This qualitative difference is largely the result of our possession of language and, by virtue of language, an ability to have thoughts about thoughts and to imagine alternatives to our current reality. The philosopher Daniel C. Dennett suggests that we would do well to draw a distinction between pain, which a great many animals experience, and suffering, which depends on a degree of self-consciousness only a few animals appear to command. Suffering, in this view, is not just lots of pain but pain intensified by human emotions like loss, sadness, worry, regret, self-pity, shame, humiliation and dread.

Consider castration. No one would deny the procedure is painful to animals, yet animals appear to get over it in a way humans do not. (Some rhesus monkeys competing for mates will bite off a rival's testicle; the very next day the victim may be observed mating, seemingly little the worse for wear.) Surely the suffering of a man able to comprehend the full implications of castration, to anticipate the event and contemplate its aftermath, represents an agony of another order.

By the same token, however, language and all that comes with it can also make certain kinds of pain *more* bearable. A trip to the dentist would be a torment for an ape that couldn't be made to understand the purpose and duration of the procedure.

As humans contemplating the pain and suffering of animals, we do need to guard against projecting onto them what the same experience would feel like to us. Watching a steer force-marched up the ramp to the kill-floor door, as I have done, I need to remind myself that this is not Sean Penn in *Dead Man Walking*, that in a bovine brain the concept of nonexistence is blissfully absent. "If we fail to find suffering in the [animal] lives we can see," Dennett writes in *Kinds of Minds*, "we can rest assured there is no invisible suffering somewhere in their brains. If we find suffering, we will recognize it without difficulty."

Which brings us — reluctantly, necessarily — to the American factory farm, the place where all such distinctions turn to dust. It's not easy to draw lines between pain and suffering in a modern egg or confinement hog operation. These are places where the subtleties of moral philosophy and animal cognition mean less than nothing, where everything we've learned about animals at least since Darwin has been simply . . . set aside. To visit a modern CAFO (Confined Animal Feeding Operation) is to enter a world that, for all its technological sophistication, is still designed according to Cartesian principles: animals are machines incapable of feeling pain. Since no thinking person can possibly believe this anymore, industrial animal agriculture depends on a suspension of disbelief on the part of the people who operate it and a willingness to avert your eyes on the part of everyone else.

From everything I've read, egg and hog operations are the worst. Beef cattle in America at least still live outdoors, albeit standing ankle deep in their own waste, eating a diet that makes them sick. And broiler chickens, although they do get their beaks snipped off with a hot knife to keep them from cannibalizing one another under the stress of their confinement, at least don't spend their eight-week lives in cages too small to ever stretch a wing. That fate is reserved for the American laying hen, who passes her brief span piled together with a half-dozen other hens in a wire cage whose floor a single page of this magazine could carpet. Every natural instinct of this animal is thwarted, leading to a range of behavioral "vices" that can include cannibalizing her cagemates and rubbing her body against the wire mesh until it is featherless and bleeding. Pain? Suffering? Madness? The operative suspension of disbelief depends on more neutral descriptors, like "vices" and "stress." Whatever you want to call what's going on in those cages, the ten percent or so of hens that can't bear it and simply die is built into the cost of production. And when the output of the others begins to ebb, the hens will be "force-molted" — starved of food and water and light for several days in order to stimulate a final bout of egg-laying before their life's work is done.

Simply reciting these facts, most of which are drawn from poultry-trade magazines, makes me sound like one of those animal people, doesn't it? I don't mean to, but this is what can happen when . . . you look. It certainly wasn't my intention to ruin anyone's breakfast. But now that I probably have spoiled the eggs, I do want to say one thing about the bacon, mention a single practice (by no means the worst) in modern hog production that points to the compound madness of an impeccable industrial logic.

Piglets in confinement operations are weaned from their mothers ten days after birth (compared with thirteen weeks in nature) because they gain weight faster on their hormone- and antibiotic-fortified feed. This premature weaning leaves the pigs with a lifelong craving to suck and chew, a desire they gratify in confinement by biting the tail of the animal in front of them. A normal pig would fight off his molester, but a demoralized pig has stopped caring. "Learned helplessness" is the psychological term, and it's not uncommon in confinement operations, where tens of thousands of hogs spend their entire lives ignorant of sunshine or earth or straw, crowded together beneath a metal roof upon metal slats suspended over a manure pit. So it's not surprising that an animal as sensitive and intelligent as a pig would get depressed, and a depressed pig will allow his tail to be chewed on to the point of infection. Sick pigs, being underperforming "production units," are clubbed to death on the spot. The USDA's recommended solution to the problem is called "tail docking." Using a pair of pliers (and no anesthetic), most but not all of the tail is snipped off. Why the little stump? Because the whole point of the exercise is not to remove the object of tail-biting so much as to render it *more* sensitive. Now, a bite on the tail is so painful that even the most demoralized pig will mount a struggle to avoid it.

Much of this description is drawn from *Dominion*, Matthew Scully's recent book in which he offers a harrowing description of a North Carolina hog operation. Scully, a Christian conservative, has no patience for lefty rights talk, arguing instead that while God did give man "dominion" over animals ("Every moving thing that liveth shall be meat for you"), he also admonished us to show them mercy. "We are called to treat them with kindness, not because they have rights or power or some claim to equality but . . . because they stand unequal and powerless before us."

Scully calls the contemporary factory farm "our own worst nightmare" and, to his credit, doesn't shrink from naming the root cause of this evil: unfettered capitalism. (Perhaps this explains why he resigned from the Bush administration just before his book's publication.) A tension has always existed between the capitalist imperative to maximize efficiency and the moral imperatives of religion or community, which have historically served as a counterweight to the moral blindness of the market. This is one of "the cultural contradictions of capitalism" — the tendency of the economic impulse to erode the moral underpinnings of society. Mercy toward animals is one such casualty.

More than any other institution, the American industrial animal farm offers a nightmarish glimpse of what capitalism can look like in the absence of moral or regulatory constraint. In these places life itself is redefined — as protein production — and with it suffering. *That* venerable word becomes "stress," an economic problem in search of a cost-effective solution, like tail-docking or beak-clipping or, in the industry's latest plan, by simply engineering the "stress gene" out of pigs and chickens. "Our own worst nightmare" such a place may well be; it is also real life for the billions of animals unlucky enough to have been born beneath these grim steel roofs, into the brief, pitiless life of a "production unit" in the days before the suffering gene was found.

Vegetarianism doesn't seem an unreasonable response to such an evil. Who would want to be made complicit in the agony of these animals by eating them? You want to throw *something* against the walls of those infernal sheds, whether it's the Bible, a new constitutional right or a whole platoon of animal rightists bent on breaking in and liberating the inmates. In the shadow of these factory farms, Coetzee's notion of a "stupefying crime" doesn't seem far-fetched at all.

But before you swear off meat entirely, let me describe a very different sort of animal farm. It is typical of nothing, and yet its very existence puts the whole moral question of animal agriculture in a different light. Polyface Farm occupies 550 acres of rolling grassland and forest in the Shenandoah Valley of Virginia. Here, Joel Salatin and his family raise six different food animals — cattle, pigs, chickens, rabbits, turkeys and sheep — in an intricate dance of symbiosis designed to allow each species, in Salatin's words, "to fully express its physiological distinctiveness."

What this means in practice is that Salatin's chickens live like chickens; his cows, like cows; pigs, pigs. As in nature, where birds tend to follow herbivores, once Salatin's cows have finished grazing a pasture, he moves them out and tows in his "eggmobile," a portable chicken coop that houses several hundred laying hens — roughly the natural size of a flock. The hens fan out over the pasture, eating the short grass and picking insect larvae out of the cowpats — all the while spreading the cow manure and eliminating the farm's parasite problem. A diet of grubs and grass makes for exceptionally tasty eggs and contented chickens, and their nitrogenous manure feeds the pasture. A few weeks later, the chickens move out and the sheep come in, dining on the lush new growth as well as on the weed species (nettles, nightshade) that the cattle and chickens won't touch.

Meanwhile, the pigs are in the barn turning the compost. All winter long, while the cattle were indoors, Salatin layered their manure with straw, wood chips — and corn. By March, this steaming compost layer cake stands three feet high, and the pigs, whose powerful snouts can sniff out and retrieve the fermented corn at the bottom, get to spend a few happy weeks rooting through the pile, aerating it as they work. All you can see of these pigs, intently nosing out the tasty alcoholic morsels, are their upturned pink hams and corkscrew tails churning the air. The finished compost will go to feed the grass; the grass, the cattle; the cattle, the chickens; and eventually all of these animals will feed us.

I thought a lot about vegetarianism and animal rights during the day I spent on Joel Salatin's extraordinary farm. So much of what I'd read, so much of what I'd accepted, looked very different from here. To many animal rightists, even Polyface Farm is a death camp. But to look at these animals is to see this for the sentimental conceit it is. In the same way that we can probably recognize animal suffering when we see it, animal happiness is unmistakable, too, and here I was seeing it in abundance.

For any animal, happiness seems to consist in the opportunity to express its creaturely character — its essential pigness or wolfness or chickenness. Aristotle speaks of each creature's "characteristic form of life." For domesticated species, the good life, if we can call it that, cannot be achieved apart from humans — apart from our farms and, therefore, our meat-eating. This, it seems to me, is where animal rightists betray a profound ignorance about the

workings of nature. To think of domestication as a form of en-
slavement or even exploitation is to misconstrue the whole relationship, to project a human idea of power onto what is, in fact, an
instance of mutualism between species. Domestication is an evolutionary, rather than a political, development. It is certainly not a
regime humans imposed on animals some ten thousand years ago.

Rather, domestication happened when a small handful of especially opportunistic species discovered through Darwinian trial
and error that they were more likely to survive and prosper in an
alliance with humans than on their own. Humans provided the animals with food and protection, in exchange for which the animals provided the humans their milk and eggs and — yes — their
flesh. Both parties were transformed by the relationship: animals
grew tame and lost their ability to fend for themselves (evolution
tends to edit out unneeded traits), and humans gave up their
hunter-gatherer ways for the settled life of agriculturists. (Humans
changed biologically, too, evolving such new traits as a tolerance
for lactose as adults.)

From the animals' point of view, the bargain with humanity has
been a great success, at least until our own time. Cows, pigs, dogs,
cats and chickens have thrived, while their wild ancestors have lan-
guished. (There are ten thousand wolves in North America, fifty
million dogs.) Nor does their loss of autonomy seem to trouble
these creatures. It is wrong, the rightists say, to treat animals as
"means" rather than "ends," yet the happiness of a working animal
like the dog consists precisely in serving as a "means." Liberation is
the last thing such a creature wants. To say of one of Joel Salatin's
caged chickens that "the life of freedom is to be preferred" betrays
an ignorance about chicken preferences — which on this farm are
heavily focused on not getting their heads bitten off by weasels.

But haven't these chickens simply traded one predator for another — weasels for humans? True enough, and for the chickens
this is probably not a bad deal. For brief as it is, the life expectancy
of a farm animal would be considerably briefer in the world beyond the pasture fence or chicken coop. A sheep farmer told me
that a bear will eat a lactating ewe alive, starting with her udders.
"As a rule," he explained, "animals don't get 'good deaths' surrounded by their loved ones."

The very existence of predation — animals eating animals — is the cause of much anguished hand-wringing in animal rights circles. "It must be admitted," Singer writes, "that the existence of carnivorous animals does pose one problem for the ethics of Animal Liberation, and that is whether we should do anything about it." Some animal rightists train their dogs and cats to become vegetarians. (Note: cats will require nutritional supplements to stay healthy.) Matthew Scully calls predation "the intrinsic evil in nature's design . . . among the hardest of all things to fathom." *Really?* A deep Puritan streak pervades animal rights activists, an abiding discomfort not only with our animality but with the animals' animality too.

However it may appear to us, predation is not a matter of morality or politics; it, also, is a matter of symbiosis. Hard as the wolf may be on the deer he eats, the herd depends on him for its well-being; without predators to cull the herd, deer overrun their habitat and starve. In many places, human hunters have taken over the predator's ecological role. Chickens also depend for their continued well-being on their human predators — not individual chickens, but chickens as a species. The surest way to achieve the extinction of the chicken would be to grant chickens a "right to life."

Yet here's the rub: the animal rightist is not concerned with species, only individuals. Tom Regan, author of *The Case for Animal Rights*, bluntly asserts that because "species are not individuals . . . the rights view does not recognize the moral rights of species to anything, including survival." Singer concurs, insisting that only sentient individuals have interests. But surely a species can have interests — in its survival, say — just as a nation or community or a corporation can. The animal rights movement's exclusive concern with individual animals makes perfect sense given its roots in a culture of liberal individualism, but does it make any sense in nature?

Consider this hypothetical episode: In 1611 Juan da Goma (a.k.a. Juan the Disoriented) made accidental landfall on Wrightson Island, a six-square-mile rock in the Indian Ocean. The island's sole distinction is as the only known home of the Arcania tree and the bird that nests in it, the Wrightson giant sea sparrow. Da Goma and his crew stayed a week, much of that time spent in a failed bid to recapture the ship's escaped goat — who happened to be pregnant. Nearly four centuries later, Wrightson Island is home to 380 goats that have consumed virtually every scrap of vegetation in their reach. The youngest Arcania tree on the island is more than three hundred years old, and only fifty-two sea sparrows remain. In the animal rights view, any one of those goats have at least as much right to life as the last Wrightson sparrow on earth, and the trees, because they are not sentient, warrant no moral consideration whatsoever. (In the mid-1980s a British environmental group set out to shoot the goats, but was forced to cancel the expedition after the Mammal Liberation Front bombed its offices.)

The story of Wrightson Island (invented by the biologist David Ehrenfeld in *Beginning Again*) suggests at the very least that a human morality based on individual rights makes for an awkward fit when applied to the natural world. This should come as no surprise: morality is an artifact of human culture, devised to help us negotiate social relations. It's very good for that. But just as we recognize that nature doesn't provide an adequate guide for human social conduct, isn't it anthropocentric to assume that our moral system offers an adequate guide for nature? We may require a different set of ethics to guide our dealings with the natural world, one as well suited to the particular needs of plants and animals and habitats (where sentience counts for little) as rights suit us humans today.

To contemplate such questions from the vantage of a farm is to appreciate just how parochial and urban an ideology animal rights really is. It could thrive only in a world where people have lost contact with the natural world, where animals no longer pose a threat to us and human mastery of nature seems absolute. "In our normal life," Singer writes, "there is no serious clash of interests between human and nonhuman animals." Such a statement assumes a decidedly urbanized "normal life," one that certainly no farmer would recognize.

The farmer would point out that even vegans have a "serious clash of interests" with other animals. The grain that the vegan eats is harvested with a combine that shreds field mice, while the farmer's tractor crushes woodchucks in their burrows, and his pesticides drop songbirds from the sky. Steve Davis, an animal scientist at Oregon State University, has estimated that if America were to adopt a strictly vegetarian diet, the total number of animals killed every year would actually *increase*, as animal pasture gave way to row crops. Davis contends that if our goal is to kill as few animals as possible, then people should eat the largest possible animal that can live on the least intensively cultivated land: grass-fed beef for everybody. It would appear that killing animals is unavoidable no matter what we choose to eat.

When I talked to Joel Salatin about the vegetarian utopia, he pointed out that it would also condemn him and his neighbors to importing their food from distant places, since the Shenandoah Valley receives too little rainfall to grow many row crops. Much the same would hold true where I live, in New England. We get plenty of rain, but the hilliness of the land has dictated an agriculture based on animals since the time of the Pilgrims. The world is full of places where the best, if not the only, way to obtain food from the land is by grazing animals on it — especially ruminants, which alone can transform grass into protein and whose presence can actually improve the health of the land.

The vegetarian utopia would make us even more dependent than we already are on an industrialized national food chain. That food chain would in turn be even more dependent than it already is on fossil fuels and chemical fertilizer, since food would need to travel farther and manure would be in short supply. Indeed, it is doubtful that you can build a more sustainable agriculture without animals to cycle nutrients and support local food production. If our concern is for the health of nature — rather than, say, the internal consistency of our moral code or the condition of our souls — then eating animals may sometimes be the most ethical thing to do.

There is, too, the fact that we humans have been eating animals as long as we have lived on this earth. Humans may not need to eat meat in order to survive, yet doing so is part of our evolutionary heritage, reflected in the design of our teeth and the structure of our digestion. Eating meat helped make us what we are, in a social and biological sense. Under the pressure of the hunt, the human brain grew in size and complexity, and around the fire where the meat was cooked, human culture first flourished. Granting rights to animals may lift us up from the brutal world of predation, but it will entail the sacrifice of part of our identity — our own animality.

Surely this is one of the odder paradoxes of animal rights doctrine. It asks us to recognize all that we share with animals and then demands that we act toward them in a most unanimalistic way. Whether or not this is a good idea, we should at least acknowledge that our desire to eat meat is not a trivial matter, no mere "gastronomic preference." We might as well call sex — also now technically unnecessary — a mere "recreational preference." Whatever else it is, our meat-eating is something very deep indeed.

Are any of these good enough reasons to eat animals? I'm mindful of Ben Franklin's definition of the reasonable creature as one who can come up with reasons for whatever he wants to do. So I decided I would track down Peter Singer and ask him what he thought. In an e-mail message, I described Polyface and asked him about the implications for his position of the Good Farm — one where animals got to live according to their nature and to all appearances did not suffer.

"I agree with you that it is better for these animals to have lived and died than not to have lived at all," Singer wrote back. Since the utilitarian is concerned exclusively with the sum of happiness and suffering and the slaughter of an animal that doesn't comprehend that death need not involve suffering, the Good Farm adds to the total of animal happiness, provided you replace the slaughtered animal with a new one. However, he added, this line of thinking doesn't obviate the wrongness of killing an animal that "has a sense of its own existence over time and can have preferences for its own future." In other words, it's OK to eat the chicken, but he's not so sure about the pig. Yet, he wrote, "I would not be sufficiently confident of my arguments to condemn someone who purchased meat from one of these farms."

Singer went on to express serious doubts that such farms could be practical on a large scale, since the pressures of the marketplace will lead their owners to cut costs and corners at the expense of the animals. He suggested, too, that killing animals is not conducive to treating them with respect. Also, since humanely raised food will be more expensive, only the well-to-do can afford morally defensible animal protein. These are important considerations, but they don't alter my essential point: what's wrong with animal agriculture — with eating animals — is the practice, not the principle.

What this suggests to me is that people who care should be working not for animal rights but animal welfare — to ensure that farm animals don't suffer and that their deaths are swift and painless. In fact, the decent-life-merciful-death line is how Jeremy Bentham justified his own meat-eating. Yes, the philosophical father of animal rights was himself a carnivore. In a passage rather less frequently quoted by animal rightists, Bentham defended eating animals on the grounds that "we are the better for it, and they are never the worse . . . The death they suffer in our hands commonly is, and always may be, a speedier and, by that means, a less painful one than that which would await them in the inevitable course of nature."

My guess is that Bentham never looked too closely at what happens in a slaughterhouse, but the argument suggests that, in theory at least, a utilitarian can justify the killing of humanely treated animals — for meat or, presumably, for clothing. (Though leather and fur pose distinct moral problems. Leather is a byproduct of raising domestic animals for food, which can be done humanely. However, furs are usually made from wild animals that die brutal deaths — usually in leg-hold traps — and since most fur species aren't domesticated, raising them on farms isn't necessarily more humane.) But whether the issue is food or fur or hunting, what should concern us is the suffering, not the killing. All of which I was feeling pretty good about — until I remembered that utilitarians can also justify killing retarded orphans. Killing just isn't the problem for them that it is for other people, including me.

During my visit to Polyface Farm, I asked Salatin where his animals were slaughtered. He does the chickens and rabbits right on the farm, and would do the cattle, pigs and sheep there too if only the USDA would let him. Salatin showed me the open-air abattoir he built behind the farmhouse — a sort of outdoor kitchen on a concrete slab, with stainless-steel sinks, scalding tanks, a feather-plucking machine and metal cones to hold the birds upside down while they're being bled. Processing chickens is not a pleasant job, but Salatin insists on doing it himself because he's convinced he can do it more humanely and cleanly than any processing plant. He slaughters every other Saturday through the summer. Anyone's welcome to watch.

I asked Salatin how he could bring himself to kill a chicken.

"People have a soul; animals don't," he said. "It's a bedrock be-

lief of mine." Salatin is a devout Christian. "Unlike us, animals are
not created in God's image, so when they die, they just die."

The notion that only in modern times have people grown uneasy about killing animals is a flattering conceit. Taking a life is mo-
mentous, and people have been working to justify the slaughter of
animals for thousands of years. Religion and especially ritual has
played a crucial part in helping us reckon the moral costs. Native
Americans and other hunter-gatherers would give thanks to their
prey for giving up its life so the eater might live (sort of like saying
grace). Many cultures have offered sacrificial animals to the gods,
perhaps as a way to convince themselves that it was the gods' desires that demanded the slaughter, not their own. In ancient
Greece, the priests responsible for the slaughter (priests! — now
we entrust the job to minimum-wage workers) would sprinkle holy
water on the sacrificial animal's brow. The beast would promptly
shake its head, and this was taken as a sign of assent. Slaughter
doesn't necessarily preclude respect. For all these people, it was
the ceremony that allowed them to look, then to eat.

Apart from a few surviving religious practices, we no longer have
any rituals governing the slaughter or eating of animals, which perhaps helps to explain why we find ourselves where we do, feeling
that our only choice is to either look away or give up meat. Frank
Perdue is happy to serve the first customer; Peter Singer, the second.

Until my visit to Polyface Farm, I had assumed these were the
only two options. But on Salatin's farm, the eye contact between
people and animals whose loss John Berger mourned is still a fact
of life — and of death, for neither the lives nor the deaths of these
animals have been secreted behind steel walls. "Food with a face,"
Salatin likes to call what he's selling, a slogan that probably scares
off some customers. People see very different things when they
look into the eyes of a pig or a chicken or a steer — a being without a soul, a "subject of a life" entitled to rights, a link in a food
chain, a vessel for pain and pleasure, a tasty lunch. But figuring out
what we do think, and what we can eat, might begin with the looking.

We certainly won't philosophize our way to an answer. Salatin
told me the story of a man who showed up at the farm one Saturday morning. When Salatin noticed a PETA bumper sticker on the

man's car, he figured he was in for it. But the man had a different agenda. He explained that after sixteen years as a vegetarian, he had decided that the only way he could ever eat meat again was if he killed the animal himself. He had come to *look*.

"Ten minutes later we were in the processing shed with a chicken," Salatin recalled. "He slit the bird's throat and watched it die. He saw that the animal did not look at him accusingly, didn't do a Disney double take. The animal had been treated with respect when it was alive, and he saw that it could also have a respectful death — that it wasn't being treated as a pile of protoplasm."

Salatin's open-air abattoir is a morally powerful idea. Someone slaughtering a chicken in a place where he can be watched is apt to do it scrupulously, with consideration for the animal as well as for the eater. This is going to sound quixotic, but maybe all we need to do to redeem industrial animal agriculture in this country is to pass a law requiring that the steel and concrete walls of the CAFOs and slaughterhouses be replaced with . . . glass. If there's any new "right" we need to establish, maybe it's this one: the right to look.

No doubt the sight of some of these places would turn many people into vegetarians. Many others would look elsewhere for their meat, to farmers like Salatin. There are more of them than I would have imagined. Despite the relentless consolidation of the American meat industry, there has been a revival of small farms where animals still live their "characteristic form of life." I'm thinking of the ranches where cattle still spend their lives on grass, the poultry farms where chickens still go outside and the hog farms where pigs live as they did fifty years ago — in contact with the sun, the earth and the gaze of a farmer.

For my own part, I've discovered that if you're willing to make the effort, it's entirely possible to limit the meat you eat to nonindustrial animals. I'm tempted to think that we need a new dietary category, to go with the vegan and lactovegetarian and piscatorian. I don't have a catchy name for it yet (humanocarnivore?), but this is the only sort of meat-eating I feel comfortable with these days. I've become the sort of shopper who looks for labels indicating that his meat and eggs have been humanely grown (the American Humane Association's new "Free Farmed" label seems to be catching on), who visits the farms where his chicken and pork come from and who asks kinky-sounding questions about touring slaughterhouses. I've actually found a couple of small processing plants willing to let a customer onto the kill floor, including one, in Cannon Falls, Minnesota, with a glass abattoir.

The industrialization — and dehumanization — of American animal farming is a relatively new, evitable and local phenomenon: no other country raises and slaughters its food animals quite as intensively or as brutally as we do. Were the walls of our meat industry to become transparent, literally or even figuratively, we would not long continue to do it this way. Tail-docking and sow crates and beak-clipping would disappear overnight, and the days of slaughtering four hundred head of cattle an hour would come to an end. For who could stand the sight? Yes, meat would get more expensive. We'd probably eat less of it, too, but maybe when we did eat animals, we'd eat them with the consciousness, ceremony and respect they deserve.

KATHA POLLITT

Learning to Drive

FROM THE NEW YORKER

"OVER THERE, the red Jeep. Park!" Ben, my gentle Filipino driving instructor, has suddenly become severe, abrupt, commanding. A slight man, he now looms in his seat; his usually soft voice has acquired a threatening edge. In a scenario that we have repeated dozens of times, and that has kinky overtones I don't even want to think about, he is pretending to be the test examiner, barking out orders as we tool along the streets above Columbia University in the early morning. "Pull out when you are ready!" "Right turn!" "Left turn!" "Straight!" "All right, Ms. Pollitt, pull over." He doesn't even need to say the words. From the rueful look on his once again kindly face, I know that I have failed.

What did I do this time? Did I run a red light, miss a stop sign, fail to notice one of the many bicyclists who sneak up into my blind spot whenever I go into reverse? Each of these mistakes means automatic failure. Or did I fail on points? Five for parallel-parking more than fourteen inches from the curb, ten for rolling when I paused for the woman with the stroller (but at least I saw her! I saw her!), fifteen for hesitating in the intersection so that a driver in a car with New Jersey plates honked and gave me the finger? This time it was points, Ben tells me: in our five-minute practice test, I racked up sixty. New York State allows you thirty. "Observation, Kahta, observation! This is your weakness." This truth hangs in the air like mystical advice from a sage in a martial-arts movie. "That and lining up too far away when you go to park." The clock on the dashboard reads 7:47. We will role-play the test repeatedly during my two-hour lesson. I will fail every time.

Observation is my weakness. I did not realize that my mother was a secret drinker. I did not realize that the man I lived with, my soul mate, made for me in Marxist heaven, was a dedicated philanderer, that the drab colleague he insinuated into our social life was his long-standing secret lover, or that the young art critic he mocked as silly and second rate was being groomed as my replacement. I noticed that our apartment was becoming a grunge palace, with papers collecting dust on every surface and kitty litter crunching underfoot. I observed — very good, Kahta! — that I was spending many hours in my study, engaged in arcane e-mail debates with strangers, that I had gained twenty-five pounds in our seven years together and could not fit into many of my clothes. I realized it was not likely that the unfamiliar pink-and-black-striped bikini panties in the clean-clothes basket were the result, as he claimed, of a simple laundry-room mixup. But all this awareness was like the impending danger in one of those slow-motion dreams of paralysis, information that could not be processed. It was like seeing the man with the suitcase step off the curb and driving forward anyway.

I am a fifty-two-year-old woman who has yet to get a driver's license. I'm not the only older woman who can't legally drive — Ben recently had a sixty-five-year-old student, who took the test four times before she passed — but perhaps I am the only fifty-two-year-old feminist writer in this situation. How did this happen to me? For decades, all around me women were laying claim to forbidden manly skills — how to fix the furnace, perform brain surgery, hunt seals, have sex without love. Only I, it seems, stood still, as the machines in my life increased in both number and complexity. When I was growing up, not driving had overtones of New York hipness. There was something beatnik, intellectual, European about being disconnected from the car culture: the rest of America might deliquesce into one big strip mall, but New York City would remain a little outpost of humane civilization, an enclave of ancient modes of transportation — the subway, the bus, the taxi, the bicycle, the foot. Still, my family always had a car — a Buick, a Rambler, some big, lumbering masculine make. My father would sit in it and smoke and listen to the ballgame in the soft summer evening, when he and my mother had had a fight.

"I am trying so hard to help you, Kahta," Ben says. "I feel perhaps I am failing you as your teacher." In a lifetime in and out of academia, I have never before heard a teacher suggest that his student's difficulties might have something to do with him. The truth is, Ben is a natural pedagogue — organized, patient, engaged with his subject, and always looking for new ways to explain some tricky point. Sometimes he illustrates what I should have done by using a pair of toy cars, and I can see the little boy he once was — intent, happy, lost in play. Sometimes he makes up analogies:

"Kahta, how do you know if you've put in enough salt and pepper when you are making beef stew?"

"Um, you taste it?"

"Riiight, you taste it. So what do you do if you've lost track of which way the car is pointing when you parallel-park?"

"I dunno, Ben. You taste it?"

"You just let the car move back a tiny bit and see which way it goes! You taste the direction! Then you —"

"Correct the seasonings?"

"Riiight . . . You adjust!"

Because it takes me a while to focus on the task at hand, Ben and I have fallen into the habit of long lessons — we drive for two hours, sometimes three. We go up to Washington Heights and drive around the winding, hilly roads of Fort Tryon Park and the narrow crooked Tudoresque streets near Castle Village. What a beautiful neighborhood! we exclaim. Look at that Art Deco subway station entrance! Look at those Catholic schoolgirls in front of Mother Cabrini High, in those incredibly cute sexy plaid uniforms! I am careful to stop for the old rabbi, I pause and make eye contact with the mother herding her two little boys. It's like another, secret New York up here, preserved from the forties, in which jogging yuppies in electric-blue spandex look like time travelers from the future among the staid elderly burghers walking their dogs along the leafy sidewalks overlooking the Hudson. In that New York, the one without road-raging New Jersey drivers or sneaky cyclists, in which life is lived at twenty miles an hour, I feel sure I could have got my license with no trouble. I could have been living here all along, coming out of the Art Deco entrance at dusk, with sweet-smelling creamy-pink magnolias all around me.

I spend more time with Ben than with any other man just now. There are days when, except for an exchange of smiles and hellos with Mohammed at the newsstand and my suppertime phone call with a man I am seeing who lives in London, Ben is the only man I talk to. In a way, he's perfect — his use of the double brake is protective without being infantilizing, his corrections are firm but never condescending or judgmental, he spares my feelings but tells the truth if asked. ("Let's say I took the test tomorrow, Ben. What are my chances?" "I'd say maybe fifty-fifty." I must be pretty desperate — those don't seem like such bad odds to me.) He's a big improvement on my former lover, who told a mutual friend that he was leaving me because I didn't have a driver's license, spent too much time on e-mail, and had failed in seven years to read Anton Pannekoek's *Workers' Councils* and other classics of the ultra-left. Ben would never leave me because I don't have a driver's license. Quite the reverse. Sometimes I feel sad to think that these lessons must one day come to an end — will I ever see those little streets again, or drive around Fort Tryon Park in the spring? "Will you still be my teacher, Ben, after I get my license, so I can learn how to drive on the highway?" Ben promises that he will always be there for me, and I believe him.

In at least one way, I am like the other older women learning to drive: I am here because I have lost my man. Most women in my situation are widows or divorcées who spent their lives under Old World rules, in which driving was a male prerogative and being ferried about a female privilege. My lover's mother lived in the wilds of Vermont for years with her Marxist-intellectual husband. With the puritanical zeal for which German Jews are famous, she kept the house spotless, grew all their fruits and vegetables, and raised her son to be a world-class womanizer — while earning a Ph.D. that would enable her to support her husband's life of reading and writing, and, of course, driving. She didn't learn to drive until after his death, when she was over sixty. To hear her tell it now, the whole process took five minutes. When she asked if I'd got my license yet — which she did every time we spoke — she adopted a tone of intense and invasive concern. It was as if she were asking me if the Thorazine had started to work.

Ben is not my first driving teacher. When I was twenty-seven, I took lessons from Mike, a young and rather obnoxious Italian American. "That's OK, I can walk to the curb from here," he would say when I parked too wide. After a month of lessons, I took the test in the Bronx and didn't even notice that I'd hit a stop sign when I parked. Automatic failure. Mike drove me back to Manhattan in hostile silence and didn't call to schedule a lesson again. Ben would never do that.

That was it for driving until four years ago, when I bought a house on the Connecticut shore and signed up for lessons with an instructor I'll call Tom. He was Italian American also, middle-aged, overweight, and rather sweet, but liable to spells of anger and gloom, as if he had raised too many sons like Mike. On bad days, as we drove around the back roads and shopping centers of Clinton and Madison and Guilford, Tom would seethe about the criminal propensities of the black inhabitants of New Haven. On good days, he liked to talk about religion. For example, he believed that Jesus Christ was a space alien, which would explain a lot — the Star of Bethlehem, the walking on water, the Resurrection. Besides, Tom said, "no human being could be that good." He made me memorize his special method of sliding backward into a parking space, failed to impress upon me the existence of blind spots, and, like his predecessor, lost interest in me when I flunked the road test.

I should have taken the test again immediately, but instead I spent several years driving around the shoreline with my lover in the passenger seat, as Connecticut law permits. He had special methods, too — for instance, on tricky maneuvers at an intersection he would urge me to "be one car" with the car in front, which means just do what that car is doing. Ben looked a little puzzled when I told him about that. What if the car in front is doing something really stupid? "Listen to your inner voice," he tells me when I continue going back as I parallel-park, even though I know I am about to go over the curb, which is an automatic failure on the test. "You are right, Kahta, you knew! Your inner voice is trying to help you!" You can't listen to your inner voice and be one car, too, is what Ben is getting at.

What was my lover thinking, I wonder, when we cruised Route 1, shuttling between our little house and the bookstore, the movie theater, Al Forno for pizza, the Clam Castle for lobster rolls, Hammonasset Beach to watch the twilight come over that long expanse of shining sand? Was he daydreaming about the young art critic, thinking about how later he would go off on his bicycle and call the drab colleague from the pay phone at the Stop & Shop? Was he thinking what a drag it was to have a girlfriend who couldn't pass a simple road test, even in small-town Connecticut, who did not care about the value-price transformation problem, and who never once woke him up with a blow job, despite being told many times that this was what all men wanted? Perhaps the young art critic is a better girlfriend on these and other scores, and he no longer feels the need for other women. Or perhaps the deception was the exciting part for him, and he will betray her, too, which is, of course, what I hope.

Now as I drive around upper Manhattan with Ben I spend a lot of time ignoring the road and asking myself, "If I had got my driver's license, would my lover have left me?" Perhaps my procrastination about the road test was symbolic to him of other resistances. "In the end," he said as he was leaving, ostensibly to "be alone" but actually, as I soon discovered, to join the young art critic on Fire Island, "our relationship revolves around you." "That's not true!" I wept. He also said, "Every day you wake up happy and cheerful and I'm lonely and miserable." "No, I don't!" I stormed. He continued, "You never read the books I recommend." I protested that I was reading one such book at that very moment — *A World Full of Gods: Pagans, Jews, and Christians in the Roman Empire,* by Keith Hopkins. "I mean serious political books," he said. "Books that are important to me." OK, point taken. Then came the coup de grâce: "I finally saw that you would never change."

What can you say to that? Change what? If I had read Anton Pannekoek's *Workers' Councils,* if I had given up e-mail for blow jobs at dawn, if I had got my license, would we still be together, driving north to buy daylilies at White Flower Farm while learnedly analyzing the Spartacist revolution of 1919? Perhaps, it occurs to me, as a demented cabbie cuts me off on Riverside Drive, it's a lucky thing I didn't get my license. I would still be living with a womanizer, a liar, a cheat, a manipulator, a maniac, a psychopath. Maybe my incompetence protected me.

New York State puts out an official booklet of rules of the road, but there are no textbooks that teach the art of driving itself. The closest is a tattered test result, much passed about by teachers, from the days when examiners filled out a form by hand. "I know his mother!" I exclaim when Ben gives me a copy. The test result happens to belong to a young writer, sometimes written up in gossip columns as a member of an all-boy fast crowd. "You see, Kahta! He failed to anticipate the actions of others. He didn't stop for pedestrians. And he forgot his turn signals, too." Ben shakes his head sorrowfully over the young writer's terrible score — seventy points off! I find this failure oddly cheering.

Mostly, though, driving is a skill transmitted by experience, one to one. In this, it resembles few activities, most of which can be learned from a book, or so we tell ourselves — think how many sex manuals are published every year, not to mention those educational sex videos advertised in high-toned literary publications aimed at people who were fantasizing about Mr. Rochester and Mr. Darcy while their classmates were steaming up the windows of their parents' cars. That was another accusation my lover flung at me the day he left: "You bought *The Joy of Sex,* but you just put it in a drawer!" "Why was it my job to improve our sex life?" I retorted. "You could have opened that book any time." I suppose the truth was that, given his multiple exhausting commitments, he didn't need to.

Sometimes when I am driving I become suddenly bewildered — it is as if I had never turned left or parallel-parked before. How many times have I turned the wheel while angling back into my parking space? I become hot and flushed and totally confused, and for some reason I keep turning the wheel until it's maxed out, and then look frantically at Ben.

"What do I do now, Ben? How far back do I turn it? How do I know when it's where it's supposed to be?"

"Beef stew, Kahta! Remember?"

"You mean I should just let it go back a tiny bit to see where it will go?"

"Riiight. You see, you are learning! Beef-stew it!"

But what if I get my license and I have one of these episodes of befuddlement when I'm alone at the wheel? Ben often has to remind me not to zone out, as I so frequently do even while I'm telling myself to stay focused. For example, I'll be staring at the red light, determined not to let my mind wander, and then I start wondering why red means "stop" and green means "go." Is there some optic science behind this color scheme? Is it arbitrary? Perhaps it derives from an ancient custom, the way the distance between rail-road tracks is derived from the distance between the wheels on Roman carts. I think how sad and romantic street lights look when blurred in the rain, and how before electricity no one could experience that exact romantic sadness, because nothing could have looked like that. I savor the odd fact that a street scene that seems so old-fashioned now is actually a product of modernity, and then it hits me that this is the sort of idea my lover was always having, and I wonder if I will ever have my mind back wholly to myself or if I will always feel invaded, abandoned, bereft.

"Kahta," Ben says gently, "the light has been green for some time now. Please, go!"

My lover used to joke that I had missed my chance to rid myself of my former husband forever by failing to run him over while an unlicensed, inexperienced driver. Actually, my ex and I get on very well. He's an excellent father, and when I have a computer problem he helps me over the phone, although he refuses to come and fix the machine himself. Now when I am careering up Riverside Drive I sometimes fantasize that I see my lover and his new girl-friend in the crosswalk. I wave my arms helplessly as the car, taking on a life of its own, homes into them like a magnet smashing into a bar of iron. Sometimes I put the drab colleague in the crosswalk, too, and run all three of them down. No jury would believe it had been an accident, although Ben would surely testify in my favor. I'd go to jail for decades, and the case would be made into a movie for one of those cable channels for women — *Out of Control: The Katha Pollitt Story*. What a disappointing end to my struggle for personal growth! Yet one not without consolations: in jail, after all, I would not need to drive. I could settle into comfy middle age, reorganizing the prison library and becoming a lesbian.

Twelve years ago, I saw a therapist who urged me to learn to drive to set an example for my daughter, who was then a toddler. She pointed out that my mother had never learned to drive, and waited in silence, as they do, for me to see a connection. Well, it's obvious, isn't it? My mother was a kind of professional helpless person. If she was alone in the house and couldn't open a jar, she would take it to the corner bar and ask one of the drunks to open it for her. "Don't be like your mother," my father would say in exasperation when I displayed particular ineptitude in the face of the physical world. And, except for the matter of driving, I'm not. I'm meaner and stronger and I'm not drinking myself to death. I own a special tool for twisting recalcitrant lids. Unlike my mother, I can time a meal so that the rice, the meat, and the vegetables all come out ready together. But it's true that my culinary skills deteriorated precipitously while I was living with my former lover, a fabulous cook who had once prepared dinner for the mayor of Bologna and who took over the kitchen the minute he moved in. Gradually, I forgot what I knew and lost the confidence to try new recipes, nor did I ever learn to use any of the numerous appliances he collected: the espresso machine with cappuccino attachment, the Cuisinart mini-prep, or the deep-fat fryer he bought the day after I said I was going on a diet.

My father made my mother sign up with a driving school. In fact, she was taking a lesson at the very moment word came over the car radio that President Kennedy had been shot. She claimed that this event so traumatized her that she could never get back behind the wheel. I didn't believe her — she'd never liked JFK, who had invaded Cuba and brought the world to the brink of nuclear war with the missile crisis. I think she was just afraid, the way I am — afraid of killing myself, afraid of killing someone else. I was fourteen when my mother gave up on her license, the same age that my daughter is now, but I give myself bonus points, because I'm still taking lessons. "You can do it, Mom," my daughter calls to me over her cereal when I dash out the door for my lesson. "Just keep your hands on the wheel." In a weak moment, I mentioned to her that sometimes at a red light I forget and put my hands in my lap — that would earn a warning from the examiner right there. I am trying to set her a good example, as that long-ago therapist urged — the example of a woman who does not fall apart because the man she loved lied to her every single minute of their life together and then left her for a woman young enough to be his daughter. "I'm going to be a little obsessed for a while," I told her. "I'm going to spend a lot of time talking on the phone with my friends and I may cry sometimes, but basically I'm fine. Also, I'm going on a huge diet, and I don't want any teenage anorexia from you."

"Mom!" She gave me the parents-are-weird eye-roll. The truth is, though, she's proud of me. When I do something new — figure out what's wrong with the computer without having to call my ex-husband, or retake the big study I vacated for my lover when he moved in, or give away my schlumpy old fat clothes and buy a lot of beautiful velvet pants and tops in deep jewel colors — she pumps her arm and says, *"Mujer de metal!"*

Ben is not just a great driving instructor; he is an interesting conversationalist. On our long lessons, he tells me all about growing up in Manila: the beauty of going to Mass with his mother every day, and how sad it was to lose touch with his sisters when they married and became part of their husbands' families. When he says that he prays for me to pass the driving test, I am so moved — I picture him surrounded by clouds of incense and tropical flowers, dressed in ornate robes, like the Infant of Prague. "Do you think I'm a weird Asian, Kahta?" Ben asks me. "Not at all," I say firmly, although how could I tell? Ben is the only Asian I know. He tells me that Asians repress their anger — which makes me wonder if he is secretly angry at me for making so many mistakes — and that Westerners don't understand their jokes. I tell him that mostly I know about Asians from reading ancient Chinese poetry and the novels of Shusako Endo. "What about the Kama Sutra?" he asks, and we laugh and insist we've never read it, never even looked at it, and then we laugh some more, because we know we are both lying. "See that pedestrian? He's Bob Marley's son," Ben says, pointing to a handsome young black man with short dreadlocks who's entering Riverside Church. And while I am wondering how Ben would know that — maybe Bob Jr. took lessons from him? — he cracks up: "You believed me!" Ben can be quite a humorist. And yet sometimes I worry about him, going home after a long day to his studio in Floral Park, Long Island. He's forty-four, and it will be years before he can marry his fiancée, who is forty and a schoolteacher back in the Philippines. When he gets home, he has three beers, which seems like a lot to drink alone. ("It used to be two, now three.") If I believed in God, I would pray for him — to get his own driving school, and be able to bring his fiancée over and move with her to a nice apartment in Castle Village, on the side that looks out over the river.

Some mornings, I know I mystify Ben. "Did you notice that hazard, Kahta? That double-parked SUV?" I admit I have no idea what he's talking about. "Always look ahead, Kahta. Look at the big picture, not just what's right in front of you. Observation!" Other days, though, I know I'm making progress. I zip up West End Avenue, enjoying the fresh green of the old plane trees and the early-morning quiet. I perform the physical work of driving, but with a kind of Zen dispersal of attention, so that as I am keeping an even pace and staying in my lane I am also noticing the bakery van signaling a right turn, and the dog walker hesitating on the curb with his cluster of chows and retrievers. A block ahead, I see a school bus stopping in front of the same Italianate apartment building where my daughter, my lover, and I used to wait for the bus when she was in elementary school, and I am already preparing to be careful and cautious, because you never know when a little child might dart out into the street. At that moment, it seems possible that I will pass the driving test, if not this time, then the next. One morning soon, I will put my license in my pocket, I will get into the car, turn the key, and enjoy the rumbly throat-clearing sound of the engine starting up. I will flick the turn signal down, so it makes that satisfying, precise click. I will pull out when I am ready and drive — it doesn't even matter where. I will make eye contact with pedestrians, I will be aware of cyclists coming up behind me; the smooth and confident trajectory of my vehicle will wordlessly convey to cabbies and Jersey drivers that they should keep at least three car lengths away, and more should it be raining. I will listen to my inner voice, I will look ahead to get the big picture, I will observe. I will beef-stew it. I will be *mujer de metal.*

ELAINE SCARRY

Citizenship in Emergency

FROM BOSTON REVIEW

FOR THE PAST YEAR, we have spoken unceasingly about the events of September 11, 2001. But one aspect of that day has not yet been the topic of open discussion: the difficulty we had as a country defending ourselves; as it happened, the only successful defense was carried out not by our professional defense apparatus but by the passengers on Flight 93, which crashed in Pennsylvania. The purpose of this essay is to examine that difficulty, and the one success, and ask if they suggest that something in our defense arrangements needs to be changed. Whatever the ultimate answer to that question, we at least need to ask it, since defending the country is an obligation we all share.

The difficulty of defense on September 11 turned in large part on the pace of events. We need to look carefully at the timelines and timetables on that day. But as we do, it is crucial to recall that the word "speed" did not surface for the first time on September 11. It has been at the center of discussions of national defense for the last fifty years. When we look to any of our literatures on the subject, we find in the foreground statements about the speed of our weapons, of our weapons' delivery systems, and of the deliberations that will lead to their use.

Throughout this period, the heart of our defense has been a vast missile system, all parts of which are described as going into effect in "a matter of minutes": a presidential decision must be made in "a matter of minutes"; the presidential order must be transmitted in "a matter of minutes"; the speed of the missile launch must be carried out in "a matter of minutes"; and the missile must reach its target in "a matter of minutes."

The matter-of-minutes claim is sometimes formally folded into the names of our weapons (as in the Minuteman missile) and other times appears in related banner words such as "supersonic" and "hair-trigger." Thousands of miles separating countries and continents can be contracted by "supersonic" missiles and planes that carry us there in "a matter of minutes"; and thousands of miles separating countries and continents can be contracted by focusing on the distance that has to be crossed not by the weapon itself but by the hand gesture that initiates the launch — the distance of a hair.

"Speed" has occupied the foreground not only of our *descriptive* statements about our national defense but also our *normative* statements. Our military arrangements for defending the country have often been criticized for moving increasingly outside the citizenry's control. The constitutional requirement for a congressional declaration of war has not been used for any war since World War II: the Korean War, the Vietnam War, and the war in former Yugoslavia were all carried out at the direction of the president and without a congressional declaration, as were the invasions of Panama, Grenada, and Haiti; the recent "Authorization for the Use of Military Force Against Iraq" once again fails to fulfill the requirement for a congressional declaration. Speed has repeatedly been invoked to counter ethical, legal, or constitutional objections to the way our weapons policies and arrangements have slipped further and further beyond democratic structures of self-governance.

This bypassing of the Constitution in the case of conventional wars and invasions has been licensed by the existence of nuclear weapons and by the country's formal doctrine of "presidential first use," which permits the president, acting alone, to initiate nuclear war. Since the president has genocidal injuring power at his personal disposal, obtaining Congress's permission for much lesser acts of injury (as in conventional wars) has often struck presidents as a needless bother: President Bush Sr. boasted, "I didn't have to get permission from some old goat in the United States Congress to kick Saddam Hussein out of Kuwait." The most frequent argument used to excuse the setting aside of the Constitution is that the pace of modern life simply does not allow time for obtaining the authorization of Congress, let alone the full citizenry. Our ancestors who designed the Constitution — so the argument goes — could not have envisioned the supersonic speed at which the country's defense would need to take place. So the congressional requirement is an anachronism. With planes and weapons traveling faster than the speed of sound, what sense does it make to have a lot of sentences we have no time to hear?

Among the many revelations that occurred on September 11 was a revelation about our capacity to act quickly. Speed — the realpolitik that has excused the setting aside of the law for fifty years — turns out not to have been very *real* at all. The description that follows looks at the timetables of American Airlines Flight 77 — the plane that hit the Pentagon — and United Airlines Flight 93 — the plane that crashed in Pennsylvania when passengers successfully disabled the hijackers' mission. Each of the two planes was a small piece of U.S. ground. Their juxtaposition indicates that a form of defense that is external to the ground that needs to be defended does not work as well as a form of defense that is internal to the ground that needs to be protected. This outcome precisely matches the arguments that were made at the time of the writing of the Constitution about why the military had to be "held within a civil frame": about why military actions, whether offensive or defensive, must be measured against the norms of civilian life, must be brought into contact with the people with whom one farms or performs shared labor, or the people with whom one raises children, or the people with whom one goes to church or a weekly play or movie. Preserving such a civil frame was needed to prevent the infantilization of the country's population by its own leaders, and because it was judged to be the only plausible way actually to defend the home ground.

When the plane that hit the Pentagon and the plane that crashed in Pennsylvania are looked at side by side, they reveal two different conceptions of national defense: one model is authoritarian, centralized, top-down; the other, operating in a civil frame, is distributed and egalitarian. Should anything be inferred from the fact that the first form of defense failed and the second succeeded? This outcome obligates us to review our military structures and to consider the possibility that we need a democratic, not a top-down, form of defense. At the very least, the events of September 11 cast doubt on a key argument that, for the past fifty years, has been used to legitimize an increasingly centralized, authoritarian model of defense — namely, the argument based on speed.

American Airlines Flight 77 was originally scheduled to fly from Washington to Los Angeles. The plane approached the Pentagon at a speed of 500 miles per hour. It entered the outermost of the building's five rings, ring E, then cut through ring D and continued on through ring C, and eventually stopped just short of ring B. Two million square feet were damaged or destroyed. Before September 11, the Pentagon was five corridors deep, five stories high, and in its overall shape five-sided. Three of the Pentagon's five sides were affected (one had to be leveled and rebuilt; the other two were badly damaged by smoke and water).

One hundred and eighty-nine people died — 64 on the plane, 125 working in the Pentagon. Many others were badly burned. Twenty-three thousand people work in the Pentagon. Two factors prevented many more people from being killed or badly burned. First, the building is stacked horizontally, not vertically like the World Trade Center towers — it is built like layers of sedimentary rock that have been turned on their side and lie flush with the ground. Second, one of the sections hit was being renovated and was therefore relatively empty of people when the plane entered.

While we continue to lament the deaths and injuries, and continue to find solace in the fact that the number of deaths and injuries was not higher, one key fact needs to be held on to and stated in a clear sentence: on September 11, the Pentagon could not defend the Pentagon, let alone the rest of the country.

The U.S. military had precious little time to respond on September 11 (and this fact has been accurately acknowledged by almost everyone, both inside and outside the country, who has spoken about the day). But by the standards of speed that have been used to justify setting aside constitutional guarantees for the last fifty years, the U.S. military on September 11 had a great deal of time to protect the Pentagon. It had more than minutes. The pilots of the F-15s and F-16s that flew on that day made no mistakes, displayed no inadequacies, and showed no lack of courage — but what they tried to do now appears to have been a structural impossibility.

One hour and twenty-one minutes go by between the moment FAA controllers learn that multiple planes have been taken and the moment the Pentagon is struck. Controllers hear the hijackers on the first seized plane (American Flight 11) say "we have some planes" at 8:24 A.M., a sentence indicating that the plane from which the voice comes is not the sole plane presently imperiled. The information that "some planes" have been taken is available one hour and twenty-one minutes before the Pentagon is hit by the third seized plane at 9:45 A.M.

Fifty-eight minutes go by between the attack on the first World Trade Center tower (at 8:47 A.M.) and the crash into the Pentagon (9:45 A.M.). This means that for almost one hour before the Pentagon is hit, the military knows that the hijackers have multiple planes and that those hijackers have no intention to land those planes safely.

The crash of American Flight 77 into the Pentagon comes fifty-five minutes after that plane has itself disappeared from radio contact (at 8:50 A.M.). So for *fifty-five minutes,* the military knows three things:

1. the hijackers have multiple planes;
2. the hijackers, far from having any intention of landing the planes safely, intend to injure as many people on the ground as possible; and
3. Flight 77 has a *chance* of being one of those planes, since it has just disappeared from radio.

When, six minutes later, the plane loses its transponder (so that its radar image as well as its radio contact is now lost), the chance that it is one of the seized planes rises.

By the most liberal reading, then, the country had *one hour and twenty-one minutes* to begin to respond. By the most conservative reading, the country had *fifty-five minutes* to begin to respond. The phrase "begin to respond" does not mean that an F-15 or F-16 could now attack the plane that would hit the Pentagon. At the one-hour-and-twenty-one-minute clock time, the plane that will eventually hit the Pentagon is only four minutes into its flight and has not yet been hijacked. It means instead that a warning threshold has just been crossed and a level of readiness might therefore begin: at one hour and twenty-one minutes, fighter pilots could be placed on standby on the ground with engines running; at fifty-five minutes, fighter planes could be following the third plane, as well as any other planes that are wildly off course and out of radio contact.

One hour and twenty-one minutes and *fifty-five minutes* are each a short time — a short, short time. But by the timetables that we have for decades accepted as descriptive of our military weapons, by the timetables we have accepted as explanations for why we must abridge our structures of self-governance — by the intoxicating timetables of "rapid response," the proud specifications of eight minutes, twelve minutes, four minutes, one minute — by these timetables, the September 11 time periods of one hour and twenty-one minutes or of fifty-five minutes are very long periods indeed.

The transition from the moment Flight 77's radio is off (at 8:50 A.M.) to the moment it disappears from secondary radar (8:56 A.M.) is crucial, for it begins to confirm the inference that this is one of the hijacked planes. A sequence of confirmations now follows. While the FAA controllers have been unable to reach the plane, now the airline company also discovers its inability to reach Flight 77 on a separate radio (shortly after 9 A.M.). At 9:25 a passenger, Barbara Olson, places a phone call to her husband, Theodore Olson, in the U.S. Justice Department, stating that the plane is under the control of hijackers. Because the passenger is well known to the Justice Department listener, no time need be lost assessing the honesty and accuracy of the report. This means that twenty minutes prior to the moment the Pentagon is hit, the Justice Department has direct, reliable voice confirmation of the plane's seizure.

So for *twenty minutes* prior to the hitting of the Pentagon, the military is in a position to know three things (the third of which differs decisively from what it knew at the fifty-five-minute marker):

1. the hijackers have multiple planes;
2. the hijackers intend to injure as many people as possible;
3. Flight 77 is *certainly* one of the hijacked planes: it has disappeared from radio, disappeared from secondary radar, disappeared from the company radio, and has been described to the Justice Department as "hijacked" by a passenger whose word cannot be doubted.

The steadily mounting *layers of verification* listed in number 3 continue. At 9:33 A.M., an FAA air traffic controller (according to the *New York Times*) sees on radar a "fast moving blip" or "fast moving primary target" making its way toward Washington airspace: this level of verification comes *twelve minutes* prior to the plane's crash into the Pentagon. At 9:36 A.M. an airborne C-130 sees the plane and identifies it as a "757 moving low and fast." This further confirmation comes *nine minutes* prior to the collision. No one can suppose that in nine minutes planes could be scrambled and reach the hijacked plane (even if we have, for decades, listened dutifully to descriptions of much more complicated military acts occurring in nine minutes). But certainly the layers of alert, of scrambling, of takeoff, of tracking, could have begun one hour and twenty minutes earlier, or fifty-five minutes earlier, not nine minutes earlier. Nine minutes is presumably the time frame in which only the last act of military defense need be carried out by the fighter planes — if there is any reasonable last act to be taken, a question to which I will return.

During much of its flight, American Flight 77 was over countryside (rather than over densely populated urban areas). Here is a list of the six successive layers of verification, which will help us picture where the plane was at each stage:

- loss of radio (55 minutes remain)
- loss of transponder (49 minutes remain)
- loss of contact with the airline company (approximately 36 minutes remain)
- a passenger calls the Justice Department (20 minutes remain)
- a radar image is seen moving toward Washington whose source is not using its secondary radar (12 minutes remain)
- a C-130 sights a Boeing 757 flying fast and low (9 minutes remain)

Assuming an air speed of 500 miles an hour, we can infer that at the time we learn that both the radio and the transponder are off (*the second layer of confirmation*), the plane would be 410 miles from Washington with many miles of sparsely populated land beneath it. By *the fourth confirmation* (Barbara Olson's phone call), it would be 166 miles from Washington. By *the sixth confirmation,* that given by the C-130, the plane destined for the Pentagon would still be 75 miles from Washington and the possibility of minimizing injury to those on the ground would be rapidly vanishing with each passing mile.

Again, the point here is not to say, "Why couldn't these airmen shoot down the plane?" Time made that extremely difficult. But much smaller units of time have been invoked to explain our battle readiness over the last fifty years and to license the centralization of injuring power rather than a decentralized and distributed authorization across the full citizenry, which is, according to the U.S. Constitution, our legal right and our legal responsibility to protect. There is a second, profound reason the act could not be (ought not to have been) carried out — the problem of consent, to which I will return when we come to United Flight 93.

Let us see what actions the military undertook during this time (actions described in the *New York Times* and *Aviation Week and Space Technology*). Fourteen National Guard planes are responsible for defending the country. Five of those planes — two F-15s from Otis Air Force Base on Cape Cod and three F-16s from Langley in Virginia — were called into action on September 11. These five planes were not the only military planes in the air that day. Once the Pentagon was hit, the FAA ordered all aircraft down — a beautifully choreographed landing of 4,546 planes over a period of three hours. When the FAA announced the order, 206 military planes were in U.S. airspace (most engaged in routine exercises, actions unconnected to the immediate defense of the country); 90 remained in the air after the grounding (their duties have not been entered into the public record). But it is only the five National Guard planes that were called into action against the seized passenger airliners that will be described here.

The two National Guard F-15s that took off from Otis attempted to address the events taking place in New York City. They were called into action one minute before the first World Trade Center tower was hit; by the time the second tower was hit, they were seventy-one miles — eight minutes — away from Manhattan. Should they then have continued down to the Washington area? (By this time, the plane destined for the Pentagon had its radio and transponder off and was reachable by neither air controllers nor the airline company.) The answer is no. The two F-15s needed to stay near New York City, where it was reasonable to worry that a third hijacked plane could approach. From September 11, 2001, until March 21, 2002, New York airspace was protected twenty-four hours a day by F-15s, F-16s, and AWACS planes.

The three F-16s at Langley received their first order from Hunt-ress Defense Section at 9:24 A.M. This is a late start: twenty-two minutes after the second World Trade Center tower has been hit, thirty-four minutes after the plane destined for the Pentagon has lost its radio, twenty-eight minutes after it has disappeared from secondary radar, and fifteen minutes after the airline company has failed to reach the plane on its own radio. By 9:30 A.M. the Langley F-16s are in the air, traveling at 600 miles per hour toward New York City. Soon they are instructed to change their course and are told that Reagan National Airport is the target. They are flying at 25,000 feet. The hijacked plane is flying at 7,000 feet. The F-16s reach Washington, D.C., at some unspecified time after the 9:45 A.M. collision of Flight 77 into the Pentagon. As they pass over the city, they are asked to look down and confirm that the Pentagon is on fire — confirmation that by this point civilians on the ground have already provided.

There are profoundly clear reasons why the military could not easily intercept the plane and bring it down in a rural area. But each of those reasons has counterparts in our long-standing military arrangements, which should now be subjected to rigorous questioning. First, Flight 77's path was hard to track, since its transponder had been turned off. Yes, that's true — and so, too, any missiles fired on the United States or its allies will surely be traveling without a transponder; their paths will not be lucid; their tracking will not be easy. Second, the fact that Flight 77's radio was not working couldn't be taken as a decisive sign that it was a hijacked plane, since at least eleven planes then in the skies had nonworking radios (nine of the eleven were unconnected to the hijackings). Yes, that's true — and with missile defense there are likely to be not eleven but hundreds of decoys and false targets that will have to be nimbly sorted through. As difficult as it was to identify the third seized plane, it must be acknowledged that the flight had elements that made it far easier to identify than the enemy missiles our nation has spoken blithely about for decades: the direct voice confirmation provided by the passenger phone call to the Justice Department, most notably, will not have any counterpart in a missile attack, nor can we reasonably expect six layers of verification of any one enemy plane or missile.

A third crucial explanation for the failure to protect the Pentagon is that an F-16 cannot shoot down a passenger plane by arrogating the right to decide whether the lives on board can be sacrificed to avert the *possibility* of even more lives being lost on the ground. Yes, that is true — and yet for decades we have spoken about actions that directly imperil the full American citizenry (including presidential first use of nuclear weapons against a population that the president acting alone has decided is "the enemy") without ever obtaining the American citizenry's consent to those actions.

Each of these three explanations for why the attack on the Pentagon could not be easily averted raises key questions about our long-standing descriptions of the country's defense, and yet so far does not appear to have in any way altered those descriptions. September 11 has caused the United States and its allies to adjust their timetables only in those cases where the scenario imagined closely approximates the events that occurred in the terrorist attack itself. In England, the *Observer* reports, "MI5 has warned Ministers that a determined terrorist attempt to fly a jet into the Sellafield nuclear plant in Cumbria could not be prevented because it is only *two minutes'* flying time from transatlantic flight paths."

While two minutes' time makes it impossible to defend Cumbria against terrorists, two minutes is apparently plenty of time for the United States and its NATO allies to carry out missile defense. Here is a post–September 11 description of England's Joint Rapid Reaction Force, described in the *Scotsman:* "A new satellite communications system has been installed to allow planners in Northwood to transmit target co-ordinates to the royal Navy's nuclear submarines equipped to fire Tomahawk cruise missiles. HMS *Trafalgar* and HMS *Triumph* in the Indian Ocean both have this system. *Within minutes* of the Prime Minister giving permission to fire from Downing Street, General Reith could pass on the orders to the submarine nominated to launch the precision attack." What would be the response by Western democracies if a terrorist used chemical, biological, or even nuclear weapons? In an article in *News of the World* describing advice given to Tony Blair by his defense ministers, we learn that "one of his most trusted advisers believes that a highly effective way of preventing such an attack is to threaten states that succor the terrorists with a nuclear wipe-out, within minutes of such an attack, without waiting for intelligence reports, United Nations resolutions or approval from NATO."

Does the Bush administration have plans in place for such an attack? Might it be our duty to inquire?

The plane that took the Pentagon by surprise could not be stopped despite a *one-hour-and-twenty-one-minute* warning that multiple planes had been hijacked, despite a *fifty-eight-minute* warning that the hijackers intended to maximize the number of casualties, despite a *fifty-five-minute* warning that Flight 77 might *possibly* be a hijacked flight, and despite a *twenty-minute* warning that Flight 77 was *certainly* a hijacked flight. Yet so confident are we of our ability to get information, of our power to decipher complex lines of responsibility, of the existence of evil and of the transparency of that evil, that we are still today talking about two or three minutes to send cruise missiles and even nuclear genocide to foreign populations. This despite eleven months — 475,000 minutes — in which we have been unable to determine who sent anthrax to the U.S. Senate and various television communication centers.

United Airlines Flight 93 was a small piece of American territory — roughly 600 cubic meters overall. It was lost to the country for approximately forty minutes when terrorists seized control. It was restored to the country when civilian passengers who became citizen soldiers regained control of the ground — in the process losing their own lives.

The passengers on Flight 93 were able to defend this ground for two reasons. First, they were able to identify the threat accurately because it was in their immediate sensory horizon (unlike the F-16s that hoped to intercept the plane that hit the Pentagon, the passengers on Flight 93 did not need to decipher their plane's flight path from the outside, nor make inferences and guesses about lost radio contact). The passengers were also able to get information from unimpeachable sources external to the plane: crucially, they did not rely on information from a single central authority but obtained it from an array of sources, each independent of the others. Second, it was their own lives they were jeopardizing, lives over which they exercised authority and consent. On the twin bases of sentient knowledge and authorization, their collaborative work met the democratic standard of "informed consent."

When the U.S. Constitution was completed it had two provisions for ensuring that decisions about warmaking were distributed rather than concentrated. The first was the provision for a congressional declaration of war — an open debate in both the House and the Senate involving what would today be 535 men and women. The second was a major clause of the Bill of Rights — the Second Amendment right to bear arms — that rejected a standing executive army (an army at the personal disposal of president or king) in favor of a militia, a citizens' army distributed across all ages, geography, and social classes. Democracy, it was argued, was impossible without a distributed militia: self-governance was perceived to be logically impossible without self-defense (exactly what do you "self-govern" if you have ceded the governing of your own body and life to someone else?).

United Flight 93 was like a small legislative assembly or town meeting. The assembly structure is audible in the public record of conversations (a detailed record that was made available by the *Pittsburgh Post-Gazette* and *U.S. News & World Report*). The residents on that ground conferred with one another, as well as with people not on the plane. Records from the onboard telephones show that twenty-four phone calls were made between 9:31 A.M. and 9:54 A.M.; additional calls were made from cell phones. In approximately *twenty-three minutes,* the passengers were able collectively to move through the following sequence of steps:

1. *Identify the location throughout the plane of all hijackers and how many people each is holding.* We know that passengers registered this information in detail because they voiced the information to people beyond the plane: Todd Beamer relayed the information to Lisa Jefferson (a Verizon customer-service operator); Jeremy Glick relayed it to his wife; Sandy Bradshaw to her husband; Mark Bingham to his mother; Marion Britton to a close friend; Elizabeth Wainio to her stepmother; and CeeCee Lyles to her husband.

In terms of democratic self-defense, these conversations are crucial (both at step 1 and at each of the seven steps listed below) to preserving the civil frame that the founders identified as so essential to military defense. The conversations enabled extraordinary events to be tested against the norms of everyday life. They were both intimate and an act of record-making — how else to explain Mark Bingham's self-identification to his mother: "This is Mark Bingham"? He both gave his mother the statement that the plane had been seized by hijackers ("You believe me, don't you?") and in effect notarized the statement by giving a verbal signature.

2. *Hear from sources outside the plane the story of the World Trade Center.* This information was key: it informed the passengers that they would almost certainly not be making a safe landing; it also informed them that many people on the ground would also suffer death or injury from their plane.

3. *Verify from multiple sources outside the plane the World Trade Center story.* Jeremy Glick, for example, told his wife that the account of the World Trade Center attacks was circulating among the passengers. He explicitly asked her to confirm or deny its truth: "Is it true?"

4. *Consult with each other and with friends outside the plane about the appropriate action.* Jeremy Glick told his family the passengers were developing a plan "to rush" the hijackers, and he asked their advice. Todd Beamer told Lisa Jefferson the passengers will "take" the terrorists. (She cautioned: "Are you sure that's what you want to do?") Tom Burnett told his wife "[a group of us] is going to do something." (She urged him to lay low and not make himself visible.) Sandy Bradshaw told her husband she was at that moment filling coffee pots with boiling water, which she planned to throw at the hijackers; she asked if he had a better plan. (He told her she had the best plan, and to go ahead.)

5. *Take a vote.* Jeremy Glick described the voting process to his wife as it was under way.

6. *Prepare themselves for taking a dire action that may result in death.* CeeCee Lyles, unable to reach her husband, left a recorded message of herself praying, then later reached him and prayed with him; Tom Burnett asked his wife to pray while he and others on the plane acted; Todd Beamer and Lisa Jefferson together recited the Twenty-third Psalm.

7. *Take leave of people they love.* Each of the passengers who was in conversation with a family member stated aloud his or her love for the listener; Todd Beamer asked Lisa Jefferson to convey his love to his family. The family members reciprocated: "I've got my arms around you," Elizabeth Wainio's stepmother told her.

8. *Act.*

Many passengers described the plan to enter the cockpit by force. Not every passenger assumed death was certain. Jeremy Glick left his phone off the hook, telling his wife, "Hold the phone. I'll be back." Todd Beamer also left the phone line open — either because he expected to come back or as an act of public record-keeping. The two open lines permitted members of the Glick household and Lisa Jefferson to overhear the cries and shouts that followed, indicating that action was being taken. CeeCee Lyles, still on the phone with her husband, cried, "They're doing it! They're doing it!" Confirmation is also provided by Sandy Bradshaw's sudden final words to her husband: "Everyone's running to first class. I've got to go. Bye."

The passengers on United Flight 93 could act with speed because they resided on the ground that needed to be defended. Equally important, they could make the choice — formalized in their public act of an open vote — between certain doom and uncertain (but possibly more widespread) doom. They could have hoped that the hijackers would change their planned course; they could have known that death by either avenue was certain, but one avenue would take them to their deaths in several minutes (rushing the hijackers and crashing the plane) and the other avenue would perhaps give them another half hour or hour of life (waiting for the plane to reach its final target). They could have chosen the second; many people have chosen a delayed death when given the same choice. It is, in any event, the right of the people who themselves are going to die to make the decision, not the right of a pilot in an F-16 or the person giving orders to the pilot in the F-16 — as both civilian and military leaders have repeatedly acknowledged since September 11.

It may be worth noting that the hijackers themselves correctly foresaw that the threat to their mission would come from the passengers ("citizen soldiers") and not from a military source external to the plane. The terrorists left behind multiple copies of a manual, five pages in Arabic. The manual is a detailed set of instructions for the hours before and after boarding the plane — what its translators and interpreters have described (in the *New York Review of Books*) as "an exacting guide for achieving the unity of body and spirit necessary for success." The ritualized set of steps includes: taking a mutual pledge to die; carrying out a ritual act of washing, invocation, and prayer; and dressing according to prescribed recommendations on the tightness or looseness of clothing.

The manual does not tell the terrorists what to do if an F-15 or F-16 approaches the plane they have seized. It instead gives elaborate instructions on what to do if passengers offer resistance. We should not ordinarily let ourselves be schooled by terrorists. But terrorists who seek to carry out a mission successfully have to know what the greatest threat to their mission is — and the handbook indicates that the great obstacles were perceived to be, first, the passengers, and second, the reluctance the hijackers might feel about killing any resisting passengers. They are instructed at length and in elaborate detail to kill any resister and to regard the killing as "a sacred drama," a death carried out to honor their parents. (That the hijackers would unblinkingly crash into a skyscraper, taking thousands of lives, yet balk at the idea of killing people with their own hands, and therefore require detailed counseling to get them through it, is perhaps no more surprising than the fact that we listen every day to casualty rates brought about by the military yet would not keenly kill in hand-to-hand combat.)

I have intended here to open a conversation about our general capacity for self-defense. I have compared the fates of the plane that hit the Pentagon and the plane that crashed in Pennsylvania. The military was unable to thwart the action of Flight 77 despite fifty-five minutes in which clear evidence existed that the plane might be held by terrorists, and despite twenty minutes in which clear evidence existed that the plane was certainly held by terrorists. In the same amount of time — twenty-three minutes — the passengers of Flight 93 were able to gather information, deliberate, vote, and act.

September 11 involved a partial failure of defense. If ever a country has been warned that its defense arrangements are defective, the United States has been warned. Standing quietly by while our leaders build more weapons of mass destruction and bypass more rules and more laws (and more citizens) simply continues the unconstitutional and — as we have recently learned — ineffective direction we have passively tolerated for fifty years. We share a responsibility to deliberate about these questions, as surely as the passengers on Flight 93 shared a responsibility to deliberate about how to act.

The failures of our current defense arrangements put an obligation on all of us to review our procedures for protecting the country. "All of us" means "all of us who reside in the country," not "all of us who work at the Pentagon" or "all of us who convene when there is a meeting of the Joint Chiefs of Staff." What the Joint Chiefs think, or what analysts at the Pentagon think, is of great interest (as are the judgments of men and women who by other avenues of expertise have thoughtful and knowledgeable assessments of security issues); it would be a benefit to the nation if such people would begin to share those views with the public. But such views can in no way preempt or abridge our own obligation to review matters, since the protection of the country falls to everyone whose country it is.

More particularly, September 11 called into question a key argument that has been used to legitimate the gradual shift from an egalitarian, all-citizen military to one that is external to — independent of — civilian control: the argument about speed. The egalitarian model turned out to have the advantage of swiftness, as well as obvious ethical advantages. This outcome has implications for three spheres of defense.

1. *Defense against aerial terrorism.* To date, the egalitarian model of defense is the only one that has worked against aerial terrorism. It worked on September 11 when passengers brought down the plane in Pennsylvania. It worked again on December 22, 2001, when the passengers and crew on an American Airlines flight from Paris to Miami prevented a terrorist (called "the shoe bomber") from blowing up the plane with plastic explosives and killing the 197 people on board. Two F-15s escorted the plane to Boston and, once the plane landed, FBI officials hurried aboard, but the danger itself was averted not by the fighter jets or the FBI but by men and women inside the plane, who restrained the six-foot-four-inch man using his own hair, leather belts, earphone wires, and sedatives injected by two physicians.

When a passenger plane is seized by a terrorist, defense from the outside (by a fighter jet, for example) appears to be structurally implausible from the perspective of time, and structurally impossible from the perspective of consent. The problem of time — time to ascertain that a plane has been seized, time to identify accurately which plane it is, time to arrive in the airspace near the seized plane — was dramatically evident in the case of the plane that hit the Pentagon, even though much more time and many more layers of verification were available that day than are likely to be available in any future instance. The time difficulty was evident again on January 5, 2002, when a fifteen-year-old boy took off without authorization from St. Petersburg–Clearwater International Airport, crossed the airspace of MacDill Air Force Base (headquarters for the U.S. war in Afghanistan), and crashed into the twenty-eighth floor of a forty-two-story skyscraper in Tampa. Two F-15s "screamed" toward him from the south (as the *Tampa Tribune* reported), but reached him only after he had completed his twenty-five-minute flight. The time problem was visible once more on June 19, 2002, when a pilot and passenger in a Cessna 182 accidentally crossed into forbidden airspace near the Washington Monument, flew there for twelve miles (coming within four miles of the White House), and then crossed out again before armed F-16s from Andrews Air Force Base could reach the plane.

Even if the nearly insurmountable problems of time and perfect knowledge can one day be solved, how can the problem of consent be solved? There is no case in war when a soldier is authorized to kill two hundred fellow soldiers; how can an airman be authorized to kill two hundred fellow citizens? How can anyone other than the passengers themselves take their lives in order to save some number of the rest of us on the ground? During the seven months that F-15s and F-16s, armed with air-to-air missiles, flew round-the-clock over New York and Washington, what instructions did they have in the event that a passenger plane was seized? What instructions do they now have for their more intermittent flights? Are such instructions something only high-ranking officials should be privy to, or might this be something that should be candidly discussed in public?

It seems reasonable to conclude that on September 11 the Pentagon could have been defended in one way and one way only, by the passengers on the American Airlines flight. This would have required three steps: that multiple passengers on the plane be informed about the World Trade Center attacks; that the passengers decide to act, or not to act; and that, in the event they choose to act, they be numerous enough to carry out their plan successfully. As far as we know, none of these steps took place — in part because, as far as we know, there were not enough passengers on board who knew about the World Trade Center. It is possible that one or more of these steps did take place, even though they were not recorded.

In stating that the egalitarian model is our best and only defense against aerial terrorism, I do not mean that passengers in any one case *must* choose to act, or that, having so chosen, they will be successful. I mean only that this is the one form of defense available to us as a country, which passengers are at liberty to exercise or refrain from exercising. Measures taken by the nation that are internal to the plane (locks on cockpit doors, the presence of air marshals, the cessation of round-the-clock fighter jets over New York and Washington) are compatible with this form of defense.

2. *National defense in the immediate present.* The contrast between the plane that hit the Pentagon and the plane that crashed in Pennsylvania invites consideration of the need to return to an egalitarian and democratic military, not only in the specific case of aerial terrorism but in all measures we take for the nation's defense in the present year. Some may argue that we cannot generalize from one day. Can we generalize from zero days? One day is what we have. What makes this non-risky is that rather than requiring us to come up with some new system of government, all it requires is returning to, and honoring, the framework of our own laws.

Since September 11 we have witnessed many actions taken in the name of homeland defense that are independent of, or external to, civilian control. Foreign residents have been seized and placed in circumstances that violate our most basic laws; the war against Afghanistan was under way before we had even been given much explanation of its connection to the terrorists, who were from Saudi Arabia or Lebanon or Egypt or the United Arab Emirates, not from Afghanistan; that war now seems to be over, even though we don't know whether we eliminated the small circle around Osama bin Laden, for whose sake we believed we were there; we are now tripping rapidly ahead to the next war, listening passively to weekly announcements about an approaching war with Iraq that has no visible connection to the events of September 11; the president's formulation of this future war sometimes seems to include (or at least not to exclude) the use of nuclear weapons and the animation of our nuclear first-use policy. The decoupling of all defense from the population itself lurches between large outcomes (presidential declaration of war) and the texture of everyday life. According to the former chairman of the Federal Communications Commission, the federal agency called the National Communications System has "proposed that government officials be able to take over the wireless networks used by cellular telephones in the event of an emergency," thereby preempting the very form of defense that did work (the citizenry) and giving their tools to the form of defense that did not work (the government).

We are defending the country by ceding our own powers of self-defense to a set of managers external to ourselves. But can these powers be ceded without relinquishing the very destination toward which we are traveling together, as surely as if our ship had been seized? The destination for which we purchased tickets was a country where no one was arrested without his or her name being made public, a country that did not carry out wars without the authorization of Congress (and the widespread debate among the population that such a congressional declaration necessitates), a country that does not threaten to use weapons of mass destruction. Why are we sitting quietly in our seats?

In the short run, returning to an egalitarian model of defense means: no war with Iraq unless it has been authorized by Congress and the citizenry; no abridgment of civil liberties; no elimination of the tools that enable citizens to protect themselves and one another (such as cell phones) — and, above all, no contemplated use of nuclear weapons.

3. *National defense in the long run.* Europeans often refer to nuclear weapons as "monarchic weapons" precisely because they are wholly external to any powers of consent or dissent exercised by the population. In the long run, the return to an egalitarian model of national defense will require the return to a military that uses only conventional weapons. This will involve a tremendous cost: it will almost certainly, for example, mean the return of a draft. But a draft means that a president cannot carry out a war without going through the citizenry, and going through the citizenry means that the arguments for going to war get tested tens of thousands of times before the killing starts.

Our nuclear weapons are the largest arsenal of genocidal weapons anywhere on earth. These weapons, even when not in use, deliver a death blow to our democracy. But even if we are willing to give up democracy to keep ourselves safe, on what basis have we come to believe that they keep us safe? Their speed? A Cessna plane (of the kind that proved impossible to intercept in Florida and Washington) travels at approximately 136 feet per second; a Boeing 757 (of the kind that proved impossible to intercept as it approached the Pentagon) travels at 684 feet per second; a missile travels at 6,400 feet per second. On what have we based our confidence about intercepting incoming missiles, since the problem of deciphering information and decoupling it from decoys will (along with speed) be much greater in the case of the missile than in the cases of the planes?

Nuclear weapons are an extreme form of aerial terrorism. It is with good reason that we have worked to prevent the proliferation throughout the world of nuclear weapons (and also biological and chemical weapons of mass destruction). But in the long run, other countries will agree to abstain from acquiring them, or to give them up in cases where they already have them, only when and if the United States agrees to give them up. The process of persuading Iraq, China, North Korea, India, Pakistan, as well as our immediate allies to give them up will commence on the day we agree to restore within our own country a democratic form of self-defense.

SUSAN SONTAG

Looking at War

FROM THE NEW YORKER

I

IN JUNE 1938, Virginia Woolf published *Three Guineas,* her brave, unwelcomed reflections on the roots of war. Written during the preceding two years, while she and most of her intimates and fellow writers were rapt by the advancing Fascist insurrection in Spain, the book was couched as a tardy reply to a letter from an eminent lawyer in London who had asked, "How in your opinion are we to prevent war?" Woolf begins by observing tartly that a truthful dialogue between them may not be possible. For though they belong to the same class, "the educated class," a vast gulf separates them: the lawyer is a man and she is a woman. Men make war. Men (most men) like war, or at least they find "some glory, some necessity, some satisfaction in fighting" that women (most women) do not seek or find. What does an educated — that is, privileged, well-off — woman like her know of war? Can her reactions to its horrors be like his?

Woolf proposes they test this "difficulty of communication" by looking at some images of war that the beleaguered Spanish government has been sending out twice a week to sympathizers abroad. Let's see "whether when we look at the same photographs we feel the same things," she writes. "This morning's collection contains the photograph of what might be a man's body, or a woman's; it is so mutilated that it might, on the other hand, be the body of a pig. But those certainly are dead children, and that undoubtedly is the section of a house. A bomb has torn open the side;

there is still a bird-cage hanging in what was presumably the sitting room." One can't always make out the subject, so thorough is the ruin of flesh and stone that the photographs depict. "However different the education, the traditions behind us," Woolf says to the lawyer, "we" — and here women are the "we" — and he might well have the same response: "War, you say, is an abomination; a barbarity; war must be stopped at whatever cost. And we echo your words. War is an abomination; a barbarity; war must be stopped."

Who believes today that war can be abolished? No one, not even pacifists. We hope only (so far in vain) to stop genocide and bring to justice those who commit gross violations of the laws of war (for there are laws of war, to which combatants should be held), and to stop specific wars by imposing negotiated alternatives to armed conflict. But protesting against war may not have seemed so futile or naïve in the 1930s. In 1924, on the tenth anniversary of the national mobilization in Germany for the First World War, the conscientious objector Ernst Friedrich published *War Against War!* (*Krieg dem Kriege!*), an album of more than 180 photographs that were drawn mainly from German military and medical archives, and almost all of which were deemed unpublishable by government censors while the war was on. The book starts with pictures of toy soldiers, toy cannons, and other delights of male children everywhere, and concludes with pictures taken in military cemeteries. This is photography as shock therapy. Between the toys and the graves, the reader has an excruciating photo tour of four years of ruin, slaughter, and degradation: wrecked and plundered churches and castles, obliterated villages, ravaged forests, torpedoed passenger steamers, shattered vehicles, hanged conscientious objectors, naked personnel of military brothels, soldiers in death agonies after a poison gas attack, skeletal Armenian children.

Friedrich did not assume that heart-rending, stomach-turning pictures would speak for themselves. Each photograph has an impassioned caption in four languages (German, French, Dutch, and English), and the wickedness of militarist ideology is excoriated and mocked on every page. Immediately denounced by the German government and by veterans' and other patriotic organizations — in some cities the police raided bookstores, and lawsuits were brought against public display of the photographs — Friedrich's declaration of war against war was acclaimed by left-wing writers, artists, and intellectuals, as well as by the constituencies of the numerous antiwar leagues, who predicted that the book would have a decisive influence on public opinion. By 1930, *War Against War!* had gone through ten editions in Germany and been translated into many languages.

In 1928, in the Kellogg-Briand Pact, fifteen nations, including the United States, France, Great Britain, Germany, Italy, and Japan, solemnly renounced war as an instrument of national policy. Freud and Einstein were drawn into the debate four years later, in an exchange of letters published under the title "Why War?" *Three Guineas*, which appeared toward the close of nearly two decades of plangent denunciations of war and war's horrors, was at least original in its focus on what was regarded as too obvious to be mentioned, much less brooded over: that war is a man's game — that the killing machine has a gender, and it is male. Nevertheless, the temerity of Woolf's version of "Why War?" does not make her revulsion against war any less conventional in its rhetoric, and in its summations, rich in repeated phrases. Photographs of the victims of war are themselves a species of rhetoric. They reiterate. They simplify. They agitate. They create the illusion of consensus.

Woolf professes to believe that the shock of such pictures cannot fail to unite people of good will. Although she and the lawyer are separated by the age-old affinities of feeling and practice of their respective sexes, he is hardly a standard-issue bellicose male. After all, his question was not, What are your thoughts about preventing war? It was, How in your opinion are we to prevent war? Woolf challenges this "we" at the start of her book, but after some pages devoted to the feminist point she abandons it.

"Here then on the table before us are photographs," she writes of the thought experiment she is proposing to the reader as well as to the spectral lawyer, who is eminent enough to have K.C., King's Counsel, after his name — and may or may not be a real person. Imagine a spread of loose photographs extracted from an envelope that arrived in the morning mail. They show the mangled bodies of adults and children. They show how war evacuates, shatters, breaks apart, levels the built world. A bomb has torn open the side of a house. To be sure, a cityscape is not made of flesh. Still, sheared-off buildings are almost as eloquent as body parts (Kabul;

Sarajevo; East Mostar; Grozny; sixteen acres of lower Manhattan after September 11, 2001; the refugee camp in Jenin). Look, the
photographs say, *this* is what it's like. This is what war *does*. And *that*,
that is what it does, too. War tears, rends. War rips open, eviscer-
ates. War scorches. War dismembers. War *ruins*. Woolf believes that
not to be pained by these pictures, not to recoil from them, not to
strive to abolish what causes this havoc, this carnage, is a failure of
imagination, of empathy.

But surely the photographs could just as well foster greater mili-
tancy on behalf of the Republic. Isn't this what they were meant to
do? The agreement between Woolf and the lawyer seems entirely
presumptive, with the grisly photographs confirming an opinion
already held in common. Had his question been, How can we best
contribute to the defense of the Spanish Republic against the
forces of militarist and clerical fascism?, the photographs might
have reinforced a belief in the justness of that struggle.

The pictures Woolf has conjured up do not in fact show what war
— war in general — does. They show a particular way of waging
war, a way at that time routinely described as "barbaric," in which
civilians are the target. General Franco was using the tactics of
bombardment, massacre, torture, and the killing and mutilation of
prisoners that he had perfected as a commanding officer in Morocco in the 1920s. Then, more acceptably to ruling powers, his
victims had been Spain's colonial subjects, darker-hued and in-
fidels to boot; now his victims were compatriots. To read in the pictures, as Woolf does, only what confirms a general abhorrence of
war is to stand back from an engagement with Spain as a country
with a history. It is to dismiss politics.

For Woolf, as for many antiwar polemicists, war is generic, and
the images she describes are of anonymous, generic victims. The
pictures sent out by the government in Madrid seem, improbably,
not to have been labeled. (Or perhaps Woolf is simply assuming
that a photograph should speak for itself.) But to those who are
sure that right is on one side, oppression and injustice on the
other, and that the fighting must go on, what matters is precisely
who is killed and by whom. To an Israeli Jew, a photograph of a
child torn apart in the attack on the Sbarro pizzeria in downtown
Jerusalem is first of all a photograph of a Jewish child killed by a
Palestinian suicide bomber. To a Palestinian, a photograph of a

child torn apart by a tank round in Gaza is first of all a photograph of a Palestinian child killed by Israeli ordnance. To the militant, identity is everything. And all photographs wait to be explained or falsified by their captions. During the fighting between Serbs and Croats at the beginning of the recent Balkan wars, the same photographs of children killed in the shelling of a village were passed around at both Serb and Croat propaganda briefings. Alter the caption: alter the use of these deaths.

Photographs of mutilated bodies certainly can be used the way Woolf does, to vivify the condemnation of war, and may bring home, for a spell, a portion of its reality to those who have no experience of war at all. But someone who accepts that in the world as currently divided war can become inevitable, and even just, might reply that the photographs supply no evidence, none at all, for renouncing war — except to those for whom the notions of valor and of sacrifice have been emptied of meaning and credibility. The destructiveness of war — short of total destruction, which is not war but suicide — is not in itself an argument against waging war, unless one thinks (as few people actually do) that violence is always unjustifiable, that force is always and in all circumstances wrong: wrong because, as Simone Weil affirms in her sublime essay on war, "The Iliad, or, The Poem of Force," violence turns anybody subjected to it into a thing. But to those who in a given situation see no alternative to armed struggle, violence can exalt someone subjected to it into a martyr or a hero.

In fact, there are many uses of the innumerable opportunities that a modern life supplies for regarding — at a distance, through the medium of photography — other people's pain. Photographs of an atrocity may give rise to opposing responses: a call for peace; a cry for revenge; or simply the bemused awareness, continually restocked by photographic information, that terrible things happen. Who can forget the three color pictures by Tyler Hicks that the *New York Times* ran on November 13, 2001, across the upper half of the first page of its daily section devoted to America's new war? The triptych depicted the fate of a wounded Taliban soldier who had been found in a ditch by some Northern Alliance soldiers advancing toward Kabul. First panel: the soldier is being dragged on his back by two of his captors — one has grabbed an arm, the other a leg — along a rocky road. Second panel: he is surrounded, gazing up in terror as he is pulled to his feet. Third panel: he is supine with arms outstretched and knees bent, naked from the waist down, a bloodied heap left on the road by the dispersing military mob that has just finished butchering him. A good deal of stoicism is needed to get through the newspaper each morning, given the likelihood of seeing pictures that could make you cry. And the disgust and pity that pictures like Hicks's inspire should not distract from asking what pictures, whose cruelties, whose deaths you are *not* being shown.

II

Awareness of the suffering that accumulates in wars happening elsewhere is something constructed. Principally in the form that is registered by cameras, it flares up, is shared by many people, and fades from view. In contrast to a written account, which, depending on its complexity of thought, references, and vocabulary, is pitched at a larger or smaller readership, a photograph has only one language and is destined potentially for all.

In the first important wars of which there are accounts by photographers, the Crimean War and the American Civil War, and in every other war until the First World War, combat itself was beyond the camera's ken. As for the war photographs published between 1914 and 1918, nearly all anonymous, they were — insofar as they did convey something of the terrors and devastation endured — generally in the epic mode, and were usually depictions of an aftermath: corpse-strewn or lunar landscapes left by trench warfare; gutted French villages the war had passed through. The photographic monitoring of war as we know it had to wait for a radical upgrade of professional equipment: lightweight cameras, such as the Leica, using 35-millimeter film that could be exposed thirty-six times before the camera needed to be reloaded. The Spanish Civil War was the first war to be witnessed ("covered") in the modern sense: by a corps of professional photographers at the lines of military engagement and in the towns under bombardment, whose work was immediately seen in newspapers and magazines in Spain and abroad. Pictures could be taken in the thick of battle, military censorship permitting, and civilian victims and exhausted, begrimed soldiers studied up close. The war America waged in Vietnam, the first to be witnessed day after day by television cameras, introduced the home front to a new intimacy with death and destruction. Ever since, battles and massacres filmed as they unfold have been a routine ingredient of the ceaseless flow of domestic, small-screen entertainment. Creating a perch for a particular conflict in the consciousness of viewers exposed to dramas from everywhere requires the daily diffusion and rediffusion of snippets of footage about the conflict. The understanding of war among people who have not experienced war is now chiefly a product of the impact of these images.

Nonstop imagery (television, streaming video, movies) surrounds us, but, when it comes to remembering, the photograph has the deeper bite. Memory freeze-frames; its basic unit is the single image. In an era of information overload, the photograph provides a quick way of apprehending something and a compact form for memorizing it. The photograph is like a quotation, or a maxim or proverb. Each of us mentally stocks hundreds of photographs, subject to instant recall. Cite the most famous photograph taken during the Spanish Civil War, the Republican soldier "shot" by Robert Capa's camera at the same moment he is hit by an enemy bullet, and virtually everyone who has heard of that war can summon to mind the grainy black-and-white image of a man in a white shirt with rolled-up sleeves collapsing backward on a hillock, his right arm flung behind him as his rifle leaves his grip — about to fall, dead, onto his own shadow.

It is a shocking image, and that is the point. Conscripted as part of journalism, images were expected to arrest attention, startle, surprise. As the old advertising slogan of *Paris Match,* founded in 1949, had it: "The weight of words, the shock of photos." The hunt for more dramatic — as they're often described — images drives the photographic enterprise, and is part of the normality of a culture in which shock has become a leading stimulus of consumption and source of value. "Beauty will be convulsive, or it will not be," André Breton proclaimed. He called this aesthetic ideal "surrealist," but, in a culture radically revamped by the ascendancy of mercantile values, to ask that images be jarring, clamorous, eye-opening seems like elementary realism or good business sense. How else to get attention for one's product or one's art? How else to make a dent when there is incessant exposure to images, and overexposure to a handful of images seen again and again? The image as shock and the image as cliché are two aspects of the same presence. Sixty-five years ago, all photographs were novelties to some degree. (It would have been inconceivable to Virginia Woolf — who did appear on the cover of *Time* in 1937 — that one day her face would become a much reproduced image on T-shirts, book bags, refrigerator magnets, coffee mugs, mouse pads.) Atrocity photographs were scarce in the winter of 1936–37: the depiction of war's horrors in the photographs Woolf discusses in *Three Guineas* seemed almost like clandestine knowledge. Our situation is altogether different. The ultra-familiar, ultra-celebrated image — of an agony, of ruin — is an unavoidable feature of our camera-mediated knowledge of war.

Photography has kept company with death ever since cameras were invented, in 1839. Because an image produced with a camera is, literally, a trace of something brought before the lens, photographs had an advantage over any painting as a memento of the vanished past and the dear departed. To seize death in the making was another matter: the camera's reach remained limited as long as it had to be lugged about, set down, steadied. But, once the camera was emancipated from the tripod, truly portable, and equipped with a range finder and a variety of lenses that permitted unprecedented feats of close observation from a distant vantage point, picture-taking acquired an immediacy and authority greater than any verbal account in conveying the horror of mass-produced death. If there was one year when the power of photographs to define, not merely record, the most abominable realities trumped all the complex narratives, surely it was 1945, with the pictures taken in April and early May in Bergen-Belsen, Buchenwald, and Dachau, in the first days after the camps were liberated, and those taken by Japanese witnesses such as Yosuke Yamahata in the days following the incineration of the populations of Hiroshima and Nagasaki, in early August.

Photographs had the advantage of uniting two contradictory features. Their credentials of objectivity were inbuilt, yet they always had, necessarily, a point of view. They were a record of the real — incontrovertible, as no verbal account, however impartial, could be (assuming that they showed what they purported to show) — since a machine was doing the recording. And they bore witness to the real, since a person had been there to take them.

The photographs Woolf received are treated as windows on the war: transparent views of what they show. It was of no interest to her that each had an "author" — that photographs represent the view of someone — although it was precisely in the late 1930s that the profession of bearing individual witness to war and war's atrocities with a camera was forged. Before, war photography had mostly appeared in daily and weekly newspapers. (Newspapers had been printing photographs since 1880.) By 1938, in addition to the older popular magazines that used photographs as illustrations — such as *National Geographic* and *Berliner Illustrierte Zeitung*, both founded in the late nineteenth century — there were large-circulation weekly magazines, notably the French *Vu*, the American *Life*, and the British *Picture Post*, devoted entirely to pictures (accompanied by brief texts keyed to the photos) and "picture stories" (four or five pictures by the same photographer attached to a story that further dramatized the images); in a newspaper, it was the photograph — and there was only one — that accompanied the story.

In a system based on the maximal reproduction and diffusion of images, witnessing requires star witnesses, renowned for their bravery and zeal. War photographers inherited what glamour going to war still had among the anti-bellicose, especially when the war was felt to be one of those rare conflicts in which someone of conscience would be impelled to take sides. In contrast to the 1914–18 war, which, it was clear to many of the victors, had been a colossal mistake, the second "world war" was unanimously felt by the winning side to have been a necessary war, a war that had to be fought. Photojournalism came into its own in the early 1940s — wartime. This least controversial of modern wars, whose necessity was sealed by the full revelation of Nazi infamy in Europe, offered photojournalists a new legitimacy. There was little place for the left-wing dissidence that had informed much of the serious use of photographs in the interwar period, including Friedrich's *War Against War!* and the early work of Robert Capa, the most celebrated figure in a generation of politically engaged photographers whose work centered on war and victimhood.

In 1947, Capa and a few friends formed a cooperative, the Magnum Photo Agency. Magnum's charter, moralistic in the way of the founding charters of other international organizations and guilds created in the immediate postwar period, spelled out an enlarged, ethically weighted mission for photojournalists: to chronicle their own time as fair-minded witnesses free of chauvinistic prejudices. In Magnum's voice, photography declared itself a global enterprise. The photographer's beat was "the world." He or she was a rover, with wars of unusual interest (for there were many wars) a favorite destination.

The memory of war, however, like all memory, is mostly local. Armenians, the majority in diaspora, keep alive the memory of the Armenian genocide of 1915; Greeks don't forget the sanguinary civil war in Greece that raged through most of the second half of the 1940s. But for a war to break out of its immediate constituency and become a subject of international attention it must be regarded as something of an exception, as wars go, and represent more than the clashing interests of the belligerents themselves. Apart from the major world conflicts, most wars do not acquire the requisite fuller meaning. An example: the Chaco War (1932–35), a butchery engaged in by Bolivia (population one million) and Paraguay (three and a half million) that took the lives of a hundred thousand soldiers, and which was covered by a German photojournalist, Willi Ruge, whose superb closeup battle pictures are as forgotten as that war. But the Spanish Civil War, in the second half of the 1930s, the Serb and Croat wars against Bosnia in the mid-1990s, the drastic worsening of the Israeli-Palestinian conflict that began in 2000 — these relatively small wars were guaranteed the attention of many cameras because they were invested with the meaning of larger struggles: the Spanish Civil War because it was a stand against the Fascist menace, and was understood to be a dress rehearsal for the coming European, or "world," war; the Bosnian war because it was the stand of a small, fledgling European country wishing to remain multicultural as well as independent against the dominant power in the region and its neo-Fascist program of ethnic cleansing; and the conflict in the Middle East because the United States supports the State of Israel. Indeed, it is felt by many who champion the Palestinian side that what is ultimately at stake, by proxy, in the struggle to end the Israeli domination of the territories captured in 1967 is the strength of the forces opposing the juggernaut of American-sponsored globalization, economic and cultural.

The memorable sites of suffering documented by admired photographers in the fifties, sixties, and early seventies were mostly in

Asia and Africa — Werner Bischof's photographs of famine victims in India, Don McCullin's pictures of war and famine in Biafra, W. Eugene Smith's photographs of the victims of the lethal pollution of a Japanese fishing village. The Indian and African famines were not just "natural" disasters: they were preventable; they were crimes of the greatest magnitude. And what happened in Minamata was obviously a crime; the Chisso Corporation knew that it was dumping mercury-laden waste into the bay. (Smith was severely and permanently injured by Chisso goons who were ordered to put an end to his camera inquiry.) But war is the largest crime, and, starting in the mid-sixties, most of the best-known photographers covering wars set out to show war's "real" face. The color photographs of tormented Vietnamese villagers and wounded American conscripts that Larry Burrows took and *Life* published, starting in 1962, certainly fortified the outcry against the American presence in Vietnam. Burrows was the first important photographer to do a whole war in color — another gain in verisimilitude and shock.

In the current political mood, the friendliest to the military in decades, the pictures of wretched hollow-eyed GIs that once seemed subversive of militarism and imperialism may seem inspirational. Their revised subject: ordinary American young men doing their unpleasant, ennobling duty.

III

The iconography of suffering has a long pedigree. The suffering most often deemed worthy of representation is that which is understood to be the product of wrath, divine or human. (Suffering brought on by natural causes, such as illness or childbirth, is scantily represented in the history of art; that brought on by accident virtually not at all — as if there were no such thing as suffering by inadvertence or misadventure.) The statue group of the writhing Laocoön and his sons, the innumerable versions in painting and sculpture of the Passion of Christ, and the immense visual catalogue of the fiendish executions of the Christian martyrs — these are surely intended to move and excite, to instruct and exemplify. The viewer may commiserate with the sufferer's pain — and, in the case of the Christian saints, feel admonished or inspired by model faith and fortitude — but these are destinies beyond deploring or contesting.

It seems that the appetite for pictures showing bodies in pain is almost as keen as the desire for ones that show bodies naked. For a long time, in Christian art, depictions of Hell offered both of these elemental satisfactions. On occasion, the pretext might be a biblical decapitation story (Holofernes, John the Baptist) or massacre yarn (the newborn Hebrew boys, the eleven thousand virgins) or some such, with the status of a real historical event and of an implacable fate. There was also the repertoire of hard-to-look-at cruelties from classical antiquity — the pagan myths, even more than the Christian stories, offer something for every taste. No moral charge attaches to the representation of these cruelties. Just the provocation: Can you look at this? There is the satisfaction of being able to look at the image without flinching. There is the pleasure of flinching.

To shudder at Goltzius's rendering, in his etching *The Dragon Devouring the Companions of Cadmus* (1588), of a man's face being chewed off his head is very different from shuddering at a photograph of a First World War veteran whose face has been shot away. One horror has its place in a complex subject — figures in a landscape — that displays the artist's skill of eye and hand. The other is a camera's record, from very near, of a real person's unspeakably awful mutilation; that and nothing else. An invented horror can be quite overwhelming. (I, for one, find it difficult to look at Titian's great painting of the flaying of Marsyas, or, indeed, at any picture of this subject.) But there is shame as well as shock in looking at the closeup of a real horror. Perhaps the only people with the right to look at images of suffering of this extreme order are those who could do something to alleviate it — say, the surgeons at the military hospital where the photograph was taken — or those who could learn from it. The rest of us are voyeurs, whether we like it or not.

In each instance, the gruesome invites us to be either spectators or cowards, unable to look. Those with the stomach to look are playing a role authorized by many glorious depictions of suffering. Torment, a canonical subject in art, is often represented in painting as a spectacle, something being watched (or ignored) by other people. The implication is: No, it cannot be stopped — and the mingling of inattentive with attentive onlookers underscores this.

The practice of representing atrocious suffering as something to be deplored, and, if possible, stopped, enters the history of images with a specific subject: the sufferings endured by a civilian population at the hands of a victorious army on the rampage. It is a quintessentially secular subject, which emerges in the seventeenth century, when contemporary realignments of power become material for artists. In 1633, Jacques Callot published a suite of eighteen etchings titled *The Miseries and Misfortunes of War*, which depicted the atrocities committed against civilians by French troops during the invasion and occupation of his native Lorraine in the early 1630s. (Six small etchings on the same subject that Callot had executed prior to the large series appeared in 1635, the year of his death.) The view is wide and deep; these are scenes with many figures, scenes from a history, and each caption is a sententious comment in verse on the various energies and dooms portrayed in the images. Callot begins with a plate showing the recruitment of soldiers; brings into view ferocious combat, massacre, pillage, and rape, the engines of torture and execution (strappado, gallows tree, firing squad, stake, wheel), and the revenge of the peasants on the soldiers; and ends with a distribution of rewards. The insistence in plate after plate on the savagery of a conquering army is startling and without precedent, but the French soldiers are only the leading malefactors in the orgy of violence, and there is room in Callot's Christian humanist sensibility not just to mourn the end of the independent duchy of Lorraine but to record the postwar plight of destitute soldiers who squat on the side of the road, begging for alms.

Callot had his successors, such as Hans Ulrich Franck, a minor German artist who, in 1643, toward the end of the Thirty Years' War, began making what would be (by 1656) a suite of twenty-five etchings depicting soldiers killing peasants. But the preeminent concentration on the horrors of war and the vileness of soldiers run amok is Goya's, in the early nineteenth century. *The Disasters of War*, a numbered sequence of eighty-three etchings made between 1810 and 1820 (and first published, except for three plates, in 1863, thirty-five years after his death), depicts the atrocities perpetrated by Napoleon's soldiers, who invaded Spain in 1808 to quell the insurrection against French rule. Goya's images move the viewer close to the horror. All the trappings of the spectacular have been eliminated: the landscape is an atmosphere, a darkness,

barely sketched in. War is not a spectacle. And Goya's print series is
not a narrative: each image, captioned with a brief phrase lament-
ing the wickedness of the invaders and the monstrousness of the
suffering they inflicted, stands independent of the others. The cu-
mulative effect is devastating.

The ghoulish cruelties in *The Disasters of War* are meant to
awaken, shock, wound the viewer. Goya's art, like Dostoyevsky's,
seems a turning point in the history of moral feelings and of sorrow — as deep, as original, as demanding. With Goya, a new standard for responsiveness to suffering enters art. (And new subjects
for fellow feeling: for example, the painting of an injured laborer
being carried away from a construction site.) The account of war's
cruelties is constructed as an assault on the sensibility of the viewer.
The expressive phrases in script below each image comment on
the provocation. While the image, like all images, is an invitation
to look, the caption, more often than not, insists on the difficulty
of doing just that. A voice, presumably the artist's, badgers the
viewer: Can you bear this? One caption declares, *"No se puede mirar"*
("One can't look"). Another says, *"Esto es malo"* ("This is bad").
"Esto es peor" ("This is worse"), another retorts.

The caption of a photograph is traditionally neutral, informa-
tive: a date, a place, names. A reconnaissance photograph from the
First World War (the first war in which cameras were used extensively for military intelligence) was unlikely to be captioned "Can't
wait to overrun this!" or the x-ray of a multiple fracture to be anno-
tated "Patient will probably have a limp!" It seems no less inappropriate to speak for the photograph in the photographer's voice, offering assurances of the image's veracity, as Goya does in *The
Disasters of War,* writing beneath one image, *"Yo lo vi"* ("I saw this").
And beneath another, *"Esto es lo verdadero"* ("This is the truth"). Of
course the photographer saw it. And, unless there's been some
tampering or misrepresenting, it is the truth.

Ordinary language fixes the difference between handmade images like Goya's and photographs through the convention that artists "make" drawings and paintings while photographers "take"
photographs. But the photographic image, even to the extent that
it is a trace (not a construction made out of disparate photographic traces), cannot be simply a transparency of something that
happened. It is always the image that someone chose; to photo-

graph is to frame, and to frame is to exclude. Moreover, fiddling with the picture long antedates the era of digital photography and Photoshop manipulations: it has always been possible for a photograph to misrepresent. A painting or drawing is judged a fake when it turns out not to be by the artist to whom it had been attributed. A photograph — or a filmed document available on television or the Internet — is judged a fake when it turns out to be deceiving the viewer about the scene it purports to depict.

That the atrocities perpetrated by Napoleon's soldiers in Spain didn't happen exactly as Goya drew them hardly disqualifies *The Disasters of War.* Goya's images are a synthesis. Things *like* this happened. In contrast, a single photograph or filmstrip claims to represent exactly what was before the camera's lens. A photograph is supposed not to evoke but to show. That is why photographs, unlike handmade images, can count as evidence. But evidence of what? The suspicion that Capa's *Death of a Republican Soldier* — recently retitled *The Falling Soldier,* in the authoritative compilation of Capa's work — may not show what it has always been said to show continues to haunt discussions of war photography. Everyone is a literalist when it comes to photographs.

Images of the sufferings endured in war are so widely disseminated now that it is easy to forget that, historically, photographers have offered mostly positive images of the warrior's trade, and of the satisfactions of starting a war or continuing to fight one. If governments had their way, war photography, like much war poetry, would drum up support for soldiers' sacrifices. Indeed, war photography begins with such a mission, such a disgrace. The war was the Crimean War, and the photographer, Roger Fenton, invariably called the first war photographer, was no less than that war's "official" photographer, having been sent to the Crimea in early 1855 by the British government, at the instigation of Prince Albert. Acknowledging the need to counteract the alarming printed accounts of the dangers and privations endured by the British soldiers dispatched there the previous year, the government invited a well-known professional photographer to give another, more positive impression of the increasingly unpopular war.

Edmund Gosse, in *Father and Son,* his memoir of a mid-nineteenth-century English childhood, relates how the Crimean War penetrated even his stringently pious, unworldly family, which belonged to an evangelical sect called the Plymouth Brethren: "The declaration of war with Russia brought the first breath of outside life into our Calvinist cloister. My parents took in a daily newspaper, which they had never done before, and events in picturesque places, which my Father and I looked out on the map, were eagerly discussed." War was, and still is, the most irresistible — and picturesque — news, along with that invaluable substitute for war, international sports. But this war was more than news. It was bad news. The authoritative, pictureless London newspaper to which Gosse's parents had succumbed, the *Times*, attacked the military leadership whose incompetence was responsible for the war's dragging on, with so much loss of British life. The toll on the soldiers from causes other than combat was horrendous — twenty-two thousand died of illnesses; many thousands lost limbs to frostbite during the long Russian winter of the protracted siege of Sebastopol — and several of the military engagements were disasters. It was still winter when Fenton arrived in the Crimea for a four-month stay, having contracted to publish his photographs (in the form of engravings) in a less venerable and less critical weekly paper, the *Illustrated London News*, exhibit them in a gallery, and market them as a book upon his return home.

Under instructions from the War Office not to photograph the dead, the maimed, or the ill, and precluded from photographing most other subjects by the cumbersome technology of picture-taking, Fenton went about rendering the war as a dignified all-male group outing. With each image requiring a separate chemical preparation in the darkroom and a long exposure time, he could photograph British officers in open-air staff meetings or common soldiers tending the cannons only after asking them to stand or sit together, follow his directions, and hold still. His pictures are tableaux of military life behind the front lines; the war — movement, disorder, drama — stays off camera. The one photograph Fenton took in the Crimea that reaches beyond benign documentation is *The Valley of the Shadow of Death*, whose title evokes the consolation offered by the biblical psalmist as well as the disaster in which six hundred British soldiers were ambushed on the plain above Balaklava — Tennyson called the site "the valley of Death" in his memorial poem, "The Charge of the Light Brigade." Fenton's memorial photograph is a portrait of absence, of death without the dead. It is the only photograph that would not have needed to be staged, for all it shows is a wide rutted road, studded with rocks and cannonballs, that curves onward across a barren rolling plain to the distant void.

A bolder portfolio of after-the-battle images of death and ruin, pointing not to losses suffered but to a fearsome British triumph over the enemy, was made by another photographer who had visited the Crimean War. Felice Beato, a naturalized Englishman (he was born in Venice), was the first photographer to attend a number of wars: besides being in the Crimea in 1855, he was at the Sepoy Rebellion (what the British call the Indian Mutiny) in 1857–58, the Second Opium War in China, in 1860, and the Sudanese colonial wars in 1885. Three years after Fenton made his anodyne images of a war that did not go well for England, Beato was celebrating the fierce victory of the British army over a mutiny of native soldiers under its command, the first important challenge to British rule in India. Beato's *Ruins of Sikandarbagh Palace,* an arresting photograph of a palace in Lucknow that has been gutted by bombardment, shows the courtyard strewn with the rebels' bones.

The first full-scale attempt to document a war was carried out a few years later, during the American Civil War, by a firm of Northern photographers headed by Mathew Brady, who had made several official portraits of President Lincoln. The Brady war pictures — most were shot by Alexander Gardner and Timothy O'Sullivan, although their employer was invariably credited with them — showed conventional subjects, such as encampments populated by officers and foot soldiers, towns in war's way, ordnance, ships, and also, most famously, dead Union and Confederate soldiers lying on the blasted ground of Gettysburg and Antietam. Though access to the battlefield came as a privilege extended to Brady and his team by Lincoln himself, the photographers were not commissioned, as Fenton had been. Their status evolved in rather typical American fashion, with nominal government sponsorship giving way to the force of entrepreneurial and freelance motives.

The first justification for the brutally legible pictures of a field of dead soldiers was the simple duty to record. "The camera is the eye of history," Brady is supposed to have said. And history, invoked as truth beyond appeal, was allied with the rising prestige of a certain notion of subjects needing more attention, known as realism, which was soon to have a host of defenders among novelists as well as photographers. In the name of realism, one was permitted — required — to show unpleasant, hard facts. Such pictures also convey "a useful moral" by showing "the blank horror and reality of war, in opposition to its pageantry," as Gardner wrote in a text accompanying O'Sullivan's picture of fallen Confederate soldiers, their agonized faces clearly visible. "Here are the dreadful details! Let them aid in preventing another such calamity falling upon the nation." But the frankness of the most memorable pictures in an album of photographs by Gardner and other Brady photographers, which Gardner published after the war, did not mean that he and his colleagues had necessarily photographed their subjects as they found them. To photograph was to compose (with living subjects, to pose); the desire to arrange elements in the picture did not vanish because the subject was immobilized, or immobile.

Not surprisingly, many of the canonical images of early war photography turn out to have been staged, or to have had their subjects tampered with. Roger Fenton, after reaching the much shelled valley near Sebastopol in his horse-drawn darkroom, made two exposures from the same tripod position: in the first version of the celebrated photograph he was to call *The Valley of the Shadow of Death* (despite the title, it was not across this landscape that the Light Brigade made its doomed charge), the cannonballs are thick on the ground to the left of the road; before taking the second picture — the one that is always reproduced — he oversaw the scattering of cannonballs on the road itself. A picture of a desolate site where a great deal of dying had indeed recently taken place, Beato's *Ruins of Sikandarbagh Palace*, involved a more thorough theatricalization of its subject, and was one of the first attempts to suggest with a camera the horrific in war. The attack occurred in November 1857, after which the victorious British troops and loyal Indian units searched the palace room by room, bayoneting the 1,800 surviving Sepoy defenders who were now their prisoners and throwing their bodies into the courtyard; vultures and dogs did the rest. For the photograph he took in March or April 1858, Beato constructed the courtyard as a deathscape, stationing some natives by two pillars in the rear and distributing human bones about the foreground.

At least they were old bones. It's now known that the Brady team rearranged and displaced some of the recently dead at Gettysburg; the picture titled *The Home of a Rebel Sharpshooter, Gettysburg* in fact shows a dead Confederate soldier who was moved from where he had fallen on the field to a more photogenic site, a cove formed by several boulders flanking a barricade of rocks, and includes a prop rifle that Gardner leaned against the barricade beside the corpse. (It seems not to have been the special rifle a sharpshooter would have used, but a common infantryman's rifle; Gardner didn't know this or didn't care.)

Only starting with the Vietnam War can we be virtually certain that none of the best-known photographs were setups. And this is essential to the moral authority of these images. The signature Vietnam War horror photograph, from 1972, taken by Huynh Cong Ut, of children from a village that has just been doused with American napalm running down the highway, shrieking with pain, belongs to the universe of photographs that cannot possibly be posed. The same is true of the well-known pictures from the most widely photographed wars since.

That there have been so few staged war photographs since the Vietnam War probably should not be attributed to higher standards of journalistic probity. One part of the explanation is that it was in Vietnam that television became the defining medium for showing images of war, and the intrepid lone photographer, Nikon or Leica in hand, operating out of sight much of the time, now had to compete with, and endure the proximity of, TV crews. There are always witnesses to a filming. Technically, the possibilities for doctoring or electronically manipulating pictures are greater than ever — almost unlimited. But the practice of inventing dramatic news pictures, staging them for the camera, seems on its way to becoming a lost art.

IV

Central to modern expectations, and modern ethical feeling, is the conviction that war is an aberration, if an unstoppable one. That peace is the norm, if an unattainable one. This, of course, is not the way war has been regarded throughout history. War has been the norm and peace the exception.

Descriptions of the exact fashion in which bodies are injured and killed in combat is a recurring climax in the stories told in the *Iliad*. War is seen as something men do, inveterately, undeterred by the accumulation of suffering it inflicts; to represent war in words or in pictures requires a keen, unflinching detachment. When Leonardo da Vinci gives instructions for a battle painting, his worry is that artists will lack the courage or the imagination to show war in all its ghastliness: "Make the conquered and beaten pale, with brows raised and knit, and the skin above their brows furrowed with pain . . . and the teeth apart as with crying out in lamentation . . . Make the dead partly or entirely covered with dust . . . and let the blood be seen by its color flowing in a sinuous stream from the corpse to the dust. Others in the death agony grinding their teeth, rolling their eyes, with their fists clenched against their bodies, and the legs distorted." The concern is that the images won't be sufficiently upsetting: not concrete, not detailed enough.

Pity can entail a moral judgment if, as Aristotle suggests, pity is considered to be the emotion that we owe only to those enduring undeserved misfortune. But pity, far from being the natural twin of fear in the dramas of catastrophic misfortune, seems diluted — distracted — by fear, while fear (dread, terror) usually manages to swamp pity. Leonardo is suggesting that the artist's gaze be, literally, pitiless. The image should appall, and in that *terribilità* lies a challenging kind of beauty.

That a gory battlescape could be beautiful — in the sublime or awesome or tragic register of the beautiful — is a commonplace about images of war made by artists. The idea does not sit well when applied to images taken by cameras: to find beauty in war photographs seems heartless. But the landscape of devastation is still a landscape. There is beauty in ruins. To acknowledge the beauty of photographs of the World Trade Center ruins in the months following the attack seemed frivolous, sacrilegious. The most people dared say was that the photographs were "surreal," a hectic euphemism behind which the disgraced notion of beauty cowered. But they *were* beautiful, many of them — by veteran photographers such as Gilles Peress, Susan Meiselas, and Joel Meyerowitz and by many little-known and nonprofessional photographers.

The site itself, the mass graveyard that had received the name Ground Zero, was, of course, anything but beautiful. Photographs tend to transform, whatever their subject; and as an image something may be beautiful — or terrifying, or unbearable, or quite bearable — as it is not in real life.

Transforming is what art does, but photography that bears witness to the calamitous and the reprehensible is much criticized if it seems "aesthetic"; that is, too much like art. The dual powers of photography — to generate documents and to create works of visual art — have produced some remarkable exaggerations about what photographers ought or ought not to do. These days, most exaggeration is of the puritanical kind. Photographs that depict suffering shouldn't be beautiful, as captions shouldn't moralize. In this view, a beautiful photograph drains attention from the sobering subject and turns it toward the medium itself, inviting the viewer to look "aesthetically," and thereby compromising the picture's status as a document. The photograph gives mixed signals. Stop this, it urges. But it also exclaims, What a spectacle!

Take one of the most poignant images from the First World War: a column of English soldiers blinded by poison gas — each rests his hand on the shoulder of the man ahead of him — stumbling toward a dressing station. It could be an image from one of the searing movies made about the war — King Vidor's *The Big Parade,* of 1925, or G. W. Pabst's *Westfront 1918,* Lewis Milestone's *All Quiet on the Western Front,* and Howard Hawks's *Dawn Patrol,* all from 1930. The way in which still photography finds its perfection in the reconstruction of battle scenes in the great war movies has begun to backfire on the photography of war. What assured the authenticity of Steven Spielberg's much admired re-creation of the Omaha Beach landing on D-day in *Saving Private Ryan* (1998) was that it was based on, among other sources, the photographs taken with immense bravery by Robert Capa during the landing. But a war photograph seems inauthentic, even though there is nothing staged about it, when it looks like a still from a movie. Sebastião Salgado, a photographer who specializes in world misery (including but not restricted to the effects of war), has been the principal target of the new campaign against the inauthenticity of the beautiful. Particularly with the seven-year project he calls *Migrations: Humanity in Transition,* Salgado has come under steady attack for producing spectacular, beautifully composed big pictures that are said to be "cinematic."

The sanctimonious Family of Man–style rhetoric that accompanies Salgado's exhibitions and books has worked to the detriment of the pictures, however unfair this may be. The pictures have also been sourly treated in response to the highly commercialized situations in which, typically, Salgado's portraits of misery are seen. But the problem is in the pictures themselves, not the way they are exhibited: in their focus on the powerless, reduced to their powerlessness. It is significant that the powerless are not named in the captions. A portrait that declines to name its subject becomes complicit, if inadvertently, in the cult of celebrity that has fueled an insatiable appetite for the opposite sort of photograph: to grant only the famous their names demotes the rest to representative instances of their occupations, their ethnicities, their plights. Taken in thirty-five countries, Salgado's migration pictures group together, under this single heading, a host of different causes and kinds of distress. Making suffering loom larger, by globalizing it, may spur people to feel they ought to "care" more. It also invites them to feel that the sufferings and misfortunes are too vast, too irrevocable, too epic to be much changed by any local, political intervention. With a subject conceived on this scale, compassion can only flounder — and make abstract. But all politics, like all history, is concrete.

It used to be thought, when candid images were not common, that showing something that needed to be seen, bringing a painful reality closer, was bound to goad viewers to feel — feel more. In a world in which photography is brilliantly at the service of consumerist manipulations, this naïve relation to poignant scenes of suffering is much less plausible. Morally alert photographers and ideologues of photography are concerned with the issues of exploitation of sentiment (pity, compassion, indignation) in war photography, and how to avoid rote ways of arousing feeling.

Photographer-witnesses may try to make the spectacular *not* spectacular. But their efforts can never cancel the tradition in which suffering has been understood throughout most of Western history. To feel the pulse of Christian iconography in certain wartime or disaster-time photographs is not a sentimental projection. It would be hard not to discern the lineaments of the Pietà in

W. Eugene Smith's picture of a woman in Minamata cradling her deformed, blind, and deaf daughter, or the template of the Descent from the Cross in several of Don McCullin's pictures of dying American soldiers in Vietnam.

The problem is not that people remember through photographs but that they remember only the photographs. This remembering through photographs eclipses other forms of understanding — and remembering. The concentration camps — that is, the photographs taken when the camps were liberated, in 1945 — are most of what people associate with Nazism and the miseries of the Second World War. Hideous deaths (by genocide, starvation, and epidemic) are most of what people retain of the clutch of iniquities and failures that have taken place in postcolonial Africa.

To remember is, more and more, not to recall a story but to be able to call up a picture. Even a writer as steeped in nineteenth-century and early-modern literary solemnities as W. G. Sebald was moved to seed his lamentation-narratives of lost lives, lost nature, lost cityscapes with photographs. Sebald was not just an elegist; he was a militant elegist. Remembering, he wanted the reader to remember, too.

Harrowing photographs do not inevitably lose their power to shock. But they don't help us much to understand. Narratives can make us understand. Photographs do something else: they haunt us. Consider one of the most unforgettable images of the war in Bosnia, a photograph of which the *New York Times* foreign correspondent John Kifner wrote, "The image is stark, one of the most enduring of the Balkan wars: a Serb militiaman casually kicking a dying Muslim woman in the head. It tells you everything you need to know." But of course it doesn't tell us everything we need to know.

From the identification supplied by the photographer, Ron Haviv, we learn that the photograph was taken in the town of Bijeljina in April 1992, the first month of the Serb rampage through Bosnia. From behind, we see a uniformed Serb soldier, a youthful figure with sunglasses perched on the top of his head, a cigarette between the second and third fingers of his raised left hand, rifle dangling in his right hand, right leg poised to kick a woman lying face down on the sidewalk between two other bodies.

The photograph doesn't tell us that she is Muslim, but she is not likely to have been labeled in any other way, or why would she and the two others be lying there, as if dead (why "dying"?), under the gaze of some Serb soldiers? In fact, the photograph tells us very little — except that war is hell, and that graceful young men with guns are capable of kicking in the head overweight older women lying helpless, or already killed.

The pictures of Bosnian atrocities were seen soon after they took place. Like pictures from the Vietnam War, such as Ron Haberle's documents of the massacre by a company of American soldiers of some five hundred unarmed civilians in the village of My Lai in March 1968, they became important in bolstering indignation at this war which had been far from inevitable, far from intractable; and could have been stopped much sooner. Therefore one could feel an obligation to look at these pictures, gruesome as they were, because there was something to be done, right now, about what they depicted. Other issues are raised when the public is invited to respond to a dossier of hitherto unknown pictures of horrors long past.

An example: a trove of photographs of black victims of lynching in small towns in the United States between the 1890s and the 1930s, which provided a shattering, revelatory experience for the thousands who saw them in a gallery in New York in 2000. The lynching pictures tell us about human wickedness. About inhumanity. They force us to think about the extent of the evil unleashed specifically by racism. Intrinsic to the perpetration of this evil is the shamelessness of photographing it. The pictures were taken as souvenirs and made, some of them, into postcards; more than a few show grinning spectators, good churchgoing citizens, as most of them had to be, posing for a camera with the backdrop of a naked, charred, mutilated body hanging from a tree. The display of the pictures makes us spectators, too.

What is the point of exhibiting these pictures? To awaken indignation? To make us feel "bad"; that is, to appall and sadden? To help us mourn? Is looking at such pictures really necessary, given that these horrors lie in a past remote enough to be beyond punishment? Are we the better for seeing these images? Do they actually teach us anything? Don't they rather just confirm what we already know (or want to know)?

All these questions were raised at the time of the exhibition and afterward when a book of the photographs, *Without Sanctuary,* was published. Some people, it was said, might dispute the need for this grisly photographic display, lest it cater to voyeuristic appetites and perpetuate images of black victimization — or simply numb the mind. Nevertheless, it was argued, there is an obligation to "examine" — the more clinical "examine" is substituted for "look at" — the pictures. It was further argued that submitting to the ordeal should help us understand such atrocities not as the acts of "barbarians" but as the reflection of a belief system, racism, that by defining one people as less human than another legitimatizes torture and murder. But maybe they *were* barbarians. Maybe *this* is what barbarians look like. (They look like everybody else.)

That being said, whom do we wish to blame? More precisely, whom do we believe we have the right to blame? The children of Hiroshima and Nagasaki were no less innocent than the young African-American men (and a few women) who were butchered and hanged from trees in small-town America. More than a hundred thousand German civilians, three fourths of them women, were incinerated in the RAF firebombing of Dresden on the night of February 13, 1945; seventy-two thousand civilians were killed by the American bomb dropped on Hiroshima. The roll call could be much longer. Again, whom do we wish to blame? What atrocities from the incurable past do we think we are obliged to see?

Probably, if we are Americans, we think that it would be "morbid" to go out of our way to look at pictures of burned victims of atomic bombing or the napalmed flesh of the civilian victims of the American war on Vietnam but that we have some kind of duty to look at the lynching pictures — if we belong to the party of the right-thinking, which on this issue is now large. A stepped-up recognition of the monstrousness of the slave system that once existed, unquestioned by most, in the United States is a national project of recent decades that many Euro-Americans feel some tug of obligation to join. This ongoing project is a great achievement, a benchmark of civic virtue. But acknowledgment of American use of disproportionate firepower in war (in violation of one of the cardinal laws of war) is very much not a national project. A museum devoted to the history of America's wars that included the vicious war the United States fought against guerrillas in the Philippines from 1899 to 1902 (expertly excoriated by Mark Twain), and that fairly presented the arguments for and against using the atomic bomb in 1945 on the Japanese cities, with photographic evidence that showed what those weapons did, would be regarded — now more than ever — as an unpatriotic endeavor.

V

Consider two widespread ideas — now fast approaching the stature of platitudes — on the impact of photography. Since I find these ideas formulated in my own essays on photography, the earliest of which was written thirty years ago, I feel an irresistible temptation to quarrel with them.

The first idea is that public attention is steered by the attentions of the media — which means images. When there are photographs, a war becomes "real." Thus, the protest against the Vietnam War was mobilized by images. The feeling that something had to be done about the war in Bosnia was built from the attentions of journalists: "the CNN effect," it was sometimes called, which brought images of Sarajevo under siege into hundreds of millions of living rooms night after night for more than three years. These examples illustrate the determining influence of photographs in shaping what catastrophes and crises we pay attention to, what we care about, and ultimately what evaluations are placed on these conflicts.

The second idea — it might seem the converse of what has just been described — is that in a world saturated, even hypersaturated, with images, those which should matter to us have a diminishing effect: we become callous. In the end, such images make us a little less able to feel, to have our conscience pricked.

In the first of the six essays in *On Photography*, which was published in 1977, I argued that while an event known through photographs certainly becomes more real than it would have been if one had never seen the photographs, after repeated exposure it also becomes less real. As much as they create sympathy, I wrote, photographs shrivel sympathy. Is this true? I thought it was when I wrote it. I'm not so sure now. What is the evidence that photographs have a diminishing impact, that our culture of spectacle neutralizes the moral force of photographs of atrocities?

The question turns on a view of the principal medium of the news, television. An image is drained of its force by the way it is used, where and how often it is seen. Images shown on television are, by definition, images of which, sooner or later, one tires. What looks like callousness has its origin in the instability of attention that television is organized to arouse and to satiate, by its surfeit of images. Image-glut keeps attention light, mobile, relatively indifferent to content. Image-flow precludes a privileged image. The whole point of television is that one can switch channels, that it is normal to switch channels: to become restless, bored. Consumers droop. They need to be restimulated, jump-started, again and again. Content is no more than one of these stimulants. A more reflective engagement with content would require a certain intensity of awareness — just what is weakened by the expectations brought to images disseminated by the media. The leaching out of content is what contributes most to the deadening of feeling.

The argument that modern life consists of a menu of horrors by which we are corrupted and to which we gradually become habituated is a founding idea of the critique of modernity — a tradition almost as old as modernity itself. In 1800, Wordsworth, in the Preface to *Lyrical Ballads,* denounced the corruption of sensibility produced by "the great national events which are daily taking place, and the increasing accumulation of men in cities, where the uniformity of their occupations produces a craving for extraordinary incident, which the rapid communication of intelligence hourly gratifies." This process of overstimulation acts "to blunt the discriminating powers of the mind" and "reduce it to a state of almost savage torpor."

Wordsworth singled out the blunting of mind produced by "daily" events and "hourly" news of "extraordinary incident." (In 1800!) Exactly what kind of events and incidents was discreetly left to the reader's imagination. Some sixty years later, another great poet and cultural diagnostician — French, and therefore as licensed to be hyperbolic as the English are prone to understate — offered a more heated version of the same charge. Here is Baudelaire writing in his journal in the early 1860s: "It is impossible to glance through any newspaper, no matter what the day, the month or the year, without finding on every line the most frightful traces of human perversity . . . Every newspaper, from the first line to the last, is nothing but a tissue of horrors. Wars, crimes, thefts, lecheries, tortures, the evil deeds of princes, of nations, of private individuals; an orgy of universal atrocity. And it is with this loathsome appetizer that civilized man daily washes down his morning repast."

Newspapers did not yet carry photographs when Baudelaire wrote. But this doesn't make his accusatory description of the bourgeois sitting down with his morning newspaper to breakfast with an array of the world's horrors any different from the contemporary critique of how much desensitizing horror we take in every day, via television as well as the morning paper. Newer technology provides a nonstop feed: as many images of disaster and atrocity as we can make time to look at.

Since *On Photography* was published, many critics have suggested that the agonies of war — thanks to television — have devolved into a nightly banality. Flooded with images of the sort that once used to shock and arouse indignation, we are losing our capacity to react. Compassion, stretched to its limits, is going numb. So runs the familiar diagnosis. But what is really being asked for here? That images of carnage be cut back to, say, once a week? More generally, that we work toward an "ecology of images," as I suggested in *On Photography*? But there *isn't* going to be an ecology of images. No Committee of Guardians is going to ration horror, to keep fresh its ability to shock. And the horrors themselves are not going to abate.

The view proposed in *On Photography* — that our capacity to respond to our experiences with emotional freshness and ethical pertinence is being sapped by the relentless diffusion of vulgar and appalling images — might be called the conservative critique of the diffusion of such images. I call this argument conservative because it is the sense of reality that is eroded. There is still a reality that exists independent of the attempts to weaken its authority. The argument is in fact a defense of reality and the imperiled standards for responding to it more fully. In the more radical — cynical — spin on this critique, there is nothing to defend, for, paradoxical as it may sound, there is no reality anymore. The vast maw of modernity has chewed up reality and spat the whole mess out as images. According to a highly influential analysis, we live in a "society of spectacle." Each thing has to be turned into a spectacle to be real — that is, interesting — to us. People themselves become images: celebrities. Reality has abdicated. There are only representations: media.

Fancy rhetoric, this. And very persuasive to many, because one of the characteristics of modernity is that people like to feel they can anticipate their own experience. (This view is associated in particular with the writings of the late Guy Debord, who thought he was describing an illusion, a hoax, and of Jean Baudrillard, who claims to believe that images, simulated realities, are all that exists now; it seems to be something of a French specialty.) It is common to say that war, like everything else that seems to be real, is *médiatique*. This was the diagnosis of several distinguished French day-trippers to Sarajevo during the siege, among them André Glucksmann: that the war would be won or lost not by anything that happened in Sarajevo, or Bosnia generally, but by what happened in the media. It is often asserted that "the West" has increasingly come to see war itself as a spectacle. Reports of the death of reality — like the death of reason, the death of the intellectual, the death of serious literature — seem to have been accepted without much reflection by many who are attempting to understand what feels wrong, or empty, or idiotically triumphant in contemporary politics and culture.

To speak of reality becoming a spectacle is a breathtaking provincialism. It universalizes the viewing habits of a small, educated population living in the rich part of the world, where news has been converted into entertainment — a mature style of viewing that is a prime acquisition of the "modern," and a prerequisite for dismantling traditional forms of party-based politics that offer real disagreement and debate. It assumes that everyone is a spectator. It suggests, perversely, unseriously, that there is no real suffering in the world. But it is absurd to identify "the world" with those zones in the rich countries where people have the dubious privilege of being spectators, or of declining to be spectators, of other people's pain, just as it is absurd to generalize about the ability to respond to the sufferings of others on the basis of the mind-set of those consumers of news who know nothing at first hand about war and terror. There are hundreds of millions of television watchers who are far from inured to what they see on television. They do not have the luxury of patronizing reality.

VI

Is there an antidote to the perennial seductiveness of war? And is this a question a woman is more likely to pose than a man? (Probably yes.)

Could one be mobilized actively to oppose war by an image (or a group of images), as one might be enrolled among the opponents of capital punishment by reading, say, Dreiser's *An American Tragedy* or Turgenev's "The Execution of Troppmann," an account of a night spent with a notorious criminal who is about to be guillotined? A narrative seems likely to be more effective than an image. Partly it is a question of the length of time one is obliged to look, and to feel. No photograph, or portfolio of photographs, can unfold, go further, and further still, as does *The Ascent* (1977), by the Ukrainian director Larisa Shepitko, the most affecting film about the horror of war I know.

Among single antiwar images, the huge photograph that Jeff Wall made in 1992 entitled *Dead Troops Talk (A vision after an ambush of a Red Army Patrol, near Moqor, Afghanistan, winter 1986)* seems to me exemplary in its thoughtfulness, coherence, and passion. The antithesis of a document, the picture, a Cibachrome transparency seven and a half feet high and more than thirteen feet wide and mounted on a light box, shows figures posed in a landscape, a blasted hillside, that was constructed in the artist's studio. Wall, who is Canadian, was never in Afghanistan. The ambush is a made-up event in a conflict he had read about. His imagination of war (he cites Goya as an inspiration) is in the tradition of nineteenth-century history painting and other forms of history-as-spectacle that emerged in the late eighteenth and early nineteenth centuries — just before the invention of the camera — such as tableaux vivants, wax displays, dioramas, and panoramas, which made the past, especially the immediate past, seem astonishingly, disturbingly real.

The figures in Wall's visionary photowork are "realistic," but, of course, the image is not. Dead soldiers don't talk. Here they do.

Thirteen Russian soldiers in bulky winter uniforms and high boots are scattered about a pocked, blood-splashed pit lined with loose rocks and the litter of war: shell casings, crumpled metal, a boot that holds the lower part of a leg. The soldiers, slaughtered in the Soviet Union's own late folly of a colonial war, were never buried. A few still have their helmets on. The head of one kneeling figure, talking animatedly, foams with his red brain matter. The atmosphere is warm, convivial, fraternal. Some slouch, leaning on an elbow, or sit, chatting, their opened skulls and destroyed hands on view. One man bends over another, who lies on his side in a posture of heavy sleep, perhaps encouraging him to sit up. Three men are horsing around: one with a huge wound in his belly straddles another, who is lying prone, while the third, kneeling, dangles what might be a watch before the laughing man on his stomach. One soldier, helmeted, legless, has turned to a comrade some distance away, an alert smile on his face. Below him are two who don't seem quite up to the resurrection and lie supine, their bloodied heads hanging down the stony incline.

Engulfed by the image, which is so accusatory, one could fantasize that the soldiers might turn and talk to us. But no, no one is looking out of the picture at the viewer. There's no threat of protest. They're not about to yell at us to bring a halt to that abomination which is war. They are not represented as terrifying to others, for among them (far left) sits a white-garbed Afghan scavenger, entirely absorbed in going through somebody's kit bag, of whom they take no note, and entering the picture above them (top right), on the path winding down the slope, are two Afghans, perhaps soldiers themselves, who, it would seem from the Kalashnikovs collected near their feet, have already stripped the dead soldiers of their weapons. These dead are supremely uninterested in the living: in those who took their lives; in witnesses — or in us. Why should they seek our gaze? What would they have to say to us? "We" — this "we" is everyone who has never experienced anything like what they went through — don't understand. We don't get it. We truly can't imagine what it was like. We can't imagine how dreadful, how terrifying war is — and how normal it becomes. Can't understand, can't imagine. That's what every soldier, and every journalist and aid worker and independent observer who has put in time under fire and had the luck to elude the death that struck down others nearby, stubbornly feels. And they are right.

FRANCIS SPUFFORD

The Habit

FROM GRANTA

"I CAN ALWAYS TELL when you're reading somewhere in the house," my mother used to say. "There's a special silence, a *reading* silence." I never heard it, this extra degree of hush that somehow traveled through walls and ceilings to announce that my seven-year-old self had become about as absent as a present person could be. The silence went both ways. As my concentration on the story in my hands took hold, all sounds faded away. My ears closed. Flat on my front with my chin on my hands or curled in a chair like a prawn, I'd be gone. I didn't hear doorbells ring, I didn't hear suppertime called, I didn't notice footsteps approaching of the adult who'd come to retrieve me. They had to shout "Francis!" near my head or, laughing, "Chocolate!"

I laughed too. Reading catatonically wasn't something I chose to do, it just happened, and I was happy for it to be my funny characteristic in the family, a trademark oddity my parents were affectionate toward. Though I never framed the thought then, stopping my ears with fiction was nonnegotiable. There were things to block out.

I was three when my sister Bridget was born. She was a small baby. Instead of following the nice upward graph of weight gain and turning into a rosy, compact toddler, she puked and thinned out. Instead of hitting the developmental milestones, and sitting up, and crawling, she just lay there. Her bones started to show through. By the time she was a few months old it was clear that something was wrong, but it took the doctors quite a while to come up with a diagnosis, because the odds were so long against the particular biological booby prize she had won. My parents were not related by blood. They came from different parts of the country. They had nothing obvious in common physically, except height and shortsightedness and a certain earnest bearing. When she was twenty, my mother had disconcerted the male students who wanted to seduce her by not knowing the rules of the game: not so much resisting as failing to notice that there was something to resist. At the same age my father had been frequently mistaken for a curate, which will happen if you go into a pub in a steel town when you're on an industrial-archaeology field trip and order yourself a half pint of lemonade to drink. But it turned out that they shared something else. Lost and unnoticed somewhere on the braid of their DNA, both carried an identical sequence of G's, A's, T's and C's. The sequence was recessive — it produced no symptoms in the carrier, and it would remain inactive if they had a child with anyone who didn't also have it. Put together two carriers, on the other hand, and each time a sperm fertilized an egg you rolled the dice. I was lucky: I inherited the trait only in the same passive form that my parents had. Bridget wasn't. In her the sequence activated, and made her unable to process an amino acid called cystine. Instead of waste cystine being flushed out of her tissues, it accumulated, as crystals. It accumulated fastest of all in the organs that were supposed to act as filters, her kidneys. There were only about twenty other living sufferers in Britain, only a few hundred in the world, and most of them were found in a cluster in the Appalachians, where hillbillies had been upping the odds by marrying their cousins for generation after generation. It was a ridiculously rare disease, a disaster it was almost absurd to be afflicted by, like being struck by a meteorite. By the time that the Great Ormond Street Children's Hospital in London made the connection between Bridget's failure to thrive and the condition called cystinosis, which appeared in the obscure footnotes of medical literature, she had one kidney already defunct, and the other about to give in. It was the autumn of 1967. Only a little time before, she'd have died right then. But the hospital had an experimental therapy that might offer her a few years of life. They offered a plan that would keep her on, but not over, the brink of starvation. My parents threw themselves into doing what was necessary. They crawled out of bed hourly during the night to adjust the tube that fed sugar water, drop by drop, up Bridget's nose, down her throat past her gag reflex, and straight into her stomach. They coaxed her into taking a daily fistful of pills. They did the four-hour round-trip rail journey to London again and again. They ran a large overdraft. They were brave. Family photographs from the time show them gray-skinned with fatigue, but always smiling, always determinedly broadcasting the message that this was all right, this was manageable, this could be sustained.

I was much too young to take in the causes and effects. I remember being asked which name I liked better, Bridget or Sophie, just after she was born; then nothing until, a year or so later, a generic scene of all four of us in my parents' bed on a Sunday morning, me playing with a drift of red and white Lego pieces, Bridget already well into the routine of existing with a fingertip grasp on the medical precipice. What I could see was that she was emaciated. Her legs dangled out of her frocks like strings. In her, the round family face we all shared became a neat little billiard ball very tightly stretched with skin, a sweet little death's-head. She could talk long before she could walk. The sugar water was the staple part of her diet, leaving her faintly nauseated a lot of the time, but it was important to tempt her to put aside the sick feeling, when she could, and to eat a little bit, a very little bit, of protein. My parents weighed out minuscule delicacies on a pair of white scales so small they would have made a more natural part of a drug dealer's equipment. "Look, Bridget," they said, "how about a quarter of an ounce of chicken?" They drafted Bridget's imaginary friend, Ben, and gave him a new passion for hiding the silver key to the sewing machine case at the bottom of pipkins of cold milk; a key that would be revealed only if all the milk was drunk.

And what I understood about Bridget's fragility made the whole world fragile. It was compounded by my mother, in her early thirties, developing osteoporosis, the brittle-bone condition women don't usually get till after the menopause. Bridget sat on rugs at family picnics, looking as if a breath of wind would blow her away; my mother sported ever-changing plaster casts as she collected fractures. Arm casts, leg casts, a complete upper-body cast. Whatever my life had been like before Bridget was born, it was over: cause for a sibling envy so fierce that I didn't dare show it, or even feel it much, in case it cracked the thinned skeleton of what was left.

It hurt to look at Bridget's situation face-on, and I shied away from it. Consequently, although she was a familiar presence, I never really got to know her very well as an individual human proposition. Other people always praised her sense of humor. They seemed to see someone using a dry wit to cope. What wit? I thought. I never found her jokes funny. The ho-ho-ho-ing that greeted them struck me as forced; more than that, as a handy getout for the people who laughed. It was like the famous putdown she had apparently come up with when I was six or so, and she was three, still rug-bound and entirely dependent on verbal comebacks. "You," she was supposed to have said, crushingly, "are a little piece of fluff" — and immediately this had been adopted into the family myth as evidence that Bridget could take care of herself, oh yes. I distrusted it for that very reason. In truth, I don't know now whether her jokes were funny or not. I wish I could remember more of them. I dismissed them *a priori*, on principle. I could never believe in a self-possession large enough to encompass the ruin I perceived; therefore she had none. I just saw raw vulnerability.

So when I read stories obsessively as a child I was striking a kind of deal that allowed me to turn away. Sometime in childhood I made a bargain that limited, so I thought, the power over me that real experience had, the real experience that comes to us in act and incident and through the proximate, continuous existence of those we love. All right, I said, I'll let a quantity of *that* stream over me, if I can have a balancing portion of *this*, the other kind of experience, which is controlled, and repeatable, and comes off the page. I learned to pump up the artificial realities of fiction from page to mind at a pressure that equalized with the pressure of the world, so that (in theory) the moment I actually lived in could never fill me completely, whatever was happening.

Thirty years have gone by since then. My life has changed, and so has the content of my reading. But the bargain holds. Still, when I reach for a book, I am reaching for an equilibrium. I am reading to banish pity, and brittle bones. I am reading to evade guilt, and avoid consequences, and to limit time's hold on me.

*

One January day when I was four, the au pair from Denmark who was helping out my parents while my sister was in the hospital took me for a walk in the Keele Woods, near where we lived. She'd been reading me the chapter in *Winnie-the-Pooh* where Pooh and Piglet go round and round the spinney in the snow, trying to catch the Woozle. "Let's go and find Piglet," she said. The woods were under snow as well that day. The snow was deep and powdery on the paths, and the trees were smoothed white masses bowed under the weight of winter, like melted candles. We passed through a zone of little fir trees near the bottom of the steps down into the woods, leaving behind a trail of big footprints and a trail of little ones. (It's not a coincidence that Pooh and Piglet walking together in Ernest Shepard's illustrations have exactly the relative sizes of an adult and child going hand in hand.) And there, perched on the hollow stump of an oak, was Piglet, wearing a small red scarf just like in the pictures. The soft toy versions of the Disney characters did not exist yet. She had sewn him herself from gray and white cotton ticking. It was wonderful.

Looking back, I see that moment almost as the first step in a seduction. As a ten-year-old, as a teenager, as an adult, I've always wanted life to be more storylike; I've always reached out for treats, setups, situations that can be coaxed by charm and by the right kind of suggestively narrative talk into yielding something like the deliberate richness of an invented scene. Friends and lovers have known me as someone willing to say aloud sentences they thought could exist only on the page, in the hope that real time could be arranged and embroidered. I'd like words to be magic; or magnetic, attracting the events they name. Perhaps I first saw the chance of that when we found Piglet in the snow.

But at four I was only a hearer of stories. It isn't until we're reading stories privately, on our own account, that story's full seducing power can be felt. For the voice that tells us a story aloud is always more than a carrier wave bringing us the meaning; it's a companion through the events of the story, ensuring that the feelings it stirs in us are held within the circle of attachment connecting the adult reading to the child listening. To hear a story is a social act. Social rules, social promises, social bonds sustain us during it. It is only when we read it stumblingly for ourselves that we feel the full force of the story's challenge.

I learned to read around my sixth birthday. I was making a dinosaur in school from crepe bandage and toilet rolls when I started to feel as if an invisible pump was inflating my head from the inside. My face became a cluster of bumps, my feet dangled limp and too far away to control. The teacher carried me home on her shoulders. I gripped the dinosaur in one hand. It was still wet with green and purple poster paint. After that, things turned delirious. I had mumps, and one by one my sister, my mother and my father all caught it from me. The house stayed convalescent in feeling till the last of us was better. It was a long quiet time of curtains closed during the day, and wan slow-moving adults, and bedsheets that seemed as big as the world when you lay in them, each wrinkle a canyon. On my sixth birthday my class came up the road and sang "Happy Birthday to You" in the front garden. It was too nice. I hid behind the curtain in my dressing gown and would not show myself at the upstairs window. Perhaps, for the very first time in my life, I was impatient to be done with a human encounter and to get back to my book. When I caught the mumps, I couldn't read; when I went back to school again, I could. The first page of *The Hobbit* was a thicket of symbols, to be decoded one at a time and joined hesitantly together. Primary schools in Britain now sometimes send home a photocopy of a page of Russian or Arabic to remind parents of that initial state when writing was a wall of spiky unknowns, an excluding briar hedge. By the time I reached *The Hobbit*'s last page, though, writing had softened, and lost the outlines of the printed alphabet, and become a transparent liquid, first viscous and sluggish, like a jelly of meaning, then ever thinner and more mobile, flowing faster and faster, until it reached me at the speed of thinking and I could not entirely distinguish the suggestions it was making from my own thoughts. I had undergone the acceleration into the written word that you also experience as a change in the medium. In fact, writing had ceased to be a thing — an object in the world — and become a medium, a substance you look through.

I. N. In. *A.* In a. *H, o, l, e.* In a hole. *I, n, t, h, e, g, r, o, u, n, d.* In a hole in the ground. *L-i-v-e-d-a-h-o-b-b-i-t.* In a hole in the ground lived a hobbit . . . And then I never stopped again.

The reading flowed when I was six, with the yellow hardback copy of *The Hobbit* in my hands; and the pictures came. I went to the door of the hobbit hole with Bilbo as he let in more and more dwarves, attracted by the sign Gandalf had scratched there in the glossy green paint. I jogged along with him on his pony out of the Shire, away from raspberry jam and crumpets and toward dragons. In *The Lord of the Rings*, this journey would become a transit from a little, naïve space of comfort and tended fields into a dangerous world that besieged it. This time, it was only the natural progression of a story outward from home. Bilbo's life in Bag End was like real life, or at any rate like a bachelor fantasy of it, in which fifty is only just grown up, and the highest felicities are a pipe and convivial male company. The farther away from Bag End Bilbo went, the more purely he inhabited the world of adventure, and even of epic. But Bilbo went on sounding like himself: chatty, fussy, scared, resourceful, prosy — ordinary. "Dear me! Dear me! I am sure this is all very uncomfortable." He took me to the mountains and the caverns and the hollow halls that the dwarves had sung about back at Bag End, in a kind of promise that the book kept. I was ordinary too; if Bilbo could be there, so could I. Tolkien made him more extravagantly cowardly than I thought of myself as being. "Then he fell flat on the floor, and kept on calling out 'struck by lightning, struck by lightning!' over and over again; and that was all they could get out of him for a long time." The angle from which Tolkien looked at Bilbo set a limit on how scary events in *The Hobbit* could be. Nothing too awful could happen to someone like Bilbo, even if the goblins did set fire to the tree he was hiding in, and sing about skin cracking, eyes glazing, fat melting and bones blackening.

I find now, rereading *The Hobbit*, that Tolkien described few things in the detail I remember. His was a speedy, storyteller's art. It made a few precise suggestions, supplied a few nodal adjectives from which the web of an imagined world could grow in a child's mind, and didn't linger. I made the pictures. I was lucky that my first book put me in the hands of a writer with such a conscious and decided idea of what a reader's imagination needed. Tolkien had trained himself on the hard, nuggetlike specifics of Anglo-Saxon and Viking poetry, with its names for things that were almost spells, and its metaphors that were almost riddles. At six I had no idea that the sea had once been the whale-path, or that Tolkien had any predecessors when he had Bilbo boast to Smaug that he was "the clue-finder, the web-cutter, the stinging fly." What I did know explicitly was that while Tolkien's words were authoritative, his occasional black-and-white drawings in the text counted only as suggestions that I was free to accept or refuse. What Middle-earth looked like was my business. Illustrations — I decided — were limitations. I had not been able to picture Bilbo's face, but I was comfortable with that. It seemed that he existed in a story-space in which it was not necessary that the points of Tolkien's description of a hobbit (round stomach, bright clothes, hairy feet, clever fingers, good-natured expression) should coalesce into one definite image; and in that, Bilbo was like my parents and my sister, whose ultimately familiar faces I found wouldn't come either when I shut my eyes and tried to summon them in the brown and purple dark behind my eyelids. No: the natural destiny of a story was to be a rich, unresolved swirl in my visual cortex, and any illustrator who tried to pin it down was taking a liberty.

At the same time, I couldn't read quite a lot of the words in *The Hobbit*. I had accelerated into reading faster than my understanding had grown. If I press my memory for the sensation of reading the second half of the book, when I was flying through the story, I remember, simultaneous with the new liquid smoothness, a constant flicker of incomprehensibility. There were holes in the text corresponding to the parts I couldn't understand. Words like "prophesying," "rekindled" and "adornment" had never been spoken in my hearing. No one had ever told me aloud to "behold" something, and I didn't know that "vessels" could be cups and bowls as well as ships. I could say these words over, and shape my mouth around their big sounds. I could enjoy them. They were obviously the special vocabulary that was apt for the slaying of dragons and the fighting of armies: words that conjured the sound of trumpets. But for all the meaning I obtained from them, they might as well not have been printed. When I speeded up and my reading became fluent, it was partly because I had learned how to ignore such words efficiently. I methodically left out chunks. I marked them to be sorted out later, by slower and more patient mental processes; I allowed each one to brace a blank space of greater or lesser size in its sentence; I grabbed the gist, which seemed to survive even in sentences that were mostly hole; and I sped on.

Now that I hardly ever spell out a word I do not know, and the things that puzzle me in books do not lie in individual words but in the author's assumption of shared knowledge about the human heart (never my strong point), I still have, like everybody, words in my vocabulary that are relics of that time. The words we learned exclusively from books are the ones we pronounce differently from everyone else. Or, if we force ourselves to say them the public way, secretly we believe the proper pronunciation is our own, deduced from the page and not corrected by hearing the word aloud until it was too late to alter its sound. The classic is "misled," said not as *mis-led* but as *myzled* — the past tense of a verb, "to misle," which somehow never comes up in the present tense. In fact, misled never misled me. One of mine is "grimace." You probably think it's pronounced *grimuss,* but I know different. It's *grim-ace,* to rhyme with *face.* I'm sorry, but on this point the entire English-speaking human race except me is wrong.

I began my reading in a kind of hopeful springtime for children's writing. I was born in 1964, so I grew up in a golden age comparable to the present heyday of J. K. Rowling and Philip Pullman, or to the great Edwardian decade when E. Nesbit, Kipling and Kenneth Grahame were all publishing at once. An equally amazing generation of talent was at work as the 1960s ended and the 1970s began. William Mayne was making dialogue sing; Peter Dickinson was writing the *Changes* trilogy; Alan Garner was reintroducing myth into the bloodstream of daily life; Jill Paton Walsh was showing that children's perceptions could be just as angular and uncompromising as those of adults; Joan Aiken had begun her Dido Twite series of comic fantasies; Penelope Farmer was being unearthly with *Charlotte Sometimes;* Diana Wynne Jones's gift for wild invention was hitting its stride; Rosemary Sutcliff was just adding the final uprights to her colonnade of Romano-British historical novels; Leon Garfield was reinventing the eighteenth century as a scene for inky Gothic intrigue. The list went on and on. There was activity everywhere, a new potential classic every few months.

Unifying this lucky concurrence of good books, and making them seem for a while like contributions to a single intelligible project, was a temporary cultural consensus, a consensus about what children were and where we all were in history. Dr. Spock's great manual for liberal middle-class child-rearing had come out at the beginning of the sixties, and had helped deconstruct the last lingering remnants of the idea that a child was clay to be molded by benevolent adult authority. The new orthodoxy took it for granted that a child was a resourceful individual, neither ickily good nor reeking of original sin. And the wider world was seen as a place in which a permanent step forward toward enlightenment had taken place as well. The books my generation were offered took it for granted that poverty, disease and prejudice essentially belonged in the past. Postwar society had ended them. As the 1970s went on, these assumptions would lose their credibility. Gender roles were about to be shaken up; the voices that a white, liberal consensus consigned to the margins of consciousness were about to be asserted as hostile witnesses to its nature. People were about to lose their certainty that liberal solutions worked. Evil would revert to being an unsolved problem. But it hadn't happened yet, and till it did, the collective gaze of children's stories swept confidently across past and future, and across all the international varieties of the progressive, orange-juice-drinking present, from Australia to Sweden, from Holland to the broad, clean suburbs of America.

For me, walking up the road at age seven or eight to spend my pocket money on a paperback, the outward sign of this unity was the dominance of Puffin Books. In Britain, almost everything written for children passed into the one paperback imprint. On the shelves of the children's section in a bookshop, practically all the stock would be identically neat soft-covered octavos, in different colors, with different cover art, but always with the same sans-serif type on the spine and the same little logo of an upstanding puffin. Everything cost about the same. For 17½p — then 25p and then 40p as the 1970s inflation took hold — you could have any of the new books, or any of the children's classics, from old ones like *The Wind in the Willows* or *Alice* to the ones that were only a couple of decades into their classichood, like the Narnia books. (C. S. Lewis had died the year before I was born, most unfairly making sure I would never meet him.) To a British reading child in the sixties or the seventies, how securely authoritative Puffins seemed, with the long, trustworthy descriptions of the story inside the front cover, always written by the same arbiter, the Puffin editor Kaye Webb, and their astonishingly precise recommendation to "girls of eleven and above, and sensitive boys." It was as if Puffin were part of the administration of the world. They were the department of the welfare state responsible for the distribution of narrative.

Bookshops were nice, but the real home of the massed possibilities of story was the public library. Before I discovered it, my life beyond home encompassed only the university — the solitary rooms I found my parents working in. My father's office in the Chancellor's Building smelled of floor polish and the butterscotches he sucked when he was concentrating. It was a modernist box whose glass and concrete he'd fitted out with the old desk and the heraldic panels he had brought with him from Cambridge, pouring the spirit of the history he studied into the future he believed in: the civilized welfare state that educated all its talented sons and daughters. The past flowed into the future without any break for him, because the student revolution and the counterculture had happened while his attention was elsewhere. Princess Margaret had come to a University of Keele function in 1965 or thereabouts and made a beeline for my parents, the youngest people in the room, hoping they would be groovy. "Do you know anything about pop music?" she asked. "No," they said, embarrassed. And it was true. As a teenager I would test them with pictures of Elvis, unable to believe that two people who had been young in the fifties could really fail to recognize him. I gave them clues. Memphis? No. Blue suede shoes? No. Rock 'n' roll? "Ah yes," said my father proudly, "the music with the very strong *beat!*"

Keele University ran a free bus service for the cleaners who came up from the towns of the Potteries to Keele Park to wax the floors of the university departments and clean the students' rooms. Anyone could use it, and from when I was about seven or so, I regularly rode the bus down the hill on my own to visit the library in Newcastle-under-Lyme. The bus turned out of the park gates, and suddenly, instead of being inside the small horizon of the campus, cupped on the hilltop round its lakes and woods, the view opened onto a long valley full of housing estates and pit winding-gear and factories. In the fields sloping down to the town, bullocks nosed at blackberry bushes on rainy mornings. Rooks cawed in the trees. At night the valley twinkled with sodium lights. Beyond the new roundabout at the foot of Keele Bank, the weirdly centerless conurbation of the Potteries began, as large as a city altogether, but never as concentrated. There were five small-town provincial High Streets, five sets of Victorian civic architecture. Newcastle's core was red sandstone, scorched by nineteenth-century industrial soot. As I first remember it, it still had a cattle market, and one of those courtly antique grocery emporiums smelling of cheese and coffee beans, where the money my parents paid over for food in neat waxed-paper packages vanished into the ceiling up pneumatic tubes, and the change came jingling down other tubes into round brass dishes the size of an ashtray. But both those holdouts from the past had vanished by the time I was taking myself to the library. The shops along the Ironmarket had posters of Slade, 10cc and the Osmonds for sale. When I bought a packet of Sweet Cigarettes for 4p in decimal currency there was a cigarette card of the space race inside. Down Bridge Street there was an Indian restaurant where I had been with my dad and adventurously eaten a biryani. When my Coke came, it had a slice of lemon floating in it. Amazing sophistication!

The town seemed just as glamorous to me as the parkland up the hill, only with a different orientation, a different job to do in my imagination. For a long time, just as I set any wild scene in Keele Woods, whenever I read a story set somewhere urban, I borrowed Newcastle in my mind's eye as the setting. Newcastle figured as London, as Paris; tweaked with columns, it was Rome; with a few pointy bits on the roofs it was Chinese. Later, when I read *To Kill a Mockingbird*, I made it into the Deep South.

The library was a brand-new concrete and glass block at the end of the Ironmarket. In the window, leaflets about passing your driving test were stapled to a corkboard, and there was a poster, put up well in advance, encouraging you to PLANT A TREE IN SEVENTY-THREE. To get to the children's section, you turned sharp left inside and down the stairs into a long basement room lit by the blue-white of fluorescent tubes. The issue desk was at the far end, next to the floor-level picture books and colored stools for the tinies; two or three wire twirlers of paperbacks tried to tempt you on your way out, like the chocolates for impulse purchasers at supermarket checkouts, but at that time library budgets ran to hardbacks as a matter of course, and anyway, paperbacks were for owning yourself. The library's true treasure was the A–Z Children's

Hardback Fiction, running the whole length of the right-hand wall
on metal shelves arranged in big U-shaped bays. Every book had its
dustwrapper sealed onto the cover in heavy-duty plastic, soup-
proof, thumb-proof, spaghetti-hoop-proof. Every book bore a yellow Dewey Decimal code number on a sticker on the spine. I approached them slowly, not with reverence exactly, but with the feeling that the riches in the room needed to be handled with some
kind of grateful attention to their ordered abundance. Also, I knew
that once I'd chosen my four books, the multiple possibilities of
the library would shrink down to that finite handful. I hated to be
hurried out of the great, free bazaar.

Books, it seemed to me, could vary more than virtually anything
else that went around in the world under one name. They infused
me with incompatible, incomparable emotions. Arthur Ransome's
Swallows and Amazons series, for example, idylls of meticulous detail, instructive about semaphore and surveying and gold refining.
They let me try out a counterlife for size: a wonderful alternative
to my own small, dreamy, medically unlucky family of four. Ransome's brothers and sisters were robust. They milled around. The
parents waved the adventurers off at the dock on page one, and no
intense spotlight of anxiety fell on anyone. They reminded me of
my cousins in Cambridgeshire, who messed about in canoes on
Fen rivers. The stories blended with the life I imagined my cousins
had. Without having to feel disloyal, I could experiment, reading
Arthur Ransome, with the idea of belonging to that other version
of family life that existed over at my aunt and uncle's house, with
its dinghy in the garage and its big Pyrex pots of stew and mounds
of boiled potatoes at mealtimes, instead of our Elizabeth David–inspired experiments with risotto and pasta.

When I made my choice, I knew that I could have melancholy
under my arm on the way to the bus stop; or laughter; or fear;
or enchantment. Or longing. I didn't just want to see in books
what I saw anyway in the world around me, even if it was perceived
and understood and articulated from angles I could never have
achieved; I wanted to see things I never saw in life. More than I
wanted books to do anything else, I wanted them to take me away. I
wanted exodus.

Exodus: and not least from school. I had two friends, but they
played soccer most break times, leaving me at loose ends in a play-

ground that never seemed to be intelligible the way a story was. There was no narrator. I would banish my uncertainty by walking around and around the white line at the edge. Pace, pace, pace, corner; pace, pace, pace, corner; looking neither to right nor to left until the whistle blew. I abolished loneliness, I abolished school, by thinking myself into the schools I had read about. From Angela Brazil and the Chalet School books through to the unexpected rebirth of the genre at Hogwarts in the Harry Potter books — where a new atmosphere, both magical and democratic, still does not displace such key features as the sneering rich boy and the contest for the house cup — school stories explore what are essentially autonomous towns of children. As a perceptive critic of Harry Potter pointed out, what makes the school setting liberating is that school rules are always arbitrary rules, externally imposed. You can break them, when you get into scrapes, without feeling any guilt, or without its affecting the loyalty to the institution that even unruly characters feel, right down from Angela Brazil to Joanne Rowling. Harry loves Hogwarts. The rules of conduct that really count are worked out by the children themselves, and exist inside the school rules like a live body inside a suit of armor. School stories are about children judging each other, deciding about each other, getting along with each other. The adults whose decisions would be emotionally decisive — parents — are deliberately absent.

Soon my parents were absent too. At the age of ten I was sent away to boarding school, a choir school, my parents having discovered the miserable miles I was covering round the playground. At first I hated the way that even sleeping wasn't private. You were in bed, but the bed wasn't truly your bed, the sheets weren't your sheets. I pulled the covers over me as if they were the bedroom door I hadn't got, but it never entirely worked. The pocket of warmth you made as you curled up was still an ambiguous, only semi-boundaried zone. Rustles and snuffles and coughs came from the beds four feet to the left and four feet to the right. You could hear the world that had rung electric bells at you all day, and called you by your surname, and required you to be on your guard all the time, still going on; and though the oblivion that came when your mind's grip on your surroundings softened, and frayed, and parted, was truly private, sleep being a kingdom whose doors opened equally everywhere, it never seemed to last for more than a moment before morning came and the long cycle of the school day began again. Boarding school was a town of children, just as the stories said, but what the stories hadn't told me was how strange it would feel, at first, to live for weeks at a time with boys' social hierarchies omnipresent and the deep connections of family nowhere.

It took three years, but I got used to it eventually. I found the compensations in boarding school, from having teachers who seemed actually pleased when I knew things to the astonishing comfort of fitting in. I had, not just a few best friends, but a role I could play. Other boys knew what I was when they saw me coming, and had a workable set of expectations about it. It turned out that school — this school, anyway — had an actual niche for someone bookish who was willing to play bookish, and live up to the images of cleverness that were current in our shared world of comics and war films and TV programs. I could be Brains in *Thunderbirds*, I could be Q in *Live and Let Die*. I could be the officer there invariably was on the escape committee at Stalag Luft 17 who wore glasses and came up with cunning plans. In short, I could be a prof. It was a mask, but it felt as if it bore a friendly relationship to my face.

And beneath these satisfactions, I had a feeling as if a long-tied private knot had been loosened. My family's unending medical crisis had gone into lovely, unexpected remission. The prediction had been that Bridget would die by the time she was eight or so, but by chance she had survived long enough for medicine to move on. They still couldn't do anything about the cystinosis itself. Cystine crystals were still forming, an accident happening in every one of her cells. But transplant surgery had arrived by 1975, pioneered as a solution to quite different diseases but perhaps adaptable to her problem. The doctors thought that a transplanted kidney could probably be protected by careful management from going the way of her own; maybe it would give her more life, maybe it could even give a semblance of an ordinary life. So in the year that she was eight and I was eleven, her medical notes, by now a mass of paper it took a trolley to move, were transferred to the kidney unit at Guy's Hospital, and to save time looking for a compatible kidney my father donated her one of his. He and Bridget were trundled into the theater together on two gurneys. They disappeared through the red rubber doors; my mother took me to spend the afternoon in a little stamp dealer's shop under Waterloo Bridge. I should have been terrified, with two of the three people I loved most going under the knife at once, but I had cultivated blind faith in doctors as an essential fear-limiting tool, and I don't remember being afraid during that long, edgy afternoon, nor noticing what my mother was feeling either. I remember the stamps. They were the ordinary pre-decimal British definitives, in strips, in little glassine envelopes. The queen on them was a young woman, her black-and-white photograph an oval island on a rectangle of pale, clear color. The halfpenny stamp was orange, the penny blue, the thruppence purple.

The operation had its costs. My father's hair turned white at forty-one. The steroids they pumped into Bridget to stop her body from rejecting the kidney made her bloat up, turning her abruptly from a very thin person into a very fat one, so drastic and irreversible a transformation that for the rest of her life it was hard to find more than occasional reminders of the person she had been before — in a glimpse of the back of her neck, for example, always slender even when she was most enpudgified. But it seemed to work. Suddenly, for the first time, Bridget could walk distances and eat normal food. The crated bottles of sugar water faded out of her life, leaving nothing behind but a hatred for sweet things and a counterbalancing taste for vicious little salad dressings, heavy on the pepper and the Tabasco. Suddenly her life had no fixed expiration date anymore. The year after the transplant, she stumped to the top of a Scottish mountain. It was a small mountain, but it was a mountain. The wind on the summit blew her tartan cape around her ears, but she herself was anchored: solid enough, decisively enough there in the flesh that there was no danger of the wind blowing her away. Gravity had hold of her. I didn't have to see her anymore as thistledown, or bird bones, or a crushable paper sculpture. Something in me that had been vigilant for years relaxed.

I wish I'd been brave enough as a teenager to try the experiment of facing the emotions that all this left pooled in the sump of my psyche. Books might have helped here, too: they can be instruments of hope and discovery, after all, as well as of escape. But I wasn't. It's not that the story of my life as a reader from thirteen

onward has followed one grim line of evasion. I hoped. I discovered. But when it came to it, whenever fear presented itself to me
and asked to be addressed, I always turned back to books as the
medium into which I was used to pouring my troublesome emotions.

Bridget died when she was twenty-two, of cystine deposits in the
brain, the one organ that can't be transplanted. "I'm sick of living
at the frontiers of medical knowledge," she said soon before the
end. She lingered long enough for my father to read her the whole
of *The Lord of the Rings* aloud.

I still go into bookshops when things go wrong. And as I walk
down the aisles, I remember that in every novel there are reverses,
that all plots twist and turn, that sadness and happiness are just the
materials authors use, in arrangements I know very well; and at
that thought the books seem to kindle into a kind of dim life all
around me, each one unfolding its particular nature into my
awareness without urgency, without haste, as if a column of gray,
insubstantial smoke were rising from it, softening the air, filling it
with words and actions which are all provisional, which could all be
changed for others, according to taste. Among these drifting pillars, the true story of my life looks no different; it is just a story
among stories, and after I have been reading for a while, I can
hardly tell anymore which is my own.

The Love of My Life

FROM THE SUN

THE FIRST TIME I cheated on my husband, my mother had been dead for exactly one week. I was in a café in Minneapolis watching a man. He watched me back. He was slightly pudgy, with jet-black hair and skin so white it looked as if he'd powdered it. He stood and walked to my table and sat down without asking. He wanted to know if I had a cat. I folded my hands on the table, steadying myself; I was shaking, nervous at what I would do. I was raw, fragile, vicious with grief. I would do anything.

"Yes," I said.

"I thought so," he said slowly. He didn't take his eyes off me. I rolled the rings around on my fingers. I was wearing two wedding bands, my own and my mother's. I'd taken hers off her hand after she died. It was nothing fancy: sterling silver, thick and braided.

"You look like the kind of girl who has a cat."

"How's that?" I asked.

He didn't answer. He just kept looking at me steadily, as if he knew everything about me, as if he owned me. I felt distinctly that he might be a murderer.

"Are you mature?" he asked intently.

I didn't know what he meant. I still don't. I told him that I was.

"Well then, prove it and walk down the street with me."

We left the café, his hand on my arm. I had monstrous bruises on my knees from falling on them after I walked into my mother's hospital room and first saw her dead. He liked these. He said he'd been admiring them from across the room. They were what had drawn him to me. Also, he liked my boots. He thought I looked intriguing. He thought I looked mature. I was twenty-two. He was older, possibly thirty. I didn't ask his name; he didn't ask mine. I walked with him to a parking lot behind a building. He stopped and pressed me against a brick wall and kissed me, but then he wasn't kissing me. He was biting me. He bit my lips so hard I screamed.

"You lying cunt," he whispered into my ear. "You're not mature." He flung me away from him and left.

I stood, unmoving, stunned. The inside of my mouth began to bleed softly. Tears filled my eyes. *I want my mother,* I thought. *My mother is dead.* I thought this every hour of every day for a very long time: *I want my mother. My mother is dead.*

It was only a kiss, and barely that, but it was, anyway, a crossing. When I was a child I witnessed a leaf unfurl in a single motion. One second it was a fist, the next an open hand. I never forgot it, seeing so much happen so fast. And this was like that — the end of one thing, the beginning of another: my life as a slut.

When my mother was diagnosed with cancer, my husband, Mark, and I took an unspoken sexual hiatus. When she died seven weeks later, I couldn't bear Mark to touch me. His hands on my body made me weep. He went down on me in the gentlest of ways. He didn't expect anything in return. He didn't make me feel that I had to come. I would soak in a hot bath, and he would lean into it to touch me. He wanted to make me feel good, better. He loved me, and he had loved my mother. Mark and I were an insanely young, insanely happy, insanely in-love married couple. He wanted to help. *No, no, no,* I said, but then sometimes I relented. I closed my eyes and tried to relax. I breathed deep and attempted to fake it. I rolled over on my stomach so I wouldn't have to look at him. He fucked me and I sobbed uncontrollably.

"Keep going," I said to him. "Just finish." But he wouldn't. He couldn't. He loved me. Which was mysteriously, unfortunately, precisely the problem.

I wanted my mother.

We aren't supposed to want our mothers that way, with the pining intensity of sexual love, but I did, and if I couldn't have her, I couldn't have anything. Most of all I couldn't have pleasure, not even for a moment. I was bereft, in agony, destroyed over her

death. To experience sexual joy, it seemed, would have been to ne-
gate that reality. And more, it would have been to betray my
mother, to be disloyal to the person she had been to me: my hero,
a single mother after she bravely left an unhealthy relationship
with my father when I was five. She remarried when I was eleven.
My stepfather had loved her and been a good husband to her for
ten years, but shortly after she died, he'd fallen in love with someone else. His new girlfriend and her two daughters moved into my
mother's house, took her photos off the walls, erased her. I needed
my stepfather to be the kind of man who would suffer for my
mother, unable to go on, who would carry a torch. And if he
wouldn't do it, I would.

We are not allowed this. We are allowed to be deeply into basketball, or Buddhism, or *Star Trek*, or jazz, but we are not allowed to be
deeply sad. Grief is a thing that we are encouraged to "let go of," to
"move on from," and we are told specifically how this should be
done. Countless well-intentioned friends, distant family members,
hospital workers, and strangers I met at parties recited the famous
five stages of grief to me: denial, anger, bargaining, depression,
and acceptance. I was alarmed by how many people knew them,
how deeply this single definition of the grieving process had per-
meated our cultural consciousness. Not only was I supposed to feel
these five things, I was meant to feel them in that order and for a
prescribed amount of time.

I did not deny. I did not get angry. I didn't bargain, become depressed, or accept. I fucked. I sucked. Not my husband, but people
I hardly knew, and in that I found a glimmer of relief. The people I
messed around with did not have names; they had titles: the Prematurely Graying Wilderness Guide, the Technically Still a Virgin
Mexican Teenager, the Formerly Gay Organic Farmer, the Quietly
Perverse Poet, the Failing but Still Trying Massage Therapist, the
Terribly Large Texas Bull Rider, the Recently Unemployed Graduate of Juilliard, the Actually Pretty Famous Drummer Guy. Most of
these people were men; some were women. With them, I was not in
mourning; I wasn't even me. I was happy and sexy and impetuous
and fun. I was wild and enigmatic and terrifically good in bed. I
didn't care about them or have orgasms. We didn't have heart-to-
heart talks. I asked them questions about their lives, and they told

me everything and asked few questions in return; they knew nothing about me. Because of this, most of them believed they were falling instantly, madly in love with me.

I did what I did with these people, and then I returned home to Mark, weak-kneed and wet, bleary-eyed and elated. *I'm alive,* I thought in that giddy, postsex daze. *My mother's death has taught me to live each day as if it were my last,* I said to myself, latching on to the nearest cliché, and the one least true. I didn't stop to think: What if it *had* been my last day? Did I wish to be sucking the cock of an Actually Pretty Famous Drummer Guy? I didn't think to ask that because I didn't want to think. When I did think, I thought, *I cannot continue to live without my mother.*

I lied — sometimes to the people I messed around with (some of them, if they'd known I was married, would not have wanted to mess around with me), but mostly to Mark. I was not proud of myself. I was in love with him and wanted to be faithful to him and wanted to want to have sex with him, but something in me wouldn't let me do it. We got into the habit of fucking in the middle of the night, both of us waking from a sound sleep to the reality of our bodies wet and hard and in the act. The sex lasted about thirty seconds, and we would almost always both come. It was intensely hot and strange and surreal and darkly funny and ultimately depressing. We never knew who started it. Neither of us recalled waking, reaching for each other. It was a shard of passion, and we held on to it. For a while it got us through.

We like to say how things are, perhaps because we hope that's how they might actually be. We attempt to name, identify, and define the most mysterious of matters: sex, love, marriage, monogamy, infidelity, death, loss, grief. We want these things to have an order, an internal logic, and we also want them to be connected to one another. We want it to be true that if we cheat on our spouse, it means we no longer want to be married to him or her. We want it to be true that if someone we love dies, we simply have to pass through a series of phases, like an emotional obstacle course from which we will emerge happy and content, unharmed and unchanged.

After my mother died, everyone I knew wanted to tell me about either the worst breakup they'd had or all the people they'd known who'd died. I listened to a long, traumatic story about a girlfriend who suddenly moved to Ohio, and to stories of grandfathers and old friends and people who lived down the block who were no longer among us. Rarely was this helpful.

Occasionally I came across people who'd had the experience of losing someone whose death made them think, *I cannot continue to live.* I recognized these people: their postures, where they rested their eyes as they spoke, the expressions they let onto their faces and the ones they kept off. These people consoled me beyond measure. I felt profoundly connected to them, as if we were a tribe.

It's surprising how relatively few of them there were. People don't die anymore, not the way they used to. Children survive childhood; women, the labors of birth; men, their work. We survive influenza and infection, cancer and heart attacks. We keep living on and on: 80, 90, 103. We live younger, too; frightfully premature babies are cloistered and coddled and shepherded through. My mother lived to the age of forty-five and never lost anyone who was truly beloved by her. Of course, she knew many people who died, but none who made her wake to the thought: *I cannot continue to live.*

And there is a difference. Dying is not your girlfriend moving to Ohio. Grief is not the day after your neighbor's funeral, when you felt extremely blue. It is impolite to make this distinction. We act as if all losses are equal. It is un-American to behave otherwise: we live in a democracy of sorrow. Every emotion felt is validated and judged to be as true as any other.

But what does this do to us, this refusal to quantify love, loss, grief? Jewish tradition states that one is considered a mourner when one of eight people dies: father, mother, sister, brother, husband, wife, son, or daughter. This definition doesn't fulfill the needs of today's diverse and far-flung affections; indeed, it probably never did. It leaves out the step-relations, the long-term lovers, the chosen family of a tight circle of friends; and it includes the blood relations we perhaps never honestly loved. But its intentions are true. And, undeniably, for most of us that list of eight does come awfully close. We love and care for oodles of people, but only a few of them, if they died, would make us believe we could not continue to live. Imagine if there was a boat upon which you could put only four people, and everyone else known to and beloved by you would then cease to exist. Who would you put on that boat? It would be painful, but how quickly you would decide: *You and you and you and you, get in. The rest of you, goodbye.*

For years, I was haunted by the idea of this imaginary boat of life, by the desire to exchange my mother's fate for one of the many living people I knew. I would be sitting across the table from a dear friend. I loved her, him, each one of these people. Some I said I loved like family. But I would look at them and think, *Why couldn't it have been you who died instead? You, goodbye.*

I didn't often sleep with Mark, but I slept beside him, or tried to. I dreamed incessantly about my mother. There was a theme. Two or three times a week she made me kill her. She commanded me to do it, and I sobbed and got down on my knees, begging her not to make me, but she would not relent. In each dream, like a good daughter, I ultimately complied. I tied her to a tree in our front yard, poured gasoline over her head, and lit her on fire. I made her run down the dirt road that passed by the house where I'd grown up, and I ran her over with my truck; I dragged her body, caught on a jagged piece of metal underneath until it came loose, and then I put my truck in reverse and ran her over again. I took a miniature baseball bat and beat her to death with it. I forced her into a hole I'd dug and kicked dirt and stones on top of her and buried her alive. These dreams were not surreal. They took place in the plain light of day. They were the documentary films of my subconscious and felt as real to me as life. My truck was really my truck; our front yard was our actual front yard; the miniature baseball bat sat in our closet among the umbrellas. I didn't wake from these dreams crying; I woke shrieking. Mark grabbed me and held me. He wetted a washcloth with cool water and put it over my face. These dreams went on for months, years, and I couldn't shake them. I also couldn't shake my infidelities. I couldn't shake my grief.

What was there to do with me? What did those around me do? They did what I would have done — what we all do when faced with the prospect of someone else's sorrow: they tried to talk me out of it, neutralize it, tamp it down, make it relative and therefore not so bad. We narrate our own lesser stories of loss in an attempt to demonstrate that the sufferer is not really so alone. We make grossly inexact comparisons and hope that they will do. In short, we insist on ignoring the precise nature of deep loss because there is nothing we can do to change it, and by doing so we strip it of its meaning, its weight, its own fiercely original power.

The first person I knew who died was a casual friend of my mother's named Barb. Barb was in her early thirties, and I was ten. Her hair was brown and shoulder length, her skin clear and smooth as a bar of soap. She had the kind of tall body that made you acutely aware of the presence of its bones: a long, knobby nose; wide, thin hips; a jaw too pointed to be considered beautiful. Barb got into her car and started the engine. Her car was parked in a garage and all the doors were closed and she had stuffed a Minnesota Vikings cap into a small hole in the garage wall to make it even more airtight. My mother explained this to me in detail: the Vikings hat, the sitting in the car with the garage door closed on purpose. I was more curious than sad. But in the months that followed, I thought of Barb often. I came to care for her. I nurtured an inflated sense of my connection to her.

Recently, another acquaintance of mine died. He was beautiful and young and free-spirited and one hell of a painter. He went hiking one day on the Oregon coast and was never seen again. Over the course of my life, I have known other people who've died. Some of them have died the way we hoped they would — old, content, at their time; others, the way we hoped they wouldn't — by murder or suicide, in accidents, or too young of illnesses. The deaths of those people made me sad, afraid, and angry; they made me question the fairness of the world, the existence of God, and the nature of my own existence. But they did not make me suffer. They did not make me think, *I cannot continue to live.* In fact, in their deaths I felt more deeply connected to them, not because I grieved for them, but because I wanted to attach myself to what is interesting. It is interesting to be in a Chinese restaurant and see a poster of the smiling face of an acquaintance, who is one hell of a painter, plastered on the front door. It is interesting to be able to say, *I know him,* to feel a part of something important and awful and big. The more connections like this we have, the more interesting we are.

*

There was nothing interesting to me about my mother's death. I did not want to attach myself to it. It was her life that I clung to, her very, very interesting life. When she died, she was about to graduate from college, and so was I. We had started together. Her college was in Duluth, mine in Minneapolis. After a lifetime of struggle and sacrifice, my mother was coming into her own. She wanted to major in six subjects, but the school wouldn't let her, so she settled on two.

My mother had become pregnant when she was nineteen and immediately married my father, a steelworker in western Pennsylvania when the steel plants were shutting down, a coal miner's son born about the time that the coal was running out. After three children and nine years of misery, my mother left him. My father had recently moved us to a small town near Minneapolis in pursuit of a job prospect. When they divorced, he went back to Pennsylvania, but my mother stayed. She worked as a waitress and in a factory that made small plastic containers that would eventually hold toxic liquids. We lived in apartment complexes full of single mothers whose children sat on the edges of grocery-store parking lots. We received free government cheese and powdered milk, food stamps and welfare checks.

After a few years, my mother met my stepfather, and when he fell off a roof on the job and hurt his back, they took the twelve-thousand-dollar settlement and spent every penny on forty acres of land in northern Minnesota. There was no house; no one had ever had a house on this land. My stepfather built a one-room tar-paper shack, and we lived in it while he and my mother built us a house from scrap wood and trees they cut down with the help of my brother, my sister, and me. We moved into the new house on Halloween night. We didn't have electricity or running water or a phone or an indoor toilet. Years passed, and my mother was happy — happier than she'd ever been — but still, she hungered for more.

Just before she died, she was thinking about becoming a costume designer, or a professor of history. She was profoundly interested in the American pioneers, the consciousness of animals, and the murders of women believed to be witches. She was looking into graduate school, though she feared that she was too old. She couldn't believe, really, that she was even getting a degree. I'd had to convince her to go to college. She'd always read books but thought that she was basically stupid. To prepare, she shadowed me during my senior year of high school, doing all the homework that I was assigned. She photocopied my assignment sheets, wrote the papers I had to write, read the books. I graded her work, using my teacher's marks as a guide. My mother was a shaky student at best.

She went to college and earned straight A's.

She died on a Monday during spring break of our senior year. After her funeral, I immediately went back to school because she had begged me to do so. It was the beginning of a new quarter. In most of my classes, we were asked to introduce ourselves and say what we had done over the break. "My name is Cheryl," I said. "I went to Mexico."

I lied not to protect myself, but because it would have been rude not to. To express loss on that level is to cross a boundary, to violate personal space, to impose emotion in a nonemotional place.

We did not always treat grief this way. Nearly every culture has a history, and some still have a practice, of mourning rituals, many of which involve changes in the dress or appearance of those in grief. The wearing of black clothing or mourning jewelry, cutting the hair, and body scarification or ritual tattooing all made the grief-stricken immediately visible to the people around them. Although it is true that these practices were sometimes ridiculously restrictive and not always in the best interest of the mourner, it is also true that they gave us something of value. They imposed evidence of loss on a community and forced that community to acknowledge it. If, as a culture, we don't bear witness to grief, the burden of loss is placed entirely upon the bereaved, while the rest of us avert our eyes and wait for those in mourning to stop being sad, to let go, to move on, to cheer up. And if they don't — if they have loved too deeply, if they do wake each morning thinking, *I cannot continue to live* — well, then we pathologize their pain; we call their suffering a disease.

We do not help them: we tell them that they need to get help.

Nobody knew about my sexual escapades. I kept waiting for them to cure me, or for something to cure me of them. Two years had passed since my mother's death, and I still couldn't live without her, but I also couldn't live with myself. I decided to tell Mark the truth. The list was long. I practiced what I would say, trying to say it in the least painful way. It was impossible. It was time.

Mark sat in the living room playing his guitar. He was working as an organizer for a nonprofit environmental agency, but his real ambition was to be a musician. He had just formed his first band and was writing a new song, finding it as he went along. I told him that I had something to tell him and that it was not going to be easy. He stopped playing and looked at me, but he kept his hands on the guitar, holding it gently. This man whom I'd loved for years, had loved enough to marry, who had been with me through my mother's death and the aftermath, who'd offered to go down on me in the gentlest of ways, who would do anything, anything for me, listened as I told him about the Technically Still a Virgin Mexican Teenager, the Prematurely Graying Wilderness Guide, the Recently Unemployed Graduate of Juilliard.

He fell straight forward out of his chair onto his knees and then face down onto the floor. His guitar went with him and it made clanging, strumming, hollow sounds as it went. I attempted to rub his back. He screamed for me to get my hands off him.

Later, spent, he calmly told me that he wanted to kill me. He promised he would if I'd given him AIDS.

Women are used to the bad behavior of men. But I had broken the rules. Even among our group of alternative, left-wing, hippie, punk-rock, artsy politicos, I was viewed by many as the worst kind of woman: the whore, the slut, the adulteress, the liar, the cheat. And to top it all off, I had wronged the best of men. Mark had been faithful to me all along.

He moved out and rented a room in the attic of a house. Slowly we told our friends. The Insanely Young, Insanely Happy, Insanely In-Love Married Couple was coming apart. First they were in disbelief. Next they were mad, or several of them were — not at us, but at me. One of my dearest friends took the photograph of me she kept in a frame in her bedroom, ripped it in half, and mailed it to me. Another made out with Mark. When I was hurt and jealous about this, I was told that perhaps it was exactly what I needed: a taste of my own medicine. I couldn't rightfully disagree, but still my heart was broken. I lay alone in our bed feeling myself almost levitate from the pain.

We couldn't decide whether to get divorced or not. We went to a marriage counselor and tried to work it out. Months later, we stopped the counseling and put the decision on hold. Mark began to date. He dated one of those women who, instead of a purse, carry a teeny-weeny backpack. He dated a biologist who also happened to be a model. He dated a woman I'd met once who'd made an enormous pot of very good chili of which I'd eaten two bowls.

His sex life temporarily cured me of mine. I didn't fuck anyone, and I got crabs from a pair of used jeans I'd bought at a thrift store. I spent several days eradicating the translucent bugs from my person and my apartment. Then the Teeny-Weeny Backpack Woman started to play tambourine in Mark's budding band. I couldn't take it anymore. I went to visit a friend in Portland and decided to stay. I met a man: a Punk Rocker Soon to Be Hopelessly Held under the Thumb of Heroin. I found him remotely enchanting. I found heroin more enchanting. Quickly, without intending to, I slipped into a habit. *Here,* I thought. *At last.*

By now Mark pretty much hated me, but he showed up in Portland anyway and dragged me back home. He set a futon down for me in the corner of his room and let me stay until I could find a job and an apartment. At night we lay in our separate beds fighting about why we loved and hated each other so much. We made love once. He was cheating on someone for the first time. He was back with the Biologist Who Also Happened to Be a Model, and he was cheating on her with his own wife. *Hmmm,* we thought. *What's this?*

But it was not to be. I was sorry. He was sorry. I wasn't getting my period. I was really, really, really sorry. He was really, really, really mad. I was pregnant by the Punk Rocker Soon to Be Hopelessly Held under the Thumb of Heroin. We were at the end of the line. We loved each other, but love was not enough. We had become the Insanely Young, Insanely Sad, Insanely Messed-Up Married Couple. He wanted me gone. He pulled the blankets from my futon in his room and flung them down the stairs.

I sat for five hours in the office of an extremely overbooked abortion doctor, waiting for my abortion. The temperature in the room was somewhere around fifty-six degrees. It was packed with micro-

scopically pregnant women who were starving because we had
been ordered not to eat since the night before. The assistants of
the Extremely Overbooked Abortion Doctor did not want to clean
up any puke.

At last I was brought into a room. I was told to undress and hold
a paper sheet around myself. I was given a plastic breast and instructed to palpate it, searching for a lump of cancer hidden
within its depths, while I waited for my abortion. I waited, naked,
palpating, finding the cancer over and over again. The Extremely
Overbooked Abortion Doctor needed to take an emergency long-
distance phone call. An hour went by. Finally, she came in.

I lay back on the table and stared at a poster on the ceiling of a
Victorian mansion that was actually composed of miniature photographs of the faces of a hundred famous and important women in
history. I was told to lie still and peacefully for a while and then to
stand up very quickly and pull my underwear on while an assistant
of the Extremely Overbooked Abortion Doctor held me up. I was
told not to have sex for a very long time. The procedure cost me
four hundred dollars, half of which I was ridiculously hoping to receive from the Punk Rocker Soon to Be Hopelessly Held under the
Thumb of Heroin. I went home to my new apartment. The light on
my answering machine said I had three messages. I lay on my
couch, ill and weak and bleeding, and listened to them.

There was a message from the Punk Rocker Soon to Be Hopelessly Held under the Thumb of Heroin, only he didn't say anything. Instead he played a recording of a Radiohead song that
went, "You're so fucking special, / I wish I was special, / But I'm a
creep, I'm a weirdo."

There was a message that consisted of a thirty-second dial tone
because the person had hung up.

There was a message from Mark wondering how I was.

My mother had been dead for three years. I was twenty-five. I had
intended, by this point in my life, to have a title of my own: the
Incredibly Talented and Extraordinarily Brilliant and Successful
Writer. I had planned to be the kind of woman whose miniature
photographed face was placed artfully into a poster of a Victorian
mansion that future generations of women would concentrate on
while their cervixes were forcefully dilated by the tip of a plastic

tube about the size of a drinking straw and the beginnings of babies were sucked out of them. I wasn't anywhere close. I was a pile of shit.

Despite my mother's hopes, I had not graduated from college. I pushed my way numbly through that last quarter, but I did not, in the end, receive my bachelor's degree because I had neglected to do one assignment: write a five-page paper about a short story called "The Nose," by Nikolai Gogol. It's a rollicking tale about a man who wakes up one morning and realizes that his nose is gone. Indeed, his nose has not only left him but has also dressed in the man's clothes, taken his carriage, and gone gadding about town. The man does what anyone would do if he woke up and found that his nose was gone: he goes out to find it. I thought the story was preposterous and incomprehensible. Your nose does not just up and leave you. I was told not to focus on the unreality of it. I was told that the story was actually about vanity, pretentiousness, and opportunism in nineteenth-century Russia. Alternately, I could interpret it as a commentary on either male sexual impotency or divine Immaculate Conception. I tried dutifully to pick one of these concepts and write about it, but I couldn't do it, and I could not discuss with my professor why this was so. In my myopic, grief-addled state, the story seemed to me to be about something else entirely: a man who woke up one morning and no longer had a nose and then went looking for it. There was no subtext to me. It was simply a story about what it was about, which is to say, the absurd and arbitrary nature of disappearance, our hungry ache to resurrect what we've lost, and the bald truth that the impossible can become possible faster than anyone dreams.

All the time that I'd been thinking, *I cannot continue to live*, I'd also had the opposite thought, which was by far the more unbearable: that I *would* continue to live, and that every day for the rest of my life I would have to live without my mother. Sometimes I forgot this, like a trick of the brain, a primitive survival mechanism. Somewhere, floating on the surface of my subconscious, I believed — I still believe — that if I endured without her for one year, or five years, or ten years, or twenty, she would be given back to me; that her absence was a ruse, a darkly comic literary device, a terrible and surreal dream.

*

What does it mean to heal? To move on? To let go? Whatever it means, it is usually said and not done, and the people who talk about it the most have almost never had to do it. I cannot say anything about healing, but I can say that something happened as I lay on the couch bleeding and listening to my answering machine play the Radiohead song and then the dial tone and then Mark's voice wondering how I was: I thought about writing the five-page paper about the story of the man who lost his nose. I thought about calling Mark and asking him to marry me again. I thought about becoming the Incredibly Talented and Extraordinarily Brilliant and Successful Writer. I thought about taking a very long walk. I decided to do all of these things immediately, but I did not move from the couch. I didn't set out the next day, either, to write the paper about the guy who lost his nose. I didn't call Mark and ask him to marry me again. I didn't start to work on becoming the Incredibly Talented and Extraordinarily Brilliant and Successful Writer. Instead I ordered pizza and listened to that one Lucinda Williams CD that I could not ever get enough of, and, after a few days, I went back to my job waiting tables. I let my uterus heal and then slept at least once with each of the five guys who worked in the kitchen. I did, however, hold on to one intention, and I set about fulfilling it: I was going to take a long walk. One thousand six hundred and thirty-eight miles, to be exact. Alone.

Mark and I had filed the papers for our divorce. My stepfather was going to marry the woman he'd started dating immediately after my mother died. I wanted to get out of Minnesota. I needed a new life and, unoriginally, I was going west to find it. I decided to hike the Pacific Crest Trail — a wilderness trail that runs along the backbone of the Sierra Nevada and the Cascade Mountains, from Mexico to Canada. Rather, I decided to hike a large portion of it — from the Mojave Desert in California to the Columbia River at the Oregon-Washington border. It would take me four months. I'd grown up in the country, done a good amount of camping, and taken a few weekend backpacking trips, but I had a lot to learn: how, for example, to read a topographical map, ford a river, handle an ice ax, navigate using a compass, and avoid being struck by lightning. Everyone who knew me thought that I was nuts. I proceeded anyway, researching, reading maps, dehydrating food and packing it into plastic bags and then into boxes that would be mailed at roughly two-week intervals to the ranger stations and post offices I'd occasionally pass near.

I packed my possessions and stored them in my stepfather's barn. I took off my wedding ring and put it into a small velvet box and moved my mother's wedding ring from my right hand to my left. I was going to drive to Portland first and then leave my truck with a friend and fly to L.A. and take a bus to the start of the trail. I drove through the flatlands and Badlands and Black Hills of South Dakota, positive that I'd made a vast mistake.

Deep in the night, I pulled into a small camping area in the Bighorn Mountains of Wyoming and slept in the back of my truck. In the morning I climbed out to the sight of a field of blue flowers that went right up to the Tongue River. I had the place to myself. It was spring and still cold, but I felt compelled anyway to go into the river. I decided I would perform something like a baptism to initiate this new part of my life. I took my clothes off and plunged in. The water was like ice, so cold it hurt. I dove under one time, two times, three times, then dashed out and dried off and dressed. As I walked back to my truck I noticed my hand: my mother's wedding ring was gone.

At first I couldn't believe it. I had believed that if I lost one thing, I would then be protected from losing another; that my mother's death would inoculate me against further loss. It is an indefensible belief, but it was there, the same way I believed that if I endured long enough, my mother would be returned to me.

A ring is such a small thing, such a very small thing.

I went down on my hands and knees and searched for it. I patted every inch of ground where I had walked. I searched the back of my truck and my pockets, but I knew. I knew that the ring had come off in the river. Of course it had; what did I expect? I went to the edge of the water and thought about going back in, diving under again and again until I found it, but it was a useless idea, and I was defeated by it before I even began. I sat down on the edge of the water and cried. Tears, tears, so many kinds of tears, so many ways of crying. I had collected them, mastered them; I was a priestess, a virtuoso of crying.

I sat in the mud on the bank of the river for a long time and waited for the river to give the ring back to me. I waited and thought about everything. I thought about Mark and my boat of life. I thought what I would say to him then, now, forever: *You, get in.* I thought about the Formerly Gay Organic Farmer and the Quietly Perverse Poet and the Terribly Large Texas Bull Rider and the Five Line Cooks I Had on Separate Occasions over the Course of One Month. I thought about how I was never again going to sleep with anyone who had a title instead of a name. I was sick of it. Sick of fucking, of wanting to fuck the wrong people and not wanting to fuck the right ones. I thought about how if you lose a ring in a river, you are never going to get it back, no matter how badly you want it or how long you wait.

I leaned forward and put my hands into the water and held them flat and open beneath the surface. The soft current made rivulets over my bare fingers. I was no longer married to Mark. I was no longer married to my mother.

I was no longer married to my mother. I couldn't believe that this thought had never occurred to me before: that it was her I'd been faithful to all along, and I knew that I couldn't be faithful any longer.

If this were fiction, what would happen next is that the woman would stand up and get into her truck and drive away. It wouldn't matter that the woman had lost her mother's wedding ring, even though it was gone to her forever, because the loss would mean something else entirely: that what was gone now was actually her sorrow and the shackles of grief that had held her down. And in this loss she would see, and the reader would know, that the woman had been in error all along. That, indeed, the love she'd had for her mother was too much love, really; too much love and also too much sorrow. She would realize this and get on with her life. There would be what happened in the story and also everything it stood for: the river, representing life's constant changing; the tiny blue flowers, beauty; the spring air, rebirth. All of these symbols would collide and mean that the woman was actually lucky to have lost the ring, and not just to have lost it, but to have loved it, to have ached for it, and to have had it taken from her forever. The story would end, and you would know that she was the better for it. That she was wiser, stronger, more interesting, and, most of all, finally starting down her path to glory. I would show you the leaf when it unfurls in a single motion: the end of one thing, the beginning of another. And you would know the answers to all the questions without being told. Did she ever write that five-page paper about the guy who lost his nose? Did she ask Mark to marry her again? Did she stop sleeping with people who had titles instead of names? Did she manage to walk 1,638 miles? Did she get to work and become the Incredibly Talented and Extraordinarily Brilliant and Successful Writer? You'd believe the answers to all these questions to be yes. I would have given you what you wanted then: to be a witness to a healing.

But this isn't fiction. Sometimes a story is not about anything except what it is about. Sometimes you wake up and find that you actually have lost your nose. Losing my mother's wedding ring in the Tongue River was not OK. I did not feel better for it. It was not a passage or a release. What happened is that I lost my mother's wedding ring and I understood that I was not going to get it back, that it would be yet another piece of my mother that I would not have for all the days of my life, and I understood that I could not bear this truth, but that I would have to.

Healing is a small and ordinary and very burnt thing. And it's one thing and one thing only: it's doing what you have to do. It's what I did then and there. I stood up and got into my truck and drove away from a part of my mother. The part of her that had been my lover, my wife, my first love, my true love, the love of my life.

JUDITH THURMAN

Swann Song

FROM THE NEW YORKER

OF THE GARMENTS I have loved and lost, there is one whose perfection gave me such happiness that I've spent decades hoping it
will surface in some thrift shop, and when I'm in Paris I never fail
to check at the Père-Lachaise of couture, Didier Ludot's grimly
glamorous little resale boutique in the Palais Royal. This first de-
luxe, not to say decent, piece of clothing that I ever owned was a
sable-brown Cossack-style maxiskirt by Yves Saint Laurent that
zipped up both sides like a sleeping bag. It was made of thick al-
paca blanket wool, lined in black silk, and ingeniously constructed
without darts so that, despite its weight, it had no bulk at the hips
or waist. I bought it in 1969 at the Rive Gauche boutique on Bond
Street, in London, which had been inaugurated with great fanfare
that year by Princess Margaret and was managed very profitably by
a former fashion journalist named Lady Rendlesham. Saint Laurent has always had a penchant for aristocratic sales help.

While he didn't invent designer ready-to-wear — Pierre Cardin
did — Saint Laurent was the first couturier to make a cult of it, as-
sociating the cachet of an exalted label with a line of factory-made
clothing and accessories of high quality and audacious chic (he designed them himself, at least for a while) that were marketed glob-
ally to a hip, baby-boom clientele. "The Rive Gauche notion of luxury had less to do with money than with attitude," Laurence
Benaïm writes in her authoritative biography of Saint Laurent,
which was published in France in 1993. Benaïm also notes that in
1966, when the Rive Gauche line was launched, the ready-to-wear
prices were about a tenth of the couture. But a tenth of the un-

thinkable was still hard for me to imagine. Except for my youth, and an inclination toward idolatry, I was hardly the target Rive Gauche customer, and I have never, unfortunately, had a Saint Laurent body — leggy and broad-shouldered, with the flat hips, shortish waist, and high, shapely haunches and bosom of the African and Caribbean models he was among the first to employ. At the time, though, I was grateful for the mercy of a long skirt: ruthless minis were the rule. I was also thrilled to have something so certifiably Parisian in a closet filled with the picturesque ethnic frippery that is back in style this year, but which stank of the embroidered sheepskin coat from Afghanistan that I'd bought in an open-air stall next to Gandalf's Garden off the King's Road. Badly cured hippie fur, patchouli, diesel exhaust, mildew, hashish rolled with stale tobacco, maté, and paraffin heating oil are the scents that summon up my remembrance of the late sixties.

I was then writing wine-dark Plathian poetry in a bed-sit with imitation William Morris wallpaper facing a garage south of the river, and paying my rent by tutoring a Hollywood mogul's eleven-year-old son in Berkeley Square. When my pupil's English lesson was finished, the butler served us tea, a repast at which we were supposed to speak French. Since teatime was off the meter, I felt entitled to wrap up whatever solid refreshments we hadn't consumed to take home, and I confess that, in addition to scones and sandwiches, I sometimes also pocketed a handful of raw brown sugar lumps, and on the way to the tube station, which, like Rive Gauche, was on Bond Street, I would eat them furtively, like stolen candy. One Friday, I noticed a discreet Final Reductions sign in the shop window, which emboldened me to cross its intimidatingly smart threshold for the first time. The carpet, as I recall, was the color of a blood orange, and there were little mauve chairs, and futuristic lighting, and a black-and-white portrait of Himself in the style of *Blow-Up*. Not much was left on the sale rack, but the marvelously refined skirt with its cavalry swagger and feline nap had been marked down to fifteen pounds — one of its zippers was "as seen." I had a week's pay in my pocket: fifteen pounds. Many of my romances would begin, like this one, as a chance encounter sparked by an obscure hunger, a neat coincidence, and a fatal attraction for the defective. That is how I joined the ranks of *celles qui s'adonnent à Yves Saint Laurent* (in the words of the 1977 ad for his perfume

Opium — a publicity campaign that was widely protested as pro-drug and anti-Asian): one of those women addicted to Yves Saint Laurent.

January 7 of this year, reading from a prepared speech in a gravelly whisper, Saint Laurent, who is sixty-five, announced his retirement. The Spring 2002 haute couture show would be his last, taking the form of a retrospective. His forty-four years in fashion had, he said, been haunted by aesthetic phantoms. "I have grappled with anguish and I have been through sheer hell . . . I have known those fair-weather friends we call tranquilizers and drugs. I have known the prison of depression and the confinement of a hospital. But one day I was able to come through all of that, dazzled yet sober. It was Marcel Proust who taught me that 'the magnificent and pitiful family of the hypersensitive are the salt of the earth.'"

French television provided live coverage of this rare and emotional press conference, which generated nearly as much nasty backbiting as it did fulsome piety. The fashion press scrambled to compose its tributes. The funereal windows of Didier Ludot were promptly dressed with vintage Saint Laurent, and so, with a brighter, mod flair, were the windows of the Galeries Lafayette, the vast department store that occupies two square blocks behind the Opéra Garnier. Grasset reissued Benaïm's biography, and bookstores on both banks also gave prominence to a six-pound coffeetable tome of film stills (*Yves Saint Laurent: 5, Avenue Marceau*) from a documentary made by David Teboul, who spent three months with his crew in Saint Laurent's atelier. Teboul's made-for-television hagiography, Warholian in *longueur* but without the consolation of sex, brutality, or weirdness, was to be screened at the Centre Pompidou on January 22, immediately following the Saint Laurent couture show, and, later in the week, on television. It should have been called *Merci, Monsieur,* the refrain of its dialogue. The ash grows longer on the master's cigarette as he labors over his sketchpad. His French bulldog, Moujik, dismembers a stuffed toy. His muse, model, and collaborator Loulou de la Falaise, the director of YSL accessories, unfurls a bolt of matronly flowered chiffon and drapes it on a stoic model. (La Falaise has always been the quintessential Rive Gauche *haute bohémienne,* and her 1977 wedding to Thadée Klossowski, the younger son of Balthus — a party hosted by Saint Laurent at the Chalet des Îles in the Bois de Boulogne — was, notes Benaïm, the first great social stir-fry of "punks and baronesses.") A plump seamstress with a bad haircut irons the canvas lapel of what will become an exquisitely banal suit jacket. Every feeble nod or hoarse croak from the subject is received like a pontifical blessing by a tired-looking staff of aging parishioners who, except for la Falaise — a woman who flaunts her well-worn beauty with mermaid nonchalance and whose expression of ironical detachment belies her vigilant subservience — are touchingly unglamorous. But Teboul's homage is perhaps more revealing than it was meant to be. It leaves the impression that 5, Avenue Marceau is less a couture atelier than a mad king's private theater where the actors conspire, elaborately, to humor his fantasies.

The backbiting in the press was encouraged, in part, by Pierre Bergé — Saint Laurent's formidably astute business partner and ex-lover, who has, for four decades, sheltered the master from the unpleasant realities of accounts payable. Saint Laurent has always maintained that he has no precise idea how much money he has; he just knows there's enough to permit him to decorate beautiful houses and collect precious things. In 1994, when Bergé was being investigated for insider trading (he was cleared the next year), the judge accepted Saint Laurent's convincing protestations of fiscal imbecility. In 1993, Bergé had sold the YSL ready-to-wear business to the pharmaceutical and cosmetics giant Sanofi, which, in a complicated deal with the luxury mogul François Pinault, resold it two years ago for a billion dollars to the Gucci Group. Domenico De Sole, Gucci's chief executive, confided the design of the Rive Gauche line to the dashing American Tom Ford. After a tepid start, Ford has, with lots of grommeting, whipstitching, ruching, animal prints, peasant ruffles, and skin-tight leather, begun to make it profitably decadent again (though not too kinky for the American market). Since the turn of the millennium, most of the "Saint Laurents" featured in the glossies or worn by celebrities to awards ceremonies have been the pretender's handiwork. This has understandably rankled the royalists. After the press conference, Bergé announced with a flash of Nixonian bitterness that the game of haute couture was finished because the player with the marbles was packing them up and going home.

*

The crowd outside the Centre Pompidou, in the Place Beaubourg, on the night of January 22 was behaving as if there were a Prada warehouse sale inside rather than the retrospective of a great designer's lifework. Two thousand of the elect held tickets, five hundred of them for standing room, which everyone knew meant three hours on one's feet. The flood surge of bodies when the doors finally opened was terrifying, and it's a miracle that none of Saint Laurent's original couture clients — a beautifully wrought, hand-painted set of tiny porcelain old-lady dolls — got trampled to death. The publicists themselves had been so mobbed by importunate style faxers begging for a seat that they'd stopped answering the phones. I had been told there would be absolutely no admission without an invitation corresponding to the name and gender on one's passport, but it was impossible to disengage a limb from the crush, much less a document.

More than one guest who made it past the barricades was secretly gratified by the rumor, later confirmed, that Gwyneth Paltrow — a fixture, with bodyguards and camera-ready pancake makeup, at every other couture event — had, among other upstart celebrities, been turned away. It was a show of loyalty on both sides: creator's and audience's. Jeanne Moreau, Lauren Bacall, Bianca Jagger, Paloma Picasso, Nan Kempner, Diane von Furstenberg, Betty Catroux, and, of course, Catherine Deneuve, muse and spokeswoman for the house — who first became addicted to Saint Laurent when he dressed her for *Belle de Jour* — shared a front row with three French first ladies, an Arab princess, and the designer's mother. Jean-Paul Gaultier's platinum buzz cut and Sonia Rykiel's electrostatic carotene pageboy glowed in the dark. Hubert de Givenchy was conspicuous for his height and distinction. Vivienne Westwood, in clashing plaids and matching red hair, teetered off on platform stilettos to find a ladies' room. Many of the spectators were wearing a treasured piece of YSL, though I assume that none of them except me, ever the bargain hunter, had bought her early-seventies décolleté tuxedo jacket — structured shoulders, tapered waist, jet buttons — at the Council Thrift Shop on East Eighty-fourth Street. Outside in the cobbled square, under a light drizzle, a battalion of well-armed riot policemen with rakish berets nervously scanned a huge throng of fashion fundamentalists, some weeping, who watched the simulcast on giant screens.

After a predictably interminable delay, the epic défilé began un-furling to a soundtrack of the Beatles, African drums, Callas, Mo-zart, jazz, and the Stones. A hundred and seven "girls" modeled three hundred archival designs, beginning with a breezy peacoat and wide-legged white trousers from 1962. The stream of vintage creations was punctuated, erratically, by some forty outfits for Spring 2002, including a suite of draped chiffon gowns in opaline colors (ravishing, though their novelty was imperceptible). The finale was a cortège of sixty tuxedos impossible to date but repre-senting every conceivable variation: cropped, skirted, slim, pad-ded, flared, strict, high-waisted, pleated, racy, flat-hipped, classic. The majority of the models had been culled from this season's crop of inhumanly lovely teenagers, although Naomi Campbell and Claudia Schiffer, magnificently sullen and goofy, respectively, who rarely work the catwalk anymore, consented to appear. But they were all outclassed by the womanly splendor of their elders: Mounia, Katouscha, and Jerry Hall.

Most couture shows last about twenty minutes. This one roiled on for more than an hour, in waves of staggering beauty, fauvish color, and perverse extravagance — a jacket costing half a mil-lion francs, for example, perfectly replicating van Gogh's *Irises* in seven hundred hours' worth of hand-beading by Lesage. There were sumptuously embellished tributes to other painters: Picasso, Matisse, Braque, Dali, and Warhol; to poets and writers, among them Aragon and Cocteau; and to exotic native populations — Russian moujiks, Forbidden City courtesans, Castilian matadors, and African queens. There was plenty of cerebral whimsy to offset the noirish sex play: feather minis suitable for a showgirl's wedding to a peer; a minuscule suede tunic from the sixties worn with high-heeled waders; swanky cocktail dresses that exposed a nipple; a transparent black baby-doll disco nightie trimmed with fur; quite a bit of immaculately white-collared *Belle de Jour* respectability beg-ging to be corrupted; a strong dose of double-breasted androgyny; and a backless evening gown cut to the cleft of the buttocks, then scored with lace. But while Saint Laurent can sometimes be pedan-tically outré, he's never trashy. And he displayed such encyclopedic formal invention and technical virtuosity that the occasional bomb — like a series of umbrella-shaped flowered tea frocks in what looked like shower-curtain fabric, or a shapeless wool shift worn with a dowager's turban — were like a sorbet between courses rather than a disappointment.

The event itself had the gestalt of those imperial funerals that the French Republic orchestrates with elegiac pomp and poignance for its national heroes (and, much more rarely, heroines), whether they have contributed to the glory of the *patrie* with a pen or a sword — or, as in this case, a number 2 pencil. And it was impossible to be unmoved by the pure-heartedness of Saint Laurent's love of women; or by his appearance of leonine decrepitude; or by the tragic grimace — the expression of a man walking the plank and still riven to his core by the conflicting imperatives of resistance and surrender — with which he took his final steps down the runway. The dauphin of couture had become its King Lear.

Yves Mathieu-Saint-Laurent (he dropped the Mathieu when he opened his own couture house) was born on August 1, 1936, in Oran, Algeria. His prosperous middle-class parents, Lucienne and Charles, who owned a house in town and a villa at the beach, prided themselves on employing French, rather than Arab, servants. Yves's father was an insurance executive who also managed a chain of movie theaters. His mother was a pretty and stylish provincial coquette with great legs, who, Saint Laurent says enigmatically, "is still a child." In pictures from the family albums she also looks rather terrifyingly sunny, at least from the point of view of a fragile and depressive homosexual son who identified so passionately with Proust that he sometimes traveled under the pseudonym M. Swann and of whom Bergé has said, "He was born with a nervous breakdown." But she encouraged his precocious talents, even to the point of letting him cut up her clothes to make rag dolls, and when he was fourteen or fifteen and had begun to design ensembles influenced by Dior and Balenciaga for her and his two younger sisters, she paid a local dressmaker to run them up.

One of the most eloquent photographs of the neurasthenic aesthete as a young man is an all-boy class portrait that seems to date from his last year at the Lycée Lamoricière, in Oran, and for which he has removed his glasses. Whether or not his fellow students are as cocky and virile as they look, it is painfully obvious that the wraith in the back row, out of focus, twenty pounds thinner than the pompadoured, *pied noir* Romeos on either side, is an alien object of locker room contempt, and perhaps of abuse. Even Proust managed to survive his military service, but when Mathieu-Saint-Laurent, Yves, was drafted into the army, in 1960, at the height of the Algerian war, and sentenced once again to the torture of a barracks full of straight boys, it shattered him so badly that he was confined in the isolation ward of a military hospital, where the doctors tranquilized him into a stupor. A common enough story: so many of those dreamy, provincial child outcasts who become the somebodies of art and literature are first driven to mobilize their powers by an urgent necessity to be somebody else.

Saint Laurent arrived in Paris for the first time in December of 1953, with his chic mother, having won third prize in the dress category of a design competition sponsored by the International Wool Secretariat. (The next year he came in first. Karl Lagerfeld took top honors in the coat category.) Through his parents' connections, he met Michel de Brunhoff, who was the editor of French *Vogue* and an intimate friend of Dior. De Brunhoff encouraged the promising teenager to study at the school run by the Chambre Syndicale de la Couture, which he did briefly. Two years later, the editor was impressed, indeed "flabbergasted," by the prowess and sophistication of a fashion portfolio that Yves, now eighteen, had brought back to Paris from his *villégiature* in Oran. It included some sketches of an A-line dress — a shape that Dior was working on but hadn't yet shown except to de Brunhoff, who now persuasively recommended his protégé to the man who, in 1947, had created the voluminously skirted, wasp-waisted New Look that revived the morale of the fashion world and, with it, the postwar French economy. Saint Laurent's first coup as an assistant at the House of Dior was a graphically arresting black evening gown with long sleeves, a décolleté nicked like a rifle sight, and an episcopal-looking sash of white taffeta. Carmel Snow featured this dress in the 1955 fall fashion issue of *Harper's Bazaar*, photographed by Avedon on a model who was herself as elegant as a calligrapher's brushstroke. Her name was Dovima. He posed her at the Cirque d'Hiver, with two elephants.

A year later, Dior, who was only fifty-two, died of a heart attack at the Italian spa where he had gone for his annual weight loss and liver cure, defying the advice of his astrologer, who'd warned him that the trip boded ill. Marcel Boussac, the textile magnate who

owned the couture house, briefly considered shutting it down before deciding to give Dior's "preferred assistant" a shot. Saint
Laurent's first collection, the Trapeze, presented in January of
1958, was greeted with delirious acclaim on both sides of the Atlantic. I have always believed, heretically, that the Trapeze — while
flattering to the trapezoidal bodies of women in advanced stages of
pregnancy — was just a couture version of the muumuu. But both
the originals and the Ohrbach's copies sold briskly and made their
obscure twenty-one-year-old creator a *Life* cover boy.

Saint Laurent's youth, his mother told Benaïm, "ceased abruptly
in 1958," when the embalming fluid of celebrity started flowing in
his veins. "In achieving his oldest dreams," the biographer continues, "he closed the door on his life. Yves becomes a purveyor of illusions." The flimsiest but most seductive and persistent of those illusions, which the women's-wear industry now treats as a sacred
truth, is that the essence of being in fashion is to live dangerously.
Poor, addled Talitha Getty, one of Yves's millionaire junkie friends
from Marrakesh and an early muse — who once posed on her roof
in the medina wearing a Rive Gauchiste caftan and a ring on every
finger and died at thirty-one of a heroin overdose, orphaning her
toddler son — has been cited by a number of young designers as
their inspiration for Fall 2002. Saint Laurent's own epic bingeing
and self-imposed quarantine from reality begin here. "I had to request an audience in order to see him," a friend recalls.

Before Saint Laurent was drafted into the army and cracked up,
there were six collections for the Dior label — not all of them,
Benaïm notes, gratifying to the expectations of his backers and
fans. The comfy but erotically challenged "sack dress" inspired innumerable cartoons. The hobble skirt was unpopular with couture clients, who had to disrobe in order to use a toilet. A series of
jewel- and lace-encrusted evening gowns that paid homage to
Goya's infantas were so ornate that critics complained about the
Dior *femme relique* — the woman mummified by her opulence. But
there was also a biker's jacket, the *blouson noir;* an early "car
coat"; and a regal wedding gown for the new empress of Iran,
Farah Diba. "Saint Laurent designs for women who lead double
lives," Catherine Deneuve once said astutely, and these tentative
experiments express the contradictory impulses that he would
continue so masterfully to explore. He drew upon the vocabulary

of proletarian work clothes and menswear, radically simplifying a woman's wardrobe and purging it of its fussy, bourgeois gestures. He replaced the tailored blouse under a suit jacket with a "see-through" chiffon halter, a T-shirt, or nothing. He gave women sporty pockets for their Miltowns and cigarettes. But he also perceived that tribal fetish worship, the past and its splendors, the Orient and its mysteries, the art world and its sacrileges, the underground, the flea market, the souk, the steppes, and the gay demimonde were all ripe for creative plunder. Saint Laurent was the designer who, in 1971, with his widely execrated but enduringly influential "Libération" collection (the title refers not to the liberation of women but to the liberation of France in 1944), invented "retro" in the form of, among other beguilingly updated throwbacks, an absinthe-green fox chubby. Proust taught him well: art, elegance, snobbery, nostalgia, and vice distilled with supreme purity make an eau de vie that goes straight to the head.

The army doctors had told Saint Laurent that he would be subject to "relapses" of his malaise. Discharged to the care of his lover, he and Bergé "honeymooned" in the Canary Islands. Meanwhile, Marcel Boussac, unhappy with his dauphin's performance, had installed Marc Bohan on Dior's throne. Bergé sued for breach of contract and won a settlement. An American investor named J. Mack Robinson (who was pointed out to me at the retrospective, proudly sitting in the second row) committed seven hundred thousand dollars to the founding of Yves Saint Laurent Couture, and in December of 1961 the partners opened their house on the Rue Spontini. Chanel was, at the same moment, back in business on the Rue Cambon. The jewelry designer Robert Goossens once compared the old queen of fashion to its Young Turk by noting that Chanel embodied Bergé and Saint Laurent in one.

In a television interview broadcast in 1968, Chanel anointed Saint Laurent as her spiritual heir (though there is some question as to whether they ever actually met), and in his farewell press conference he paid homage to the predecessor "who taught me so much, and who, as we all know, liberated women. It was this that enabled me, years later . . . to liberate fashion." But the notion that any revolution can be concluded or claimed as a definitive victory is itself a relic of the past. What Chanel liberated was the natural line of the body, which entailed, as most liberations do, a new form of tyranny — the oppressive maintenance of a svelte, toned silhouette. Hers is the virile glamour of renunciation. She freed women to dress with the sobriety and nonchalance of English gentlemen, though she stopped short of putting them into trousers. That was Saint Laurent's claim to immortality. He showed his first tailored pants in 1962, and went on to commandeer other staples of a gentleman's and an officer's wardrobe: the business suit, the jumpsuit, the pea coat, the short, the trenchcoat, the motorcycle jacket, the safari jacket, and, most famously, the tuxedo. Yet, for all his often proclaimed debt to the "street," he was more romantic than Chanel was about the rich — she who slept her way out of poverty. And as a gay man, or perhaps simply as a man, he was more sentimental than she was about femininity. Indeed, no one has been so religiously gallant toward women or resistant to the temptation of modern fashion to make clothes as difficult, ironic, contemptuous, or ugly as modern art. Saint Laurent takes it upon himself to anticipate every potential humiliation in the bulge of a seam, the pucker of a pleat, the mockery of a bow. His cutting and drapery are a lover's discourse with the female body.

Bergé has been calling Saint Laurent "the last couturier" for years, at least since the time of his retrospective at the Metropolitan Museum in 1983. Even then the vitality of his great work — his legacy — was behind him. The only news that he delivered this January was at the press conference. But the pathos of his eclipse is proportional to the radiance of his imagination and the supreme good fortune of his timing. He came of age as an artist at the moment everything changed. With all the talent in the world, it isn't possible to be a Saint Laurent today — any more than it's possible to be an Elvis — even if one is Saint Laurent.

On the morning after the Beaubourg show, *Le Monde* published a brief interview that the designer, who was declining interviews, gave to Laurence Benaïm. "What motivated the announcement of your retirement?" she asked him. "We are living in a world of disorder and decadence," he replied. "The struggle for elegance and beauty has been causing me much sadness . . . I have been feeling marginal and alone." There was something so ingenuous about this remark, as if the speaker had just awakened from a coma to perceive the disarray of Western civilization, that I thought of Proust's last scenes, in which the Narrator returns to Paris after his long wartime convalescence in a nursing home and discovers that the world of the salons is a grotesque and degraded parody of all that he remembers. But then he is introduced to a young girl, Gilberte's daughter — Swann's grandchild — a tall beauty of sixteen, "rich in hopes," "a masterpiece . . . formed from those very years which I myself had lost." And this encounter permits him to understand that "the cruel law of art is that people die . . . after exhausting every form of suffering, so that over our heads may grow the grass not of oblivion but of eternal life [upon which] gaily and without a thought for those who are sleeping beneath them, future generations may come to enjoy their *déjeuner sur l'herbe*." I can't think of a more hopeful insight to reconcile one with the "magnificent and pitiful" family picnic that is the fashion world. But Saint Laurent couldn't know about, and therefore take heart from, Marcel's moment of existential truth because, he told Benaïm, he's never finished reading *In Search of Lost Time*. Perhaps now he will.

JOHN EDGAR WIDEMAN

Whose War

FROM HARPER'S MAGAZINE

NOBODY ASKED ME, but I need to say what I'm thinking in this new year in New York City, five months after the Twin Towers burned, after long stretches of fall weather eerily close to perfect — clear blue skies, shirtsleeve warmth — through December, a bizarre hesitation, as if nature couldn't get on with its life and cycle to the next season, the city enclosed in a fragile, bell-jar calm till shattered by a siren, a plane's roar overhead.

I grew up in Homewood, an African-American community in Pittsburgh where people passing in the street might not have known each other's names but we knew something about each other's stories, so we always exchanged a greeting. We greeted each other because it feels good but also because we share the burden of racism, understand how it hurts, scars, deforms, but yes, it can be survived, and here we are, living proof meeting on the ground zero of a neighborhood street. The burning and collapse of the World Trade Center has conferred a similar sort of immediate intimacy upon all Americans. We've had the good luck to survive something awful, but do we truly understand, as Homewood people are disciplined to understand by the continuing presence of racism, that it ain't over yet. There's the next precarious step, and the next down the street, and to survive we must attend to the facts of division as well as the healing wish for solidarity.

Staring up at a vast, seamless blue sky, it's hard to reckon what's missing. The city shrinks in scale as the dome of sky endlessly recedes. Piles of steel and concrete are whims, the vexed arc of the city's history a moment lasting no longer than the lives of victims consumed in the burning towers. The lives lost mirror our own fragility and vulnerability, our unpredictable passage through the mysterious flow of time that eternally surrounds us, buoys us, drowns us. Ourselves the glass where we look for the faces of those who have disappeared, those we can no longer touch, where we find them looking back at us, terrified, terrifying.

A few moments ago I was a man standing at a window, nine stories up in an apartment building on the Lower East Side of New York, staring out at a building about a hundred yards away, more or less identical to his, wondering why he can't finish a piece of writing that for days had felt frustratingly close to being complete, then not even begun. Wondering why anybody, no matter how hard they'd plugged away at articulating their little piece of the puzzle, would want to throw more words on a pile so high the thing to be written about has disappeared. A man with the bright idea that he might call his work in progress "a speech to be performed because no one's listening." Like singing in the shower: no one hears you, but don't people sing their hearts out anyway, because the singing, the act itself, is also a listening to itself, so why not do your best to please yourself.

And the man standing at the window retracts his long arms from the top of the upper pane he's lowered to rest on as he stares. Then all of him retracts. Picture him standing a few moments ago where there's emptiness now. Picture him rising from a couch where he'd been stretched out, his back cushioned against the couch's arm, then rising and walking to the window. Now visualize the film running backward, the special effect of him sucked back like red wine spilled from the lip of a jug returning to fill the jug's belly, him restored exactly, legs stretched out, back against the couch's cushioned arm. Because that's who I am. What I'm doing and did. I'm the same man, a bit older now, but still a man like him, restless, worried, trying to fashion some tolerable response with words to a situation so collapsed, so asphyxiated by words, words, it's an abomination, an affront to dead people, to toss any more words on the ruins of what happened to them.

I, too, return to the couch, return also to the thought of a person alone singing in a shower. A sad thought, because all writing pretends to be something it's not, something it can't be: something or someone other, but sooner or later the writing will be snuffed back into its jug, back where I am, a writer a step, maybe two, behind my lemming words scuffling over the edge of the abyss.

I'm sorry. I'm an American of African descent, and I can't applaud my president for doing unto foreign others what he's inflicted on me and mine. Even if he calls it ole-time religion. Even if he tells me all good Americans have nothing to fear but fear itself and promises he's gonna ride over there and kick fear's ass real good, so I don't need to worry about anything, just let him handle it his way, relax and enjoy the show on TV, pay attention to each breath I take and be careful whose letters I open and listen up for the high alerts from the high-alert guy and gwan and do something nice for a Muslim neighbor this week. Plus, be patient. Don't expect too much too soon. These things take time. Their own good time. You know. The sweet by-and-by. Trust me.

I'm sorry. It all sounds too familiar. I've heard the thunder, seen the flash of his terrible swift sword before. I wish I could be the best kind of American. Not doubt his promises. Not raise his ire. I've felt his pointy boots in my butt before. But this time I can't be Tonto to his Lone Ranger. Amos to his Andy. Tambo to his Bones. Stepin to his Fetchit. I'm sorry. It's too late. I can't be as good an American as he's telling me to be. You know what I'm saying. I must be real. Hear what I'm saying. We ain't going nowhere, as the boys in the hood be saying. Nowhere. If you promote all the surviving Afghans to the status of honorary Americans, Mr. President, where exactly on the bus does that leave me. When do I get paid. When can I expect my invitation to the ranch. I hear Mr. Putin's wearing jingle-jangle silver spurs around his dacha. Heard you fixed him up with an eight-figure advance on his memoirs. Is it true he's iced up to be the Marlboro man after he retires from Russia. Anything left under the table for me. And mine.

Like all my fellow countrymen and -women, even the ones who won't admit it, the ones who choose to think of themselves as not implicated, who maintain what James Baldwin called "a willed innocence," even the ones just off boats from Russia, Dominica, Thailand, Ireland, I am an heir to centuries of legal apartheid and must negotiate daily, with just about every step I take, the foul muck of unfulfilled promises, the apparent and not so apparent effects of racism that continue to plague America (and, do I need to add, plague the rest of the Alliance as well). It's complicated muck, muck that doesn't seem to dirty Colin Powell or Oprah or Michael Jordan or the black engineer in your firm who received a bigger raise than all her white colleagues, muck so thick it obscures the presence of millions of underclass African Americans living below the poverty line, hides from public concern legions of young people of color wasting away in prison. How can I support a president whose rhetoric both denies and worsens the muck when he pitches his crusade against terror as a holy war, a war of good against evil, forces of light versus forces of darkness, a summons to arms that for colored folks chillingly echoes and resuscitates the Manichaean dualism of racism.

I remain puzzled by the shock and surprise nonblack Americans express when confronted by what they deem my *"anger"* (most would accept the friendly amendment of *"rage"* or *"bitterness"* inside the quotes). Did I see in their eyes a similar shock and surprise on September 11. Is it truly news that some people's bad times (slavery, colonial subjugation, racial oppression, despair) have underwritten other people's good times (prosperity, luxury, imperial domination, complacency). News that a systematic pattern of gross inequities still has not been corrected and that those who suffer them are desperate (*angry, bitter, enraged*) for change.

For months an acrid pall of smoke rose from smoldering ruins, and now a smokescreen of terror hovers, *terror* as the enemy, terror as the problem, terror as the excuse for denying and unleashing the darkness within ourselves.

To upstage and camouflage a real war at home the threat of terror is being employed to justify a phony war in Afghanistan. A phony war because it's being pitched to the world as righteous retaliation, as self-defense after a wicked, unwarranted sucker punch when in fact the terrible September 11 attack as well as the present military incursion into Afghanistan are episodes in a long-standing vicious competition — buses bombed in Israel, helicopters strafing Palestinian homes, economic sanctions blocking the flow of food and medicine for Iraq, no-fly zones, Desert Storms, and embassy bombings — for oil and geopolitical leverage in the Middle East.

A phony war that the press, in shameless collusion with the military, exploits daily as newsy entertainment, a self-promoting concoction of fiction, fact, propaganda, and melodrama designed to keep the public tuned in, uninformed, distracted, convinced a real war is taking place.

A phony war because its stated objective — eradicating terrorism — is impossible and serves to mask unstated, alarmingly open-ended goals, a kind of fishing expedition that provides an opportunity for America to display its intimidating arsenal and test its allies' loyalty, license them to crush internal dissent.

A phony war, finally, because it's not waged to defend America from an external foe but to homogenize and coerce its citizens under a flag of rabid nationalism.

The Afghan campaign reflects a global struggle but also reveals a crisis inside America — the attempt to construct on these shores a society willing to sacrifice democracy and individual autonomy for the promise of material security, the exchange of principles for goods and services. A society willing to trade the tumultuous uncertainty generated by a government dedicated to serving the interests of many different, unequal kinds of citizens for the certainty of a government responsive to a privileged few and their self-serving, single-minded, ubiquitous, thus invisible, ideology: profit. Such a government of the few is fabricating new versions of freedom. Freedom to exploit race, class, and gender inequities without guilt or accountability; freedom to drown in ignorance while flooded by information; freedom to be plundered by corporations. Freedom to drug ourselves and subject our children's minds to the addictive mix of fantasy and propaganda, the nonstop ads that pass for a culture.

A phony war but also a real war, because as it bumbles and rumbles along people are dying and because like all wars it's a sign of failure and chaos. When we revert to the final solution of kill or be killed, all warring parties in the name of clan tribe nation religion violate the first law of civilization — that human life is precious. In this general collapse, one of the first victims is language. Words are deployed as weapons to identify, stigmatize, eliminate, the enemy. One side boasts of inflicting casualties, excoriates the other side as cowards and murderers. One side calls civilians it kills collateral damage, labels civilian deaths by its opponents terrorism.

From their initial appearance in English to describe the bloody dismantling of royal authority during the French Revolution (Burke's "thousands of those Hell-hounds called Terrorists . . . are let loose on the people") the words *terror* and *terrorist* have signified godless savagery. Other definitions — government by a system of coercive intimidation — have almost entirely disappeared. Seldom if ever perceived neutrally as a tool, a set of practices and tactics for winning a conflict, terror instead is understood as pure evil. Terror and terrorists in this Manichaean scheme are excluded even from the problematic dignity of conventional warfare.

One side's use of *terrorist* to describe the other is never the result of a reasoned exchange between antagonists. It's a refusal of dialogue, a negation of the other. The designation terrorist is produced by the one-way gaze of power. Only one point of view, one vision, one story, is necessary and permissible, since what defines the gaze of power is its absolute, unquestionable authority.

To label an enemy a terrorist confers the same invisibility a colonist's gaze confers upon the native. Dismissing the possibility that the native can look back at you just as you are looking at him is a first step toward blinding him and ultimately rendering him or her invisible. Once a slave or colonized native is imagined as invisible, the business of owning him, occupying and exploiting his land, becomes more efficient, pleasant.

A state proclaiming itself besieged by terrorists asserts its total innocence, cites the unreasonableness, the outrageousness, of the assaults upon it. A holy war may be launched to root out terrorism, but its form must be a punitive crusade, an angry god's vengeance exacted upon sinners, since no proper war can exist when there is no recognition of the other's list of grievances, no awareness of the relentless dynamic binding the powerful and powerless. Perhaps that's why the monumental collapsing of the towers delivered such a shocking double dose of reality to Americans — yes, a war's been raging and yes, here's astounding proof we may have already lost it. It's as if one brick snatched away, one sledgehammer blow, demolished our Berlin Wall.

Regimes resisting change dismiss challenges to their authority by branding them terrorist provocations. In the long bloody struggles that often follow, civil protests, car bombings, kidnappings, assassinations, guerrilla warfare in the mountains, full-scale conventional military engagements, blur one into the other. At first the

media duly reports on the frightening depredations of terrorists —
Algerian terror, Mau Mau terror, Palestinian terror, Israeli terror,
South African terror — then bears witness as fighters from the
Mau Mau, the Palmach, the PLO, emerge to become leaders of
new states. George Washington, inaugurated as America's first
president only a few blocks from the ruins of the World Trade Center, would have been branded a terrorist if the word had been invented in 1775. Clearly not all terrorists become prime ministers
or presidents, but if and when they do they rewrite the history of
their struggle to attain legitimacy. This turnabout clarifies the relationship between power and terror. Terrorists are those who have
no official standing, no gaze, no voice in the established order,
those determined by all means possible to usurp power in order to
be seen and heard. Some former terrorists survive to accomplish
precisely that. Others survive long enough to decry and denounce
the terrorist threat nibbling at the edges of their own regime.

The destruction of the World Trade Center was a criminal act, the
loss of life an unforgivable consequence, but it would be a crime of
another order, with an even greater destructive potential, to allow
the evocation of the word *terror* to descend like a veil over the
event, to rob us of the opportunity to see ourselves as others see us.

The terror that arises from fear of loss, fear of pain, death, anni-
hilation, prostrates us because it's both rational and irrational. Rational because our sense of the world's uncertainty is accurate. Rational because reason confirms the difference between what is
knowable and unknowable, warns us that in certain situations we
can expect no answers, no help. We are alone. Irrational because
that's all we have left when reason abandons us. Our naked emotions, our overwhelmed smallness.

Terror thrives in the hour of the wolf, the hour of Gestapo raids
on Jewish ghettos, of blue-coated cavalry charges on Native American villages. Those predawn hours when most of us are born or
die, the hour when cops smash through doors to crack down on
drugs or on dissidents, the hour of transition when sleep has trans-
ported the body furthest from its waking state, when our ability to
distinguish dream from not-dream weakens. Terror manifests itself
at this primal juncture between sleep and waking because there we
are eternally children, outside time, beyond the protections and
consolations of society, prey to fear of the dark.

To a child alone, startled from sleep by a siren, the hulking bear silhouetted in the middle of the dark room is real. The child may remember being assured that no bears live on the Lower East Side of New York, may know his parents' bed is just down the hall, may even recall tossing his bulky down parka over the back of the chair instead of hanging it neatly in the closet like he's been told a million times to do. None of this helps, because reason has deserted him. Even if things get better when his mother knocks and calls him for breakfast, the darkness has been branded once again, indelibly, by agonizing, demoralizing fear, by a return to stark terror.

For those who don't lose a child's knack for perceiving the aural archaeology within the sound of words, words carry forward fragments, sound bites that reveal a word's history, its layered onomatopoeic sources, its multiplicity of shadowed meanings. *Terror* embeds a grab bag of unsettling echoes: tear (as in rip) (as in run fast), terra (earth, ground, grave, dirt, unfamiliar turf), err (mistake), air (terra firma's opposite element), eerie (strange, unnatural), error (of our ways), roar-r-r (beasts, machines, parents, gods). Of course any word's repertoire is arbitrary and precise, but that's also the point, the power of puns, double entendre, words migrating among languages, Freudian slips, Lacan's "breaks," all calling attention to the unconscious, archaic intentionality buried in the words.

But the word *terror* also incarcerates. Like the child pinned to its bed, not moving a muscle for fear it will arouse the bear, we're immobilized, paralyzed by terror. Dreading what we might discover, we resist investigating terror's source. Terror feeds on ignorance, confines us to our inflamed, tortured imaginings. If we forget that terror, like evil, resides in us, is spawned by us no matter what name we give it, then it makes good sense to march off and destroy the enemy. But we own terror. We can't offload it onto the back of some hooded, barbaric, shadowy other. Someone we can root out of his cave and annihilate. However, we continue to be seduced by the idea that we might be able to cleanse ourselves of terror, accomplish a final resolution of our indeterminate nature. But even if we could achieve freedom from terror, what would we gain by such a radical reconfiguration of what constitutes being human. What kind of new world order would erase the terror we're born with, the terror we chip away at but never entirely remove. What system could anticipate, translate, or diffuse the abiding principle of uncertainty governing the cosmos. Systems that promise a world based on imperishable, impregnable truth deliver societies of truncated imagination, of history and appetite denied, versions of Eden where there is no dreaming, no rebellion, no Eros, where individuality is sacrificed for interchangeability, eternal entertainment, becalmed ego, mortality disguised as immortality by the absence of dread.

Power pales (turns white with terror — imagines its enemies black — invents race) when power confronts the inevitability of change. By promising to keep things as they are, promising to freeze out or squeeze out those not already secure within the safety net of privilege, Mr. Bush won (some say stole) an election. By launching a phony war he is managing to avoid the scrutiny a first-term, skin-of-its-teeth presidency deserves. Instead he's terrorizing Americans into believing that we require a wartime leader wielding unquestioned emergency powers. Beneath the drumbeat belligerence of his demands for national unity, if you listen you'll hear the bullying, the self-serving, the hollowness, of his appeals to patriotism. Listen carefully and you'll also hear what he's not saying: that we need, in a democracy full of contradictions and unresolved divisions, opposition voices.

Those who mount a challenge to established order are not the embodiment of evil. Horrifically bloody, criminal acts may blot the humanity of the perpetrators and stimulate terror in victims and survivors, but the ones who perpetrate such deeds are not the source of the terror within us. To call these people terrorists or evil, even to maintain our absolute distinction between victims and perpetrators, exercises the blind, one-way gaze of power, perpetuates the reign of the irrational and supernatural, closes down the possibility that by speaking to one another we might formulate appropriate responses, even to the unthinkable.

Although trouble may always prevail, being human offers us a chance to experience moments when trouble doesn't rule, when trouble's not totally immune to compassion and reason, when we make choices, and try to better ourselves and make other lives better.

Is war a preferable alternative. If a child's afraid of the dark, do we solve the problem by buying her a gun.

Biographical Notes

ANDRÉ ACIMAN is the author of *Out of Egypt: A Memoir* (Farrar, Straus and Giroux/Riverhead) and *False Papers* (FSG/Picador) as well as the coauthor and editor of *Letters of Transit* (New Press). He was born in Alexandria and has lived in Egypt, Italy, and France. Educated at Harvard, he has taught comparative literature at Princeton and Bard College and now teaches at The Graduate Center (CUNY). He is the recipient of a Whiting Writers' Award and a Guggenheim fellowship. A contributor to the *New York Times, The New Yorker, The New Republic, The New York Review of Books,* and *Commentary,* he is currently working on a novel.

DONALD ANTRIM is the author of three novels: *Elect Mr. Robinson for a Better World, The Hundred Brothers,* and *The Verificationist.* He has contributed to *The New Yorker, Harper's Magazine,* and *Paris Review,* and has been awarded fellowships from the John Simon Guggenheim Memorial Foundation, the National Endowment for the Arts, and the Dorothy and Lewis B. Cullman Center for Scholars and Writers at the New York Public Library. He lives in Brooklyn, New York.

RACHEL COHEN writes for *The Threepenny Review, McSweeney's, Modern Painters,* and other publications, and has received fellowships from the New York Foundation for the Arts and the MacDowell Colony. Cohen won the 2003 PEN/Jerard Fund Award for her book of interlocking essays on figures in American cultural history, *A Chance Meeting,* which is forthcoming from Random House in spring 2004. She teaches in the Sarah Lawrence MFA nonfiction program and lives in Brooklyn.

BRIAN DOYLE is the editor of *Portland Magazine* at the University of Portland, in Oregon. He is the author of four essay collections, most recently *Leaping: Revelations & Epiphanies,* and editor of *God Is Love,* a collection of the best spiritual essays from *Portland Magazine*. Doyle's own essays have appeared in *The American Scholar, The Atlantic Monthly, Harper's Magazine, Orion, Commonweal,* and *The Georgia Review,* among other periodicals, and in *The Best American Essays* of 1998 and 1999.

JOSEPH EPSTEIN'S most recent books include *Fabulous Small Jews,* a collection of stories, and *Envy,* a book in the Oxford University Press series on the seven deadly sins. He served as guest editor of *The Best American Essays 1993.*

MARSHALL JON FISHER has written on a wide range of topics for *The Atlantic Monthly,* and his work has also appeared in *DoubleTake, Harper's Magazine, Discover,* and other magazines. He is the coauthor (with David E. Fisher) of *Tube: The Invention of Television* (1996) and *Strangers in the Night: A Brief History of Life on Other Worlds* (1998). He lives in the Berkshires with his wife and two sons.

CAITLIN FLANAGAN is a contributing editor of *The Atlantic Monthly* and a two-time finalist for the National Magazine Award for her reviews and criticism. Her work has appeared in the *New York Times* and other national and international publications. She is currently writing a book entitled *Housewife Heaven,* to be published by Little, Brown. She lives in Los Angeles with her husband and sons.

IAN FRAZIER writes humor, essays, reporting, and other nonfiction. His books include *Dating Your Mom, Great Plains, Coyote v. Acme,* and *On the Rez.* He was the guest editor of *The Best American Essays 1997.* He lives in Montclair, New Jersey.

ATUL GAWANDE is a surgical resident in Boston and, since 1998, a staff writer for *The New Yorker.* A graduate of Harvard Medical School, Oxford University, and Stanford University, he has been a laboratory researcher, a senior health policy adviser to President Bill Clinton, and a research fellow at the Harvard School of Public Health. His first book, *Complications: A Surgeon's Notes on an Imperfect Science,* was published by Metropolitan Books in 2002.

ADAM GOPNIK writes the "New York Journal" for *The New Yorker* and is the author of *Paris to the Moon.* His new book, *The King in the Window,* an adventure story for children, will appear in 2004.

FRANCINE DU PLESSIX GRAY was born in the French embassy in Warsaw, where her father was a member of the diplomatic corps. After receiving a degree in philosophy from Barnard College, she worked as a reporter and book editor, and in the 1960s she began publishing fiction and political essays in *The New Yorker.* Her work has appeared in such periodicals as *The New York Review of Books, The New York Times Magazine, The*

New Republic, Rolling Stone, and *Vanity Fair.* She is the author of three novels — *Lovers and Tyrants* (1976), *World Without End* (1981), and *October Blood* (1985) — as well as a number of award-winning nonfiction books, including *Divine Disobedience: Profiles in Catholic Radicalism* (1970), *Hawaii: The Sugar-Coated Fortress* (1972), *Soviet Women: Walking the Tightrope* (1990), and a collection of essays on the political, domestic, and literary scene, *Adam & Eve in the City* (1987). She has written three biographies: *Rage and Fire: A Life of Louise Colet* (1994); *At Home with the Marquis de Sade: A Life,* which was a finalist for the 1999 Pulitzer Prize in biography; and, most recently, a brief life of the French philosopher Simone Weil. A member of the American Academy of Arts and Letters, she has taught at the College of the City of New York, Yale, Columbia, Brown, Princeton, and Vassar College. She is currently at work on a family memoir.

EDWARD HOAGLAND has published eight collections of essays, most recently *Balancing Acts* and *Tigers & Ice;* five books of fiction, including *Seven Rivers West;* and two travel books, *Notes from the Century Before: A Journal from British Columbia* and *African Calliope: A Journey to the Sudan,* both of which were reissued in 1995. He also writes criticism and is the editor of the Penguin Nature Classics series. He is a member of the American Academy of Arts and Letters and has taught at ten colleges, currently at Bennington. He was guest editor of *The Best American Essays 1999.*

MYRA JEHLEN has published several volumes of literary criticism, including *American Incarnation: The Individual, the Nation, and the Continent* and, most recently, *Readings at the Edge of Literature.* She teaches literature at Rutgers University.

JANE KRAMER has written *The New Yorker*'s "Letter from Europe" for more than twenty years. She is the author of nine books, among them *The Last Cowboy, Europeans, The Politics of Memory,* and, most recently, *Lone Patriot,* and has been the recipient of many awards, including a National Book Award and a National Magazine Award. With *Europeans,* she became the first woman — as well as the first American — to win the Prix Européen de l'Essai "Charles Veillon," Europe's most important award for nonfiction. She divides her time between Europe and New York.

BEN METCALF was born in Illinois and raised in that state and in Virginia. He currently makes his home in New York City, where he is a senior editor of *Harper's Magazine.*

FREDERIC MORTON is the author of seven books of fiction and three of nonfiction. His work has been translated into fifteen languages. He has twice been a National Book Award finalist: for *The Rothschilds* (1962) and *A Nervous Splendor: Vienna 1888/1889* (1979). Both are still in print. A musical based on *The Rothschilds* ran on Broadway from 1970 to 1972; a musical based on *A Nervous Splendor* will open in Vienna next year. He has contributed to *Harper's Magazine, The Atlantic Monthly, Esquire, Playboy,* the *New York Times* (op-ed and other sections), *Holiday, The Hudson Review, The Nation,* and other publicatons. He was a columnist for the *Village Voice* for three years and is currently contributing editor at *Vanity Fair.* His short fiction has appeared in *The Best American Short Stories* and other anthologies. He received the Author of the Year Award of the National Anti-Defamation League and the City of Vienna's Gold Medal of Honor.

MICHAEL POLLAN is a contributing writer for the *New York Times,* where many of his essays and articles have appeared. He is the author of *The Botany of Desire* (2001), *A Place of My Own* (1997), and *Second Nature* (1991). His essay "Why Mow?" appeared in *The Best American Essays 1990.* He is currently living in Berkeley, California, where he teaches in the Graduate School of Journalism at the University of California.

KATHA POLLITT is a poet, essayist, and columnist for *The Nation.* She is the author of *Antarctic Traveller,* a book of poems, and two collections of prose: *Reasonable Creatures: Essays on Women and Feminism* and *Subject to Debate: Sense and Dissents on Women, Politics, and Culture.* She has won many awards and prizes for her work, including a National Book Critics Circle Award, a National Magazine Award, and Guggenheim and Whiting grants. She lives in New York City.

ELAINE SCARRY, the Walter M. Cabot Professor of Aesthetics and the General Theory of Value at Harvard University, is the author of *The Body in Pain, On Beauty and Being Just, Dreaming by the Book,* and many articles on war and the social contract.

SUSAN SONTAG is the author of four novels, *The Benefactor, Death Kit, The Volcano Lover,* and *In America;* a collection of stories, *I, Etcetera;* a play, *Alice in Bed;* and five books of essays, including *On Photography, Illness as Metaphor,* and *Under the Sign of Saturn* — all published by Farrar, Straus and Giroux. She has also written and directed four feature-length films and directed plays in the United States and Europe, her most recent theater work being a staging of Beckett's *Waiting for Godot* in besieged Sarajevo. She served as guest editor of *The Best American Essays 1992.* "Looking at War" is taken from her latest book, *Regarding the Pain of Others,* which was published by Farrar, Straus and Giroux in 2003.

FRANCIS SPUFFORD is the author of three books of nonfiction. *I May Be Some Time* (1996), a cultural history of polar exploration, won several literary prizes in Britain. *The Child That Books Built* (2002), a memoir, expands on the themes of "The Habit." *The Backroom Boys* (2003) explores the creativity of engineers. He has also edited two literary anthologies and, with Jenny Uglow, *Cultural Babbage* (1996), a collection of essays on technology and the imagination. He lives and works in London.

CHERYL STRAYED is the author of *Torch*, a novel set in rural northern Minnesota, where she grew up. Her works of fiction and memoir have been published in several magazines and anthologies, including *DoubleTake, Nerve, Hope, The Sun,* and *The Best New American Voices 2003.* A graduate of the MFA program in fiction writing at Syracuse University, she lives in Portland, Oregon, and is at work on a book-length memoir. This is her second appearance in *The Best American Essays.*

JUDITH THURMAN'S essays on literature, fashion, and culture appear regularly in *The New Yorker,* where she is a staff writer. She is the author of two biographies: *Isak Dinesen: The Life of a Storyteller* (St. Martin's Press, 1982) won the National Book Award for nonfiction; *Secrets of the Flesh: A Life of Colette* (Knopf, 1999) won the Los Angeles Times Book Prize and the Salon Book Prize, both for biography. Thurman lives in Manhattan with her son, William.

JOHN EDGAR WIDEMAN is a two-time winner of the PEN/Faulkner Award and has been a nominee for the National Book Critics Circle Award. His novels include *A Glance Away, The Lynchers, Sent for You Yesterday, Reuben, Philadelphia Fire, The Cattle Killing,* and *Two Cities.* Along with several short story collections, Wideman has written four memoirs: *Brothers and Keepers, Fatheralong, Hoop Roots,* and, most recently, *The Island: Martinique.* His story "Weight" won the 2000 O'Henry Prize. He teaches at the University of Massachusetts at Amherst.

Notable Essays of 2002

Selected by Robert Atwan

AMARTYA SEN
Civilizational Imprisonments. *The New Republic,* June 10.
ELIZABETH SEWELL
A Cautionary Tale. *Society,* July/ August.
BARBARA SJOHOLM
Across the Maelstrom. *Michigan Quarterly Review,* Summer.
FLOYD SKLOOT
The Memory Lingers On. *Southwest Review,* vol. 87, nos. 2 and 3.
LAUREN SLATER
I Gave Up My Breasts to Save My Life. *Self,* August.
MARK SLOUKA
A Year Later. *Harper's Magazine,* September.
PAULA SPECK
Disappearing. *The Distillery,* July.
Three Guns. *The Gettysburg Review,* Summer.
JENNY SPINNER
(My Father's Dead) If Only I Could Tell You. *Fourth Genre,* Fall.
SHELBY STEELE
The Age of White Guilt. *Harper's Magazine,* November.
MICHAEL STEINBERG
Elegy for Ebbets. *New Letters,* vol. 68, nos. 3 and 4.
SHERYL ST. GERMAIN
Bodies of Water: A Suite from the South. *Southern Humanities Review,* Winter.

GAY TALESE
On the Bridge. *The New Yorker,* December 2.
BARRY TARGAN
Abstract Nature. *Sewanee Review,* Winter.

SALLIE TISDALE
Second Chair. *Antioch Review,* Fall.

DOUGLAS UNGER
Autobiography. *The Iowa Review,* vol. 32, no. 3.
JEFFREY UTZINGER
You're Going to Hell for This. *The Cream City Review,* Fall.

ROBERT VIVIAN
Doctor Whisper. *The Georgia Review,* Fall.

GARRY WALLACE
Kane Cemetery. *Owen Wister Review,* Spring.
JOHN WENKE
Scars. *North Dakota Quarterly,* Spring.
PAUL WEST
My Father Weightless. *Harper's Magazine,* December.
JOHN EDGAR WIDEMAN
Looking at Emmett Till. *Creative Nonfiction,* no. 19.
LEON WIESELTIER
Hitler Is Dead. *The New Republic,* May 27.
S. L. WISENBERG
Irving Berlin: The Margin and the Mainstream. *Crab Orchard Review,* Spring/Summer.

XIAODA XIAO
Devil's Trill. *The Massachusetts Review,* Autumn.

LEE ZACHARIAS
The Village Idiot. *The Gettysburg Review,* Autumn.
PAUL ZIMMER
Small Places. *Shenandoah,* Spring.

Best Theme Issues of 2002

The American Scholar, "The World's Eye," ed. Anne Fadiman, Summer.

Audubon, "This Land Is Your Land," ed. David Seideman, January/February.

Granta, "What We Think of America," ed. Ian Jack, Spring.

Many Mountains Moving, "The Literature of Spirituality," guest ed. Cathy Capozzoli, vol. 5, no. 1.

Natural Bridge, Special Irish Issue, guest ed. Eamonn Wall, Spring.

New Letters, "The Game of Baseball," ed. James McKinley, vol. 68, nos. 3 and 4.

River City, Elvis Presley Issue, ed. Tom Carlson, Summer.

The South Atlantic Quarterly, "Dissent from the Homeland: Essays after September 11," eds. Stanley Hauerwas and Frank Lentricchia, Spring.

THE B·E·S·T AMERICAN SERIES ™

THE BEST AMERICAN SHORT STORIES® 2003
Walter Mosley, guest editor • Katrina Kenison, series editor

"Story for story, readers can't beat the *Best American Short Stories* series" (*Chicago Tribune*). This year's most beloved short fiction anthology is edited by the award-winning author Walter Mosley and includes stories by Dorothy Allison, Mona Simpson, Anthony Doerr, Dan Chaon, and Louise Erdrich, among others.

0-618-19733-8 PA $13.00 / 0-618-19732-X CL $27.50
0-618-19748-6 CASS $26.00 / 0-618-19752-4 CD $35.00

THE BEST AMERICAN ESSAYS® 2003
Anne Fadiman, guest editor • Robert Atwan, series editor

Since 1986, the *Best American Essays* series has gathered the best non-fiction writing of the year and established itself as the best anthology of its kind. Edited by Anne Fadiman, author of *Ex Libris* and editor of the *American Scholar*, this year's volume features writing by Edward Hoagland, Adam Gopnik, Michael Pollan, Susan Sontag, John Edgar Wideman, and others.

0-618-34161-7 PA $13.00 / 0-618-34160-9 CL $27.50

THE BEST AMERICAN MYSTERY STORIES™ 2003
Michael Connelly, guest editor • Otto Penzler, series editor

Our perennially popular anthology is a favorite of mystery buffs and general readers alike. This year's volume is edited by the best-selling author Michael Connelly and offers pieces by Elmore Leonard, Joyce Carol Oates, Brendan DuBois, Walter Mosley, and others.

0-618-32965-X PA $13.00 / 0-618-32966-8 CL $27.50
0-618-39072-3 CD $35.00

THE BEST AMERICAN SPORTS WRITING™ 2003
Buzz Bissinger, guest editor • Glenn Stout, series editor

This series has garnered wide acclaim for its stellar sports writing and top-notch editors. Now Buzz Bissinger, the Pulitzer Prize–winning journalist and author of the classic *Friday Night Lights,* continues that tradition with pieces by Mark Kram Jr., Elizabeth Gilbert, Bill Plaschke, S. L. Price, and others.

0-618-25132-4 PA $13.00 / 0-618-25130-8 CL $27.50

THE BEST AMERICAN TRAVEL WRITING 2003
Ian Frazier, guest editor • Jason Wilson, series editor

The Best American Travel Writing 2003 is edited by Ian Frazier, the author of *Great Plains* and *On the Rez*. Giving new life to armchair travel this year are William T. Vollmann, Geoff Dyer, Christopher Hitchens, and many others.

0-618-11881-0 PA $13.00 / 0-618-11881-0 CL $27.50
0-618-39074-X CD $35.00

THE BEST AMERICAN SCIENCE AND NATURE WRITING 2003
Richard Dawkins, guest editor • Tim Folger, series editor

This year's edition promises to be another "eclectic, provocative collection" (*Entertainment Weekly*). Edited by Richard Dawkins, the eminent scientist and distinguished author, it features work by Bill McKibben, Steve Olson, Natalie Angier, Steven Pinker, Oliver Sacks, and others.

0-618-17892-9 PA $13.00 / 0-618-17891-0 CL $27.50

THE BEST AMERICAN RECIPES 2003–2004
Edited by Fran McCullough and Molly Stevens

"The cream of the crop . . . McCullough's selections form an eclectic, unfussy mix" (*People*). Offering the very best of what America is cooking, as well as the latest trends, time-saving tips, and techniques, this year's edition includes a foreword by Alan Richman, award-winning columnist for *GQ*.

0-618-27384-0 CL $26.00

THE BEST AMERICAN NONREQUIRED READING 2003
Edited by Dave Eggers • Introduction by Zadie Smith

Edited by Dave Eggers, the author of *A Heartbreaking Work of Staggering Genius* and *You Shall Know Our Velocity,* this genre-busting volume draws the finest, most interesting, and least expected fiction, nonfiction, humor, alternative comics, and more from publications large, small, and on-line. *The Best American Nonrequired Reading 2003* features writing by David Sedaris, ZZ Packer, Jonathan Safran Foer, Andrea Lee, and others.

0-618-24696-7 $13.00 PA / 0-618-24696-7 $27.50 CL
0-618-39073-1 $35.00 CD

HOUGHTON MIFFLIN COMPANY   www.houghtonmifflinbooks.com